D0065934

HUMAN HELPLESSNESS

Theory and Applications

HUMAN HELPLESSNESS

Theory and Applications

Edited by

JUDY GARBER
Department of Psychology
University of Minnesota
Minneapolis, Minnesota

MARTIN E. P. SELIGMAN
Department of Psychology
University of Pennsylvania
Philadelphia, Pennsylvania

ACADEMIC PRESS 1980
A Subsidiary of Harcourt Brace Jovanovich, Publishers
New York   London   Toronto   Sydney   San Francisco

ACADEMIC PRESS, INC.
111 Fifth Avenue, New York, New York 10003

United Kingdom Edition published by
ACADEMIC PRESS, INC. (LONDON) LTD.
24/28 Oval Road, London NW1 7DX

Library of Congress Cataloging in Publication Data
Main entry under title:

Human helplessness.

  Bibliography: p.
  Includes index.
  1. Helplessness (Psychology) I. Garber, Judy.
II. Seligman, Martin E. P.
BF575.H4H85   155.2'32   79−6773
ISBN 0−12−275050−0

To Marty Seligman, for his support, encouragement, and most of all, his trust.

—JG

To my mother, Irene Brown Seligman.
—MEPS

Contents

I

THEORETICAL ISSUES

1

Learned Helplessness in Humans: _→ reviews article_
An Attributional Analysis   **3**

LYN Y. ABRAMSON, JUDY GARBER, AND MARTIN E. P. SELIGMAN

5

Knowing More (or Less) Than You Can Show: Understanding Control through the Mindlessness–Mindfulness Distinction   97

BENZION CHANOWITZ AND ELLEN LANGER

6

On the Distinction between Anxiety and Depression: Perceived Control, Certainty, and Probability of Goal Attainment   131

JUDY GARBER, SUZANNE M. MILLER, AND LYN Y. ABRAMSON

II

CONCEPTUAL APPLICATIONS

7

A Cognitive–Expectancy Theory of Therapy for Helplessness and Depression   173

STEVEN D. HOLLON AND JUDY GARBER

8

Learned Helplessness and Intellectual Achievement   197

CAROL S. DWECK AND BARBARA G. LICHT

9

Helplessness and the Coronary-Prone Personality   223

DAVID C. GLASS AND CHARLES S. CARVER

10

Personality and Locus of Control   245

HERBERT M. LEFCOURT

11

Aging and Control   261

RICHARD SCHULZ

12

Coping with Undesirable Life Events   **279**

ROXANE L. SILVER AND CAMILLE B. WORTMAN

List of Contributors

Numbers in parentheses indicate the pages on which the authors' contributions begin.

LYN Y. ABRAMSON (3,59,131), Department of Psychology, State University of New York at Stony Brook, Stony Brook, New York 11794

LAUREN B. ALLOY (59), Department of Psychology, Northwestern University, Evanston, Illinois 60201

CHARLES S. CARVER (223), Department of Psychology, University of Miami, Coral Gables, Florida 33124

BENZION CHANOWITZ (97), Department of Psychology, Graduate Center, City University of New York, New York, New York 10036

CAROL S. DWECK (197), Department of Psychology, University of Illinois, Champaign, Illinois 61820

JUDY GARBER (3, 131, 173), Department of Psychology, University of Minnesota, Minneapolis, Minnesota 55455

DAVID C. GLASS (223), The Graduate School and University Center, City University of New York, New York, New York 10036

STEVEN D. HOLLON (173), Department of Psychology, University of Minnesota, Minneapolis, Minnesota 55455

ELLEN LANGER (97), Department of Psychology and Social Relations, Harvard University, Cambridge, Massachusetts 02138

HERBERT M. LEFCOURT (245), Department of Psychology, University of Waterloo, Waterloo, Ontario, Canada N2L3G1

BARBARA G. LICHT (197), Department of Psychology, Florida State University, Tallahassee, Florida 32306

TCHIA LITMAN-ADIZES (35), Department of Psychology, University of California, Los Angeles, Los Angeles, California 90024

SUZANNE M. MILLER (71, 131), Department of Psychology, Temple University, Philadelphia, Pennsylvania 19122

RICHARD SCHULZ (261), Institute on Aging, Portland State University, Portland, Oregon 97207

MARTIN E. P. SELIGMAN (3), Department of Psychology, University of Pennsylvania, Philadelphia, Pennsylvania 19174

ROXANE LEE SILVER (279), Department of Psychology, Northwestern University, Evanston, Illinois 60201

BERNARD WEINER (35), Department of Psychology, University of California, Los Angeles, Los Angeles, California 90024

CAMILLE B. WORTMAN (279), Research Center for Group Dynamics, Institute for Social Research, University of Michigan, Ann Arbor, Michigan 48106

Preface

The original theory of learned helplessness, proposed 15 years ago, was an elegant, although simple, statement of the effects of uncontrollability on behavior. Through a series of carefully controlled laboratory experiments originally conducted on dogs and later extended to include rats, cats, fish, and humans, the theory has been tested, confirmed in certain aspects, and disputed in others. There have been well over 300 journal articles, reviews, and chapters written reporting the results of these investigations of the effects of uncontrollability. In 1975, the second editor of this volume, Martin Seligman, wrote the first book on the topic to explicate the theory of learned helplessness and to suggest its potential application to such human problems as depression, development, and death. Since then, interest and research in human helplessness has grown considerably.

Because the original helplessness formulation was based on experiments with animals, the theory required modification to cope with the more complex phenomenon of helplessness in humans. In response to challenging new data, human helplessness theory recently has been reformulated (Abramson, Seligman, & Teasdale, 1978). The present volume is devoted to the burgeoning field of human helplessness since the reformulation.

The reformulated theory of learned helplessness in humans has begun to play an important role in our understanding of a variety of psychological problems. It continues to attract careful and critical attention among basic researchers while having real-world applications. The breadth of topics represented by the chapters in this volume samples both basic scientific thinking about helplessness and its application to real human problems.

The goal of this book is to provide a progress report on the creative application of the concept of helplessness to a range of significant psychological problems and to provide a means for sharing new ideas for future research directions. The present volume attempts to synthesize theoretical, empirical, and applied perspectives on human helplessness into an integrated whole. We have drawn upon the special expertise of a variety of researchers from experimental, personality, social, developmental, and clinical psychology. We hope that this collection of original chapters will attract the interest of a diverse audience who will find new applications of the central concepts discussed here. The volume is directed toward scholars, scientists, and students, especially those interested in the theoretical issues of control and helplessness and their conceptual application to real-world problems.

The book divides into two sections emphasizing new developments, conceptions, and applications of human helplessness. Part I addresses various unresolved theoretical issues concerning the concepts of control and helplessness: What is the role of attributions in human helplessness? How do we distinguish between the cognitive and motivational components of helplessness? Why is having control desirable, and under what conditions will individuals voluntarily relinquish control? Must you know you have control in order to have it, or can you have control without knowing it? What are the emotional and behavioral consequences of degrees of control and certainty? What is the distinction between helplessness and hopelessness, and between anxiety and depression? The individual chapters discuss these unresolved theoretical issues and provide a framework for future empirical investigations.

The second half of the book explores helplessness in real life. Human helplessness research has expanded beyond the experimental laboratory into the classroom, psychiatric clinic, medical hospital, and nursing home. Investigators from various areas of psychology have applied the theoretical concepts of uncontrollability and helplessness to such diverse phenomena as depression and therapy, academic achievement and sex differences, coronary proneness and personality, aging and death, and victimization and bereavement. It is our hope that these chapters will stimulate continued research into these real-life concerns as well as provide a model and inspiration for further application of human helplessness to other human problems.

We also hope that the reference section will provide a unified and complete compilation of the relevant literature on human helplessness.

As with any edited volume, it could not have been completed without the efforts of many individuals. We would like to express our gratitude to the staff of Academic Press for their patience and assistance. We, of course, would like to thank each of the contributors for being part of this volume. Finally, most sincere appreciation to Steve Hollon who provided continued support, patience, and unselfish encouragement.

I

THEORETICAL ISSUES

1

Learned Helplessness in Humans:
An Attributional Analysis

LYN Y. ABRAMSON
JUDY GARBER
MARTIN E. P. SELIGMAN

INTRODUCTION

The phrase "learned helplessness" first was used by Overmier and Seligman (1967) and Seligman and Maier (1967) to describe the debilitated escape–avoidance responding shown by dogs exposed to uncontrollable shocks in the laboratory. Over the past decade, research in the area of learned helplessness has proliferated. The debilitating consequences of experience with uncontrollable events have been observed in cats (Masserman, 1971; Seward & Humphrey, 1967; Thomas & Dewald, 1977), in fish (Frumkin & Brookshire, 1969; Padilla, 1973; Padilla, Padilla, Ketterer, & Giacolone, 1970), and in rats (Braud, Wepman, & Russo, 1969; Maier, Albin, & Testa, 1973; Maier & Testa, 1975; Seligman & Beagley, 1975; Seligman, Rosellini, & Kozak, 1975). (In a recent paper, Maier and Seligman [1976] extensively review work on learned helplessness in animals.)

More recently, investigators have documented the existence of learned helplessness in humans (Fosco & Geer, 1971; Gatchel & Proctor, 1976; Glass & Singer, 1972; Hiroto, 1974; Hiroto & Seligman, 1975; Klein, Fencil-Morse & Seligman, 1976; Klein & Seligman, 1976; Krantz, Glass, & Snyder, 1974; Miller & Seligman, 1975; Racinskas, 1971; Rodin, 1976; Roth, 1973;

3

Roth & Bootzin, 1974; Roth & Kubal, 1975; Thornton & Jacobs, 1971; among others). Seligman (1972, 1973, 1974, 1975) has argued that learned helplessness plays a part in a wide variety of human conditions, including child development, stomach ulcers, depression, and death. Other investigators have argued that the learned helplessness model is useful in examining intellectual achievement (Dweck & Licht, 1980), crowding (Rodin, 1976), victimization (Wortman & Silver, 1980), the coronary prone personality (Glass & Carver, 1980), and aging (Schulz, 1980).

The typical learned helplessness experiment involves what is known as the *triadic design* in which one group of subjects receives controllable events, a second group of subjects yoked to the first group receives uncontrollable events of the same intensity and duration, while a third group of subjects is not exposed to either controllable or uncontrollable events. The experiment by Hiroto (1974) is typical of human helplessness studies and provides an analogue to the original animal studies. College student volunteers were exposed to either loud controllable noises that they could terminate by pressing a button four times or uncontrollable noises that terminated independently of their responses, while others were not exposed to any noises. Subjects subsequently were tested on a hand shuttle box task in which noise termination was controllable for all subjects. The results of this test phase closely paralleled the results observed with animals. Whereas the groups that had originally received controllable noises or no noises adequately learned to terminate the noises in the shuttle box task, subjects who had received prior uncontrollable noises failed to terminate the noises during the shuttle box procedure.

The learned helplessness hypothesis provides a unified account of the debilitating consequences of experience with uncontrollable events in humans and animals. According to this hypothesis, learning that outcomes are uncontrollable results in three deficits: motivational, cognitive, and emotional. The motivational deficit consists of retarded initiation of voluntary responses and is seen as a consequence of the expectation that responding is futile. The cognitive deficit consists of difficulty in learning that responses produce outcomes. If one has acquired a cognitive set that X is irrelevant to Y, then it will be more difficult for one to later learn that X's produce Y's when they do. Finally, the learned helplessness model argues that depressed affect is a consequence of learning that outcomes are independent of responding.

The learned helplessness hypothesis is primarily "cognitive" in that it postulates that mere exposure to uncontrollable events is not sufficient to produce the associated helplessness deficits. Rather, the organism must come to *expect* that outcomes are uncontrollable in order to exhibit helplessness. A number of alternative noncognitive explanations for the etiology of the learned helplessness effects have been advanced. In general, however, these hypotheses have been limited to examining the effects of uncontrollable shocks on animals, rather than attempting to explain learned helplessness in both humans and animals. A description of these alternative theories can be found in a recent review by Maier and Seligman (1976).

Historically, work on learned helplessness in humans grew out of the original findings with animals. As research with humans progressed, however, a number of investigators pointed to the inadequacy of the theoretical constructs originating in animal helplessness for understanding helplessness in humans (e.g., Blaney, 1977; Buchwald, Coyne & Cole, 1978; Golin & Terrell, 1977; Miller & Norman, 1979; Wortman & Brehm, 1975; Roth & Kilpatrick-Tabak, Note 1). In a special issue of the *Journal of Abnormal Psychology* published in February 1978, Abramson, Seligman, and Teasdale presented an attributional framework in order to resolve several of the theoretical controversies about the effects of uncontrollability in humans. This chapter will review, clarify, and expand this reformulated model of learned helplessness in humans and will examine the research conducted over the past two years which tests the reformulation. Briefly, the reformulated hypothesis states that when people find themselves helpless, they implicitly or explicitly ask *why* they are helpless. The causal attributions they make influence the generality and chronicity of the helplessness deficits as well as later self-esteem. Finally, the implications of the reformulation for the helplessness model of depression (Seligman, 1975; Seligman, Klein, & Miller, 1976) will be discussed.

INADEQUACIES OF THE OLD HELPLESSNESS HYPOTHESIS

Types of Helplessness: Personal versus Universal

The first inadequacy of the old helplessness model concerns the issue of individual differences and the fact that there may be more than one type of human helplessness. How is it that subjects who are similarly exposed to uncontrollable noise's reach quite different conclusions concerning the cause of this uncontrollability? For example, after repeated unsuccessful attempts to turn off the noise, one subject may come to believe that the task is unsolvable; that is, neither that subject nor any other subject can control termination of the noise. A second subject, on the other hand, may believe that the task is indeed solvable, but that he or she is just unable to solve it; that is, although he or she cannot terminate the noise, other subjects can do so successfully. The old helplessness hypothesis does not account for these individual differences in response to uncontrollability and neglects the differential effects of such beliefs on self-esteem. Bandura (1977) similarly recognized this inadequacy and suggested a conceptual distinction between efficacy and outcome expectations. Bandura asserted, "People can give up trying because they lack a sense of efficacy in achieving the required behavior, or they may be assured of their capabilities but give up trying because they expect their behavior to have no effect on an unresponsive environment [pp. 204–205]."

Another aspect of this inadequacy becomes evident when we examine the literature concerning the relationship between helplessness and locus of control. The earlier perspectives on learned helplessness (Hiroto, 1974; Miller & Seligman, 1973; Seligman, Maier & Geer, 1968) emphasized an apparent similarity between the helplessness concept of learning that outcomes are uncontrollable and Rotter's (1966) concept of external locus of control. According to Rotter, individuals' beliefs about causality can be arrayed along the dimension of locus of control, with "internals" tending to believe that outcomes are caused by their own responding and "externals" tending to believe that outcomes are not caused by their own responding but rather by factors such as luck, fate, and chance. One method used to assess such beliefs was suggested by Rotter and his associates (James, 1957; James & Rotter, 1958; Phares, 1957; Rotter, Liverant, & Crowne, 1961). These investigators demonstrated that verbalized expectancies for future success change more when reinforcement is perceived as skill-determined (response-dependent) than when it is perceived as chance-determined (response-independent). Studies which examined the conceptual similarity of externals and helpless individuals (Klein & Seligman, 1976; Miller & Seligman, 1975) demonstrated that on tasks of skill, helpless subjects exhibited small expectancy changes, suggesting a belief in external control, whereas subjects not made helpless exhibited large expectancy changes, suggesting a belief in internal control. These findings were interpreted as indicating that helpless subjects perceived tasks of skill as if they were tasks of chance; that is, individuals who were first exposed to noncontingency subsequently responded to response-dependent tasks as if they were response-independent. Garber and Hollon (1980), however, pointed out the puzzling finding that in these studies, on postexperimental questionnaires, both helpless and nonhelpless subjects reported that they viewed the skill task as being a task of skill and that outcomes were controllable. Thus, despite the helpless subjects' smaller expectancy changes on the skill task, they reported that the task was skill-determined. Therefore, it appears that the relation between the concept of uncontrollability and external locus of control is far more complex than was implied by the old hypothesis.

The first inadequacy of the original helplessness hypothesis concerning differential responses to uncontrollability was, in part, a result of the ambiguity of the definition of control. According to the old helplessness hypothesis, an outcome was said to be uncontrollable for an individual when the occurrence of the outcome was not related to his or her responding; that is, if the probability of an outcome is the same whether or not a given response occurs, then the outcome is independent of that response. When this is true of all voluntary responses, the outcome is said to be uncontrollable for the individual (Seligman, 1975; Seligman, Maier, & Solomon, 1971). Conversely, an outcome is controllable if the probability of the outcome when some response is made is different from the probability of the outcome when the response is not made. This early definition, however, makes no distinction between cases in which an individual lacks requisite controlling responses that are available to other people and cases in which the individual as well as all other individuals do not possess controlling responses. The resolution of this inadequacy will be outlined in a later section in terms of the new distinction between personal helplessness and universal helplessness.

Generality and Chronicity of Helplessness

The second inadequacy of the old helplessness hypothesis concerns the generality of helplessness across situations and chronicity over time. Some investigators (e.g., Cole & Coyne, 1977; Hanusa & Schulz, 1977; Roth & Bootzin, 1974; Tennen & Eller, 1977; Wortman & Brehm, 1975) have argued that the phenomenon of learned helplessness is demonstrated only when an individual inappropriately generalizes the expectation of noncontingency to a new, controllable situation. However, the old hypothesis does not require an inappropriate generalization for the demonstration of helplessness. It is only necessary that a person show motivational and cognitive deficits as a consequence of the expectation of uncontrollablility. The veridicality of the belief and the extent of the situations over which it occurs are irrelevant to demonstrating helplessness.

Nonetheless, the old hypothesis is vague about generality and chronicity. Helpless individuals learn in a particular situation that certain responses and outcomes are independent. If, in a new situation, the responses called for or the outcomes desired are similar to those in the original learning situation, then the resulting deficits are likely to occur. Helplessness was considered to have generalized when it produced performance deficits on responses highly dissimilar to those about which original learning had occurred or when it extended to stimuli highly dissimilar to those about which original learning had occurred. No account was given concerning why helplessness was sometimes specific and sometimes global.

Helplessness also tends to dissipate over time. Forgetting produced by interference from prior or subsequent learning was invoked to explain this dissipation in time (Seligman, 1975); that is, forgetting of helplessness was believed to result from either earlier mastery learning (immunization) or subsequent mastery learning (therapy). Unfortunately, however, these explanations were largely *post hoc*. When helplessness dissipated rapidly, it was assumed to have had strong proactive or retroactive intereference; when it persisted, it was not.

Thus, the second inadequacy concerns the question of when and where helplessness will generalize once people believe they are helpless in one situation. In the following section, an attributional framework will be presented to resolve both the first and the second inadequacies of the old helplessness hypothesis.

THE RESOLUTION: AN ATTRIBUTIONAL ANALYSIS

The inadequacies of the old helplessness hypothesis mentioned in the foregoing discussion can be resolved by invoking a unified attributional analysis that utilizes three primary attributional dimensions: *(a)* internal–external; *(b)* stable–unstable; and *(c)* global–specific. Each of these dimensions is relevant to resolving a different inadequacy of the original helplessness hypothesis when applied to humans, and, taken together, they form a new and enriched learned helplessness theory.[1] It is noteworthy that our attributional analysis of helplessness conforms to the logic of Weiner's (1972, 1974) attributional analysis of achievement motivation.

Before discussing each attributional dimension and its role in the reformulation, it is useful to spell out the flow of events which lead to the various symptoms of helplessness. Both the old and the reformulated hypotheses emphasize that the *expectation* of noncontingency is the crucial determinant of the symptoms of learned helplessness. Objective noncontingency is predicted to lead to symptoms of helplessness "only if the expecta-

---

[1]We recognize that there are other attributional dimensions besides the ones used here. For example, the dimension of controllability is logically orthogonal to the Internal × Global × Stable dimensions (although it is empirically more frequent in the internal and unstable attribution), and as such it is a candidate for a $2 \times 2 \times 2 \times 2$ table of attributions. Although we do not detail such an analysis here, we note that the phenomena of self-blame, self-criticism, and guilt (a subclass of self-esteem deficits) in helplessness (and depression) follow from attribution of failure to factors that are controllable. Another attributional dimension, which was suggested by Miller and Norman (1979), is that of importance. Miller and Norman defined this as the relative value a person assigns to an event, and they suggested that the dimension of importance primarily affects the magnitude of the affective and performance deficits. We agree that the notion of importance needs to be considered somewhere in the model. Rather than treat it as a separate dimension, however, we have chosen to discuss it with respect to the intensity of the affective and self-esteem deficits. (See the following section on depressed affect.)

tion of noncontingency is present [Seligman, 1974, p. 48]."[2] The old model, however, did not clearly specify under what conditions the *perception* that events are noncontingent in the past or present will be transformed into an *expectation* that events will be noncontingent in the future. The reformulated helplessness hypothesis suggests that the *attribution* individuals make for the noncontingency between their responses and outcomes in the here and now is an important determinant of their subsequent expectations for future noncontingency. It is these *expectations* which, in turn, determine the generality, chronicity, and type of helplessness symptoms.

The first inadequacy can be resolved by the proposed distinction between universal helplessness and personal helplessness. Table 1.1 explicates this distinction and ultimately serves to define the attributional dimension of "internality" as it is used here. "Internality" is defined primarily in terms of a self–other dichotomy. When individuals believe that outcomes are more likely or less likely to happen to themselves than to relevant others, they attribute these outcomes to something about themselves—internal factors. Conversely, when individuals believe that outcomes are as likely to happen to themselves as to relevant others, they make external attributions.[3]

In Table 1.1, the X-axis represents the person's expectations about the relation between the desired outcome and the responses in his or her repertoire. The person believes that the outcome is either contingent on some responses in his or her repertoire or that it is not contingent on any response in his or her repertoire. the Y-axis represents the individual's expectations

[2]Neither the old nor the reformulated hypothesis requires that expectancy of noncontingency follow from every exposure to uncontrollability, nor do they exclude the possibility that the expectancy may result from other types of experiences as well. For example, for a control procedure, some studies have told subjects to listen to noise (which is inescapable) but not to try to do anything about it (Hiroto & Seligman, 1975); similarly, Glass and Singer (1972) gave subjects a panic button that "will escape noise if pressed" but discouraged them from using it ("I'd rather you didn't, but it's up to you"). These subjects did not become helpless. Because in the latter case they perceived potential response–outcome contingency, and in the first case, they had no relevant perception, these subjects did not form the relevant attributions and expectations and, therefore, did not show the associated deficits.

[3]The formulation of "internal" and "external" attributions used here resembles other attributional frameworks, although it relies more on social comparison. Heider (1958), the founder of attribution theory, distinguished between "factors within the person" and "factors within the environment" as the perceived determinants of outcomes. Similarly, according to Rotter's (1966) locus of control distinction, outcomes are perceived as being causally related either to personal characteristics or to external forces such as chance. Unlike these earlier formulations, which depended on whether factors reside "within the skin" or "outside the skin" to define internality and externality, the present formulation uses the self–other dichotomy as the criterion of internality–externality. Despite the apparent differences between these formulations, further analysis reveals some basic similarities. Heider (1958) and, later, Kelley (1967) both argued that ultimately factors that consistently covary with an outcome are considered to be its cause. In this sense, the various attributional formulations do not substantially disagree.

TABLE 1.1
Personal Helplessness and Universal Helplessness[a]

Other	Self	
	The person expects the outcome is contingent on a response in his or her repertoire	The person expects the outcome is not contingent on any response in his or her repertoire
The person expects the outcome is contingent on a response in the repertoire of a relevant other.	1	Personal helplessness 3 (Internal attribution)
The person expects the outcome is not contingent on a response in the repertoire of any relevant other.	2	Universal helplessness 4 (External attribution)

[a] From L.Y. Abramson, M.E.P. Seligman, & J. Teasdale, Learned helplessness in humans: Critique and reformulation. *Journal of Abnormal Psychology,* 1978, *87,* p. 53. Copyright 1978 by the American Psychological Association. Reprinted by permission.

about the relation between the desired outcome and the responses in the repertoires of relevant other individuals. Here, the person believes that the outcome is either contingent on at least one response in at least one other relevant person's repertoire or not contingent on any response in any relevant other's repertoire.

Although both the X-axis and Y-axis are described as dichotomies, strictly speaking, they actually are continuua. At one end, the person expects that there is a zero probability that the desired outcome is contingent on any response in his or her (or in a relevant other's) repertoire. At the other end, the person expects there is a probability of 1.0 that the desired outcome is contingent on a response in his or her (or in a relevant other's) repertoire. For the purpose of exposition, however, dichotomies rather than continuua are used here.

A second point to clarify is why we use "relevant other" rather than "random other" or "any other." This distinction is particularly important for explaining the symptoms related to self-esteem which were formerly ignored by the old helplessness hypothesis. Consider, for example, a failing graduate student in mathematics who is unable to do complex calculus problems. It is of no solace to such an individual that a "random other" (i.e., an English major) is also unable to do such calculations. The student's self-evaluation is based on the belief that his or her classmates, "relevant others," have a high probability of being able to do the calculus problems.

A special case concerning this "relevant other" distinction is that of the individual who, in the absence of an actual relevant other individual capable of producing the desired outcome, compares him or herself to an "ideal" relevant other. In this case, the individual believes that although no other individual has yet produced the desired outcome, he or she should be able to do so. Examples of this case are athletes who strive to break world records or scientists who work to make new discoveries. In such cases their self-evaluations may be based more on their "ideal" self (see Rogers, 1961) rather than on a real "relevant" other.

Cell 4 in Table 1.1 represents universal helplessness, and Cell 3 represents personal helplessness. In Cells 1 and 2 individuals do not believe that they are helpless, and therefore these cells are not relevant to our present discussion. It should be mentioned, however, that individuals in Cell 2 would be more likely to make internal attributions for their perceived control than would persons in Cell 1

Universal helplessness is characterized by the belief that an outcome is independent of all of one's own responses as well as the responses of other people (see Table 1.1, Cell 4). For example, suppose a child has leukemia and his parents use all their resources to save the child's life. Nothing they do, however, improves the child's health. Nor is there anything anyone else can do to cure the disease. The parents come to believe that there is nothing they or anyone else can do to save the child's life. They subsequently give up trying and exhibit the behavioral as well as the affective symptoms of helplessness. This example is consistent with the old helplessness hypothesis and characterizes the case of universal helplessness.

Personal helplessness, on the other hand, is the case where the individual believes that there exist responses that would contingently produce the desired outcome, although he or she does not possess them. Consider a student who studies endlessly and takes remedial courses in an attempt to get good grades. Unfortunately, however, the student fails anyway. The person eventually comes to believe that he or she is stupid and incompetent, and soon gives up trying to pass. According to the original helplessness model, this is not a clear case of uncontrollability because the person believes that there are responses (for other relevant persons) which would produce passing grades, although he or she does not seem to have them in his or her repertoire. Regardless of any voluntary response the person makes, the probability of his or her obtaining good grades remains unchanged. This is the case of personal helplessness and is a refinement of the old helplessness hypothesis.

The distinction between universal helplessness and personal helplessness clarifies the relation of uncontrollability to failure, which has been questioned by a number of investigators (e.g., Blaney, 1977; Tennen, Note 2). Arguing from an attributional stance, Tennen (Note 2) suggested that the concept of uncontrollability should be replaced with the simpler concept of failure because the terms appear to be redundant. Tennen's view, however, seems to confuse the definitions of failure and uncontrollability.

Failure refers to not obtaining a desired outcome. According to this framework, failure and uncontrollability are not synonymous. Rather, failure is a subset of uncontrollability involving bad outcomes. The original helplessness theory did not differentiate the effects of uncontrollability according to the valence of the outcome. Both good and bad outcomes occurring independently of responding were predicted to lead to helplessness deficits. Seligman (1975) noted that "not only trauma occurring independently of responses, but noncontingent positive events can produce helplessness [p. 98]." Recent evidence confirms this. Uncontrollable positive events produce the motivational and cognitive deficits in animals (Goodkin, 1976; Welker, 1976) and in humans (Eisenberger, Kaplan, & Singer, 1974; Griffiths, 1977; Eisenberger, Mauriello, Carlson, Frank, & Park, Note 3; Hirsch, Note 4; Nugent, Note 5; but see Benson & Kennelly, 1976, for a contrary view) but probably do not produce sad affect. Similarly, Cohen, Rothbart, and Phillips (1976) produced helplessness effects in the absence of failure. Therefore, the concept of uncontrollability means more than just failure, and it makes predictions concerning both failure and noncontingent success.

According to the reformulated model, failure is a subset of helplessness, primarily overlapping with personal helplessness. Failure typically means more than simply not obtaining a desired outcome. In general, failure implies that there was a possibility of success (i.e., some responses can produce the desired outcome) and that the unsuccessful attainment of the goal is attributed to internal factors. In this sense, failure would clearly fall into Cell 3 of Table 1.1, and typify the case of personal helplessness.

Thus, the attributional dimension of internality–externality defines the distinction between universal and personal helplessness and resolves the first set of inadequacies discussed earlier. Situations in which subjects believe that neither they nor any relevant other can solve the problem are instances of universal helplessness, whereas situations in which subjects believe that they cannot solve solvable problems are instances of personal helplessness. This reformulation is consistent with Bandura's (1977) conceptual distinction between efficacy and outcome expectancies. Personal helplessness involves a low efficacy expectation and a high outcome expectation (the response producing the outcome is unavailable to the person), whereas universal helplessness involves a low outcome expectation (no response produces the outcome).

Finally, according to the reformulation, helplessness and external locus of control are orthogonal. Individuals can make either internal or external attributions for their helplessness. Personally helpless individuals make internal attributions for failures, whereas universally helpless individuals make external attributions. The experimental finding that helpless individuals view skill tasks as being tasks of skill rather than chance is no longer puzzling. The individual believes that the task itself is solvable and requires skill (relevant others can solve it) but that they do not have the necessary skill. These subjects view themselves as personally helpless rather than as universally helpless (see Garber & Hollon, 1980, for a discussion of this issue).

The second set of inadequacies of the old helplessness hypothesis concerns the generality and chronicity of the expectation of response–outcome independence. The reformulated attributional analysis of helplessness makes a major new set of predictions about this topic. The helpless individual first learns that certain outcomes and responses are independent; he or she may then make an attribution about the cause. This attribution affects his or her expectations about future response–outcome relations and thereby determines the chronicity, generality, and to some extent, the intensity of the resulting deficits. Some attributions have global, others only specific, implications; some attributions have chronic, others transient, implications. Suppose, for example, you apply for a job and you are turned down. There are a number of attributions which you can make to explain this. Two of the more obvious attributions are "I am unqualified" or "The employer was biased." The former attribution, "I am unqualified," has more severe implications for your future employment than does the latter. If "I am unqualified" is true, you are more likely to be rejected on future job interviews, whereas if "The employer is biased" is true, you have a better chance of being employed in the future as long as you do not return to the same company. Because "I" is something you carry around with you, attributing causes of helplessness internally often, although not always (see later discussion), implies a more consistent outcome in the future than does attributing causes externally, for external circumstances are usually, but not always, in greater flux than are internal factors.

In an attempt to explain this consistency over time, attribution theorists (Weiner, 1974; Weiner, Frieze, Kukla, Reed, Rest, & Rosenbaum, 1971) have refined attribution theory by introducing the attributional dimension of "stable–unstable," which is orthogonal to "internal–external." Stable factors are considered to be long-lived and recurrent, whereas unstable factors are short-lived or intermittent. When an outcome occurs, an individual can attribute it to (a) an internal–stable factor (ability), (b) an internal–unstable factor (effort), (c) an external–stable factor (task difficulty), or (d) an external–unstable factor (luck).

Although the addition of the "stable–unstable" dimension is a useful and important refinement for explaining the consistency of attributions over time, a further refinement is needed to account for the generality of helplessness across situations. In particular, Abramson et al. (1978) suggested a third dimension—"global–specific"—that is orthogonal to internality and stability. Global factors affect a wide variety of situations, whereas specific

TABLE 1.2
Formal Characteristics of Attribution and Some Examples[a]

Dimension	Internal		External	
	Stable	Unstable	Stable	Unstable
Global	Lack of intelligence	Exhaustion	Unfairness of ETS[b]	Today is Friday the 13th.
	(Laziness)	(Having a cold makes me stupid.)	(People are usually unlucky on the GRE.)	(ETS gave experimental tests this time which were too hard for everyone.)
Specific	Lack of mathematical ability	Frustration with math problems	Unfairness of ETS math tests	The math test was form No. 13.
	(Math always bores me.)	(Having a cold ruins my arithmetic.)	(People are usually unlucky on math tests.)	(Everyone's copy of the math test was blurred.)

[a] From L. Y. Abramson, M. E. P. Seligman, & J. Teasdale, Learned helplessness in humans: Critique and reformulation. *Journal of Abnormal Psychology*, 1978, 87, p. 57. Copyright 1978 by the American Psychological Association. Reprinted by permission.
[b] ETS = Educational Testing Service, the maker of graduate record examinations (GRE).

factors do not. So, attributing uncontrollability to a global factor implies that helplessness will occur across situations, and a specific attribution implies helplessness only in the original situation. The global–specific dimension as well as the dimensions of stability and internality are continuua rather than dichotomies. For the sake of simplicity, we will treat them as dichotomies.

Table 1.2 describes the formal characteristics of these attributional dimensions and exemplifies them. Table 1.2 extends Table 1.1 by using the attributional dimensions of stability and globality to further subdivide the cases of personal helplessness (Table 1.1, Cell 3—Internal attribution) and universal helplessness (Table 1.1, Cell 4—External attribution). In the example in Table 1.2, crossing the three dimensions (Internal–External × Stable–Unstable × Global–Specific) yields eight kinds of attributions individuals can make concerning their poor performances on the math test of the Graduate Record Examinations.[4] These attributions have very different implications for their expectations about their performance in the next hour on the

[4] Although we have used primarily examples of vocational or achievement-related helplessness, the model also may be applied to interpersonal examples. This is particularly important because so much real-life helplessness stems from social inadequacy and rejection.

verbal part of the test (generality of helplessness deficits across situations) and for their expectations concerning how they will do on future math tests when they retake the GRE's next time (chronicity of the deficits over time).

According to this reformulated hypothesis, if the individual makes any of the four global attributions for their low math score, the deficits will extend across situations; that is, global attributions imply that when individuals confront new situations they will expect that outcomes will again be independent of their responses. So, if they attribute their poor math scores to lack of intelligence (internal, stable, global), exhaustion (internal, unstable, global), unfairness of Educational Testing Service (ETS) tests (external, stable, global), or it is an unlucky day (external, unstable, global), then when they take the verbal test in the next few minutes, they will expect that here, again, the outcome will be independent of their responses, and helplessness deficits will ensue. If, on the other hand, the individual makes any of the aforementioned specific attributions, helplessness deficits are less likely to appear during the verbal test.

In a parallel manner, the chronicity of the deficits follows from the stability dimension. Chronic deficits will ensue if the attribution is to stable factors: lack of intelligence, lack of mathematical ability, unfairness of ETS tests, or unfairness of ETS math tests. Individuals will manifest chronic deficits if they make a stable attribution because it implies to them that they will lack the controlling response in the future. If the attribution is to an unstable factor—exhaustion, frustration with math problems, unlucky day, or unlucky on math tests—they will not necessarily be helpless the next time they take the math part of the GRE.[5]

Thus, this attributional analysis of experience with uncontrollability predicts when helplessness deficits will generalize to new situations and when they will persist over time. The attributional dimensions are relevant to explaining when inappropriate, broad generalization of the expectation of noncontingency will occur. When subjects attribute their helplessness in the training phase to very global and stable factors, broad transfer of helplessness effects will be observed. Alternatively, attributing helplessness to very specific and unstable factors predicts very little transfer of helplessness.

[5]A point needs to be made concerning the correspondence between the dimensions of attributions as suggested by Weiner et al. (1971)—internal–stable, internal–unstable, external–stable, and external–unstable—and the examples used to characterize them—ability, effort, task–difficulty, and luck, respectively. We would like to reiterate Weiner's (1974) point that these examples do not map isomorphically onto these dimensions. Table 2 presents (in parentheses) attributions that systematically violate the mapping. An example of this is the fact that an internal–stable attribution for helplessness need not always be lack of ability; it could be lack of effort, laziness (global), math always bores me (specific). Thus, ability and effort are logically orthogonal to internal–stable and internal–unstable attributions, as are luck and task difficulty orthogonal to external–stable and external–unstable attributions.

Implications

We have presented here a unified attributional analysis of helplessness, emphasizing three specific dimensions in order to resolve the various inadequacies of the old helplessness hypothesis. The dimension of internality predicts the type of helplessness (universal versus personal); the dimension of globality predicts the generality of helplessness across situations; and the dimension of stability predicts the chronicity of helplessness over time. In addition to resolving these inadequacies, the attributional analysis has other important implications for the helplessness model.

The first implication is that the universal versus personal helplessness distinction deduces a fourth deficit of human helplessness—low self-esteem. A major determinant of attitudes toward the self is comparison with others (Clark & Clark, 1939; Festinger, 1954; Morse & Gergen, 1970; Rosenberg, 1965). This analysis suggests that individuals who believe that desired outcomes are not contingent on responses in their repertoire, but are contingent on responses in the repertoires of relevant others, will show lower self-esteem than will individuals who believe that desired outcomes are neither contingent on acts in their own repertoire nor contingent on acts in the repertoires of relevant others; that is, an unintelligent student who fails an exam that his or her peers have passed will have lower self-esteem (at least with respect to intelligence) than will a student who fails an exam that all of his or peers have failed as well. In the example from Table 1.2, if the individual makes any of the internal attributions for failure on the math test—lack of intelligence, lack of math ability, exhaustion, or frustration with math problems—the self-esteem deficits will occur. In contrast, none of the external attributions will produce self-esteem deficits. Thus, the dichotomy between universal and personal helplessness determines cases of helplessness with and without low self-esteem. It is important to emphasize, however, that the cognitive and motivational deficits are hypothesized to occur in both personal and universal helplessness. According to both the old and new hypotheses, then, the expectation that outcomes are noncontingently related to one's own responses is a sufficient condition for motivational and cognitive deficits, whereas according to the reformulation, low self-esteem is assumed to result from internal attributions—personal helplessness.

The second implication of this attributional analysis of helplessness is in regard to the dimensions of stability and globality. Attributions along the global–specific continuum determine the generality of helplessness effects across situations; attributions along the stable–unstable continuum determine the chronicity of helplessness effects across time. This attributional account of the generality and chronicity of symptoms of helplessness explains why debriefing after an experimental manipulation ensures that deficits are not carried outside the laboratory. In the typical helplessness experiment, subjects are presented with an unsolvable problem, tested on a second, solvable problem, and finally debriefed. During debriefing, the subject is informed that the first problem had actually been unsolvable. It is typically assumed that telling subjects that no one could have solved the problem will cause the helplessness deficit to go away. The old helplessness hypothesis, however, did not provide an explanation for why debriefing removes the cognitive and motivational deficits. What does debriefing undo and why?

According to the attributional reformulation of helplessness, debriefing presumably changes the subject's attribution from a global (and potentially harmful outside the laboratory) and possibly internal one (e.g., I'm stupid) to a more specific and external one (e.g., Psychologists are nasty; they give unsolvable problems to experimental subjects). Since the attribution for help-lessness is to a specific factor, the expectation of uncontrollability should not recur outside the laboratory anymore than it would have without the exper-imental experience of noncontingency.

A final implication concerns the question of the intensity or severity of the various deficits associated with helplessness. Severity refers to the strength of a given deficit at any one time in a particular situation and is logically independent of chronicity and generality. We suggest that the intensity of the motivational and cognitive deficits increases with the strength or *certain-ty* of the expectation of noncontingency (see Garber, Miller, & Abramson, 1980, for a discussion of the relationship between certainty and helpless-ness). The intensity of self-esteem loss and affective changes are assumed to increase with both the certainty and importance of the event the person is helpless about (see later discussion of depression). So, for example, rejection by a lover will typically produce more severe helplessness deficits than will failing your road test for your driver's license, because of the greater impor-tance of the former. Attributions to global and stable factors also may indirectly affect the severity of self-esteem and affective deficits because the individual will expect to be helpless in the near and distant future (both across other areas of his or her life and across time). The future will seem hopeless. This expectation will increase the intensity of the self-esteem and affective defi-cits. Moreover, if the attribution is internal, this may tend to increase the severity of the symptom even further, for internal attributions are typically more stable and more global. So, in the case where the individual fails his or her driving test, he or she may manifest severe helplessness deficits, despite its apparent triviality, if he or she makes a stable, global, and internal attribu-tion for failure, such as "I am generally incompetent." The symptoms of helplessness will be more intense because the individual expects to be unable to control many of the outcomes which he or she may desire in the future.

Attribution and Expectancy: Hypothetical Constructs

The attributional reformulation of helplessness, like Weiner's (1972, 1974) attributional analysis of achievement motivation, discusses the affective, cognitive, and behavioral *consequences* of making particular attributions for events. The reformulation is relatively silent with respect to specifying the properties of the attribution *process* itself. Although questions concerning whether or not people always make causal attributions for success and failure are important (e.g., Bem, 1967; Diener & Dweck, 1978; Wortman & Dintzer, 1978) and have implications for helplessness theory (e.g., Diener & Dweck, 1978; Hanusa & Schulz, 1977), the attributional reformulation is intended as an explanation of what happens once an attribution is made for uncontrollability.

Similarly, the attributional reformulation is relatively silent with respect to specifying the determinants of what particular attribution a person happens to make for uncontrollability. Attribution theorists (e.g., Heider, 1958; Jones & Davis, 1965; Kelley, 1967; Weiner, 1974) have discussed situational factors that influence the sort of attributions people make. In addition, there may be systematic biases and errors in the formulation of attributions (Heider, 1958; Kelley, 1967). One such bias may be the "attributional style" that characterizes depressed individuals (e.g., Seligman, Abramson, Semmel, & von Baeyer, 1979).

To summarize the logic of the reformulation, once an attribution is made for uncontrollability, its properties predict in what new situations and across what span of time the expectation of uncontrollability will be likely to recur. An attribution to global or stable factors predicts that the expectation will recur even when the situation changes or even after a lapse of time, respectively. Alternatively, an attribution to specific or unstable factors predicts that the expectation need not recur when the situation changes or after a lapse of time, respectively. It should be emphasized that it is the *expectation* of uncontrollability which ultimately determines whether or not helplessness deficits will recur in a new situation or with elapsed time. *The attribution predicts the recurrence of the expectations whereas the expectation determines the occurrence of the helplessness deficits.*

While we suspect that actual experiences with uncontrollability and the subsequent formation of attributions are the most salient and effective means for producing helplessness, we recognize that neither is a necessary condition for helplessness. Only the *expectation* of helplessness is necessary to produce the associated deficits, regardless of how this expectation is acquired. In addition to attributions, other sources of information such as vicarious experience, verbal persuasion, and physiological states may influence expectations of uncontrollability (see Bandura, 1977; Brown & Inouye, 1978;

DeVellis, DeVellis, & McCauley, 1978). Similarly, the expectation can change as a consequence of new evidence which may intervene between the initial attribution and the new and subsequent situation. (For further discussion of this point and its implications for the treatment of helplessness and depression, see Hollon & Garber, 1980). Therefore, using the example from Table 1.2, if individuals find out by intervening successes that they are not as stupid as they have thought or that everyone obtained low scores on the math GRE and so ETS now is under new management, then they need not expect to be helpless across situations and time. On the other hand, if the expectation of uncontrollability is present, then helplessness deficits will occur.

A final important point is that the attributional reformulation regards both attributions and expectations as *hypothetical constructs*. The reformulation is not a phenomenological theory. Attributions and expectations are hypothesized events mediating between objective uncontrollability and subsequent helplessness performance deficits. Consequently, verbal report is only one of a number of potential converging measures for assessing attributions and expectancies. An important future task for investigators working with the reformulated helplessness hypothesis is to develop an adequate technology for measuring attributions and expectations.

VALIDITY OF THE ATTRIBUTIONAL REFORMULATION

As with any new hypothesis, the validity of the reformulated model is ultimately determined by its ability to generate novel predictions that survive attempts at experimental disconfirmation. Because it is still a relatively new hypothesis, few results from such attempts are yet available. A minimum requirement, however, is that this hypothesis be consistent with the available experimental evidence. An inconsistency might cause one to seriously question the hypothesis.

Experimental Evidence

Is the reformulated hypothesis consistent with the experimental evidence on learned helplessness in humans? Is there new evidence which has been generated since Abramson et al. (1978) first presented the reformulation which tests it directly? There are three basic classes of evidence which are relevant here: (a) deficits produced by learned helplessness; (b) attributional evidence; and (c) skill–chance evidence.

Deficits Produced by Learned Helplessness

Both the old and the reformulated hypotheses explain the deficits which result from exposure to uncontrollability (e.g., inescapable noise or unsolvable discrimination problems) by proposing that subjects expect that outcomes and responses are independent in the subsequent test situation. This expectation produces the motivational deficit evidenced by failure to escape noise (Glass, Reim, & Singer, 1971; Hiroto & Seligman, 1975; Klein & Seligman, 1976; Miller & Seligman, 1976) and failure to solve anagrams (Benson & Kennelly, 1976; Gatchel & Proctor, 1976; Hiroto & Seligman, 1975; Klein et al., 1976) and the cognitive deficit evidenced by failure to see patterns in anagrams (Hiroto & Seligman, 1975; Klein et al., 1976).

The reformulated hypothesis further explains why the expectation of uncontrollability transfers to new situations and survives the time interval between tasks. In such cases it is likely that subjects have made global and stable attributions (e.g., I'm unintelligent. Problems in this laboratory are impossible) for the uncontrollability of the noise or the unsolvability of the discrimination problems. Because attributions were not assessed directly in these studies and because there was no measure of self-esteem, however, it is impossible to determine whether the global and stable attributions were internal (e.g., I'm unintelligent) or external (e.g., Laboratory tasks are impossible).

In all the studies using the typical triadic design, the nondepressed subjects who control noise, solve problems, or receive nothing during the pretreatment phase did not experience or perceive response–outcome independence, and thus, did not make attributions about such independence. Nevertheless, these subjects' attributions concerning their experience with response–outcome dependency may be of interest as well. In fact, Alloy and Abramson (1979) have found that nondepressed, nonhelpless subjects appear to have a somewhat unrealistic expectation of response–outcome *dependence,* evidenced by their tendency to overestimate the degree of control they have.

Results of earlier studies on human helplessness that were difficult to explain in terms of the original helplessness hypothesis now may be more easily explained by the reformulated hypothesis. Such studies may have tapped into the attributional dimensions of globality and stability. A good example is the study by Roth and Kubal (1975), which tested the cross-situational generality of helplessness. Subjects were led to believe that they were participating in two very separate experiments. Subjects who failed on the first task (pretraining) were told either that the test was a "really good prediction of grades in college" (important) or that the test was merely "an experiment in learning" (unimportant). Subjects in the former group showed deficits on the subsequent cognitive problems (test task). The reformulated helplessness hypothesis suggests that these subjects probably made a more global, internal, and possibly more stable attribution for their performance, and therefore, the expectation of uncontrollability recurred in the new situation, thus producing the deficits. Subjects in the "unimportant" condition probably made a more specific and less stable attribution, did not have an expectation of helplessness on the next task, and thus did not show the performance deficits. (See Cole & Coyne, 1977, for another way to induce a specific, rather than a global attribution for helplessness.)

Similarly, Douglas and Anisman (1975) found that subjects who failed on what they believed to be a simple task showed later cognitive deficits, whereas subjects who failed on a supposedly complex task did not. It is likely that subjects attributed their failure on the simple tasks to more global and internal factors (e.g., I'm stupid), whereas the other subjects attributed their failure on the complex tasks to external and more specific factors (e.g., These problems are too difficult).

The attributional reformulation also better explains the effects of therapy and immunization than does the old hypothesis. The key attributional dimension here is global–specific. Experiences with success have been shown to both reverse and prevent the deficits associated with helplessness. Klein and Seligman (1976) gave a "therapy" procedure, using 4 or 12 soluable cognitive problems, to nondepressed subjects made helpless with uncontrollable noise and to depressed subjects given no noise. The therapy worked such that these subjects subsequently controlled noise successfully and showed normal expectancy changes after success and failure. The reformulated model suggests that the therapy had the effect of inducing subjects to revise their original global attribution for the inescapable noise (e.g., I'm incompetent, or laboratory tasks are unsolvable) to a more specific attribution (I'm only incompetent on some tasks, or only some laboratory tasks are too difficult) after the experience of success on the intervening task. Thus, the intervening success experience may have changed an expectation of uncontrollability to an expectation of controllability by changing attributions.

It is noteworthy that according to this explanation, the attributional dimension of global–specific rather than internal–external is relevant here. This point is partially supported empirically by a study by Teasdale (1978), who found that whereas both real success experiences and recalling past successes were equally effective in shifting attributions for initial failure from internal to external factors, only real success reversed the helplessness performance deficits. It may be that success does not have its effect by shifting attributions along the internal–external dimension, but rather modifies attributions along the global–specific dimension, although the relevant data remains to be collected.

The effects of immunization (Jones, Nation, & Massad, 1977; Klee & Meyer, 1979; Thornton & Powell, 1974; Dyck & Breen, Note 6) may be explained similarly: Initial success experience should make the attribution for a subsequent helplessness experience less global and therefore less likely to produce an expectation of helplessness in the new test situation.

In a recent study by Koller and Kaplan (1978) the notion that debriefing alters subjects' attribution with respect to the dimensions of global–specific and stable–unstable was supported. Regardless of whether subjects had received contingent or noncontingent reinforcement during the pretreatment phase, all subjects who were later informed that "during the pretreatment the experimenter had been controlling the tone and problem solution [p. 1179]" performed well on the test task. In contrast, those subjects in the noncontingent pretreatment condition who received no such information showed the typical deficits associated with helplessness. Thus, giving subjects a specific, unstable (and external) attribution for their earlier helplessness, prevented the formation of an expectancy of uncontrollability on the next task. Moreover, subjects were explicitly told in this condition that on the next task "reinforcement would be entirely contingent upon the subject's responding." Thus, not only were subjects supplied with a specific, unstable attribution for their prior helplessness, but they were also given an explicit expectation of response–outcome dependence. These results indeed are consistent with the attributional reformulation of helplessness. (Interestingly, Koller and Kaplan [1978] misinterpreted the reformulated hypothesis and argued that their results disconfirmed the hypothesis!)

Improved rather than impaired performance shown by subjects exposed to uncontrollable events has been found in several studies (Hanusa & Schulz, 1977; Roth & Kubal, 1975; Tennen & Eller, 1977; Wortman, Panciera, Shusterman, & Hibscher, 1976). Such facilitation is not well understood, however, (see Wortman & Brehm, 1975; Roth & Kilpatrick-Taback, Note 1, for a discussion of this issue). It may be that compensatory attempts to reassert control follow experiences with uncontrollability once the person leaves the original situation in which he or she was helpless. (See Solomon & Corbit, 1973, for a relevant rebound theory.) According to an attributional analysis of facilitation, subjects who make internal, specific, and unstable attributions (e.g., effort) for their first failure may attempt to compensate by trying harder on the next task. Attempts to test the compensatory rebound hypothesis should also assess attributions. Facilitiation of performance after experience with uncontrollability may also result when individuals cannot find a controlling response but have not yet concluded that they are helpless. Again, we predict that these subjects would make an unstable and specific attribution for their trial-to-trial failures despite their belief that they would eventually find the controlling response.

The reformulated helplessness hypothesis, then, accounts for the basic helplessness results better than does the original hypothesis. However, the explanations given by the reformulated hypothesis are necessarily *post hoc* because the relevant measurements of globality, stability, and internality of attribution were not made. Recent studies which have offered alternative explanations for helplessness effects such as egotism (Frankel & Snyder, 1978) or persistence (Nation, Cooney, & Gartrell, 1979) have failed to directly assess attributions and therefore cannot be interpreted as either confirmation or disconfirmation of the reformulation. Rather, the reformulated helplessness hypothesis must be empirically validated either by measuring attributions and correlating them with deficits that occur, or by inducing the attributions and predicting deficits.

Attributional Evidence

According to the reformulation, performance deficits should occur in cases of both universal helplessness (external attribution) and personal helplessness (internal attribution). In both cases the expectation that outcomes are independent of responses is present. In addition, attributions of helplessness to stable and global factors should be more likely to result in performance deficits over time and across situations than attributions to unstable and specific factors. Four studies have directly manipulated attributions for helplessness in adults (Hanusa & Schulz, 1977; Klein et al., 1976; Tennen & Eller, 1977; Wortman et al., 1976). Klein et al. (1976) found that relative to groups receiving solvable problems or no problems at all, nondepressed subjects exposed to unsolvable discrimination problems performed poorly in a subsequent anagrams task, regardless of whether they were induced to attribute their helplessness to internal factors or to external factors.

In an attempt to manipulate attributions, Tennen and Eller (1977) gave subjects unsolvable discrimination problems that were labeled either progressively "easier" or progressively "harder." It was assumed that failure on easy problems should produce attributions to lack of ability (internal, stable, and *global),* whereas failure on hard problems should produce attributions to task difficulty (external, stable, *specific).* Paralleling the procedure used by Roth and Kubal (1975), subjects then went to what was supposed to be a second, unrelated experiment in which they were given anagrams. Attribution to inability (easy problems) produced deficits, whereas attribution to task difficulty resulted in facilitation of anagram solving. We suggest that subjects in the task–difficulty group did not show performance deficits because they made specific attributions for their helplessness and did not have an expectation of noncontingency in the test task.

Results of the two other studies that manipulated attributions at first appear to be somewhat contrary to the reformulation. Hanusa and Schulz

(1977) and Wortman et al. (1976) found that neither the subjects instructed to believe they were personally helpless (internal attribution) nor the subjects instructed to believe they were universally helpless (external attribution) on a training task showed performance deficits on a test task relative to subjects exposed to contingent events. It is interesting, however, that Wortman et al. (1976) found that personally helpless subjects reported greater emotional distress than did universally helpless subjects. One difficulty with these studies is that they did not replicate the basic helplessness findings; that is, the typical helplessness group (a group exposed to noncontingency but given no explicit attribution) did not show performance deficits on the test task. Thus, the test task may not have been sensitive to helplessness deficits. (For a discussion of the relative sensitivity of tasks to helplessness in animals, see Maier & Seligman, 1976).

A final group of studies by Dweck and her associates (Dweck, 1975, 1976; Dweck & Repucci, 1973; Dweck, Davidson, Nelson, & Enna, Note 7; Dweck, Goetz, & Strauss, Note 8) demonstrated the differential effects of attributions for failure to lack of ability versus lack of effort in fourth-grade children. Whereas attributions to lack of effort are unstable and specific (and internal), attributions to lack of ability are stable and global (as well as internal) and are more likely to lead to an expectation of failure in a new task. Dweck and Repucci (1973) found that fourth-grade girls tend to attribute their failure to lack of ability and subsequently show performance deficits on a cognitive task, whereas fourth-grade boys tend to attribute their failure to lack of effort or bad conduct and do not show performance deficits. Since boys attribute failures to lack of effort, all they need to do is to try harder on the next task, and they will perform adequately. Moreover, when children are taught to attribute failure to lack of effort rather than to lack of ability, they tend to perform better (Dweck, 1975).

Thus, there is some support for the attributional reformulation from helplessness studies which have directly assessed and manipulated attributions. These studies are not without methodological problems, however. Future research which manipulates attributions needs to avoid the problem of confounding one attributional dimension with another, particularly externality with specificity and internality with globality.

Expectancy Changes in Skill Tasks

As discussed previously, the finding that in a skill task helpless (Klein & Seligman, 1976; Miller & Seligman, 1976; Miller, Seligman, & Kurlander, 1975) and depressed (Abramson, Garber, Edwards, & Seligman, 1978; Garber & Hollon, 1980; Miller & Seligman, 1973) subjects increase their expectancy for future success less following success and/or decrease their expectancy of future success less following failure than do nonhelpless and nondepressed subjects has been interpreted as support for the learned helplessness hypothesis. It was assumed that this index measured the central helplessness deficit, that is, the general tendency of helpless subjects to perceive responding and outcomes as independent on skill tasks.

Weiner and his colleagues (Weiner et al., 1971), contrary to Rotter and his colleagues (James, 1957; James & Rotter, 1958; Phares, 1957; Rotter et al., 1961), asserted that the attributional dimension of stability rather than locus of control is the primary determinant of expectancy changes. Thus, according to Weiner (1974) and Weiner, Heckhausen, Meyer, and Cook (1972), attributions to unstable factors produce small expectancy changes, whereas attributions to stable factors produce large expectancy changes. Past outcomes are assumed to be good predictors of future outcomes only when they are caused by stable factors.

Unfortunately, due to the absence of direct assessment of individuals' attributions on the chance and skill tasks, it is difficult to validate these hypotheses for helplessness and depression. The reformulated helplessness hypothesis makes no specific predictions about expectancy changes and helplessness, because a belief in response–outcome independence or dependence is orthogonal to the stable–unstable dimension. It is possible, however, that helpless subjects make internal attributions to lack of ability for their helplessness, but when they are confronted with the 50% success rate typically used in helplessness studies, they may attribute outcomes on the skill task to an unstable (and external) factor such as chance. They may maintain their belief that they lack the stable factor of ability but conclude that in this case ability is not necessary for success on the task. After all, they succeeded sometimes in spite of their perceived lack of ability. Here, the subjects will exhibit small expectancy changes because they believe outcomes are a matter of chance (unstable factors) for themselves, although they believe that the task is a matter of skill for others (see Garber & Hollon, 1980, for a discussion of this issue related to depression).

Thus, small expectancy changes do not necessarily imply a belief in response–outcome independence, and large expectancy changes do not necessarily imply a belief in response–outcome dependence. We agree with Rizley (1978) that expectancy changes on chance and skill tasks do not directly test the learned helplessness model of depression. Nevertheless, the finding that depressives often show smaller expectancy changes on skill tasks than do nondepressed individuals (Abramson et al., 1978; Garber & Hollon, 1980; Klein & Seligman, 1976; Miller & Seligman, 1973, 1976; Miller et al., 1975; Sacco & Hokanson, 1978; although see McNitt & Thornton, 1978; Smolen, 1978; Willis & Blaney, 1978, for contrary results) is intriguing and needs to be researched further, even though it provides only limited support for the learned helplessness model. The results support the

model only in as far as both helpless and depressed individuals show the
same pattern of expectancy shifts, but the pattern itself cannot be predicted
without further information about the accompanying attributions. Thus, expectancy changes on chance and skill tasks are not really a direct way of
testing helplessness because such changes are sensitive to the attributional
dimension of stability and not to expectations about response–outcome
independence.

IMPLICATIONS OF THE ATTRIBUTIONAL ANALYSIS
FOR THE HELPLESSNESS MODEL OF DEPRESSION

Historically, the learned helplessness model of depression (Garber, Miller, & Seaman, 1979; Seligman, 1974, 1975; Seligman et al., 1976) has
emphasized the parallels between the laboratory phenomenon of learned
helplessness and clinical depression. The four lines of evidence used to
compare similarities between these phenomena have been: symptoms, etiology, therapy, and prevention. Symptom similarity has received the most
support empirically. Seligman (1975) has argued that experience with uncontrollability in the laboratory is similar to experience with events that are
typically thought to be precipitants of depression, such as loss of a loved
one, loss of a job, and so on. The cornerstone of the original learned
helplessness model of depression is that learning that outcomes are uncontrollable produces the motivational, cognitive, and emotional components
of depression. The motivational deficit of retarded initiation of responses
observed in helpless subjects parallels the passivity, psychomotor retardation, and social impairment found in naturally occurring depression. The
cognitive deficit of difficulty learning that responses produce outcomes parallels depressives' "negative cognitive set" (Beck, 1967), which involves the
belief that their actions are doomed to failure. Finally, the model claims that
depressed affect is a consequence of the belief that outcomes are uncontrollable. There are a number of inadequacies, however, of the original formulation with respect to the symptoms of depressed affect, lowered self-esteem,
and self-blame. Moreover, the old model is silent with respect to variations
in the generality, chronicity, and intensity of depression. These shortcomings will be discussed now in terms of the new attributional framework.

Before discussing the resolution of these inadequacies, we need to
address the issue of the taxonomy of depression. The syndrome of depression is a complex and heterogeneous phenomenon (see Depue & Monroe,
1978). The adequacy of the new psychiatric system of classification—DSM
III—still needs to be determined. It is therefore unclear what type of depres-

sion helplessness most appropriately models. The subclass of depressions modeled by laboratory helplessness may cut across the typical ways of classifying clinical depression. In fact, there may be a subclass of "helplessness" depression which is consistent with the symptoms, etiology, treatment, and prevention of helplessness. Its central and defining feature would be the expectation that outcomes are independent of responding. It is important to emphasize, however, that the model regards this expectation of response–outcome independence as a sufficient, but not necessary, condition for depression. Other etiological factors such as physiological states, post partum conditions, hormonal states, chemical depletions, heredity, and so on, may produce depression in the absence of the expectation of uncontrollability. Moreover, although these various causal agents may produce different types of depressions, it is also possible that more than one cause may operate on an individual at the same time to produce a particular form of depression. Thus, for example, a diathesis–stress model of depression would suggest that both genetic and psychological (e.g., helplessness) factors may interact to produce the syndrome. According to the model, then, there may exist a subset of depressions—helplessness depression—that is caused by the expectation of response–outcome independence, which is characterized by symptoms of passivity, negative cognitive set, and depressed affect, and may be treated with therapies that are designed to alter the expectation of uncontrollability.

Depressed Affect

Seligman (1974, 1975) speculated that noncontingent positive events as well as noncontingent negative events can produce helplessness and depression. According to the old hypothesis, the expectation of noncontingency regardless of the valence of the outcome produced helplessness deficits, including depressed affect. Even though there is empirical evidence that uncontrollable positive events can produce subsequent performance deficits (e.g., Eisenberger et al., 1974; Griffiths, 1977), there is no evidence of an affective deficit in these cases. Moreover, common sense as well as anecdotal evidence suggest that the expectation of good events does not typically produce depressed affect (see Seligman, 1975, p. 98, versus Maier & Seligman, 1976, p. 17, for previous inconsistent accounts). Receiving a monthly check of $1000 from a trust fund does not usually produce sadness even though the money comes noncontingently. In this case, individuals may become passive with respect to trying to obtain or to stop receiving the money (motivational deficit) or may have difficulty relearning once money becomes response-contingent again (cognitive deficit), but they do not show dysphoria. *Only those cases in which the expectation of response–outcome independence is about the lack or loss of a highly desired outcome or about the occurrence of a highly aversive outcome are sufficient for the emotional component of depression.* Thus, depressed affect is outcome-related. Affective changes result from the expectation that bad outcomes will occur and not from their expected uncontrollability. (For a discussion of the relationship of uncontrollability to another affect—anxiety—see Garber, Miller, & Abramson, 1980.) Depressed affect may occur in cases of either universal or personal helplessness, because either may involve expectations of uncontrollable important outcomes of a negative valence.

One problem with the present formulation, although it is also a problem for the psychology of motivation in general, concerns what is meant by "importance" or "highly desired" outcomes. Even though most people would very much like to receive a million dollars, we usually are not sad that we have not, even though we believe we are basically helpless with respect to this outcome. Klinger's (1975) notion of "current concerns" may be relevant here. We suggest that depressed affect results only when the outcome, which we are helpless to obtain, is "on our mind," "in the realm of possibility," or "of present concern."

The intensity of sad affect increases with the desirability of the unobtainable outcome (or with the aversiveness of the unavoidable outcome) and with the strength or certainty of the expectation of its unobtainability. Moreover, Weiner (1974) suggested that failures attributed to internal factors (e.g., lack of ability) produce greater negative affect than do failures attributed to external factors (e.g., task difficulty); hence, depressed affect may be more intense in personal helplessness than in universal helplessness. The intensity of the cognitive and motivational deficits, however, is not dependent on the type of helplessness or on the importance of the outcome.

Lowered Self-Esteem

In addition to the motivational, cognitive, and emotional deficits of helplessness, there is a fourth deficit—low self-esteem—which is important for the syndrome of depression. The old helplessness model of depression, however, failed to explain the depressive's low opinion of himself or herself. Low self-esteem has been regarded as a hallmark symptom of depression by several theoretical perspectives (Beck, 1967, 1976; Bibring, 1953; Freud, 1917/1957), and therefore an adequate model of depression should attempt to account for this symptom.

The universal versus personal helplessness distinction predicts that depressed individuals who attribute their helplessness to internal factors (personal helplessness) will show lower self-esteem than will individuals who make external attributions (universal helplessness). Ickes and Layden (1978) reported that individuals with low self-esteem tend to attribute negative outcomes to internal factors and positive outcomes to external factors, whereas the opposite was true for high self-esteem subjects. So, for example, a depressed, unemployed individual who attributes his or her joblessness to personal incompetence will show lower self-esteem than will an unemployed individual who attributes his or her joblessness to an external factor, such as the economic recession. Both depressed individuals, however, will show the other three deficits (passivity, negative cognitive set, depressed affect) because they both expect that the highly desired outcome of obtaining employment is not contingent on their responses and is unobtainable.

Other writers (e.g., Blatt, D'Afflitti, & Quinlan, 1976; Bibring, 1953) have similarly suggested that there are at least two types of depressions which differ in terms of self-regard. Blatt et al. (1976), for example, characterized depressions in terms of the dimensions of dependency, on the one hand, and low self-esteem, on the other. The universal versus personal helplessness distinction introduced by the reformulated helplessness hypothesis attempts to account for these observed differences in self-esteem.

Attributions and Depression

What are the naturally occurring attributions of depressives? There is a growing literature which has addressed this issue from a number of perspectives. One of the earlier studies to assess the attributions of depressed and nondepressed college students for failure on discrimination problems was conducted by Klein et al. (1976). Whereas depressed students tended to attribute failure to internal factors, nondepressed students tended to attribute failure to external factors.

Similarly, Rizley (1978) assessed the attributions of depressed and nondepressed students for their success or failure on a cognitive task. Depressed students attributed failure to incompetence (internal, global, stable) and success to ease of the task (external, specific, stable), whereas nondepressed subjects attributed failure to task difficulty (external, specific, stable) and success to their ability (internal, global, stable). Using a word-association task, Kuiper (1978) replicated these results for nondepressed and depressed subjects' attributions for failure. Contrary to expectation, however, depressives tended to make internal attributions for successful outcomes. Kuiper (1978) suggested that depressives may have a more general tendency to assume responsibility for outcomes regardless of their hedonic valence.

A recent study by Leon, Kendall, and Garber (in press) assessed the attributions of depressed and nondepressed children using a self-report measure of attributions administered verbally. The results parallel those found for adults, with depressed children showing a greater tendency to make internal attributions for negative outcomes and external attributions for positive outcomes than nondepressed children.

The most direct test of the attributional reformulation of learned helplessness as it relates to depression was conducted by Seligman et al. (1979) who attempted to discover a depressive *attributional style*. Using a new attributional style scale developed by Semmel, Abramson, Seligman, and von Baeyer (Note 9), Seligman et al. (1979) assessed the three dimensions of internality, globality, and stability both individually and exhaustively. Results indicated that relative to nondepressed students, depressed students attributed bad outcomes to internal, stable, and global factors. They also were more likely to attribute good outcomes to unstable, external factors than were nondepressed students.

Taken together, the aforementioned studies provide the most direct support for the reformulated helplessness hypothesis. Two additional studies provide further, although somewhat more indirect, support for the model. Hammen and Krantz (1976) examined the cognitive distortions of depressed and nondepressed women using a multiple-choice story completion questionnaire. Depressed women selected more depressed–distorted cognitions, whereas nondepressed women selected more nondepressed–nondistorted cognitions. The depressed distortions tended to be consistent with the more internal, global, and stable attributions for failure found in other studies.

Finally, Garber and Hollon (1980) found that in a skill task, depressed subjects show small expectancy changes when they estimate the probability of their own success, but do not show these small expectancy changes when estimating the probability of another subject's success. These results suggest that depressives believe they lack the ability for the skill task (personal helplessness), although they believe that others may possess the ability for the task.

The fact that depressives attribute failure to internal factors has been interpreted by some investigators (e.g., Blaney, 1977; Rizley, 1978) as disconfirming the helplessness model of depression. Similarly, Abramson and Sackeim (1977) have pointed to an apparent conceptual paradox by asking how depressed indidividuals can blame themselves for outcomes about which they believe they can do nothing. The reformulation clearly removes any contradiction between being the cause and being helpless about the same event although it does not explicitly articulate the relationship between blame or guilt and helplessness.

Generality and Chronicity of Depression

The same logic used to explain the generality and chronicity of help-lessness deficits applies to explaining the generality and chronicity of depression. According to the reformulated helplessness hypothesis, the degree of globality and stability of the attributions that depressed individuals make for their helplessness determines the generality and chronicity, respectively, of the deficits associated with depression.

The attributional reformulation may also be relevant to the issue of the continuity between laboratory-induced analogues of depression and the actual clinical syndrome found in the hospital. These mild versus severe cases of depression may differ along the global–specific and stable–unstable dimensions. The attributions of subjects made helpless in the laboratory presumably are less global and less stable than are attributions made by depressed people for their real-life helplessness. Hence, the laboratory-induced depressions are less chronic and less global and may be reversed during debriefing. We suggest, however, that they are not basically different in kind from the naturally occurring helplessness depressions. They are "analogues" to these naturally occurring helplessness depressions and differ quantitatively rather than qualitatively from them.

In summary, the reformulated model of depression improves the old hypothesis in the following ways:

1. All four classes of deficits associated with depression are explained. These deficits are: motivational, cognitive, affective, and self-esteem.
2. The hedonic valence of the outcome is important in determining the affective component of helplessness and depression. The unobtainability of highly desirable outcomes or the unavoidability of highly aversive outcomes will produce depressed affect. When individuals expect that no response in their repertoire will change the likelihood of these out-comes then the other deficits of helplessness and depression will result.
3. The generality of the depressive deficits will depend on the globality of the attribution for helplessness; the chronicity of the depressive defi-cits will depend on the stability of the attribution for helplessness; the chronicity of the depressive deficits will depend on the stability of the attribution for helplessness; and whether self-esteem is lowered will de-pend on the internality of the attribution for helplessness. Of course, these attributions will produce the depressive deficits only to the extent

that they produce global, stable, and internal expectations of future help-lessness.
4. The intensity of the deficits depends on the strength, or certainty, of the expectation of uncontrollability and, in the case of the affective and self-esteem deficits, on the importance of the outcome.

Thus, the attributional framework which was proposed to resolve the problems of human helplessness experiments also resolves some salient inadequacies of the helplessness model of depression.

VULNERABILITY, THERAPY, AND PREVENTION

Is there such a thing as an attributional style or a tendency to consistently attribute outcomes to some factors more than to others? Although the attribu-tional reformulation does not explain why people make the attributions they make, we suggest that individuals who differ in terms of their attributional style will differ in their responses to uncontrollability. So, those people who typically tend to attribute failure to global, stable, and internal factors should be most prone to general and chronic helplessness depressions with low self-esteem. Moreover, such a style may predispose these individuals to depression.

The attributional analysis provides a systematic framework for under-standing the tendency of depressives to make logical errors in interpreting reality, such as overgeneralization and arbitrary inferences (Beck, 1967). In particular, depressives' overgeneralizations may directly follow from their tendency to make global, stable, and internal attributions for undesirable outcomes (Seligman et al., 1979). Furthermore, the finding that women are more likely than men to suffer from depression (Radloff, Note 10) may be partially explained by the different attributional styles of girls and boys, with girls tending to attribute their failure to lack of ability (global, stable) and boys tending to attribute their failure to lack of effort (specific, unstable) (Dweck, 1976).

The attributional reformulation has important implications for the treat-ment of helplessness and depression. Abramson et al. (1978) suggested and Seligman (in press) elaborated upon four strategies of therapeutic interven-tion. Briefly these include:

1. Changing the estimated probability of the outcome. This is done by changing the environment in such a way as to reduce the likelihood of aversive outcomes and to increase the likelihood of desired outcomes.
2. Making the highly preferred outcomes less preferred by reducing the

aversiveness of unavoidable outcomes or the desirability of unobtainable outcomes.

3. Changing the expectation from uncontrollability to controllability when the outcomes are indeed obtainable. If the individual does not know how to emit the appropriate responses, then he or she should be trained in these skills. When the responses already are in the individual's repertoire but are not being made because the individual has a distorted expectation of response–outcome indpendence, then this expectation should be altered.

4. Changing unrealistic attributions for failure to more realistic attributions—such as external, specific, and unstable—and changing unrealistic attributions for success to internal, global, and stable factors.

An alternative view is suggested by Hollon and Garber (1980). They present a cognitive-expectancy theory of therapy for helplessness and depression that emphasizes the greater efficiency and efficacy of intervening at the level of expectation directly, rather than focusing on altering attributions. Moreover, Hollon and Garber argue that when the procedures derived from the reformulated helplessness hypothesis outlined above actually produce changes in helplessness and depression, they operate largely through expectancy–disconfirmation procedures.

Although there are no studies that directly test the therapeutic implications of the reformulated model of depression, several studies that examine the effectiveness of various therapeutic interventions are relevant here. Therapies that teach depressives to alter their cognitive distortions are more effective in reducing depressive symptomatology than is antidepressant medication (Rush, Beck, Kovacs, & Hollon, 1977) behavior therapy, no-treatment, or an attention-placebo therapy (Shaw, 1977).

Finally, the reformulation has implications for prevention of helplessness and depression as well. Individuals who consistently attribute failures to stable, global, internal factors may be at higher risk for depression than people who make unstable, specific, external attributions for failure. Preventive strategies that teach depression-prone individuals to look for a number of alternative explanations for events may cause the individuals to eventually alter their attributional style. Similar to the strategies used in therapy, procedures that produce environmental enrichment, a greater sense of personal control, and attribution training may be effective in insulating individuals from the effects of uncontrollability.

In conclusion, the reformulation of the theory of learned helplessness in humans emphasizes the importance of the attributional dimensions of internal–external, stable–unstable, global–specific in modulating helplessness defi-

cits. This attributional analysis was proposed in order to resolve the inadequacies of the original helplessness hypothesis with respect to self-esteem,
chronicity, and generality. In general, the reformulation is consistent with
and in some cases better explains the data from existing helplessness studies,
although more direct tests of the hypothesis are needed. Finally, the attributional reformulation has important implications for the helplessness model
of depression.

REFERENCE NOTES

1. Roth, A., & Kilpatrick-Tabak, B. *Developments in the study of learned helplessness in humans: A critical review.* Unpublished manuscript, Duke University, 1977.
2. Tennen, H. A. *Learned helplessness and the perception of reinforcement in depression: A case of investigator misattribution.* Unpublished manuscript, State University of New York at Albany, 1977.
3. Eisenberger, R., Mauriello, J., Carlson, J., Frank, M., and Park, D. C. *Learned helplessness and industriousness produced by positive reinforcement.* Unpublished manuscript, State University of New York at Albany, 1976.
4. Hirsch, Kenneth A. *An extension of the learned helplessness phenomenon to potentially negatively punishing and potentially positively reinforcing stimuli noncontingent upon behavior.* Unpublished manuscript, 1976. (Available from K. A. Hirsch, Galesburg Mental Health Center, Galesburg, Illinois.)
5. Nugent, J. *Variations in noncontingent experiences and test tasks in the generation of learned helplessness.* Unpublished manuscript, University of Massachusetts.
6. Dyck, D. G., & Breen, L. J. *Learned helplessness, immunization and task importance in humans.* Unpublished manuscript, University of Manitoba, 1976.
7. Dweck, C. S., Davidson, W., Nelson, S., & Enna, B. *Sex differences in learned helpless-ness: (II) The contingencies of evaluative feedback in the classroom and (III) An experimen-tal analysis.* Unpublished xanuscript, University of Illinois at Urbana-Champaign, 1976.
8. Dweck, C. S., Goetz, T., & Strauss, N. *Sex differences in learned helplessness: (IV) An experimental and naturalistic study of failure generalization and its mediators.* Unpublished manuscript, University of Illinois at Urbana-Champaign, 1977.
9. Semmel, A., Abramson, L. Y., Seligman, M. E. P., & von Baeyer, C. A scale for measuring attributional style. Unpublished manuscript, University of Pennsylvania, 1978.
10. Radloff, L. S. *Sex differences in helplessness—with implication for depression.* Unpublished manuscript, Center for Epidemiologic Studies, National Institute of Mental Health, 1976.

2

An Attributional, Expectancy–Value Analysis of Learned Helplessness and Depression[1]

BERNARD WEINER
TCHIA LITMAN-ADIZES

INTRODUCTION

In prior publications (Weiner, 1972, 1974, 1976), there has been proposed a model of achievement strivings that applies some of the principles of social perception to human motivation. This model has been influenced by three very dominant trends in contemporary psychology: *(a)* the belief that behavior is guided by cognitive processes and that humans are best described as information processors and information seekers (see Estes, 1975); *(b)* the concern with perceived responsibility, as evidenced by concepts such as locus of control (Rotter, 1966), reactance (Brehm, 1966), personal causation (de Charms, 1968), perceived freedom (Steiner, 1970), intrinsic–extrinsic motivation (Deci, 1975), and learned helplessness (Seligman, 1975); and *(c)* the rise of attribution theory in social psychology (Harvey, Ickes, & Kidd, 1976; Heider, 1958; Jones, Kanouse, Kelley, Nisbett, Valins, & Weiner, 1972; Kelley, 1967).

It now appears that a general theory of motivation has evolved from this model and that success–failure manipulations merely provided the research

[1]This chapter was written while the first author was supported by Grant MH 25687-04 from the National Institute of Mental Health.

35

site for the initial investigations. In this chapter, this general conception of motivation is elucidated. We first examine the theory as it applies to achievement strivings, for the achievement arena remains the focus of this conception. The discussion of achievement embraces diverse topics, including skill–chance settings, self-concept maintenance, and self–other evaluation. Because of space limitations, we do not discuss the empirical support for the conception in any detail. Next, to illustrate how the theory is being applied in domains related to difficulties in psychological adjustment, the areas of parole decisions, loneliness, and hyperactivity are discussed from the attributional perspective. Then, the field of emotion and linkages between attributions and affects are discussed. Finally, we examine learned helplessness and depression from the standpoint of attribution theory.

AN ATTRIBUTIONAL THEORY OF
ACHIEVEMENT MOTIVATION

The essential aspects of the theory as it has evolved from research in achievement-related contexts are shown in Table 2.1. As indicated in this table, in achievement-related contexts, a number of causes, including ability, effort, task difficulty, and luck, are used to interpret the outcome of an achievement-related event; that is, in attempting to explain (make a causal attribution for) a prior success or failure, individuals estimate, among other factors, their own or the performer's level of ability, the amount of effort that was expended, the difficulty of the task, and/or the magnitude and direction of experienced luck. There are additional perceived causes of success and failure, such as fatigue, mood, illness, and bias, as well as causes that are unique to specific situations (see, for example, Mann, 1974; Staff, Note 1). In a cross-cultural survey it was reported that even patience (Greece and Japan) and tact and unity (India) are perceived as causes of success (Triandis, 1972). But in our culture, and within the confines of academic, occupational, and athletic accomplishment, it clearly has been documented that ability and effort typically are believed to be the dominant causes of success and failure, and that task difficulty and luck are perceived to be among the remaining causes of achievement outcomes (Elig & Frieze, 1975; Frieze, 1976).

The causes of success and failure have been subsumed within a three-dimensional taxonomy (see Weiner, 1974). One dimension is the internal–external description of causes often associated with the field of locus of control (Rotter, 1966). Ability, effort, mood, and patience, for example, are properties internal to the person, whereas task difficulty, luck, and teacher

TABLE 2.1
The Current Attributional Model of Achievement Motivation (Simplified Version)

Antecedents	Causes of success and failure	Causal dimensions	Causal effects	Behavioral consequences
Specific information	Ability	Stability ⟶	Expectancy shifts	Intensity
	Effort		Affective reaction	Choice
(Social norms, past success history, time spent at the task, pattern of outcome, etc.)	Task difficulty	Locus of control ⟶	(Evaluation)	Persistence
	Luck			Resistance to extinction
	Mood	Controllability ⟶		Others
Individual differences	Fatigue			
	Teacher bias			
(In achievement needs, sex)	Others			
Reinforcement schedules				
(100% versus 50%, ratio versus interval)				
Others				
(Interpersonal communication, stereotypes, situational constraints)				

bias are external or environmental causes. We will refer to this dimension as the locus of *causality*. A second dimension of causality, labeled *stability,* characterizes causes on a stable (invariant) versus unstable (variant) continuum. Ability, the difficulty of a task, and patience are likely to be perceived as relatively fixed, whereas luck, effort, and mood are more unstable: Luck implies random variability; effort may be augmented or decreased from one episode to the next; and mood typically is conceived as a temporary state. A third dimension of causality, first proposed by Heider (1958) and then incorporated within the achievement scheme by Rosenbaum (1972), is labeled *intentionality* or, more appropriately, *controllability*. Some causes, such as effort or the bias of a teacher or a supervisor, are likely to be perceived as controllable, whereas, for example, ability, mood, or the difficulty of the task are uncontrollable causes. The controllability dimension has not been subject to a great deal of research within this attributional framework primarily because it does not appear to be independent of the locus and stability dimensions. However, applications to the areas of helping behavior (Ickes & Kidd, 1976) and parole decisions (Carroll & Payne, 1976), where the evaluations of others are involved, have proven useful, and "intention" has long been a key term in the psychological analysis of moral judgments (see Maselli & Altrocchi, 1969).

The placement of a cause within a dimension is not invariant over time or between people. For example, luck may be perceived as an internal, stable factor (He is "lucky"), or as an external, unstable cause (A "chance" event). Even effort is not always considered volitional ("I just can't seem to study for this course"). Furthermore, experimenters often can influence the perceived dimensional placement of a cause. For example, Valle and Frieze (1976) depicted task difficulty as an unstable cause by specifying that salespeople would be changing their sales territory, which was the operational anchor for level of task difficulty. Inasmuch as attribution theorists are concerned with phenomenal causality, the seeming inconsistency in the placement of causes within the dimensions is not a theoretical shortcoming, but rather a fact that must be taken into account. Furthermore, the prediction of behavior must be based upon the subjective meaning of the causes to the individual.

Other dimensions of causality, which identify the general properties of causes, are likely to emerge with further analysis. But it does appear that the main dimensions of causality in achievement-related contexts may have been determined. These dimensions are "second-order" concepts (Schütz, 1967, p. 59); that is, they are concepts used by attribution theorists to organize the causal concepts of the layperson. As such, the dimensions may not be strictly part of a "naive" psychology or ethnoscience.

DIMENSIONAL CONSEQUENCES

The dimensions of causal judgments have been integrated within an expectancy–value theory of motivation (see Atkinson, 1964; Weiner, 1972, 1974). Expectancy–value theorists maintain that the intensity of aroused motivation is determined jointly by the expectation that the response will lead to the goal and by the attractiveness of the goal object. The greater the perceived likelihood of goal attainment and the greater the incentive value of the goal, the more intense is the presumed degree of positive motivation. Causal attributions for success and failure have been shown to influence both the expectancy of success and the affective consequences (incentive value) of achievement performance (see Weiner, 1974). Thus, given the postulates of expectancy–value theory, causal ascriptions also should influence motivated behavior.

Expectancy of Success

Considering expectancy of success, it has been found, for example, that failure ascribed to low ability or to the difficulty of the task decreases the expectancy of future goal attainment more than does failure that is ascribed to bad luck or to a lack of effort. In a similar manner, success ascribed to good luck results in lesser increments in the subjective expectancy of future success at that task than does success ascribed to high ability or to the ease of the task (see Fontaine, 1974; McMahan, 1973; Rosenbaum, 1972; Valle & Frieze, 1976; Weiner, Nierenberg, & Goldstein, 1976; Pancer & Eiser, Note 2). A summary of the empirical relations between these attributions and expectancy change is depicted in Figure 2.1.

More generally, Figure 2.1 indicates that if one anticipates conditions will remain unchanged (attribution to a stable factor), then the prior outcome at a task will be foreseen again with an increased degree of certainty. But if conditions are perceived as changeable (attribution to an unstable cause), then there is some doubt that the prior success or failure will be repeated. Hence, in Figure 2.1 effort falls between ability and luck because effort may be perceived as a stable trait and because the intent to succeed often is constant over time.

Skill versus Chance Settings, the "Gambler's Fallacy," and Locus of Control

Figure 2.1 reveals that there should be differential expectancy shifts in skill (ability attribution) versus chance (luck attribution) contexts. This supposition has been confirmed in many studies. In games of chance, atypical shifts (decrements in the expectancy of success following a success and

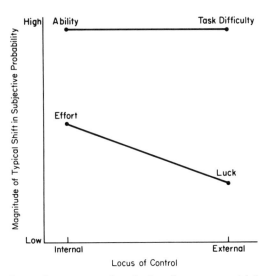

Figure 2.1. The relations between causal attributions for success and failure and the magnitude of typical expectancy shifts (increments in expectancy after a success and decrements after a failure) are shown in this figure. [From Weiner, 1974, p. 22.]

increments after a failure) frequently are reported (e.g., Jarvik, 1951; Phares, 1957; Skinner, 1942). Such shifts have been labeled the "gambler's fallacy," connoting the misconception that occurs in games of chance, where events are not perceived as independent and the same outcome is believed unlikely to recur on successive occasions (the "negative recency" effect). In addition, in chance tasks, the conviction that the future outcome will differ from the prior result increases as a function of the number of consecutive occurrences of the past event (Jarvik, 1951; Lepley, 1963). These findings are in marked contrast to data in skill situations, for with increasing success (or failure) at a skill-related task, there is increasing certainty that success (or failure) again will be experienced; that is, "positive recency" effects are displayed (see, for example, Diggory, Riley, & Blumenfeld, 1960; Zajonc & Brickman, 1969).

In other publications (e.g., Weiner, Nierenberg, & Goldstein, 1976) the attributional analysis of expectancy shifts has been compared to the beliefs espoused by social learning theorists (Phares, 1957; Rotter, 1966). According to the social learning conception, expectancy shifts are influenced by the locus of control (internal versus external) of the perceived cause of an event. To test this hypothesis, experimental studies also have compared expectancy shifts in ability-determined (internal control) versus chance-determined (external control) settings (James, 1957; Phares, 1957; Rotter, Liverant, & Crowne, 1961). These investigations again confirm that expectancies are differentially affected in these situational contexts. However, ability is an internal, stable cause, whereas luck is an external, unstable cause. Hence, the disparate expectancy shifts that have been observed can be logically imputed to either the locus of control or the stability dimension of causality. Subsequent research separating these two explanations has conclusively demonstrated that it is the stability, and not the locus, dimension of causality that accounts for the expectancy shift data (see review in Weiner et al., 1976).

Formal Analysis and Self-Concept Maintenance

McMahan (1973) and Valle and Frieze (1976) have developed more formal models of expectancy shifts based upon the concept of causal stability. Valle and Frieze (1976) postulate that predictions of expectancies *(P)* are a function of the initial expectancy *(E)* plus the degree to which outcomes *(O)* are attributed to stable causes *(S):*

$$P = f(E + O\ [f(S)])$$

In addition, Valle and Frieze (1976) also note that the perceived causes of success or failure are related to the initial expectation of success. It has been clearly documented that unexpected success or failure leads to unstable attributions, particularly luck (Feather, 1969; Feather & Simon, 1971; Frieze & Weiner, 1971).Hence, Valle and Frieze (1976) conclude that ''there is some value for the difference between the initial expectations and the actual outcome that will maximally change a person's predictions for the future. If the difference is greater than this point, the outcome will be attributed to unstable factors to such a great extent that it will have less influence on the person's future predictions [p. 581].''

These ideas have important implications for attributional-change programs and for the maintenance of one's self-concept (see Weiner, 1974). For example, assume that an individual with a high self-concept of ability believes that he or she has a high probability of success at a task. It is likely that failure would then be ascribed to luck, which may not reduce the subsequent expectancy of success and maintains a high ability self-concept. On the other hand, success would be ascribed to ability, which increases both the subsequent expectancy (certainty) of success and confirms one's self-concept. The converse analysis holds given a low self-concept of ability and low expectancy of success: Success would be ascribed to luck and failure to low ability. These attributions result in the maintenance of the initial self-concept (see Fitch, 1970; Gilmore & Minton, 1974). In addition, the foregoing analysis suggests that in change programs involving expectancies or self-concept, the perceived causes of performance must be altered, and the modification of self-perception would have to involve a gradual process (Valle & Frieze, 1976). (See Ickes and Layden, 1978, for a fuller analysis of the relation between self-esteem and attributions.)

Affective Reactions

In addition to influencing expectancy of success, causal attributions also in part determine the affective consequences of success and failure, as Table 2.1 indicates, and hence influence the "attractiveness" of goal attainment. Figure 2.2 summarizes the hypothesized relations between attributions and affect. The attributions included in Figure 2.2 are again ability, effort, task difficulty, and luck. Furthermore, the affects under consideration are esteem-related, such as pride and shame, for these have been specified as the emotional consequences of success and failure (Atkinson, 1964; McClelland, Atkinson, Clark, & Lowell, 1953). Figure 2.2 reveals that pride and shame are maximized when achievement outcomes are ascribed to personal causes and are minimized when given attributions to external factors. Thus, locus of causality influences the emotional consequences of achievement outcomes.

Figure 2.2 has found support from three sources. First of all, the relations depicted in the figure are intuitively compelling. One clearly does not expe-

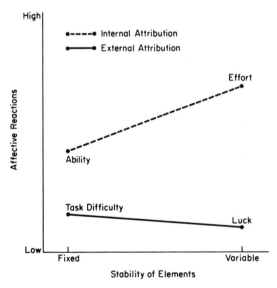

Figure 2.2. The hypothesized relations between causal attributions for success and failure and the magnitude of the achievement-related affects of pride and shame are shown graphically. [From Weiner, 1974, p. 32.]

rience pride in success when, for example, receiving an "A" from a teacher who gives only that grade or when defeating a tennis player who loses all his or her other matches. In these instances, the actor is likely to perceive that the causes of success are external. On the other hand, an "A" from a teacher who gives few high grades or a victory over a highly rated tennis player following a great deal of practice generate great positive affect. In these instances, the causes of success are likely to be perceived as some personal characteristic(s), such as high ability and/or great effort expenditure. The current movement in industry stressing that the worker be given personal credit for the product is another example that intuitively is guided by a perceived locus of causality–affect linkage.

Second, the analysis depicted in Figure 2.2 is in accord with the empirical support and the theory of achievement motivation formulated by Atkinson (1964). Atkinson postulated that the incentive values of success (pride, or I_s) and failure (shame, or I_f) are inversely related to the probabilities of success (P_s) and failure (P_f) at a task (i.e., $I_s = 1 - P_s$ and $I_f = 1 - P_f$); that is, one experiences greatest pride when succeeding at a difficult task (low P_s) and greatest shame following failure at an easy task (low P_f). Inasmuch as success at a difficult task and failure at an easy task produce internal attributions or the perception of self-responsibility (Kun & Weiner, 1973; Weiner & Kukla, 1970), Atkinson's ideas fit perfectly within the attributional conception.

Finally, scattered throughout the psychological literature are data supporting the attribution–intensity of affect linkage. For example, Feather (1967) found that self-reports of attraction for success and repulsion for failure are greater for skill-related (internal attribution) than chance-related (external attribution) tasks; Lanzetta and Hannah (1969) observed that greater punishment is administered for failure at an easy task than for failure at a difficult task, presumably because only failure at an easy task might be ascribed to a lack of effort; equity theorists such as Leventhal and Michaels (1971) report that inputs (effort) and assigned rewards covary; and Storms and McCaul (1976) as well as many others contend that internal ascriptions for aberrant behaviors magnify anxiety and feelings of inadequacy.

Thus, the relations depicted in Figure 2.2 have been, for the most part, validated. The only controversy evident in the figure is the contention that effort attributions have greater esteem-related consequences than have ability ascriptions. Some investigators have opposed this hypothesis in regard to the determinants of self-evaluation (Covington & Beery, 1976; Nicholls, 1976; Sohn, 1977). These researchers posed the following general question: "If effort is so rewarded and ascriptions to this factor generate so much pride, then why do students often hide their efforts and refuse to admit that they studied hard?" To resolve this controversy, it has been suggested that individuals strive to maintain a self-concept of high ability. Failure ascribed to a lack of effort, and success in spite of low effort, promote the view that one has ability (Kun & Weiner, 1973). Data have been gathered supporting the hypothesis that under certain conditions ability rather than effort ascriptions maximize positive and negative affective reactions.

In sum, self- versus other-perception, and affect versus evaluation, must be distinguished when examining the consequences of causal attributions. It is now evident that the relative potency of ability versus effort attributions will vary as a function of many conditions, including the importance of the task, its long-term consequences, and even the affect that is being assessed. Therefore, Figure 2.2 is in need of some elaboration.

THEORETICAL RANGE

At the outset of this chapter it was asserted that achievement merely provided the substantive area for the initial investigations and that a general theory of motivation has emerged from the attributional perspective. In this section of the chapter, these statements will be documented by examining applied behavioral problems from an attributional perspective. In addition, it will be demonstrated that the theory charted in Table 2.1 provides a general framework for a cognitive analysis of motivation and behavior. This analysis subsequently will be extended to the learned helplessness literature and depression.

Parole Decisions

A parole decision is a complex judgment in which causal attributions play a major role. Figure 2.3 depicts the parole decision process as conceptualized by Carroll and Payne (1976, 1977). The figure indicates that the decision maker is provided with a variety of information about the criminal, the crime, and other pertinent facts. This information is combined and synthesized, yielding attributions about the cause of the crime. The causal attributions, in turn, are dimensionalized and influence judgments about "goodness–badness" and risk, which are believed to be the basis for the final parole decision.

Carroll and Payne (1976), after reviewing an array of literature, contend that the parole decision process is "based on a simple two-part model. In the first part, the primary concern of the decision maker is to make the punishment fit the crime. . . . At the second part . . . the primary concern . . . is with parole risk, i.e., the probability that the person being considered for release will again violate the laws of society [p. 15]." According to Carroll and Payne, crimes that are ascribed to internal and/or intentional factors (e.g.,

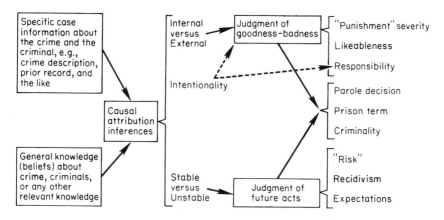

Figure 2.3. An attributional framework is provided for the parole decision process. [Adapted from Carroll & Payne, 1977, p. 200.]

personality characteristics, evil intents) should result in harsher personal evaluation (punishment) than should crimes attributed to external and/or unintentional causes (e.g., economic conditions, bad friends). This is not surprising, for we know that the law distinguishes between murder and manslaughter, and the subjective determinants of moral judgment have been well documented by Piaget, Kohlberg, and others. In addition, the risk associated with parole should depend upon the stability of the perceived cause of the original crime. If, for example, the crime is attributed to some fixed personality trait, then the decision maker is likely to expect that a crime will be committed again if the prisoner is paroled. On the other hand, if the cause of the crime has been altered (e.g., economic conditions have improved, bad friends have left, rehabilitation has been successful), then the criminal will be perceived as a good parole risk.

Given the above analysis, a criminal is least likely to be paroled if the cause of the crime is perceived as internal and/or intentional and stable (e.g., "He is a bad seed"). Conversely, parole is most likely to be granted when the crime is perceived as caused by external and/or unintentional and unstable factors (e.g., prior economic conditions). The remaining causal combinations should fall between these extremes in terms of parole likelihood. Carroll and Payne have furnished support for these hypotheses, examining professional parole decision makers and the judgments of college students when given simulated criminal cases. They find, for example, that perceptions of the locus, stability, and intentionality of causes significantly relate to indexes such as perceived responsibility for the crime, likelihood of recidivism, likability, prison term, and purpose of the sentence. In a research investigation using the college students, Carroll and Payne (1977) reported:

Averaging across eight crimes, crimes with internal causes were given an average prison term of 7.8 years, crimes with external causes were given an average of 4.4 years. Crimes with stable causes were given an average term of 7.1 years compared to 5.1 years for unstable causes. The effects of these dimensions were additive, such that the internal–stable causal information led to an average of 9.1 year sentence against the 3.6 years for external–unstable causes [p. 203].

In sum, according to Carroll and Payne, the parole decision procedure is conceptually identical to the perceived sequence of events in the achievement domain: Antecedent information is processed; a causal judgment is reached; the cause is placed within the locus, stability, and intentionality dimensions; and this influences evaluation and expectancy, which are the main determinants of the parole decision.

Affiliation and Loneliness

It has been reasoned that in our culture two sources of motivation are most dominant: achievement and social recognition (or, in Freud's more general terms, *Arbeit und Liebe*). Hence, affiliative motivation is a natural area to turn to in the development of a general theory of motivation.

An attributional analysis of affiliative motivation that is guided by the the theory diagrammed in Table 2.1 conceives of loneliness as a social failure (Gordon, 1976; Stein & Bailey, 1973). Hanusa (Note 3) and Heim (Note 4) examined the perceived causes of social success and failure and found them to be similar to the causes of achievement success and failure. Michela and Peplau (Note 5) then used scaling procedures to discover the dimensions of the causes of social failure. Thirteen causes of social failure were rated in terms of perceived similarity, and these data provided the input for a multidimensional scaling procedure. A three-dimensional scaling solution was obtained, with the dimensions labeled: (a) locus (anchored to internal causes of physical unattractiveness and shyness versus external causes of impersonal situations and lack of opportunities); (b) stability (anchored to stable causes of unpleasant personality and physical unattractiveness versus unstable causes of lack of opportunities and feeble efforts); and (c) controllability (anchored to controllable causes of feeble efforts and no social polish versus uncontrollable causes of physical unattractiveness and cliquish groups). On the basis of these data Michela and Peplau (Note 5) concluded:

The overall picture . . . seems to support rather well the applicability of Weiner's dimensional model of attributions for performance to the social failure of loneliness. Intuitive and empirical procedures for labelling dimensions converged on identification of dimensions very similar to Weiner's. This finding is all the more dramatic due to the divergent methodologies used in previous research on academic achievement compared to this study. Weiner's model was originally developed by a *deduc-*

tive process of reasoning from characteristics of specific causes to postulating general dimensions, and then empirically testing predictions dictated by the model. But the present study used an *inductive* process from the outset, namely, multidimensional scaling, to derive dimensions empirically [p. 4].

The question which then remains is whether the attributional dimensions in the affiliative domain relate to affect and expectancy in the same manner as they do in the achievement domain. Intuitively, that appears to be the case. For example, social failure ascribed to internal factors such as "physically unattractive" or "unpleasant personality" should result in greater loss of self-esteem than should attributions to external causes such as "lack of opportunities" or "cliquish groups." Furthermore, one can reasonably hypothesize that unstable causes of social failure will result in a higher expectancy of future affiliative success than will attributions to stable causes. In support of this line of reasoning, Folkes (1978) found that rejection in a romantic relationship because of perceived stable reasons ("She did not like my personality") results in a lower expectancy of establishing a relationship with the rejector than do rejections for perceived unstable reasons (a prior commitment). Both affect and expectancy, in turn, are likely to influence a variety of affiliative-related instrumental activities.

Hyperactivity and Psychostimulants

Whalen and Henker (1976) have outlined an attributional analysis of the effects of drug treatment for hyperactive children. They contend that when hyperactivity is combatted with a drug, the belief is conveyed to both the child and his or her parents that the cause of the hyperactivity is a physiological dysfunction. Hence, the involved individuals are not responsible for, or in control of, the maladaptive behavior that is exhibited. Because this physiological deficit is perceived as an uncontrollable cause, it seems intuitively reasonable that neither the child nor the parent need feel guilty or take blame for the aberrant behavior; That is, the shift in perceived causality minimizes self-blame and negative evaluations. This appears to be a beneficial and an unanticipated side effect of the treatment technique.[2]

On the other hand, Whalen and Henker (1976) also state that "the reputed physiological dysfunctions used to explain the failure of the hyperactive child are frequently viewed as stable and relatively unresponsive to behavioral change effects [p. 1123]." Thus, the perception of fixed causation "leads to demoralization about problem solutions . . . and interferes with effective coping [p. 1124]."

In sum, again there is an analysis of a psychological phenomenon from

[2]Note that in this case the attribution is still internal but has switched from controllable to noncontrollable. It is known that perceived controllability influences interpersonal evaluation, liking, and blame.

the perspective shown in Table 2.1. Individuals utilize information (treatment technique) to infer causation about an event (hyperactivity). The perceived cause (a genetic deficit) minimizes negative affect (a beneficial effect) but also weakens the perceived likelihood of recovery (a harmful effect). These two factors, in turn, influence the long-range consequences of the treatment (negatively, according to Whalen and Henker, inasmuch as expectancy is assumed to be a more potent determinant of long-term behavioral change than affect).

We will turn now from the basic theory to a more detailed analysis of emotions. A closer look at the attributional determinants of affect is necessary before presenting our analysis of learned helplessness and depression.

EMOTIONS

The field of emotions is immense, embracing the insights of many important historical figures, including Darwin (the innate bases of emotional expression), Freud (affective transformations), and James (the temporal relation of bodily processes and emotion). There is no comprehensive theory which can account for even a small portion of the data in this field. In a similar manner, the attributional framework advocated in this chapter does not lend itself to the formulation of a general theory of emotions. Nonetheless, it does provide suggestions concerning the antecedents of particular emotional experiences.

Affective Reactions in Achievement Settings

As intimated previously, prior conceptions of achievement motivation (Atkinson, 1964; McClelland et al., 1953) uniquely link achievement concerns with one particular affective dimension, labeled pride–shame. Yet there is neither experimental nor anecdotal evidence supporting the belief that the only affects one experiences in a "pure" achievement setting are pride and shame. It is equally reasonable to propose that following success or failure one experiences feelings of confidence (lack of confidence), safety (fear), contentment (agitation), or gratitude (vindictiveness). In addition, all of these affects, including pride and shame, might be experienced in contexts unrelated to achievement (e.g., pride may be sensed after winning an election, which is defined by Veroff, 1957, and others as a power concern; one may feel shame in a situation eliciting moral concerns; and so on). Weiner, Russell, and Lerman (1978, 1979) therefore initiated a series of investigations to determine the emotional reactions in achievement-related settings and to relate these feelings to the perceived causes of success and failure.

In their initial study, the general procedure was first to compile a list of nearly 250 potential affective reactions to success and failure in an academic context by means of a dictionary search. The next step was to select the ascriptions for success and failure that accounted for the majority of free-response attributions in prior investigations (see Elig & Frieze, 1975; Frieze, 1976).

Weiner et al. (1978) then proceeded with the viewpoint of "naive, skeptical phenomenologists [Davitz, 1969, p. 5]." They merely gave a cause for success or failure within a brief story format, randomly listed the affective reactions that had been compiled, and asked subjects to report the affective intensity that would be experienced in this situation. Responses were made on a rating scale anchored at the extremes.

There were three general findings of interest. First, there was a set of "outcome-dependent, attribution-independent" affects that represented general positive or negative reactions to success and failure, regardless of the "why" of the outcome. For example, given success, the affects of pleased, happy, satisfied, good, and so on, were reported as equally experienced, regardless of the attribution for the positive outcome. In a similar manner, given failure, there were a number of outcome-dependent, attribution-independent affects, such as uncheerful, displeasure, and upset.

But for both success and failure there were many affects discriminably related to specific attributions (see Table 2.2). Table 2.2 shows some of the causal attributions for success and failure and a label that best describes the affective reactions that are primarily linked to these attributions. It indeed appears that causal cognitions give rise to qualitatively distinct feelings.

In addition, certain affects were associated with causal dimensions. For example, the esteem-related affects of pride, competence, and confidence were maximized given internal attributions (e.g., ability, effort, personality). Thus, there appear to be three sources of affect in achievement contexts:

TABLE 2.2
Attributions and Dominant Discriminating Affects for Success and Failure

Attributions	Success	Failure
Ability	Competence Confidence	Incompetence
Unstable effort	Activation	Guilt, shame
Stable effort	Relaxation	Guilt, shame
Own personality	Self-enhancement	
Others effort and personality	Gratitude	Aggression
Luck	Surprise	Surprise

performance outcome, the specific causal attribution, and the properties (dimensions) of that attribution.

The methodology in the Weiner et al. (1978) investigation was guided by the belief that individuals do not have the necessary language to describe fully their affective experiences. Thus, the opportunity for expression was made available by providing a vocabulary of emotions to the subjects. Unfortunately, this respondent procedure undoubtedly encourages subjects to report affects that are not experienced or that are experienced in a manner not truly captured by the labels. Subsequent research (Weiner et al., 1979) in which subjects freely reported their emotional feelings in concerning critical incidents that were characterized by specific causal ascriptions replicated many of the findings shown in Table 2.2. In addition, when given a list of discriminating affects, subjects can identify the causal attributions for success and failure (see Weiner et al., 1979). Thus, one may be able to infer thoughts from emotions. This suggests an important methodological tool for the study of populations with limited verbal abilities, such as infants.

AN ATTRIBUTIONAL APPROACH TO LEARNED HELPLESSNESS AND DEPRESSION

With the prior discussion of attribution theory completed, it is now appropriate to consider an attributional analysis of learned helplessness. Just such an approach already has been suggested by Abramson, Seligman, and Teasdale (1978) and Miller and Norman (1979). What is proposed here builds upon their earlier attempts and at the same time points up other issues that we feel are worthy of consideration. Recall that the basic framework proposed for helplessness is that an objective noncontingency between responding and outcome produces an expectation that outcomes are uncontrollable, which generates cognitive (e.g., negative beliefs about oneself), emotional (e.g., sadness), and motivational (e.g., passivity) consequences, or a syndrome resembling depression.

Objective Noncontingency

Perhaps because the notion of learned helplessness is rooted in learning theory and animal psychology, it has been postulated that this state originates when there has been a prior *objective* noncontingency between actions and outcomes. An objective noncontingency, of course, is readily established in an experimental setting.

Attribution theory, on the other hand, is concerned with phenomenal causality. Two scientists, for example, one with a history of accomplishment (objective contingency between actions and outcomes) and the other with a history of failure (objective noncontingency) may feel equally unworthy and exhibit depressive symptoms, the former because of the distorted belief that his or her actions have not led to success. In other words, both scientists are labeled depressed, although in one case this was preceded only by subjective noncontingency, whereas in the second case the symptoms were preceded by objective and subjective noncontingency.

In sum, the "objective" stipulation in the antecedent conditions originally specified by Seligman and his colleagues appears to be unnecessary from our point of view. The expectancy–value approach to motivation advocated here is phenomenological and ahistorical—what matters is the contemporary evaluation of the physical and the social world, regardless of the veridicality or the source of one's beliefs. Indeed, an organism first trained in a classical aversive conditioning situation and exhibiting helplessness in a subsequent operant setting because of the prior noncontingency training is responding to the subjective, rather than to the objective, stimuli in the new context. The learned helplessness formulation thus already has a phenomenological flavor.

Causal Attributions

Given a perceived noncontingency between actions and outcomes, the attributional approach suggests that the next phase in the development of depression involves a "why" question, such as "Why am I not able to succeed in my work?" or "Why am I unable to establish social or emotional relationships?" This step recently has been recognized as necessary by Abramson et al. (1978) and Miller and Norman (1979).

There are, of course, a myriad of answers to such "why" questions. From the perspective outlined in this chapter, the properties (dimensional placements) of the causal ascriptions are of particular importance. This classification also has been perceived as essential in the newer conceptions of learned helplessness. We suggest that three causal dimensions are germane to the analysis of helplessness and depression: stability, locus, and controllability. However, we feel most secure in discussing the roles of stability and locus and thus will not include a detailed examination of controllability here.

Causal Stability and Expectancy of Success

It has been contended by Seligman and his colleagues that beliefs about prior noncontingency carry over to future contingent contexts. For example, given a noncontingent aversive outcome (failure), the expectancy of failure persists over time. Similar to Abramson et al. (1978), we suggest that for this to be the case, the actor must ascribe the prior perceived failure, or lack of control, to stable causes. If a cause is perceived to be invariant over time (e.g., inability or physical unattractiveness), then there is likely to be expectancy generalization on future occasions. On the other hand, if the perceived cause of a prior event is unstable ("We could not go on the picnic because of rain"), then the expectation for future positive outcomes should not necessarily be dampened ("We will have the picnic tomorrow"). (Note that the stability dimension of causality refers to temporal generalization. A principle of stimulus generalization has not been incorporated into our model, but has been suggested by Abramson et al., 1978).

Helplessness versus Hopelessness

Seligman and his associates have specified that learned helplessness involves the belief that one's responses do not influence outcomes. However, one may be helpless without being hopeless. For example, even if probabilities of reward are not increased by personal responding, positive anticipations may be sustained by the knowledge that someone else is going to help or by ascribing the current noncontingency to unstable causes.

Stated somewhat differently, outcomes can be ascribed to either internal or external causes. A low expectancy of goal attainment requires that both internal and external contributors to success be minimal and be perceived as stable. Heider (1958) illustrates this point with an example of a rower crossing a lake. The rower may make progress because of personal forces (ability and effort) or environmental forces (a favorable wind). Even if an accident has occurred so that the rower is personally helpless, hope can be maintained because of the wind.

If one assumes that an *absolutely* low expectancy of goal attainment rather than just an independence of responses and outcomes is the key antecedent of depression, then hopelessness, rather than helplessness, would be the appropriate concept to emphasize. Helplessness would then be a necessary, rather than a sufficient, antecedent. This seems to be a reasonable presumption, for if an expectancy is high due to facilitative external causes, then it does not seem intuitively reasonable to anticipate depression as a consequence of perceived personal noncontingency. For example, it is unlikely that the helpless rower will become depressed over his or her plight knowing that strong winds always blow over the lake. But depression may be experienced following a prolonged absence of wind (hopelessness).

Locus of Causality and Affective Reactions

Depression is considered by some theorists (Freud 1917/1957; Jacobson, 1971) to be an affective, rather than a cognitive, disorder. As already indicated, from the attributional perspective, affect and expectancy both are products of causal ascriptions. Nonetheless, it remains possible to examine the relative independent influence of affect and expectancy upon learned helplessness and depression despite their possible common origin.

A number of recent investigations have demonstrated the differential influence of internal versus external causal ascriptions upon feelings of depression and helplessness (as used by Seligman). As previously indicated, locus of causality is believed to be important in determining affective reactions to success and failure. Internal attributions for failure, such as low ability or lack of effort, maximize feelings of inadequacy and low self-esteem.

In one of these studies, Klein, Fencil-Morse, and Seligman (1976) demonstrated that performance deficits normally exhibited by depressives are alleviated when prior lack of control (failure) can be ascribed to external causes. More specifically, depressed subjects who were informed that the task they were attempting was exceedingly difficult did not exhibit impairment in performance following failure. These investigators therefore suggested that "the learned helplessness model of depression needs an extra construct concerning attribution of helplessness to personal failure [Klein et al., 1976, p. 515]."

Subsequently, Tennen and Eller (1977) induced repeated failure at two tasks. In one of their experimental conditions, the second task was described as relatively easy, whereas in another condition the task was described as difficult. Subjects in these two experimental conditions significantly differed in their later quality of performance on a different activity, with only persons in the internal ascription (easy task condition) exhibiting indications of helplessness. Although in this experiment expectancy of success also may have varied between the experimental conditions, it is possible to interpret the data as demonstrating that internal versus external attributions for failure ("I am inadequate" versus "The task is too hard") generate disparate affective reactions and, in turn, differential behavioral consequences. At the very least, the data "indicate that causal ascriptions concerning the inability to control reinforcement play an important role in determining subsequent performance [Tennen & Eller, 1977, p. 271].[3]

The investigations of Klein et al. (1976) and Tennen and Eller (1977) relied on the operations (perceived task difficulty) known to influence subjective causation. However, causal attributions in these studies were not assessed. An investigation by Litman-Adizes (1978) directly examined the

[3]Hanusa and Schulz (1977) have reported conflicting data, although they also maintain that their study "demonstrates the importance of attributions as mediators of subjects' responses to noncontingency experience [p. 610]." It is apparent that the influence of causal ascriptions upon subsequent performance will be dependent on many variables, such as the amount of helplessness training and the relation between the training and the testing sessions.

causal attributions of depressed college students. Litman-Adizes found that depressives tended to ascribe failure in a noncontrollable situation to a lack of ability more than did nondepressive subjects. In addition, the depressives tended to ascribe failure to the difficulty of the task less than did nondepressives. Thus, depressed subjects were more likely to take personal responsibility for failure and to minimize the role of external factors in causing poor performance.

In sum, these studies suggest that perceived noncontrol and the linked low expectancy of success (hopelessness) are not sufficient to generate learned helplessness and depression. Rather, low expectancy must be accompanied by self-attributions for prior failure and by associated affects such as blame, guilt, incompetence, and lowered self-esteem (also see Beck, 1967, 1974, 1976; Lichtenberg, 1957). Hence, given this analysis, the necessary precondition for depressive symptomatology is ascription of prior response–outcome independence to stable *and* internal causes. Miller and Seligman (1975) also present some data in support of this hypothesis. They noted that two of their subjects in a learned helplessness condition who became angry at the experimenter (ascription of noncontrol to an external source) reported little depression and performed well at a subsequent task.

The notion that depression is a consequence of internal, stable ascriptions also is in accord with the phenomenology of depression expressed by college students. Weiner et al. (1978) found that motivational indicators of depression, such as apathy and resignation, were expected to be experienced only when a hypothetical person made stable and internal ascriptions for failure (i.e., attribution for failure to lack of ability, low intrinsic motivation, or personality deficits).

In contrast to the foregoing conclusion, it also is evident that in some situations depression does occur given external ascriptions for noncontrollable "failures." This is what Abramson et al. (1978) labeled "universal helplessness." For example, catastrophic natural events, the death of a significant other, and placement in a prisoner-of-war camp, all of which are uncontrollable and aversive, often promote depression. Furthermore, these events typically are explained with external ascriptions, such as bad luck, God's will, or evil others. This would seem to indicate that depression can occur as a consequence of hopelessness plus the affect generated by an external causal ascription or the affect that is elicited by the negative event per se. Affects associated with external causality include, for example, aggression and anger (ascription to evil others) and bewilderment and astonishment (attribution to bad luck), whereas the affects produced by nonattainment of a desired goal, independent of any particular causal attribution, include upset, displeasure, and unhappiness (see Weiner et al., 1978, 1979).

If the discussion in the previous paragraph is accepted, then it appears that depression may or may not be accompanied by self-attributions. However, depression must be accompanied by expectations of nonattainment of desired goals (hopelessness) and negative affects which may be generated either by internal or external ascriptions or by the negative outcome of an event.

The Necessary versus Sufficient Status of Affect and Expectancy

To complicate matters even further, there are still additional possibilities for the genesis of depression, given an expectancy–value (affect) analysis. It is evident that many of the passive behaviors exhibited by depressives do not appear to be linked to a low expectancy of success *for that particular class of activities*. For example, eating is perceived as reducing hunger; hair-combing often is believed to increase attractiveness; reading or watching television is thought to relieve boredom; and so on. Yet these are the kinds of operant behaviors that decrease in the lives of depressed individuals. It may be that there are some overriding goals (e.g., success in life) for which these behaviors are no longer perceived as instrumental. Thus, passivity is mediated by a low expectancy of long-term goal attainment. But it also is possible that negative affect serves as a general inhibitor of activity, as Atkinson (1964) has argued. If this latter explanation has some validity, then depression could be exhibited without a mediating expectancy component (although the original source of the negative affect could have been prior failure and a low expectancy for a particular goal).

To summarize the discussion thus far, it has been contended that expectancy and affect, which are often mediated by causal attributions, are essential determinants of learned helplessness and depression. It is further suggested that there are disparate genotypes for the general class or phenotype labeled depression. The genotypic categories include *(a)* low expectation of goal attainment (hopelessness) accompanied by internal attributions and their linked affects (e.g., low self-esteem); *(b)* hopelessness accompanied by external ascriptions and their linked affects (e.g., anger); *(c)* hopelessness accompanied by general negative affects from nonattainment of a goal that are not attributionally mediated (e.g., upset); and *(d)* negative affect without a mediating low expectation of goal attainment. This analysis indicates that negative affect is a necessary, and at times sufficient, precondition for the depressive syndrome. On the other hand, low expectation of future success is often a necessary, but never a sufficient, precursor of helplessness, for failure always is accompanied by negative affect, regardless of whether or not it is attributionally mediated (internal or external ascriptions). The four genotypic categories outlined may be uniquely linked with specific symptoms, courses of illness, and responses to therapeutic treatments.

Finally, to add even more complexity, causal attributions are not fixed over time. There are likely to be primary and secondary appraisals of events, as Lazarus (1966) and others have suggested. This might be evidenced, for example, by an initial reaction of self-blame for failure and lowered self-esteem changing to blame of others and displays of aggression and anger. Such a sequence is reminiscent of the "vicissitudes of the instincts" championed by Freud and is consistent with his contention that aggression may be redirected inwardly or outwardly. Such fluctuations in affect, which from our viewpoint are indicators of cognitive (attributional) change or distortion, also could be an important aspect of the depressive disorder.

A Word about Controllability

The concept most associated with the learned helplessness analysis of depression is controllability. The learned helplessness model posits that depressed individuals perceive themselves as unable to exert any volitional control to increase the probability of desired outcomes. The lack of control is experimentally manipulated by the noncontingent conditions in the learned helplessness paradigm and is presumed to be internalized prior to the onset of depression in clinical patients. There is both experimental and clinical evidence to support this position. For example, depressed individuals have been shown to have less of a sense of control over their successes and failures in a laboratory situation than have nondepressives (Litman-Adizes, 1978). On the basis of clinical observations, Schwartz (1964) concluded: "The depressive person is quite able to conceive of himself as causing things in himself or in other people. However, he does not see himself as having control or choice over what he causes [p. 696]."

The controllability dimension thus far has been explored only minimally within our attributional analysis. One reason for this void, which has already been indicated, is that controllability does not seem to be orthogonal to the locus and stability dimensions of causality; an internal, stable cause (e.g., low ability) logically is not subject to volitional control. A question worthy of pursuit, then, is whether the uncontrollable nature of a cause warrants the positing of a third causal dimension or merely can be reduced to an internal stable description. In favor of the argument that a third dimension is necessary is the reasonable analysis that some causes are internal and unstable, as well as uncontrollable (e.g., mood and fatigue), whereas others are internal and unstable, but are subject to volitional control (e.g., effort). Thus, it would appear that controllability is not completely reducible to the locus and stability dimensions, and it could play an independent role in the etiology and description of learned helplessness and depression. However, from our perspective the conceptual status of controllability has yet to be elucidated. One interesting speculation regarding the independence of controllability from locus of causality is that internal yet uncontrollable causes can account for the seeming paradox of the coexistence of self-blame and perceived noncontrollability which are at times displayed by depressives (Abramson & Sackeim, 1977).

REFERENCE NOTES

1. Staff, P. *Sex and success of outcome as determinants of reported attributions.* Unpublished master's thesis, University of Texas at Arlington, 1976.
2. Pancer, S. M., & Eiser, J. R. *Expectations, aspirations, and evaluations as influenced by another's attributions for success and failure.* Paper presented at the American Psychological Association Convention, Chicago, September 1975.
3. Hanusa, B. H. *An extension of Weiner's attribution approach to social situations: Sex differences in social situations.* Paper presented at the Eastern Psychological Association Convention, New York, April 1975.
4. Heim, M. *Sex differences in causal attributions for achievement in social tasks.* Paper presented at the Eastern Psychological Association Convention, New York, April 1975.
5. Michela, J. L., & Peplau, L. A. *Applying attributional models of achievement to social settings.* Paper presented at the Western Psychological Association Convention, Seattle, April 1977.

3

The Cognitive Component of Human Helplessness and Depression: A Critical Analysis[1]

LAUREN B. ALLOY
LYN Y. ABRAMSON

INTRODUCTION

Over the past five years, human helplessness has become a burgeoning field. The learned helplessness phenomenon has captured the attention of social psychologists, clinical psychologists, and personality and learning theorists, among others. Originally, learned helplessness was demonstrated in animals. In the laboratory, dogs that experienced aversive outcomes which they could not control subsequently showed gross deficits in behavior, whereas dogs that experienced an equivalent number of controllable aversive events or no aversive events did not show such behavioral deficits (Overmier & Seligman, 1967; Seligman & Maier, 1967). The behavior of the dogs that experienced uncontrollable aversive events was characterized by failure to

[1]The order of authors' names is random. The research reported in this chapter was supported by a National Institute of Mental Health Predoctoral Fellowship, MH 07284-01, to L. B. Alloy and by a University of Pennsylvania Dissertation Year Fellowship to L. Y. Abramson, while both authors were at the University of Pennsylvania. Preparation of the chapter was supported by BRSG Grant RR07028-13 awarded to L. B. Alloy by the Biomedical Research Support Grant Program, Division of Research Resources, National Institutes of Health and by U.S. Public Health Service Biomedical Research Support Grant 5507 RR 07067-13 to L. Y. Abramson.

emit appropriate escape responses in new situations where aversive outcomes could be controlled. To account for these results, Maier, Seligman,
and Solomon (1969) and Seligman, Maier, and Solomon (1971) proposed
that when animals experience uncontrollable events, they form the expectation that future events will be uncontrollable as well. They then hypothesized that such an expectation leads to three deficits: motivational, cognitive,
and emotional. The motivational deficit refers to a lowered probability of
initiating voluntary responses. The logic here is that if an organism believes
that its responses do not matter, then it will fail to emit future responses. The
cognitive, or associative, deficit consists of difficulty in perceiving a relationship between responses and outcomes when a relationship does, in fact,
exist. According to the theory, proactive interference from the original expectation of no control retards the formation of subsequent expectations of
control. Finally, Maier and Seligman (1976) argued that when organisms
expect that aversive events are uncontrollable, they experience depressed
affect. Thus, according to the helplessness theory, the debilitated performance of dogs in an escape task following inescapable shock reflects two
consequences of an expectation of response–outcome independence: lowered initiation of responses and difficulty in perceiving response–outcome
relationships.

Since the original demonstration of learned helplessness in animals, a
number of investigators successfully have reproduced the phenomenon in
humans (e.g., Fosco & Geer, 1971; Hiroto, 1974; Hiroto & Seligman, 1975;
Klein & Seligman, 1976; Roth & Kubal, 1975). More recently, learned helplessness has been proposed as a laboratory model of naturally occurring
depression in humans (e.g., Abramson, Seligman, & Teasdale, 1978; Seligman, 1975; Seligman, Klein, & Miller, 1976). According to the learned
helplessness model of depression, depressed individuals are characterized
by the generalized expectation that their responses do not control outcomes.
Each component of the helplessness syndrome is hypothesized to have a
counterpart symptom in the syndrome of depression.

Surprisingly, after 5 years of intensive research on human helplessness
and depression, the basic postulates of the theory have not been tested
adequately. Instead, the majority of work on human helplessness has consisted
of studies attempting to demonstrate helplessness in a wide variety of situations (e.g., Hiroto & Seligman, 1975; Klein & Seligman, 1976; Miller &
Seligman, 1975; Roth & Bootzin, 1974; Roth & Kubal, 1975; Willis &
Blaney, 1978), studies of an applied nature (e.g., Baum, Aiello, & Calesnick,
1978; Krantz, Glass, & Snyder, 1974; Langer, Janis, & Wolfer, 1975; Langer
& Rodin, 1976; Rodin, 1976; Rodin & Langer, 1977; Schulz, 1976), and
studies attempting to demonstrate behavioral parallels between people made
helpless in the laboratory and depressed people (e.g., Kilpatrick-Tabak &

Roth, 1978; Klein & Seligman, 1976; Miller & Seligman, 1975; Miller, Seligman, & Kurlander, 1975; Price, Tryon, & Raps, 1978). The importance of such research should not be minimized, even though its theoretical implications are not clear. We believe that an adequate test of the helplessness theory involves three parts. First, the three components of helplessness (motivational, cognitive, and emotional) must be demonstrated in isolation from one another. Second, it must be shown that these three components result from the expectation of no control. Finally, it must also be shown that debilitated performance shown by people exposed to uncontrollable events is mediated by the motivational and cognitive components of helplessness.

In this chapter we discuss the hypothesized cognitive component of human helplessness and depression. We choose to focus on the cognitive or associative component because it lies at the heart of helplessness theory and distinguishes this theory from other more behavioral theories of learning and depression. We critically review prior work relevant to the demonstration of the associative component and present some new research that bears directly on its existence in isolation from the motivational component.

PRIOR RESEARCH ON THE ASSOCIATIVE COMPONENT IN HUMAN HELPLESSNESS AND DEPRESSION

Historically, it has been difficult to demonstrate the existence of the associative deficit of helplessness independently of the motivational deficit. Early helplessness studies relied on the relatively indirect method of examining people's performance on instrumental learning tasks to infer difficulty in perceiving response–outcome relationships. Later studies attempted to develop more direct methodologies for assessing people's beliefs about control.

Instrumental Learning Studies

The behavioral observation that dogs exposed to uncontrollable shocks not only refrained from emitting subsequent escape responses but also failed to follow one successful escape response with another provided the original basis for inferring an associative deficit in helpless organisms. Although simple failure to respond in the face of shock suggested a lack of motivation, failure to follow one successful response with another suggested that the dog did not relate termination of the shock to the occurrence of his own response. Similar behavior was observed in humans exposed to uncontrollable noises. Early investigators of human helplessness developed a quantitative index of the degree to which subjects exposed to uncontrollable events failed to profit from prior response–outcome sequences (Hiroto, 1974; Hiroto & Seligman, 1975; Klein, Fencil-Morse, & Seligman, 1976; Klein & Seligman, 1976; Miller & Seligman, 1975). For each subject, the average conditional probability of an escape response on a trial, given a successful escape response on the previous trial, was computed. Typically, this conditional probability was lower for depressed individuals exposed to no prior events and for individuals exposed to uncontrollable events than for those individuals exposed to controllable or no events (Hiroto, 1974; Hiroto & Seligman, 1975; Klein et al., 1976; Klein & Seligman, 1976; Miller & Seligman, 1975). These results provide only loose support for an associative deficit in helplessness and depression. As Miller and Seligman (1975) have noted, the motivational deficit alone is sufficient to account for failure to follow one successful response with another. An individual who emits very few responses is statistically unlikely to follow one successful response with another. Thus, early attempts to isolate the associative component of helplessness based on the conditional probability measure are not convincing.

A number of investigators (e.g., Benson & Kennelly, 1976; Gatchel & Proctor, 1976; Hiroto & Seligman, 1975; Klein et al., 1976; Miller & Seligman, 1975) employed an anagrams test task following uncontrollable outcomes as an alternate index of the associative deficit in helplessness. Subjects were presented with a list of 20 five-letter words in which the order of the letters was scrambled. Because there was a pattern to the anagrams, all could be solved by an identical rearrangement of letters. Solution of three consecutive anagrams within 15 seconds was taken as evidence that a subject had "broken the pattern." A consistent result was obtained in these studies. Individuals who had experienced uncontrollable outcomes in the first phase of the experiment required more trials to break the pattern than did individuals who experienced controllable or no outcomes. In addition, depressed individuals also were slower to discover the pattern than were nondepressed individuals (Miller & Seligman, 1975; Willis & Blaney, 1978).

The interpretation of the anagram pattern results is problematic. Most importantly, it is unclear why difficulty in picking up a pattern in anagrams necessarily reflects an underlying inability to perceive the relationship between one's responses and outcomes. Intuitively, difficulty in seeing patterns in anagrams seems no more intimately related to the particular cognitive deficit postulated by helplessness theory than it does to a generalized intellectual impairment. In addition, a measure of the trials required to see a pattern in anagrams is as subject to the effects of lowered response initiation as is the conditional probability measure previously discussed. Finally, it seems plausible that subjects could meet the criterion of three consecutive anagram solutions within 15 seconds without breaking the pattern (Price et al., 1978, have also commented on the inadequacy of the "trials to criterion" measure). The instrumental learning experiments, then, have not provided a definitive test of the associative component of helplessness.

Chance – Skill Studies

Miller and Seligman (1973) developed a more promising method for isolating the associative component of learned helplessness and depression. This method was based on the assumption that the helplessness cognition that outcomes and responding are independent and Rotter's (1966) concept of external control are similar. Rotter and his associates (James, 1957; James & Rotter, 1958; Phares, 1957; Rotter, Liverant, & Crowne, 1961) used tasks in which success appeared to be determined by either chance or skill. They demonstrated that verbalized expectancies for future success are affected by outcomes on previous trials. Outcomes on previous trials have a greater effect on expectancies for future success when people believe outcomes are dependent upon responses (skill-determined) than when they believe outcomes are independent of responses (chance-determined). Employing this logic, Miller and Seligman (1973, 1976) and Klein and Seligman (1976) examined verbalized expectancies of success on skill and chance tasks for nondepressed college students previously exposed to controllable, uncontrollable, or no noises and for depressed college students given no noises. In these studies, depressed students and students exposed to prior uncontrollable noises showed less expectancy change than did students exposed to prior controllable noises or no noises in an ostensible skill task, whereas the groups did not differ on a chance task (but, see Willis & Blaney, 1978; and McNitt & Thornton, 1978; for alternative findings). Hospitalized unipolar depressives showed an expectancy change pattern similar to that of the helpless and depressed students (Abramson, Garber, Edwards, & Seligman, 1978). From these results, Miller and Seligman (1973, 1976) and Klein and Seligman (1976) inferred that helpless and depressed students had acquired a generalized expectancy of response–outcome independence which interfered with seeing the relationship between their responses and outcomes.

Two conceptual problems preclude acceptance of the chance–skill method as providing an assessment of humans' cognitive representations of contingencies. The first problem with the chance–skill methodology concerns its reliance on the assumption that external locus of control is conceptually similar to the expectation of independence between responses and outcomes. Abramson et al. (1978) recently have argued that external locus of control and the expectation of response–outcome independence are orthogonal. They distinguish between cases of personal helplessness in which people attribute the independence between outcomes and their responses to internal factors and cases of universal helplessness in which people attribute the independence between outcomes and their responses to external factors. Moreover, recent developments in attribution theory (Weiner, Frieze, Kukla, Reed, Rest, & Rosenbaum, 1971; Weiner, Nierenberg, & Goldstein, 1976) suggest that changes in expectancy of success are a function of the perceived likelihood that factors which produced prior success will be present again in the future, rather than a function of people's perceptions of response–outcome contingencies. According to this view, small expectancy changes reflect attributions of task outcomes to unstable factors instead of a belief in no control.

In summary, this review of prior work suggests that although the learned helplessness hypothesis postulates that helpless and depressed people are characterized by an associative deficit, no methodology developed within the helplessness framework has yet proved adequate to assess this deficit.

A MORE DIRECT METHOD FOR ASSESSING THE ASSOCIATIVE COMPONENT?

A more direct method for isolating the cognitive component of helplessness and depression was developed by Alloy and Abramson (1979), based on prior work by Jenkins and Ward (1965). Unlike earlier attempts to measure the associative component of helplessness and depression, Alloy and Abramson (1979) asked subjects to actually quantify the degree of relationship between their responses and an outcome in a number of contingency learning problems. A contingency learning problem consists of a series of trials on which the subject makes one of two possible responses (pressing a button or not pressing a button) and receives one of two possible outcomes (a green light or no green light). At the end of the series of trials, the subject is asked to judge on a scale of 0–100 the degree of contingency that exists between button pressing and green light onset.

In the contingency learning studies discussed later in this chapter, subjects actually were asked to judge the degree of *control* their responses exerted over outcomes rather than the degree of *contingency* between responses and outcomes. "Contingency" is a general term which refers to the degree of relationship between any two events. In an instrumental learning situation, the events of interest consist of the individual's responses and some outcome or reinforcer. The relationship between responses and outcomes is best construed as one of controllability; the response exerts either some or no degree of control over the outcome (see Jenkins & Ward, 1965, and Seligman, 1975, for a discussion of the concept of controllability). Another reason for using the term "control" when interacting with the subjects is that it conveys the technical meaning of "contingency" in everyday language (Jenkins & Ward, 1965).

In contingency learning studies, it is necessary to construct an index of the objective degree of control or dependency between responses and outcomes. Similar to the studies of Jenkins & Ward (1965), the studies to be discussed used the magnitude of the difference between the conditional probability of an outcome given the occurrence of a response versus the conditional probability of that outcome given the nonoccurrence of that response as the index of degree of control. An example clarifies this "difference in probability" metric. According to this metric, if the probability of having an article accepted for publication is .90 when you mention the journal editor favorably in the article, and .10 when you mention the editor unfavorably, the degree of contingency between the manner in which you refer to the editor and having the article accepted is .80. Alternatively, if the probability of acceptance is .90 whether you mention the editor favorably or not, then the manner in which you refer to the editor and getting the article accepted are noncontingently related.

As noted earlier in this chapter, methods used to assess the cognitive component of helplessness in prior studies confounded this component with the motivational component. This type of confounding is virtually eliminated in the contingency learning studies to be described. In these studies, failure to perceive a relationship between one's own responses and the outcome cannot be ascribed to failure to emit the relevant responses. The relevant responses were simple and required little or no effort: pressing a button or not pressing a button. Moreover, subjects were instructed to and did sample these two responses fairly regularly.

Judgment of Contingency in Depressed and Nondepressed Students

In a series of four experiments, Alloy and Abramson (1979) presented depressed and nondepressed college students with one of a series of contingency problems. Some students were presented with problems in which there was a high degree of relationship between their responses and the outcome, while other students were presented with problems in which there was little relationship or no relationship between their responses and the outcome. The learned helplessness theory of depression makes a strong and a weak prediction concerning the linkage between people's perceptions of contingencies and objective contingencies. According to the strong prediction, depressed people should underestimate the degree of control their responses exert over outcomes relative to the objective degree of control. According to the weak prediction, depressed individuals merely should be more inclined to judge that their responses exert less control over outcomes than should nondepressed individuals.

Although several proponents of the learned helplessness model (e.g., Klein & Seligman, 1976; Miller & Seligman, 1973) have argued that depressed and nondepressed people should not differ in their perception of noncontingent response–outcome relationships and, moreover, that both groups will accurately detect noncontingency, Alloy and Abramson (1979) argue that the learned helplessness model does not deduce this prediction. According to Alloy and Abramson (1979), the learned helplessness model of depression makes a strong and a weak prediction about people's perceptions of noncontingency. According to the strong prediction, nondepressed people should tend to overestimate the degree of control when responses and outcomes are noncontingently related, whereas depressed people will be accurate. According to the weak prediction, there simply will be a net difference between depressed and nondepressed people's judgments of noncontingency. As noted earlier, the learned helplessness model states that an expectation of no control interferes with the detection of contingency or dependence between responses and outcomes. By this logic, Alloy and Abramson (1979) argue that an expectation of control should interfere with the detection of noncontingency or independence between responses and outcomes. Thus, depressed individuals should underestimate the degree of control their responses exert over an outcome because of their generalized expectation that they have no control, and nondepressed individuals should overestimate the degree of control their responses exert over an outcome because of their generalized expectation that they do have control.

The overall pattern of the results in the four experiments (Alloy & Abramson, 1979) provide no evidence for an associative deficit in depression. Depressed students' judgments of contingency were surprisingly accurate in all four experiments. Nondepressed students, on the other hand, overestimated the degree of control their responses exerted over outcomes when noncontingent outcomes were frequent and/or desirable and they underestimated the degree of control when contingent outcomes were undesirable. Nondepressed students also underestimated the degree of control when the passive response of not pressing the button was associated with the higher percentage of reinforcement in a hedonically charged situation.

Making a judgment about the degree of control one's responses exert over an environmental outcome is best conceived of as an instance of drawing an inference from raw data. Nondepressed students' errors in judging contingency could be either because they did not collect the appropriate raw data or because they drew incorrect inferences from a set of appropriate raw data. For example, the nondepressed students may have known the probability of green light onset associated with pressing the button and not pressing the button but may have been unable to organize these probabilities in the manner necessary for making a correct judgment of contingency. Alternatively, nondepressed students could have erred in judging contingency simply because they did not know the conditional probabilities of green light onset. Therefore, in addition to making judgments about control, subjects in the studies of Alloy and Abramson (1979) also gave independent judgments of the conditional probabilities of green light onset associated with pressing and not pressing the button. Both depressed and nondepressed students were quite accurate in judging these two conditional probabilities. Thus, nondepressed students' errors in judging degree of control appear to stem from inappropriate organization of conditional probability data rather than from the perception of these data themselves.

If, as the Alloy and Abramson (1979) studies suggest, depressed individuals do not have difficulty perceiving relationships between their responses and outcomes, why do they fail to perform adequately on instrumental learning tasks? As previously noted, the use of performance measures as indices of the associative deficit in helplessness and depression confounded this deficit with the response initiation deficit. Alloy and Abramson (1979) suggest one way of reconciling these disparate findings. They propose that depressives are characterized by a generalized expectancy of no control but that this expectancy only interferes with the initiation of responses and not with the perception of response–outcome relationships. In this view, depressed people often perform poorly on instrumental tasks because they fail to generate the response that increases the probability of the successful outcome rather than because they have trouble discerning the effect their responses exert on these outcomes. Some support for this view comes from the observation that depressed students were less likely to generate complex hypotheses for exerting control over the green light than were nondepressed students (Alloy and Abramson, 1979). This view deduces a testable prediction: Depressives should underestimate the amount of control they exert over an outcome in situations in which a complex hypothesis is required to exert control. The logic here is that depressives will be less likely to generate the appropriate hypothesis and therefore will fail to sample the potential contingency between their responses and the outcome. In situations in which the complex hypothesis required to exert control is generated for them, depressives should not underestimate their control (cf., Alloy & Abramson, 1979). Abramson, Alloy, and Rosoff (Note 1) confirm this prediction. They found that relative to nondepressed students, depressed students underestimated the degree of control they exerted over the onset of a green light when they were required to generate the relatively complex hypothesis for exerting control themselves. In addition, Abramson et al. (Note 1) showed that depressives' underestimation of control was due, in fact, to a decreased probability of performing the correct controlling response, and therefore to a failure to sample adequately the potential contingency between their responses and the outcome. Alternatively, if depressed and nondepressed subjects were given a small pool of potential hypotheses for exerting control from which to sample, both groups accurately judged the degree of control their responses exerted over the green light.

To summarize to this point, the work of Alloy and Abramson (1979) suggests that when a measure is used to assess the cognitive component of helplessness unconfounded with the motivational component, no evidence emerges for an associative deficit in depression (see also Alloy & Seligman, 1979). If anything, nondepressives appear to suffer from an "associative deficit." On the other hand, depressives do appear to generate fewer complex hypotheses for exerting control than do nondepressives (Abramson et al., Note 1). Because depressives may be less likely to generate complex hypotheses for exerting control than nondepressives, they often will exert less control in the real world. The less control they actually exert, the more their belief that they have no control will be strengthened. Thus, the expectation of no control and the consequent reduction in the generation of hypotheses for exerting control may trap the depressive in a vicious circle.

Although the work of Alloy and Abramson (1979) suggests that depressives do not show the associative component of helplessness, a second issue concerns the existence of an associative deficit in people exposed to uncontrollable events. Does the learned helplessness theory provide an adequate explanation for the helplessness phenomenon but not for depression? Alloy and Abramson (Note 2) recently completed a study addressed to this issue. Depressed and nondepressed students were exposed to controllable noises, yoked uncontrollable noises, or no noises in a typical helplessness triadic design. Following this experience, students gave judgments of control for a problem in which an objectively noncontingent outcome was either desirable or undesirable. The prediction based on the associative component of helplessness theory is that subjects exposed to uncontrollable noises will form the expectation that their responses are unrelated to outcomes, and this expectation will facilitate accurate perception of noncontingency on the subsequent judgment of noncontingency tasks. In addition, subjects exposed to controllable noises should form the expectation that their responses do contol outcomes. This expectation should interfere with the accurate perception of noncontingency. That is, subjects exposed to controllable noises are expected to overestimate the degree of control their responses exert over the noncontingent, but desirable, outcome.

The findings of the experiment by Alloy and Abramson (Note 2) are in direct opposition to the predictions of helplessness theory. Nondepressed subjects previously exposed to uncontrollable or no noises greatly overestimated their degree of control over the noncontingent–desirable outcome, while nondepressed subjects previously exposed to controllable noises accurately judged that they had little control. Depressed subjects also gave accurate judgments of control regardless of whether they previously experienced controllable, uncontrollable, or no noises. Thus, the associative component of helplessness theory does not provide an adequate account of either depressed or helpless individuals' perceptions of response–outcome relationships. Neither helpless nor depressed individuals appear to be biased toward perceiving contingent response–outcome relationships as noncontingent.

REMAINING ISSUES

An obvious question emerges concerning the generality of the judgment of contingency work to clinical populations of depressives. Although depressed college students do not appear to have an associative deficit, clinically depressed people may underestimate the degree of relationship between their responses and outcomes in the manner predicted by helplessness theory. Even if clinically depressed people do show the associative deficit, failure to obtain evidence for this deficit in helpless or more mildly depressed individuals still is problematic for the theory. According to helplessness theory, helplessness and mild depression are on a continuum with severe depression, with the expectation of no control characterizing all intensities of the syndrome. Is it the case that the learned helplessness model explains severe depression but not helplessness or mild depression? More work is needed to clarify this point.

Although the studies previously discussed did not support the helplessness theory's prediction of an associative deficit in helplessness or depression, depressives did appear to have a motivational impairment. However, to demonstrate that the motivational deficit in depression found by Abramson et al. (Note 1) is explained by the learned helplessness theory, it is necessary that this deficit be the result of an expectation of no control. Another issue is whether this motivational deficit, in part, mediates the impairment in instrumental learning shown by helpless and depressed humans as specified by the learned helplessness theory. It is interesting that the learned helplessness theory emphasized depressives' failure to initiate motor responses to control environmental outcomes. Perhaps depressives are less likely to generate voluntary "mental" responses as well as voluntary motor responses. For example, depressives may be less likely to engage actively in many cognitive strategies (e.g., hypothesis generation, attention focusing, memory search, and rehearsal).

This discussion of the cognitive and motivational components of helplessness and depression suggests new directions for future research in this area. If such research is to increase our understanding of helplessness and depression, it is important that it be guided by theory rather than by practical considerations. Only when the basic propositions of the learned helplessness theory have been fully tested, will we know where to search for the most appropriate applications.

REFERENCE NOTES

1. Abramson, L. Y., Alloy, L. B., and Rosoff, R. *Depression and the generation of complex hypotheses in the judgment of contingency.* Submitted for publication, 1980.
2. Alloy, L. B., and Abramson, L. Y. *The judgment of contingency: An experimental test of the cognitive component of the learned helplessness theory of depression.* Submitted for publication, 1980.

4

Why Having Control Reduces Stress: If I Can Stop the Roller Coaster, I Don't Want to Get Off[1]

SUZANNE M. MILLER

INTRODUCTION

Someone in the neighborhood is throwing a big, noisy party. Neighbor A is told to complain if he can no longer tolerate the music and frivolity, although he refrains from doing so (because of self-imposed restraint, etc.). Neighbor B receives no such communication. The party festivities are equally disruptive to both neighbors. Despite this, it is likely that neighbor A (who believes he can complain but never does) will be less disturbed by the festivities than will neighbor B (who will probably spend the whole night stewing and might eventually tip off the police as a "concerned citizen").

Individuals are continually faced with the prospect of aversive events such as the situation just depicted. How can we account for the fact that having control seems to reduce the stress generated by an aversive event? The resolution to this problem is not immediately evident, and no viable theoretical account of it currently exists. Why should control be stress-reducing, even when (a) the individual without control has equal predict-

[1]The preparation of this chapter was partially supported by PHS Grants MH 19604 and RR 09069.

71

ability; and *(b)* the individual with control does not actually execute the controlling response?

This chapter attempts to make sense of these issues by presenting two new hypotheses, the "internality hypothesis" and the "minimax hypothesis," to account for the evidence on controllability and human stress. The discussion begins by clarifying the ways in which "controllability" and "stress" have been used in the literature. Next, the major existing theories of controllability are briefly reviewed. Following this, the two new "expected outcome" hypotheses of controllability and their predictions are examined in some detail. Then the experimental evidence is presented and contrasted with the "expected outcome" hypotheses. Finally, the conditions under which individuals prefer not to have controllability but yield it instead to another person are discussed.

DEFINITIONS OF CONTROLLABILITY

Actual Control

Instrumental Control

The first type of controllability refers to an instrumental training space (e.g., Seligman, 1975) in which the individual is able to make a response that actually modifies the aversive event. Such a response can be either active or passive and can escape (Corah & Boffa, 1970; Gatchel & Proctor, 1976), avoid (Averill & Rosenn, 1972), or otherwise mitigate, the impact of the stimulus (Staub, Tursky, & Schwartz, 1971). The individual without control receives exactly the same physical event that the individual with control has received, but he or she has no response at hand for modifying the event. For example, in a study by Szpiler and Epstein (1976), all subjects were told that they might receive shock following countdown. The two relevant groups consisted of a group that could avoid shock by tapping rapidly during the countdown and a yoked group that tapped rapidly but believed that shock would be random.

A variant of instrumental control is the perceived instrumental control paradigm. Here, the contingencies are arranged such that the individual *believes* that control rests with him or her. However, it is the experimenter who is actually controlling the aversive event. Although this is a psychologically trivial variant of instrumental control, methodologically it is not trivial: It allows individuals in both controllable and uncontrollable conditions to experience exactly the same aversive event, supposedly without the disadvantages of the yoked control design (Church, 1964; Levis, 1976). This point will be elaborated later.

Self-Administration

In the second type of controllability, the individual is allowed to deliver the aversive event to himself or herself (Ball & Vogler, 1971; Haggard, 1943; Pervin, 1963). As with perceived (but nonveridical) instrumental control, the self-administering individual cannot change the objective aspects of the situation in any way. Thus, both the self-administering and the experimenter-administering individual receive exactly the same physical stimulus.

A salient methodological confound pervades the entire instrumental control and self-administration literatures. This is due to the fact that both procedures confound controllability—the variable of interest—with predictability. The difference here is that controllability means you can actually *do* something about the event in question, whereas predictability means that you can merely *know* something about the event, whether or not you can do anything about it (cf. Miller & Grant, Note 1). In the case of instrumental control and self-administration, the group with control has both more controllability *and* more predictability than the group without control, because timing is inevitably better for the controlling group. For example, in the instrumental control paradigm, when you escape a shock, you not only control it, but you know exactly when it will go off. In contrast, if you cannot escape a shock, you neither control it, nor do you know when it will go off. Similarly, if you avoid a shock, you both control it and know it will not occur. In the self-administration paradigm, when you deliver a shock to yourself, you not only control it, but you know exactly when it is coming. On the other hand, if it is delivered to you, you neither control it nor do you know exactly when it is coming.

Miller and Grant (1979; Note 1) have extensively reviewed the predictability literature, concluding that there are conditions under which predictable aversive events are "less stressful" than unpredictable events. In the present case, having control makes the aversive event more predictable. For instrumental control, the group with the controlling response perceives more control, as well as more predictability, than the yoked group: Feedback from (and the intention to make) a controlling response also predicts the offset of the aversive event in the case of escape, or the nonoccurrence of the aversive event in the case of avoidance. In the case of self-administration, control is also confounded with predictability because feedback from (and the intention to make) the controlling response also predicts the onset of the aversive event. The perceived (but nonveridical) instrumental control paradigm minimizes differences in predictability while varying perceived control, because the stressor actually occurs independently of responding. The subjects may believe, however, that they have more predictability from feedback just as they believe they have more control. So although actual control is unconfounded by actual predictability, perceived predictability may still be confounded with perceived controllability. Therefore, in all these procedures, any differences in stress that emerge between groups could be attributed as easily to differences in predictability as to differences in controllability.

It should be noted that the major common virtue of these procedures is that both a group with and a group without a controlling response receive exactly the same physical stimulation. This is done to insure that the groups differ only in psychological factors. The major common flaw of the procedures is that the controlling and the no controlling groups differ on more than one major psychological dimension. As previously noted, the controlling group has more predictability and more controllability than the no controlling group. Therefore, results obtained with these procedures cannot discriminate between the class of theory that says controllability reduces stress *because* it provides the individual with extra predictability and the class of theory that says controllability has stress-reducing effects *above and beyond* providing extra predictability. Because of this confounding, these two categories will not be elaborated any further in this chapter (see Miller, 1979, for a review of the evidence on instrumental control and self-administration).

Actual Control Equated for Predictability

It should be clear from the foregoing discussion that predictability must somehow be equated for subjects with and without control. Predictability and controllability *can* be kept methodologically distinct by providing the no controlling individual with an external time cue. Such a cue can be used to signal explicitly when the event will arrive in the case of self-administration, terminate in the case of instrumental escape, and occur or not occur in the case of instrumental avoidance. This effectively eliminates differences in timing between the two groups; procedures that provide such signals will be referred to as "actual control equated for predictability" procedures.

Potential Control

"Potential control" induces individuals to believe that some controlling response is available to them but they refrain from using it. In these studies, the aversive stimulation occurs on a prearranged schedule for all individuals. However, individuals with control have at hand a panic button for terminating the event, which they never actually use. This is important for theoretical reasons, because it teases apart present control and future control. Since individuals refrain from responding, they do not exercise control in the present; rather, they expect that, if need be, they will be able to execute control at some point in the future.

Thus the experimenter is faced with a procedural dilemma: How can he or she both instill a sense of potential control in an individual and at the same time insure that the response will not be acted upon? In the standard procedure, social pressure is brought to bear on individuals so that they refrain from pressing the button (e.g., Glass & Singer, 1972). Alternatively, individuals can be provided with a potential control response for terminating an aversive event that is never subsequently administered. For example, individuals can be threatened with the possibility of receiving preprogrammed electric shocks and then offered a button which they can use to turn off a given shock if necessary. No shock is ever administered; so no individual ever has to press (Miller, Grant, & Nelson, Note 2).

The potential control and equated predictability procedures are both very elegant. In both procedures, an individual with and an individual without control are exposed to the identical physical event, and this event is equally preditable for the two individuals. However, in the case of actual control equated for predictability, amount of actual responding is a minor confounding variable (as it is in instrumental control and self-administration), because the group with control responds more than the yoked group. The potential control case is by far the most elegant. Here the group with and the group without potential control do not differ in degree of actual responding. In fact, they are identical on every dimension except one: The potential control individual anticipates more future control (and predictability) than the individual without such control.

OPERATIONALIZATION OF "STRESS"

There are three main ways in which "stress" reactions have been operationalized in controllability experiments. The first is to give individuals a choice between a controllable and an uncontrollable aversive event. Or, individuals can be exposed to both controllability and uncontrollability, and then express their preference between them. The second measure is anticipatory arousal, that is, whether or not individuals are more anxious and aroused while waiting for a controllable as opposed to an uncontrollable event. Anticipatory arousal can be assessed either physiologically, via electrodermal and cardiovascular measures, or subjectively, via self-ratings of anxiety and tension. Finally, the third measure is impact arousal, that is, whether or not a controllable aversive event actually hurts less. Impact arousal can be assessed physiologically, subjectively, and behaviorally.

PREDICTABILITY HYPOTHESES OF CONTROL

There are three major hypotheses which claim that the effects of controllability are reducible to the effects of predictability. This class of hypothesis includes Seligman's (1968) safety signal view, Weiss's (1971) relevant feedback theory, and Berlyne's (1960) information-seeking view as applied to control. These hypotheses and their fit to the predictability (Miller & Grant, 1979, Note 1) and controllability (Miller, 1979) literatures have recently been reviewed at length. Hence, I will only briefly present and review them here.

The predictability hypotheses all assert that controllability is preferred and less arousing because it provides the individual with additional predictability and proceed to explain why predictability reduces stress. However, they differ on the proposed mechanism by which predictability achieves its stress-reducing effects. Seligman's safety signal hypothesis holds that when a signal (CS) reliably predicts danger, the absence of the signal ($\overline{CS}$) reliably predicts safety and relaxation. In contrast, if no signal reliably predicts danger, then no signal reliably predicts safety. Therefore, the individual never knows when he or she can relax. The crucial mechanism affecting choice of control is differential predictability, and hence differential relaxation, in anticipation of an aversive event. As noted, an individual with either instrumental control or self-administration has more predictability and safety signals than an individual without such control. During a controllable aversive event, the individual can relax more because he or she has more safety signals that the shock will not occur (avoidance), that it will go off (escape), and that it will not come on (self-administration). During uncontrollable shock, the individual has fewer safety signals and so relaxes less. Therefore, control should be preferred because it provides more safety and hence less anticipatory arousal than no control. Safety signal makes no predictions about the effects of control on impact arousal. Weiss's (1971) relevant feedback view is logically similar to the safety signal hypothesis and need not be elaborated here (see Miller, 1979).

Finally, the information-seeking theory of Berlyne (1960) is primarily about predictability, although it can be extended to controllability (see also Sokolov, 1963). The theory says that individuals seek information, and, when faced with uncertainty (unpredictability), they strive for certainty. Moreover, uncertainty causes conflict and also increases surprise and arousal. As control provides more predictability, information-seeking theory predicts (a) choice of instrumental control and self-administration, because individuals seek information; (b) less anticipatory arousal with such control, because individuals are in less conflict; (c) less impact with control, because individuals are less surprised by the aversive event.

Both the safety signal and information-seeking views fare equally well in accounting for the evidence on instrumental control and self-administration, where having control really does provide the individual with extra predictability. In both categories, the data show choice of control over no control, as well as less anticipatory arousal with control. These results are accurately predicted by each of the two hypotheses. With regard to impact arousal, controllability appears to reduce aversiveness in the case of instrumental control, but to have no effect in the case of self-administration. The first result is consistent with safety signal and inconsistent with information-seeking, whereas the second result is consistent with information-seeking and inconsistent with safety signal (see Miller, 1979, for a thorough review of this literature).

The predictability hypotheses have in common the view that controllability adds nothing above and beyond more finely tuned predictability. Moreover, they are all present-oriented: Both controlling and no controlling individuals anticipate exactly the same aversive event. The individuals with control have an advantage in the here-and-now, however, because controllability decreases their anticipatory arousal (and/or impact arousal) by reducing conflict or signalling safety. It is for these reasons that such theorizing is inadequate to account for the stress-reducing effects associated with the equated predictability and potential control paradigms. With respect to the equated predictability paradigm, both the individuals with and the individuals without control have equal predictability, because of the provision of external signals to the no controlling individuals. This means that the controlling response neither reduces surprise (information-seeking) nor signals safety (safety signal). Similarly, with respect to the potential control paradigm, both controlling and no controlling individuals are in the presence of exactly the same external signals. They differ only in that the controlling individuals have a manipulandum which they refrain from using. Since the controlling individuals never execute the response, they have no more control and receive no more safety signals or certainty than the no controlling individuals. Therefore, the predictability theories would suggest that there are no stress-reducing effects of having actual control equated for predictability or of having unexercised potential control. Yet, as we shall see, such stress-reducing effects do emerge, and I now propose an alternative class of theorizing that predicts these effects.

EXPECTED OUTCOME HYPOTHESES OF CONTROL

The Internality Hypothesis

The internality hypothesis is based on the yoked control argument of Church (1964), which appeared over 15 years ago. It was originally intended as a methodological criticism of the yoked control paradigm, but it can be translated into a general statement of why individuals want control. The hypothesis to be proposed can be distilled as follows: Individuals choose control because having control improves an aversive outcome. It does so by enabling individuals to present stimuli to themselves to suit fluctuations in their moods, thereby rendering the outcome less painful.

In the yoked control paradigm, the individual without control is presented with exactly the same physical stimuli as the individual with control has received. This is done to insure that the effects of control are not contaminated by differences in the nature of physical stimulation administered to the two individuals. The amount of shock that an individual with control receives is determined by how well he or she executes the controlling response. In contrast, the amount of shock that an individual without control receives is determined by how much shock the controlling individual has received. In the case of instrumental escape, for example, if the controlling individual performs the response within .2 seconds on a given trial, he or she receives only a .2-second shock. He or she is then matched with a no controlling individual, who is similarly administered only a .2-second shock on that trial. In this way, both individuals receive exactly the same sequence of "objective" events, the only difference being that one individual actually goes through the act of making a response.

Church (1964) accepts the fact that the stimuli are *physically* identical as administered by the experimenter (i.e., a .2-second shock in either case). However, he challenges the premise that they are necessarily *experienced* as identical by the two individuals. His view rests on the assumption that individuals typically undergo moment-to-moment fluctuations in their internal states, both physiological and psychological (e.g., mood). So, for example, a physically aversive stimulus such as shock will feel differently, depending on the individual's internal physical state *at the moment* shock is delivered. A given level of shock is going to feel intolerable anytime the individual is in a highly vulnerable internal physical state. However, the exact same level of shock is going to feel less painful anytime the individual is in a less vulnerable state.

Consider now the case of individuals who have learned that they can turn off shock by executing a controlling response. Shock is occasionally going to be turned on at a moment when they are in a highly vulnerable internal state. This will have the net result of making the shock feel particularly painful, and hence the individuals will be motivated to turn off the shock as quickly as possible (e.g., in less than .2 seconds). Conversely, anytime the shock is turned on at a moment when they are in a less vulnerable internal state, they will be slower to turn off shock (e.g., in greater than .2 seconds). This means that *although the individuals with control sometimes receive "subjectively" tolerable shocks of long duration, they never receive a "subjectively" intolerable shock of long duration.*

The yoked control individuals are in a very different situation, however. Because shock is being turned on and off without regard to fluctuations in their internal states, they are *bound to receive, at some point, a "subjectively" intolerable shock of long duration.* Therefore the two groups of individuals are actually receiving different psychological outcomes, and Church argues that this artifact pervades the entire animal literature.

The internality view thus predicts stress-reducing effects of the standard instrumental control and self-administration procedures, because the individual with control can match his or her internal state with external events. This means that *(a)* control should be chosen over no control; *(b)* control should be associated with less anticipatory arousal, because the individual is waiting for a less intense aversive event; and *(c)* control should be associated with less impact arousal, because the aversive event actually hurts less. The experimental evidence generally supports these predictions. The real value of the hypothesis, however, is the fact that control changes the expected outcome. This means that all these results should still occur, even when the individual without control is provided with equal predictability. This is because the provision of external signals does not enable the individual without control to more accurately match his internal state with external events, and so he or she cannot improve the outcome. Therefore, control should still be chosen and should lead to decreased anticipatory and impact arousal.

The internality hypothesis also predicts reduced stress as a result of potential control. Recall that the potential control individuals are given a panic button which they can use to terminate the aversive event. Therefore they *anticipate* that they will never receive a long-duration intolerable shock. If the shock should be turned on when they are in a highly vulnerable internal state, they know that they can always turn it off quickly. Although mild and even moderate "subjectively" aversive events are being turned on and off without regard to their internal states in the here-and-now, the individuals with potential control still have an advantage over the individuals without potential control. This is because they expect to shorten any subjectively *intense* shocks that occur in the future and thereby improve the anticipated outcome. The hypothesis predicts *(a)* choice of potential control over no control; *(b)* less anticipatory arousal with potential control, because the subjects anticipate an overall less aversive US; and *(c)* no effect of unexercised potential control on impact, because the response is never made. Therefore, the aversive event is experienced as subjectively identical by the two groups of individuals.

Minimax Hypothesis

Minimax hypothesis, like the internality view, says that controllability provides the individual with more than just extra predictability. Both views are, in addition, oriented toward expected outcomes; that is, an individual with control expects a less aversive *outcome* than an individual without control. According to the internality view, the mechanism by which control-lability achieves this effect is by enabling an individual to match his or her internal state with external events. According to minimax, the mechanism by which controllability achieves this effect is by providing a guaranteed upper limit on how bad the situation can become. Minimax hypothesis proposes that, in aversive situations, individuals want to minimize the max-imum danger to themselves; that is, they are inclined to "make the best of a bad situation," and controllability enables them to do so. The theory is explicitly stated as follows: "A person who has control over an aversive event insures having a lower maximum danger than a person without control. This is because a person with control attributes the cause of relief to a stable internal source—his own response—whereas a person without control attri-butes relief to a less stable, more external source [Miller, 1979]."

Consider what happens when two groups of individuals are threatened with the same high-intensity electric shock. Those with instrumental control know that all they have to do is execute the controlling response, and shock will termiante fast; that is, they have a guarantee that the maximum upper limit of duration of shock will not be greater than their reaction time. They are also assured that any future such shock will only occur up to some relatively low, maximum amount. In contrast, the individuals who do not have instrumental control have no guarantee that a high-intensity shock will go off quickly. For example, in the laboratory, individuals with control are typically told that they can and should turn off shock in the minimum time required. In contrast, individuals without control are simply told that shock will eventually be turned off. This means that the controlling individuals know that they can *always* obtain relief from a high-intensity shock. The no controlling individuals, however, can *never* know for certain whether or not they will obtain immediate relief.

So the minimax hypothesis predicts that individuals choose instrumen-tal control over no control, because instrumental control minimizes the maximum duration, intensity, and/or frequency of the aversive event. Minimax hypothesis predicts less arousal in anticipation of an instrumentally con-trolled event. Anticipatory arousal is proportional to the magnitude of the anticipated danger, and the anticipated upper limit of the event is lower with control. Thus, an individual who is waiting for a 7 MA shock that will not exceed 1 second in duration will be less aroused than will a subject who is waiting for the same 7 MA shock that might last as long as 10 seconds. The theory makes no explicit prediction about impact, as it postulates no mech-anism by which expectations about the upper limit of an impending shock affect how painful the shock will actually feel.

Identical logic applies to the case of self-administration, where the experimenter-administered procedures also give an individual fewer guaran-tees than the self-administering procedures. Individuals who can self-administer shock to themselves know that once they have had enough, they can simply not deliver any more shock. They also know that they will not self-administer six shocks if they are only scheduled to receive five. Nor will they give themselves a 2-second shock instead of the scheduled 1-second shock. In contrast, an individual whose fate is in the hands of the experimenter has none of the above guarantees. So, as with instrumental control, minimax hypothesis predicts preference for self-administered shock and less anticipatory arousal. Again, the hypothesis makes no explicit prediction about impact. Similar to the predictability views and internality hypothesis, minimax adequately handles the data on instrumental control and self-administration (see Miller, 1979).

Note that minimax differs from the internality view in explaining the effects of instrumental control and self-administration. Internality specifically relies on an individual matching his or her internal state with external events in order to improve the anticipated outcome. Minimax, on the other hand, postulates that controllability provides an individual with a guaranteed upper limit on how bad the situation can become. Such a guarantee effectively improves the expected outcome and reduces stress, independently of whether or not individuals even undergo variations in their internal states. For example, when an individual is threatened with a high-intensity shock that he can turn off himself in 1 second (controllability), he anticipates a more guaranteed outcome and shows less stress than a subject who must rely on the experimenter to turn it off in 1 second (uncontrollability). This effect occurs even though the same shock is scheduled to be turned on at a subjectively invulnerable (or vulnerable) moment for both individuals, because it is the guaranteed maximum aversiveness and not the variations in internal state that is crucial for minimax.

There is an important attributional premise which is implicit in minimax hypothesis and which should be explicitly stated. This premise accounts for the stress-reducing effects of the equated predictability and potential control procedures and also helps to clarify how minimax differs from the internality view. Minimax proposes that when individuals have control, they go on to attribute this control to an internal, stable factor: their own responding (Weiner, Frieze, Kukla, Reed, Rest, & Rosenblum, 1971); that is, when danger is controllable, the individual attributes its effects to him or herself. When danger is uncontrollable, the individual must make alternate, external attributions that are more unstable [e.g., the experimenter is controlling, luck, benevolent (or malevolent) God, bureaucracy, and the like]. This difference is crucial to the hypothesis, because "If a subject attributes the cause of relief to a stable, internal factor—such as his own response—he has a reliable predictor that in the future, danger will only occur up to some relatively low, maximum amount. In contrast, if the attribution is to some unstable, external factor—such as the experimenter's whims—future danger is not

guaranteed to be restricted to any relatively low maximum [Miller, 1979]."
Consider an individual who can turn off shock for himself. He can depend
on his own actions, and so he can predict that shock will be turned off in the
minimum time it takes for him to perform his controlling response. This
individual will show reduced arousal. Consider now an individual who must
rely on the experimenter. Even though the experimenter's actions may have
been reliable and predictable in the past, the individual cannot count on
them for the future as reliably as he can on his own response. It is always
possible that the experimenter will fall asleep or forget in the future, or
become sadistic, no matter how efficient his performance has been thus far.
This individual will show sustained arousal, because an unfamiliar experimenter is relatively less stable than his own response.

Thus, controllability and uncontrollability result in opposing attributions
for the cause of relief: The former is to an internal, stable factor, whereas the
latter is to an external, unstable factor. According to minimax, it is the
difference in the stability dimension, not the internality dimension, that is
crucial in accounting for the stress-reducing effects of control: That is, what-
ever guarantees the maximum danger must not be capricious or, in other
words, it must be stable. So there is no inherent value to having control per
se. Rather, intenral factors (such as one's own response) generally tend to be
more stable than external factors.

Therefore, minimax predicts that controllability will be preferred and
produce less anticipatory arousal even when the no controlling group is
equated for predictability. Although external signals may have given equal
predictability of onset and offset of shock in the past, they are a less stable
guarantee of future minimized danger than is an individual's own response.

Potential (but unexercised) control should also be preferred to no control, and potential control should reduce anticipatory arousal. Subjects with
a panic button believe that the maximum duration and intensity of shock on
each trial is limited to the latency of their reaction time to press the button.
They will be less aroused than their counterparts without a panic button,
who have no guaranteed maximum on each trial and so anticipate a worse
outcome. Minimax is silent about whether or not impact is reduced by
potential control or by actual control equated for predictability.

The internality hypothesis differs from minimax in stressing the internality,
and not the stability, of controlling responses. According to this view, there
is an inherent value to control per se, because it enables the individual to
most optimally match his or her internal state with external events. This is
crucial, because such matching is the means by which an individual is able
to improve an aversive outcome. The fact that an internal controlling response is also more stable than an external factor is unimportant.

Bandura (1977a, 1977b) has proposed a self-efficacy theory of the effects of control which is compatible with minimax. The theory states that

personal control endows individuals with a high sense of self-efficacy, or perceived ability, for coping with an aversive event. When individuals expect to minimize an event (by avoidance, escape, etc.), they have little reason to fear it. This means that they do not engage in repetitive perturbing ideation which, in turn, reduces their level of anxiety and arousal. In contrast, individuals who judge themselves inefficacious expect a more aversive event, which generates more stress-inducing thoughts. This, in turn, maintains a high level of anxiety and arousal.

The self-efficacy view thus places greater explicit emphasis on negative self-referent cognitions as the mediator of anticipatory arousal than minimax does. Minimax holds that arousal is proportional to the magnitude of the anticipated danger. When an individual has control, the anticipated danger is minimized, and so arousal is reduced. In essence, having control is equivalent to transforming an expected two-shock into an expected one-shock situation. However, minimax would also accept the social learning premise that the greater the danger one anticipates, the more likely one is to think about and magnify the potential perils to oneself. This can mean that the aversiveness of the subjectively anticipated event far exceeds the objective aversiveness of the event, thereby increasing anxiety and arousal beyond the actual danger. An individual who lacks some form of behavioral control is in an objectively more dangerous situation than is a subject with control. This may, in turn, activate a chain of disturbing cognitions which subjectively magnifies the anticipated event and so contributes to maintaining elevated levels of anxiety and arousal.

Social learning theory also proposes a mechanism for reduced impact. The theory assumes that self-referent negative cognitions not only precede but also accompany the onset of aversive events, particularly with prolonged rather than punctate events (e.g., "What if the shock should start to get even worse"). Such cognitions generate anticipatory arousal, which overlays impact arousal. Although controllability may not actually make the event hurt less, it eliminates negative cognitions and therefore reduces the anticipatory arousal overlay. This, in turn, reduces the net impact arousal. The anticipatory arousal premise can be appended to either the minimax or internality hypothesis to account for impact differences between controllable and uncontrollable groups.

EVIDENCE

Actual Control Equated for Predictability

There are three instrumental control studies and one self-administration study that hold predictability constant between a controllable and an uncontrollable group. All four studies still find significant stress-reducing effects as a consequence of exercising control. For example, in a study by Geer and Maisel (1972), two groups were shown slides of dead bodies, which were always preceded by a 10-second tone. Individuals who had control were told to turn the slides off when they became too aversive. Individuals without control could not escape but were told how long the slides would be on. Therefore, both groups equally could predict slide onset and offset. Electrodermal arousal was measured throughout, and the results showed less anticipatory and impact arousal for the group that could escape. Moreover, the group that could predict but not control aversive stimulation actually showed more anticipatory arousal than a third group, which could neither predict nor control the slides. Thus, if anything, predictability enhanced stress reactions under conditions where controllability decreased such reactions.

Minimax can account for the Geer and Maisel (1972) results because having a control response provides a more stable guarantee of a maximum upper limit of danger ("This slide in front of me, and any future slide, cannot last longer than my reaction time to turn it off"). The internality view, on the other hand, would say that having a control response allows the individual to match his or her internal state with external events ("Right now I feel particularly squeamish, and so I will press the button fast"). Thus both expected outcome hypotheses can easily and equally handle these data.

In a second instrumental control study by Geer, Davison, and Gatchel (1970), individuals were occasionally shocked while performing a reaction time task. One group of subjects (controllability) was then told they could reduce shock from 6 seconds to 3 seconds if they responded fast enough. The other group (uncontrollability) was simply told that all shocks would now last 3 seconds. As with the Geer and Maisel (1972) study, individuals who could control showed less electrodermal arousal, both anticipatory and impact, than individuals who could not control. In addition, the results of a replication study by Glass, Singer, Leonard, Krantz, Cohen, & Cummings (1973) showed that the controlling group also rated the shock as less painful and performed better on a behavioral posttest than the no controlling group, although there were no electrodermal differences between the groups.

Minimax hypothesis would explain the above data by saying that an individual who attributes the cause of shock duration to his or her own response has a more reliable guarantee than the no controlling individual that all present and future shocks will never exceed 3 seconds. The internality view, on the other hand, at first blush appears to have greater difficulty explaining these data. Both an individual with control and an individual without control are receiving exactly the same improved outcome—a shorter duration shock. Moreover, for both individuals, shock is actually occurring without regard to momentary internal fluctuations. All shocks, whether turned on at a subjectively tolerable or intolerable moment, are uniformly 3 seconds for all individuals. Therefore, the controlling individual has no more opportunity to somehow diminish the impact of a subjectively intolerable shock than the no controlling individual, because the latter never receives a long-duration (6-second) intolerable shock. Controlling individuals may ex-pect, however, that they will have more opportunity to match internal states with external events and thereby improve the outcome, just as they expect to have more control. Since no shock ever actually exceeds 3 seconds, this expectation is never contradicted. No controlling individuals do not expect to match their internal states with external events, and so they expect a worse outcome. It is these differential expectations, then, that account for the stress-reducing effects of control. Indeed, when a group is told it can reduce shock, but the reduction does not occur (shock still lasts 6 seconds), arousal remains high (Glass et al., 1973). Thus, induced beliefs about con-trol only reduce stress if these beliefs are not contradicted by environmental events. As Bandura (1977a and 1977b) has noted, since individuals cannot actually improve the aversive event in laboratory studies using the ''per-ceived'' control paradigm, such studies may underestimate the beneficial effects that accrue to having control in the real world.

Finally, there is one self-administration study where predictability and controllability are not confounded (Björkstrand, 1973). Here a light CS sig-naled shock onset for both groups, but one group could self-administer shock when the light came on, and the other group could not. The self-administration group showed reduced electrodermal skin conductance re-sponse to shock, but not to the signal. The minimax hypothesis must invoke an additional premise to explain these results, such as the social learning theory premise that having a controlling response reduces the anticipatory arousal component of the impact response. The internality hypothesis must also invoke a similar premise, since the controlling individual cannot choose a subjectively ''invulnerable'' moment to deliver shock to him or herself. Therefore shock per se should not actually ''hurt'' less.

Potential Control

Only one study has measured choice of potential control (Miller et al., Note 2). Here individuals were threatened with low probability shocks that would go on and off on a prearranged schedule and were then told: ''There are two groups of subjects in this experiment, and it's up to you which group you want to be in. . . . Should you decide to be in group one, I will put a button beside you that can affect the shocks. . . . On any given trial, if a shock occurs, you can stop it if need be by pressing the button. It would be up to you whether or not you ever used the button. Should you decide to be in group two, you would not have this button available to you. . . . Which group would you like to be in?" No individual was ever actually administered a shock, and so no individual ever exercised the response. Of the 32 individuals, 25 chose potential control. The majority of individuals who chose control said they did so in order to potentially limit the amount of shock they might receive. Those who chose no control said they did not think shock would ever get very bad and having the button would only focus their mind on shock.

Interestingly, choice of the button could be predicted by how stressed individuals were by the initial threat of receiving electric shock—before they knew about choice of button or no button. Individuals who were subjectively aroused by the prospect of shock subsequently opted for the button when it was offered, whereas individuals who were only minimally aroused by shock subsequently opted not to have the button. Moreover, having control reduced self-rated arousal, because over the course of the experiment individuals who chose the button decreased in anxiety to the low level of the no button group. So individuals choose potential control when aroused by upcoming aversive events, and the knowledge of such control promotes anticipatory relaxation.

Because individuals selected for themselves whether or not they would have the button, it is possible that the subsequent reduction in stress reflected simple habituation over trials rather than the presence of the button per se. In a follow-up experiment, each individual was exposed to both button and no button trials, randomized for order. Individuals who were initially made highly anxious by the prospect of electric shock subsequently reported less arousal during button than during no button trials, whereas this effect was not obtained for individuals who were not made as anxious by the prospect of shock. In fact, individuals who were the least aroused by the threat of electric shock subsequently reported more, *not* less, arousal during button than during no button trials. Typical comments of these subjects were to the effect that the option of exercising control only made them think more about shock. As with the first experiment, individuals who were benefited by control said they felt more secure with the button because they could limit shock if the need arose.

To summarize, there are three major findings from the two experiments just reported: (a) The majority of individuals prefer to have potential control; (b) they do so in order to potentially improve an aversive outcome; and (c) they show reduced anticipatory arousal when such control is available. These findings are consistent both with minimax and with the internality view, the former because potential control provides a guaranteed upper limit on the duration of any given shock and the latter because a subject can shorten the duration of a subjectively intolerable shock. There are two further findings worth highlighting: (a) A minority of individuals prefer not to have potential control; and (b) such individuals express more anticipatory anxiety when they have a button available than when they do not have a button available. This suggests that, under some circumstances, there is an emotional cost associated with potential control. A low-anxiety individual who does not have a panic button may find it easy to psychologically remove himself from the threat of electric shock and thereby relax. When such a button is provided, it may remind him of the threat and undermine his ability to psychologically withdraw himself from shock-related thoughts. These considerations bear on the issue of when and under what circumstances individuals choose to relinquish control to another person and will be elaborated later.

One study (Glass, Reim, & Singer, 1971) obtained a physiological measure of anticipatory arousal (electrodermal skin conductance level) and also found reduced arousal with potential control. The impact and post-impact effects of potential (but unexercised) control are more contradictory. None of the studies has found that potential control improves performance on a behavioral task during the aversive event (impact) (Glass, Singer, & Friedman, 1969; Glass et al., 1971; Sherrod & Downs, 1974), and only one out of three studies has found that potential control lowers the physiological response to impact (electrodermal skin conductance responses) (Corah & Boffa, 1970 versus Glass et al., 1969; Glass et al., 1971). In contrast, two out of two studies found reduced pain ratings with potential control (Corah & Boffa, 1970; Glass et al., 1969), and two out of two studies found improved post-impact performance on a behavioral task with potential control (Glass et al., 1969, 1971). These data are too inconsistent to be brought to bear on the hypotheses.

Thus, the internality and minimax views both can account equally well for the evidence on actual control equated for predictability and potential control. Both hypotheses predict preference for control and reduced anticipatory arousal with such control, and the data confirm these predictions. In addition, both hypotheses need a supplementary premise, such as reduced overlay of anticipatory arousal, to explain the possibility of reduced impact and post-impact arousal with such control.

There is a final piece of evidence which seems to discriminate between the views. Bowers (1968) told one group of individuals that they would be able to avoid shock during the experiment, whereas the other group was told that shock delivery would be random. Before the experiment proper, all individuals underwent a shock–tolerance procedure to set the level of shock that would be used. Both groups were encouraged to take as much shock as possible. For individuals who believed they would be able to avoid shock, the level rated as painful was *twice* the intensity of the shock rated as painful in the no controlling group. So the expectation of control seems to have a direct effect on increasing how much shock will be tolerated.

Minimax can explain these results on the basis that controlling individuals have a guaranteed upper limit (provided by their own response) on how bad shock can become during the experiment. Therefore, they are less concerned to leave themselves a safety margin than are individuals who have no control. The results are more of a problem for the internality hypothesis, which views individuals as concerned to match their internal states with external events. Under these circumstances, it is hard to understand why an individual would ever consent to a level of shock that may, at a subjectively vulnerable moment, feel intolerable. Even an individual with control, who can conceivably turn off such a shock and thereby shorten its duration, should prefer to forestall the possibility of its occurrence altogether. So he or she should opt for the same level of shock that the no controlling individual has judged to be subjectively tolerable. Thus, there is at least one set of data which supports minimax more than the internality view. In the next section, I review yet another set of findings which discriminates between the two hypotheses.

RELINQUISHMENT OF CONTROL

One of the main advantages of the minimax view as compared to the internality view is that the former hypothesis makes systematic predictions about when individuals will prefer to have control and when they will prefer, instead, to relinquish control to another individual. This is important, because it is obvious that in real life people often voluntarily yield control. Moreover, in the laboratory, there is always a minority of subjects who prefer to opt for uncontrollable aversive events when offered a choice (e.g., Averill, O'Brien, & DeWitt, 1977; Averill & Rosenn, 1972).

The minimax hypothesis postulates that, in stressful situations, individuals are concerned to put an upper limit on the amount of aversive stimulation they must undergo. Therefore, the hypothesis specifies that individuals should choose control only when they believe that their own responding provides the most stable guarantee of a maximum upper limit of danger. In contrast, they should relinquish control when they believe that some factor other than their own responding provides a more stable guarantee of a maximum upper limit of danger. There are three main circumstances under which internal factors will be construed as less stable than external factors. The first such circumstance is when an individual is uncertain as to whether he or she can reliably execute the response needed to produce the outcome. For example, Bandura (1977a, 1977b) has provided evidence showing that individuals who doubt their own "self-efficacy," that is, their ability to execute a given behavior, tend to avoid threatening situations and to show more stress when forced into such situations than individuals who have high efficacy expectations. The second circumstance which reduces the stability of internal factors is when an individual is uncertain that execution of the response will reliably lead to the outcome. Averill et al. (1977) conducted an experiment in which the probability of avoiding shock by pressing a button was either 1.00, .66, or .33. Preference for control decreased as the probability of shock avoidance decreased from 1.0. Finally, internal factors may be construed as less stable when the individual has to discover the response that reliably leads to the outcome. In two experiments (Gatchel & Proctor, 1976; Gatchel, McKinney, & Koebernick, 1977) controlling individuals were simply told that there was something they could do to avoid aversive noise and were provided with a microswitch. The correct controlling response was actually four presses on the microswitch, and inviduals could only learn this after several trials. Under these conditions, having an instrumental controlling response maintained high anticipatory and impact arousal. This result is in contrast to the majority of instrumental control studies, which provide individuals with an easy controlling response and which show reduced anticipatory and impact arousal as a consequence of such control.

In all of the aforementioned three circumstances, having an internal response does not guarantee stability. Therefore, uncontrollability may be more preferred and less arousing than controllability. The limited evidence cited suggests that this may well be the case. Conversely, external factors may be highly stable. Individuals should trust someone else more than they trust themselves when they believe that the response of this other person is a more stable guarantee of a maximum upper limit. For example, most people would choose having a skilled doctor administer a hypodermic to them rather than administer it to themselves. Under these circumstances, uncontrollability will again be more preferred and less arousing than controllability. This effect should decrease as the judged stability of the external controlling factor decreases. Individuals will be less likely to yield the hypodermic to a nurse than to a doctor, and to feel more stress in the nurse than in the doctor condition.

In contrast to minimax, the internality hypothesis emphasizes the internality, and not the stability, of controlling responses. It says that control is chosen in order to most optimally match one's internal state with external events, thereby improving the aversive outcome. A given individual is obviously a better judge of his or her own moment-to-moment internal fluctuations than is any external factor. This means that individuals should always choose to retain control, because this is the most effective way of optimally matching internal states with external events. When an individual chooses uncontrollability he or she is, in essence, giving up the opportunity and possibility of accomplishing this match. Therefore, even in circumstances where internal factors are not construed to be very stable, individuals should still prefer controllable over uncontrollable aversive events. For example, even an individual who is slow to turn off shock should prefer to have an escape response, because he can conserve his energy and effort until he is in a highly vulnerable internal state. Then he can marshall all his resources toward shortening a shock that is turned on at that vulnerable moment. Similarly, individuals should decline to yield up control to another individual, although they may believe that this individual has a more stable controlling response than their own. While an individual may have a generally less steady hand for administering hypodermics than a doctor does, he is nonetheless a far more accurate judge of his own internal fluctuations. Therefore he can choose the opportune moment at which to go through with the injection. The doctor does not have access to such finely tuned information and so will tend to deliver the injection at random. This is bound to make the event feel more painful, despite the fact that it is administered by a steady hand. The heart of the internality view, then, is that an aversive outcome is improved by taking account of internal states. Individuals should thus elect to retain control, because this enables them to take account of their own internal states. This, in turn, increases the likelihood of obtaining the improved outcome.

No evidence presently bears on the question of whether individuals will ever actually yield control to another person, and this has been perhaps the most salient empirical gap in the literature. Minimax is unique among the competing hypotheses in predicting that such relinquishment should occur under conditions where internal factors are construed to be less stable than external factors (see also Bandura's [1977a, 1977b] self-efficacy view). The following experiment was conducted to address this issue (Miller, Harkavey, & Hammel, Note 3). In the first part of the study, an individual's belief about how reliably he or she could execute a given response relative to another person was manipulated. In the second part of the study, performance of this response determined how much electric shock both individuals would receive. The individual could elect either to execute the response him or herself, or to allow the other individual to execute it on his or her behalf.

The design of the experiment was as follows: The rationale given to subjects was that the experimenter was interested in determining how the presence of another person affects performance on a task. Therefore, both they and another individual (actually a confederate) would be performing a reaction time task at the same time, and the speed of their performance would then be compared with already established norms. Once they had completed the test, the subject and the confederate each received feedback in the presence of the other individual about their own performance. The results were "rigged" so that subjects fell into one of the three following groups: (a) In the "superior ability" condition, the subject performed above, and the confederate below, the average; (b) in the "comparable ability" condition, the subject and the confederate each performed about average;

and finally, *(c)* in the "inferior ability" condition, the subject performed below, and the confederate above, the average.

Following this, both individuals were told that they were now in the second phase of the study, which involved their reactions to stress (in the form of electric shock to the fingers). Each individual then went through a procedure (feigned on the confederate's part) to establish their "threshold" or zero point for first sensing electric shock. They were told that the shock to be used during the experiment proper would be adjusted to feel moderately painful to each of them. This was done to instill the belief that both the subject and confederate would be receiving equivalent levels of physical stimulation and so should have equal incentive for avoiding such stimulation. At this point, the confederate was presumably escorted to the room next door to be hooked up to another shock apparatus. Finally, the subject was read the following instructions: "For this part of the experiment, there will be a series of experimental trials. At the end of each trial, you will receive an electric shock. [The other subject] will also go through these trials, and receive a shock at the end of each trial. You two are, in effect, wired together. . . . Now, *one of you will have a way of affecting the shocks* with a set of switches like this. When the white light comes on, you switch all the switches down and up, down the row, in sequence 1–2–3–4–5. If you can do it in 2 seconds, no shock will occur. It if takes longer than 2 seconds, the shock stops as soon as you finish the sequence. The switches turn off the shock for both of you, but only one of you will have the switches. Because you are in the group that stays in this room, you have the choice of who gets the switches. The other subject will not be told that you had a choice. He or she will either be given the switches or not. So, do you want the switches or do you want [the other subject] to have them?"

In sum, the speed of a subject's reaction time to turn off the shock was the crucial factor in determining how much shock would be received. Minimax hypothesis would predict that subjects in the superior ability condition should want to keep the button, because they were shown to have a reaction time faster than that of the confederate. Similarly, subjects in the comparable ability condition should opt for the button, because there should be a bias for opting for control, given no compelling evidence for relinquishing it. Conversely, subjects in the inferior ability condition should want the confederate to have the button, because he or she was shown to have the more stable response.

Before going on to present the results, one possible source of confounding should be noted. The question of interest here was whether individuals could be induced to relinquish control when they judged their own response to be less stable than that of another individual. Therefore it was important to control for the effects of having failed per se. Otherwise it could be argued that choice of control or no control in the inferior ability condition was primarily due to the increased helplessness or lowered self-esteem that such failure typically induces. To accomplish this, half of the subjects performed an irrelevant "memory" task (instead of the reaction time task) during the first part of the experiment, in which their performance was either superior, comparable, or inferior to that of the confederate. Here subjects in the inferior ability condition would have judged the confederate to be more skilled at memory tasks, but they would have had no basis for determining whether he or she was more skilled at reaction time tasks and hence at avoiding shock. Thus, although subjects in both the memory and reaction time inferior ability conditions would experience failure equally, only subjects in the reaction time inferior ability condition would construe this failure as an indication of their unreliability (relative to the other individual) to limit the amount of shock received.

In sum, relinquishing the button on the shock task is simply due to the effects of failing on a prior task, then subjects in the inferior ability conditions of both the memory and reaction time tasks should yield control equally. If, on the other hand, subjects only relinquish the button when they believe that another individual has a more stable response for minimizing danger than they do, only subjects in the reaction time inferior ability condition should yield control. Subjects in the other two reaction time conditions and in *all three* memory conditions should choose equally to keep the button.

Table 4.1 depicts the number of subjects in the reaction time superior, comparable and inferior ability conditions who opt to keep the button (control) or to yield it (no control). As can be seen, all of the superior ability subjects and the majority of the comparable ability subjects chose control. In contrast, the majority of subjects in the inferior ability condition chose no control. The difference between conditions is highly significant, and this effect has since been replicated in a follow-up study (Miller, Harkavey, & Hammel, Note 4).

The results of the reaction time task suggest that individuals prefer control only to the extent that their own response is the most stable guarantee for minimizing the maximum danger. When an external factor, such as

TABLE 4.1
Number of "Reaction Time" Subjects Who Choose to Retain or Yield Control

	Retain control	Yield control
Superior ability	8	0
Comparable ability	5	3
Inferior ability	2	6

another person, has a more stable response, then individuals prefer not to have control. However, the possibility exists that choice of no control is not dictated by stability considerations but rather by the helplessness-inducing effects of failure. What, then, happens when subjects fail on a task that does not reflect on the ability of themselves or an external factor to execute the controlling response? The number of subjects choosing control and no control in the memory task conditions is given in Table 4.2. Unlike the reaction time results, the majority of subjects chose to retain control in all three conditions, including the inferior ability condition. Therefore choice of no control is not an artifact of experience with failure.

It is noteworthy that in the superior ability condition of both the reaction time and memory groups, all subjects chose control. For the comparable ability condition of both tasks, the majority of subjects similarly chose control, and no difference emerged between the two conditions. For the inferior ability condition, however, choice of control or no control was determined by which group an individual was in: The majority of reaction time subjects opted for no control, whereas the majority of memory subjects opted for control. Thus, choice of control or no control is not a consequence of having experienced failure but seems to be dictated by an individual's desire to minimize the maximum danger to himself.

In Bandura's (1977a, 1977b) terms, subjects in the memory conditions and in the superior ability and comparable ability reaction time conditions have a high sense of their own self-efficacy or personal effectiveness for terminating shock. Conversely, subjects in the reaction time inferior ability condition have a low sense of their own self-efficacy for terminating shock and doubt their personal effectiveness. How do such estimates of one's coping ability affect the degree of anxiety and stress experienced by individuals? On the one hand, it could be argued that perceived efficacy should lower stress and anxiety, because having an internal, stable controlling response is one of the most reliable guarantees of an upper limit of danger that an individual can have. On the other hand, personal control often places heavy demands on the individual, in the form of increased responsibility; high investment of time, effort, and resources; as well as the ever-present possibility of failure (cf. Bandura, 1977a, 1977b). According to the social

TABLE 4.2
Number of "Memory Task" Subjects Who Choose to Retain or Yield Control

	Retain control	Yield control
Superior ability	8	0
Comparable ability	6	2
Inferior ability	6	2

learning view, such demands generate worry and rumination which, in turn, elevate stress and anxiety. Therefore, it is conceivable that although individuals choose to exercise personal control when it is the most effective means of minimizing aversive situations, they do so at an emotional cost. The greater the demands on the individual, the greater the emotional toll should be. In contrast, when individuals can yield control to another person who is judged to be a highly reliable guarantee of maximum danger, they may show reduced stress and anxiety. Even though the no controlling individuals have a lowered sense of self-efficacy, all of the benefits of personal control nonetheless accrue to them without any of the demands; that is, they anticipate the same less aversive outcome, but do not have to invest any time, effort, or resources in achieving this outcome. Moreover, they do not bear any of the responsibility if the situation should somehow go awry.

Some evidence from the present experiment bears on these considerations. The Multiple Affect Adjective Checklist (Zuckerman, Lubin, & Robins, 1965) was administered at various points during the experiment to assess mood change. It was found that choice of control or no control did affect subjects' ratings of mood on the anxiety subscale. Those subjects who opted to keep the button showed an increase in self-reported anxiety, whereas those who opted to yield the button showed a slight decrease in anxiety. This was true for all subjects, regardless of which task they performed and regardless of whether their performance was superior, comparable, or inferior to that of the confederate. Moreover, perceived ability per se had an effect on mood, with subjects in the superior ability condition showing the greatest increase in anxiety, and subjects in the inferior ability condition showing the least increase in anxiety. A similar effect was observed for ratings of hostility. It is also worth noting that subjects whose perceived performance was inferior to that of the confederate did not differ in depression from subjects whose perceived performance was superior or comparable to that of the confederate.

To summarize, although individuals generally choose to retain control over aversive stimulation, they only do so as long as they believe their own response is the most stable factor for limiting the maximum danger to themselves. When they believe that another individual has a more stable response for minimizing the maximum danger, then they relinquish control to that other person. This relinquishment of control cannot be explained by failure-induced self-esteem loss or by increased depression. Indeed, if anything, it is those individuals with a stable *internal* controlling response who suffer an emotional cost. They maintain higher levels of anxiety and hostility than do individuals who can yield control to a stable, *external* factor. These results are inconsistent with the internality view, which emphasizes the internality aspect of control and so does not specify conditions where individuals should prefer uncontrollability. The data are consistent with the minimax view, which emphasizes the stability aspect of control and so specifies that uncontrollability will be preferred under conditions where external factors are construed as more stable than internal factors.

SUMMARY

In conclusion, two expected outcome views have been proposed, which make sense of the literature on controllability and human stress. Controllability improves an aversive outcome by providing individuals with a guaranteed upper limit (minimax) or by enabling them to match their internal state with external events (internality). Both views are adequate to explain the stress-reducing effects of actual control equated for predictability and the effects of potential control. However, only minimax specifies conditions under which individuals will choose to relinquish rather than retain control, and these predictions are supported by the experimental evidence.

ACKNOWLEDGMENTS

I thank A. Bandura, R. Grant, M. Hammel, J. Harkavey, W. Miller, J. Nelson, and M. Seligman.

REFERENCE NOTES

1. Miller, S. M., & Grant, R. P. Predictability and human stress: Evidence, theory, and conceptual clarification. Unpublished manuscript, University of Pennsylvania, 1978.
2. Miller, S. M., Grant, R. P., & Nelson, J. Preference for potential control under threat of electric shock. Unpublished manuscript, University of Pennsylvania, 1978.
3. Miller, S. M., Harkavey, J., & Hammel, M. Relinquishment of control as a function of perceived stability of the controlling response. Unpublished manuscript, University of Pennsylvania, 1979.
4. Miller, S. M., Harkavey, J., & Hammel, M. Differential relinquishment of control among anxious and depressed populations. Unpublished manuscript, University of Pennsylvania, 1979.

5

Knowing More (or Less) Than You Can Show: Understanding Control through the Mindlessness–Mindfulness Distinction[1]

BENZION CHANOWITZ
ELLEN LANGER

INTRODUCTION

Much theoretical work has devoted itself to formalizing the concept of control. Concurrent experimental work has focused on identifying aspects of control and the effects that their variability have on the actual exercise of control. In that effort, this research has catalogued a number of apparently useful constructs, including perceived control, actual control, cognitive control, behavioral control, decisional control, locus of control (internal control versus external control), interpersonal control, personal control, self-control, prediction and control, and the illusion of control—not to mention the associated constructs of freedom, perceived freedom, reactance, power, Machiavellianism, learned helplessness, self-induced dependence, learned industriousness, self-efficacy, and perceived competence.

Despite the abundance of documentation, the concept seems to remain plagued by ambiguities. Must you know you have control in order to have control, or can you have it without knowing it? How is it that for some

[1] The research described in this chapter was supported by National Institute of Mental Health Grant 1 RO 1 MH32946-01 to Ellen Langer.

97

people failure is an occasion for slackening efforts, whereas for others it is an occasion for redoubling efforts? Is there some way of accounting for the sense that control is slipping away as hope turns into despair? Surely, is it not purely a function of "mounting" odds? Is there a coherent distinction to be made between the ability to predict and the ability to control? Does being cautious, careful, watchful, or fearful signify that you are in control or out of control? Is control some sort of basic motivation to be satisfied? And if it is, does increasing control in one domain mean you need more or less in another domain? What can it mean when one person "gives" another person control? Concurrently, what sense can the subject make, in the experimentally controlled situation, that he or she has control in the situation?

The accumlated data in control research do not seem to offer simple, straightforward answers to these questions. Much of this confusion can be traced to the failure to distinguish between the experience of exercised control and the description of exercised control. Initially, we must characterize the distinction between experience and its description. The failure to distinguish between them can lead one in everyday life to frame ongoing experience in terms of its described parts, thereby impoverishing the potentially available experience. We will begin by using a version of the definition of control that is prevalent: the intentional manipulation of material in order to produce desired outcomes. We can then make the distinction between experience and its description, apply it to the activity of control, and arrive at a new and more useful definition of control. Given the capacity in everyday life for one to confuse experience and its description, we will show that there are distinguishable ways in which one can experience that exercised manipulation of material. These ways produce distinguishable effects that reveal that certain activities, which look like and are described as "control," might better be characterized in some other fashion. Clarifying these distinctions which remain obscured in control research could serve to reduce some of the ambiguity in this area.

EXPERIENCE AND STRUCTURE

Experience of the First Order and Its Description

Think back to a particularly exciting experience that you once had—your first attempts to ride a horse or ski down a mountain, a visit to a strange country, etc. There is a distinction to be drawn, for example, between the experience of one's first attempts to drive a car and the description of those first attempts to drive a car. In describing those first attempts, you can list a number of intentionally produced gestures (e.g., I turned the ignition, I stepped on the accelerator, I turned the wheel of the car) and their effect on the car (i.e., the car started humming, the car moved forward, the car moved to the left). Part by part you break down that episode into words which you hope will relate to the listener the excitement of your experience. Somehow, though, you feel that you are inadequately recounting the experience, as if something were missing. And the impulse is to tell more, as if to capture in words and fill in the parts of the experience that were missing in the initial description. At some point, if the listener remains unmoved, you give up. Sometimes this sentiment is voiced in words such as, "the whole is greater than the sum of its parts," thereby leaving the impression that the addition of a few more described parts would equal the whole experience. We hope to show that it is misleading to say that the whole is greater. Rather, it would be more accurate to say that the whole (experience) is *other* than the sum of its describable parts. In other words, the "highlights" that constitute the description of an experience are not a part of the experience; rather, they are a product of the experience. The description of an episode can *stand for* the experience of that episode and the work that went into it, but it is not the *same as* that experience. It is not different in the sense that when you are doing something you are employing a vocabulary of gestures, whereas when you are describing something you are employing a vocabulary of words. It goes more deeply than that.

When we describe an experience retrospectively, we rely on a set of stable, categorical distinctions in order to explain to others what it was that was important or exciting in what we did. But during the experience, it is precisely those distinctions that are *at issue*. Given this perspective, experience is indescribable. It is the instability of those distinctions as we become involved with the environment that is exciting. That the Grand Canyon is beautiful is not very exciting. What is exciting during the experience is the movement to stabilize its beauty—*managing* to make sense of the heretofore unseen sight. Similarly, when we are prospectively given instruction about how to drive a car, we rely on a set of stable, categorical distinctions in order to know what to look for. That the car moves to the left as we turn the wheel is not exciting. What is exciting is the accumulating feeling of *how* the car is steered to the left as the steering wheel is turned. It lurches too far, and I pull the wheel back as the car eases into the next lane. What is exciting about my control over the car is not that I *can do it* but that I am *making it happen*.

Insofar as an object of description must be stable in order for one to be able to point at it, the description of that experience relies on already made distinctions. Yet, it was the creating of the distinction that was most exciting about the activity—what happened on the way to the made distinction. As we grope for stability in an ambiguously defined environment, our deepening involvement is providing a clearer and surer sense of the stability of that environment. After the fact, we point at the made distinction and the stabilized environment as the indicant of what was exciting, forgetting that it was out productive efforts that provided the affect. The product only *stands for* the accumulating excitment of the experience. It is not the *same as* that experience, nor is it a *part of* that excitement.

To summarize, then, as one looks at an activity in retrospect or prospect, one inevitably relies on the stability of those made distinctions in order to make it an object capable of description. The description *of* the object of experience requires a cessation of involvement *with* that object. To stand back and describe the object, one must cease the exploration that is involving one in even more sharply distinguishing and stabilizing that object. To the degree that one must hold the object in focus during description, one must cease efforts at further resolution of that object. To tell another about our exciting activity, we also must rely on achieved distinctions. All that one has to show is the product of that activity. However, what was exciting, as we became more involved in the activity, was the experience of creating those distinctions.

Experience or Its Description?

Appearances, though, can become deceptive. As people look back *at* their own activity, they can be left with the impression that the activity exclusively consisted of those shown products. The involving work that produced those distinctions is nowhere to be seen. One is likely to regard one's own activity in this way when one engages in the "same" activity repeatedly. The awareness of the "repetitiousness" of the activity (e.g., driving a car) is a signal and symptom of the fact that there are no new distinctions to be made. Instead, each instance of the activity goes through the same sequence of made distinctions. All has been learned (e.g., about driving a car), and I am not learning any more. Insofar as the object is no longer in flux, the activity becomes mechanical because I am moving from made distinction to made distinction over the course of the activity. The way I describe the activity now becomes the way I experience the activity. All I have to tell about is all I have to show. As I look forward to the next instance of driving the car, I see it as another occasion for going through the same sequence of made distinctions. Thus, anticipating and framing my experience, I go through the "routine" activity that way.

On the other hand, the awareness of the excitement of the activity (e.g., driving a car) is a signal and a symptom of the fact that new distinctions are being made. Each instance of the activity involves one in a deepening appreciation of the activity. While learning how the car responds, I am learning how the car is driven. As the picture of the car becomes more distinguished, my notion of self-as-driver becomes more coherent. Insofar as the object is in flux, the activity is creative as I am involved in making the distinctions that are giving me a handle on the car. The way I describe the activity does not do justice to the way I have experienced the activity. As I look forward to the next instance of driving the car, I look forward to another occasion for deepening my involvement with the car. Thus, anticipating and framing my experience, I go through the "exciting" activity that way.

There is a distinction to be drawn, then, between activities: (a) where, in experience, the character of what is important or relevant is at issue; where one approaches an ambiguously defined situation and is involved in looking for how it is that this relevance which makes a difference does indeed *make* a difference, locating it, and exploiting it; where looking for how it is that the turning of the steered car is related to the turning of the steering wheel, noticing it, and adjusting with it; and (b) where, in experience, the characteristic of relevance is known beforehand; where one approaches the situation already knowing how it is that what makes a difference does indeed make a difference; where knowing already how far the car will turn when you turn the wheel *before* you turn it and therefore paying little attention to the car as it is turning, noticing instead the car's proper placement after it has turned.

Yet, how is the observer, who sees only what is shown, to distinguish between the person who is mindlessly "going through the motions" of driving the car on the basis of made distinctions and the person whose mind is thoroughly occupied with the experience of driving the car while making distinctions? Certainly, it is not impossible to point at. Sitting next to a driver, one can distinguish between the expert who is barely minding the road and the novice who is barely managing the road as he or she drives down the highway—even though he or she is, for most practical purposes, going though the "same" motions. But before one can point at the difference, one must concede that there is a difference and try to characterize it. Simply going through the motions does not dictate the sort of experience that will characteristically accompany that activity. Similarly, putting someone else through the motions does not dictate the sort of experience that will characteristically accompany that activity.

This analysis is not restricted to those cases where we use our hands or feet. It holds as well for those where we use our eyes or ears. For example, as you begin to listen to the performance of a piece of music that you have heard before, you can approach with the attitude that you know beforehand what the notes will sound like when they are sounded. Each performance is taken as a repetition of that same piece of music. Consequently, you wait for the performed notes to sound like that. Or, you could approach with the attitude that each performance is different. Each performance is taken as another occasion for deepening involvement with that ever-changing piece of music. Consequently, you follow the notes as they are getting played and are more involved in the sounding of the notes. It is difficult to adopt the latter attitude when you are listening to a record for the seventh time, but it's not impossible. Conversely, it is difficult to adopt the former attitude when you are listening to the music for the first time and in live performance, but it's not impossible. The apparently structured environment *suggests* certain modes of humanly minded engagement, but it does not *dictate* that mode. Memory and imagination are the only limits of the activity.

The Emergence of Structure

The notion of structure is employed here to refer to the provisionally fixed sequence of parts that an activity is reduced to in order to make it recognizable, describable, or managable (e.g., using hands or ears). Those parts can be seen, for example, when we describe to another what Beethoven's Fifth Symphony sounds like or how to drive a car. While we will consider three ways, there are a variety of ways in which the environment can assume an apparent structure for the engaged person.

First, repeated involvement in the same activity over a period of time might seem to decompose the whole activity into a sequence of parts. These can be used as a guide for or as a description of that activity. Though people decompose that activity as a function of their own personal history, the decomposed structures of a certain activity for a number of people may often coincide. For instance, many people may learn on their own how to complete their income tax forms. After several times, they might all come to break down that activity into the same steps that will most effectively allow for the completion of that activity.

Second, a person might be provided with instructions as to how one performs a particular activity. These instructions would be provided in terms of the steps of the activity, with the implication being that each step is another part of the activity. For instance, a parent might instruct a child how to tie shoelaces by providing a step-by-step list of the parts of the activity.

Finally, the material environment to be used in an activity might be segmented in such a way as to invite the impression that the activity consists of parts that correspond to the segments. For instance, when one writes on a piece of lined paper, those lines invite a step-by-step progression down the paper along the lines.

For the issues at hand, it makes no difference whether the whole activity assumes the structure of the repetition of a single step (e.g., writing along the lines on paper) or a sequence of steps (e.g., tying the shoe-laces). The issue is that the whole activity can be resolved into a number of parts that are reflected in the segmentation that the environment assumes. Concurrently, as the person becomes involved in the activity, the mind paces itself to be synchronized with the steps that constitute the environment's structure. Conversely, the mind's pace might influence the degree to which the person will become involved in the activity. This, in turn, will influence the degree to which the person is making new distinctions during the activity that further articulate that structure. During the activity, how you make the environment happen reflects the status of the mind and vice versa. An account of this sort might indicate how a structure for activity emerges. Further analysis is necessary as we return to the problem of how one uses that structure as he or she "once again" becomes involved in that activity.

The Uses of Structure

Suppose we are interested in finding out how listening to music affects the person who hears it. As the person listens to a piece of familiar music, the tapping finger shows us that the person is following the music. Concommitantly, the revealing finger is evidence of the structure used by the person in following the music, but it does not tell us how the person is listening. How is the person using the previously generated structure for listening to the familiar music? The person could approach with the attitude that this upcoming music has been heard before. This "repetition" of the same music is followed by its fit with the previously acquired structure. Nothing new is heard because one is relying on made distinctions. Or; the person could approach with the attitude that this upcoming music is an occasion for deepening appreciation of that piece. The previously acquired structure is up for modification during the person's involvement with this performance of the music. It is a starting point for appreciating new, deeper things about the music. (We speak of "things about" rather than "interpretations of" to avoid the impression that a piece of music can exist independent of an interpreter.)

If we are interested in the music's effect, it is important to know in which way the person is following the music. The former is likely to have deadening effects, and the latter is likely to have enlivening effects. If we simply pay attention to the tapping finger, we obscure this difference. Verifying the fact that the person is going through the motions of following the music does not give us a clue to the sort of experience accompanying those motions. Does the tapping finger stand for a mind that is mechanically occupied with keeping time that echoes a previously acquired structure? Or, does each tap stand for the conclusion of another effort that the mind is creatively occupied with as it makes time and modifies the previously acquired structure? Is the present being used in the service of the past, or is the past being used in the service of the present? Depending on what is modified by what, going through the motions of an activity can be accompanied by experience that is involved in making distinctions or by experience that mimics made distinctions of past experience. If one looks, the difference can be seen. One seems excited while the other seems bored, and that disparity widens as the music goes on. But before one can tell the difference, one must recognize that there is a difference to be looked for and recognize how to look for that difference. If one wishes to know the effects of listening to music, one must know more than the fact that the person is listening. That can be seen by the motions that the tapping finger goes through. As one looks at the effects, one must also know in what way the person is listening. In seeking to understand how music effects people, we must distinguish between the ways they are listening to the music.

There is a distinction to be made between a Picasso who is painfully and ecstatically struggling to create that which will result in a distinguished product called *Guernica* and the individual who follows by more mindlessly employing a set of created distinctions with a color-by-number set in order to produce the "same" Guernica. This is not to imply that control cannot be involved in a color-by-number activity. However, there is a distinction to be made between the activity of creating distinctions and the activity of manipulating created distinctions. Both go through the same motions when we use rough data sheets. But those activities have different effects on the motioning humans.

The Uses of Structure and the Varieties of "Control"

Let us review the accepted definition of control as the intentional manipulation of material for the production of desired outcomes. Let us also bear in mind the established distinction between the description of an activity and the experience of an activity, applying it to the activity of control. Insofar as the description of exercised control is not the same as experienced control, our descriptions have failed to distinguish between the mindful and mindless experience of exercised control. Insofar as we are interested in the effects of control on *humans,* the preservation of this distinction must be of paramount concern. If one is interested in the environment, then it might not make a difference how the "controlling" person goes through the motions. We are interested in humans. The failure to clearly make this distinction has led to difficulty in the field.

As we return to the example of driving the car, we are confronted with a bewildering question. Which of the two drivers has more control over the car—the one who is barely minding or the one who is barely managing? If we were to ask the drivers themselves, what would they have to look back on as they attempted to respond? The driver who barely minded could look back and remember turning the ignition and the car starting, turning the wheel and the car being in the other lane, etc. He or she can recall trying to do something (i.e., one part of the routine) and that it was done. He or she can recall the state of the car before and after the exerted effort. However, what happened between before and after is not available for recall because he or she was not paying attention to it. In the light of years of driving, the driver knows before turning the wheel where the car will be after the wheel is turned and so does not have to watch the car get from here to there. Years of driving have revealed the segmented routine of driving to the driver. The whole activity has assumed the structure of its segmented parts. These parts can stand as a description of the activity. But now, they also stand as the experience of the activity. The made distinctions are relied upon as a guide for this episode of driving. They preclude the possibility of making new distinctions by framing the ongoing experience to conform with made distinctions. Of course, years of driving do not dictate driving in this manner. They just allow for the possiblity of driving in this manner. One *could* treat each driving episode as another opportunity for refining one's appreciation of just how the car responds to direction.

But the novice does not have this choice. The novice possesses no routine that can be relied upon as a guide for this episode of driving. He or she has not yet learned where the car will be after the wheel is turned before it is actually turned. As a matter of fact, there is yet no clear notion of what is "before" and "after." Parts of the material (e.g., this is the wheel with which the car is turned) that imply segments of the whole activity have been verbally pointed out. But that definition is ambiguous insofar as the novice has not absorbed a stable, felt sense of the moving car in response to the turning wheel. The fact that "driving" is not yet an *experientially* defined activity is reflected in the uncertainty of where the moving car is getting to as the steering wheel is turned this much. Consequently, he or she must follow the car's response to the turning wheel between before and after—*during* the car's response. With each additional episode of driving, the person is absorbing a surer sense of the car's movement. The novice is becoming a driver. The involving search for and the movements toward that stable sense are exciting. As the novice looks back at each episode, he or she realizes that distinctions have been made during the course of the activity. When the novice is asked about control, those efforts to establish that stable sense are recollectible.

The experienced driver recalls before and after effects, whereas the novice recalls during effects. However, when both drivers assert that they did control the car, the justifications for those assertions can sound exactly alike. They both say, "When I turned the ignition, the car started," etc., but they are pointing at different things. They are both showing that they can drive the car, but the novice is trying to say that he or she can "make happen" with the car.

Thus, there are conceptually distinguishable ways in which one can go through the motions of control. Going through the motions (or, for that matter, being put through the motions) does not dictate the sort of experience that will accompany those motions that constitute the activity of control. Some sort of experience inevitably accompanies the motions of individuals who are directed at producing desired outcomes. The product of those motions, after the fact, does not necessarily indicate the sort of experience sustained during those motions. As they had intended at the outset of their journey, both drivers got their cars from there to here, but the accomplished success of that venture does not indicate *how* they got their cars here.

For psychologists who are interested in the human exercise of control, a question might naturally arise. What difference does it make how one gets things done? After all, both drivers got the car to its intended destination. Isn't *that* what control is all about—the successful manipulation of material in order to produce desired outcomes? The more one achieves of the desired outcomes that were announced at the outset of the activity, the more one is in control of that activity. Shown achievements serve as a measure of control. We will endeavor to show, however, that there is something misleading about this perspective. It is misleading in that the exercise of control has distinguishable effects on humans, depending on which way the activity is experienced. Equally important, each version of experienced control provides a distinguishably different degree of control to the person that will be manifest in future engagements with that activity.

The finished product or the changed world might stand for the fact that control was exercised. For some purposes, the achievements of the activity might serve as a satisfactory account of what happened. However, it dismally fails as an account of what is happening *during* the exercise of control. By focusing on the consolidated products of an activity as a measure of the degree of control the person exercised during the activity, we preclude the possibility for observing and understanding what is going on during the exercise of control as that product is being consolidated. The aftereffects of any activity that seem visibly identical to those aftereffects visibly available after the exercise of control do not necessarily indicate that control was exercised during the former activity. As we shall see, it is not clear that one is justified in calling all instances where desired outcomes were achieved as instances in which control was exercised.

What is going on during the exercise of control? As the person is going through motions that will produce desired outcomes, that person might be involved with noticing differences and making distinctions in the material, thereby managing to produce the desired outcome, or that person might be relying on made distinctions that were generated in earlier encounters with the material as a guide for completing this activity in order to produce the desired outcome. Conceptually, these versions of engagement are distinguishable. In the former instance, the person is looking to see how the present material is different from that encountered in the past in order to arrive most efficiently at the desired outcome. In the latter instance, the person relies on how the present material is the same as that encountered in the past in order to arrive most efficiently at the desired outcome. Both use the past, but in different ways and with different effects.

For the person who is in mindful control, that is, one who is making categories, succeeding opportunities for engaging with the material to be controlled are occasions for deeping involvement. As one retrospectively considers each occasion, the result of the engagement is a more articulate display of the environment-to-be-controlled and a more substantial notion of self-as-controller for this segment of the environment. During the activity, as the distinction is being made that will bring one closer to the desired outcome, there is a sense of renewing vitality to the self-as-controller. This sense could also result from distinctions that bring one further from the desired outcome, because knowing how you went wrong can be as informative as knowing how you went right. Each difference that is noticed and made demarcates the boundary between two categories of response for future occasions, and the more articulate display of the environment is seen as inviting more opportunities than it seemed to invite before. As self and environment become more entangled with each other, each occasion provides for a reunion whose outcome is productive. The experienced excitement during the episode is a symptom of that productivity which one can point at in the environment after the episode. As a result of an accumulation of encounters, the self assumes an identity that can manage, and the environment assumes a structure that can be managed. With deepening involvement, self and environment together expose more of each other regardless of the field of play. They develop together—the baseball field and the baseball player, the violin and the violinist, the wood and the carpenter, the horse and the rider, the car and the driver, etc. As the person is confronted by an intimately known environment, the linked self that controls that environment is called out to define and be defined. Control is not dominion over something. That is another affair, as we shall see later.

In this light, the response that George Mallory gave to the question "Why do you climb Mount Everest?" is not the *non sequitur* that it is often taken to be. "Because it is there" is a very revealing, emotional response. It only seems mundane because Mallory neglected the importance of the second half of the answer, ". . . and I am here." I (the mountain climber) saw it (the mountain to be climbed) as a challenge. It is not just anybody who sees the mountain as a challenge. A tourist would not feel the urge to climb the mountain. The sight might strike the tourist as something to be photographed. Nor does the mountain represent a singular challenge. For other developed selves, the mountain calls out other challenges. For the skier, Yuichiro Miura, Mount Everest is seen as a challenging mountain to be skied down.

Contrast this exercise of control with achieving desired outcomes by manipulating material on the basis of past distinctions. For the latter, the opportunity for engaging with the material is taken as an occasion for reproducing products that are "identical" to the ones produced in earlier engagements with the material. No new distinctions are being made. The atmosphere of repetitiousness overcomes the episode. The failure of the self to become involved in making new distinctions obscures the fact that there is a self acting in the episode. The notion of self-as-controller of this material withers, and the environment assumes a rigid mechanical structure. Anybody can manipulate the material in order to produce the outcome, that is to say, nobody in particular is doing it. Once the person is in that position, there is nobody to notice differences emerging in the course of the activity. Instead, as the person works to produce the desired outcome, he or she follows the sequence of mechanically ordered cues that has come to represent the structure of the activity. What happens between those cues is nowhere to be seen.

It is no wonder, then, that many people who find themselves on assembly lines are not comforted by the assertion that they are exercising a great deal of control. Consider the person who spends the day putting chocolates in candy boxes. The pile of packed boxes at the end of a day's work would seem to represent a great deal of exercised control. Or does it?

Thus, when several people go through the same motions of bringing about an outcome, the fact that they had the same outcomes to show for that activity should not be taken to indicate that they experienced the same degree of control. The degree of success that one has in manipulating material to produce desired outcomes should not be taken as the sole measure of the degree of control that one had over the material during the episode. Taking the success in producing outcomes as a measure of control is not simply misleading. It also has damaging consequences. It obscures the fact that in the fullest exercise of control, the changing display of the material's structure must be accompanied by a changing self-as-controller. It is not enough that the world is changed. The self must change along with it. By unhinging the notions of changing self and changing world during the exercise of control, one takes the changed world as a sign that the self who effected those changes underwent a similar change. It obscures the required experience that is necessary for reworking the self. Going through the motions of painting a picture does not make one a painter. The observer who relies on a description of painting might not be able to tell if this painter is a very experienced one. But the actor can—unless the actor is under the impression that going through the motions of painting is tantamount to being a painter. This can happen when the experience and description of control are confused with each other.

CONTROL

Who Exerts Control and When Is It Exerted?

Who experiences more control—the driver who is barely minding the road or the one who is barely managing? They both claim to have control. They both reached their intended destinations. The justification of one sounds like the justification of the other. For a number of reasons, it should be clear that the latter driver exercises more control. To make this clear, let us distinguish two categories of actors: learners and nonlearners. Nonlearners are people who are no longer engaged in the activity of making distinctions; learners are people who are. An individual can be a learner or nonlearner at any level of proficiency. For example, a complete novice and a racing car driver both may be learners, whereas the daily commuter on the expressway may be a nonlearner. The beginner taking piano lessons and the concert virtuoso may both be learners, whereas the piano player at a wedding or bar mitzvah may be nonlearners. By adopting the mindless attitude, the nonlearner in our first example gives up control over what might happen between the beginning and the end of a segment of the assumed structure of the routine of driving. In the effort to move the car to the adjacent lane, the nonlearner knows beforehand where the car will be if the steering wheel is turned this much. Consequently, the expert does not follow the car's movement from here to there. At the worst, something might go wrong, and he or she will not find out about that wrong thing until it has already happened. If there is a pothole in the lane to which the car is shifting, for example, the nonlearner may only find this out as the car is falling into the hole. The mindful novice is following the whole course of the activity because its segmented routine is not yet available. In barely managing the road, he or she *manages* to avoid the pothole.[2]

Furthermore, if the nonlearner does not have the presence of mind to see the trouble that is coming, it may not be clear what sort of trouble he or she has just gotten away from. It could have been a stray cat, and therefore

[2]In this era of postmodern technology, where potholes are a roadside routine, perhaps nonlearner drivers can incorporate "watchfulness for potholes" into their mindless routine. The thrust of the example should hold, however, for other, less publicized roadside troubles.

there is no need to be careful anymore; it could have been a pothole that was indicating that this whole section of the road is full of holes; etc. But the nonlearner does not know what to look for as he or she is driving down the road. The novice, though, has seen the pothole and knows what to look for while driving down the road.

In addition, relying on made distinctions that are represented in the assumed structure of the routine activity, the expert makes it most difficult to appreciate classes of finer distinctions that are available within each segment of the routine or to adapt to new circumstances that would alter the routine of driving. The novice does not have this trouble because "finer distinctions" and "new circumstances" only make sense in the light of an "old routine." To the degree that this routine is rigidly assumed by the expert and to the degree that the future does not resemble the past, the expert then has lost control over future events in this domain of activity. Both drivers might have seemed to display the same degree of control on this journey. The greater control that the novice possesses at this moment will not be evident until some future occasion.

Finally, the fact that one can do something is less satisfying than the experience of "making happen." The beneficial psychological effects that are a "result" of mindful control of material are greater than those effects that are a result of competent but mindless manipulation of material. The former is rewarded with excitement, whereas the latter is bored. The former is enlivened, whereas the latter is deadened.

Indeed, these distinctions illustrate the fact that different forms of experience that accompany "identical" motions may or may not give rise to the experience of control. Control relies on the sort of experience you are having as you go through the motions. That difference might not be evident to the observer now, but the actor is aware that he or she is preparing for the future. If psychologists wish to study the dynamics of exercising control and the effects of exercised control, then they must know what sort of experience the subject is generating to accompany motions that the subject is being put through. The degree to which the subject was intentionally able to materially change the circumstances during this episode of an experiment is not a unilateral measure of the degree of control that this subject can exercise on future occasions. That is how the subject feels, and it is a reflection of his or her experience in the natural world. If psycholgists do not take the factor of the subject's experience into consideration, then they might be puzzled by some of the findings that are a result of experiments.

The person's deeper involvement with the material during the activity of control leads to more "mindfully experienced" activity on that person's part. That greater mindfulness offers the involved person a geater degree of control. Conversely, the degree to which the controlling person slips into mindless activity (that relies on the material assuming a rigid structure) signifies the degree of control that has been surrendered. Some of the greater control that the mindful person maintains is immediately visible. Some of it will only become evident in future occasions of that exercised control. After all, the degree to which a person has effected change or has achieved desired outcomes is not itself control and is not a measure of the control that person has over the material. "Control" is not some sort of commodity to be carried in one's pocket. It would be more useful to view control as a characterization of the way the person interacts with the material. It is the nature of the interaction that determines whether or not control is exerted. It is a state of affairs that describes how the person is prepared to act *with* the environment.

The Consequence of Exerted Control

Similarly, it is deceptive to attribute comparable amounts of control to two persons simply because they have effected the same amount of change in some past episode. They may have demonstrated the same degree of expertise—if we use gross techniques for measuring effected change in the manipulated world—but that does not mean they have the same degree of control over the material. The greater or lesser control that the mindful versus mindless person has available is distinguishable in the following ways:

1. Individuals who mindlessly manipulate material for desired outcomes by following a sequence of steps allow for the possibility of a mishap between those steps. By not following the entire course of the activity, they are liable not to find out about that wrong thing until it has interrupted the sequence. Mindful individuals who follow the entire course of the activity are not as liable to experience such a mishap. They are more capable of anticipating the trouble.

2. Mindless involvement obscures the significance of the mishap. In not seeing the trouble coming, the factors that are leading to that trouble are unseen as the episode is developing. Consequently, that trouble is made sense of as an "accident"—as something extrinsic to the episode that fortuitously intruded at that time. It allows for the possiblity that this accident will happen again, and precludes the possiblity for reorienting action so that desired outcomes will be more efficiently achieved. Mindful involvement promotes the significance of that mishap. The person is sensitive to the trouble that is developing and to the contributing factors. It becomes easier to avoid a repetition of that trouble because it is easier to see the significance of those heretofore insignificant factors. Action can thus be reoriented in that light.

3. One's capacity to reorient action is a reflection of one's view of the environment's character. Mindless involvement relies on a view that the environment is composed of an ensemble of unchanging parts. It implies that the environment has been fully articulated once control has been demonstrated over that environment. Mindful involvement continues in the recognition that the environment is constantly shifting as one becomes more involved with it. It implies that the environment is constantly offering new opportunities for grasping surer control of the material.

4. Mindful involvement with a changing environment fosters the development of the self that must keep up with those changes. That controlled management of those changes provides stimulating evidence that some one self was in control. Mindless involvement with an unchanging environment stunts the development of self. The mechanical production of "desired" outcomes implies that the involved self is one more gear in the machinery.

5. The sorts of involvement that one maintains, as selves in control of a correspondent number of domains (e.g., father-family, lawyer-law, gardner-garden, etc.), also has an effect on the person that embodies all of those selves. Those psychological benefits or deficits that accrue are evident over a period of time. The deepening involvement of the mindful person provides stimulation for that person's growth. As the environment becomes more articulate, the person feels pride in his or her experienced capacity to keep up with those changes as he or she controls. It is clear to the person that not just anybody can do it. The rigid environment that the mindless person is involved with provides no stimulation for that person's growth. With all differences made, the person does not feel that he or she makes a difference. As the notion of self-as-agent atrophies, there is a loss of initiative or motivation or desire to act.

All of these are factors that contribute to the control a person has as he or she approaches the episode in which control will be exercised. The varying character of experience that accompanies the motions of control constitutes distinctive degrees of control. The demonstrated success of the person in producing desired outcomes may provide the observer with some insight into how much control the person exerted over the material. The important constituent of that exerted control is the degree of involvement with the material as those changes were being effected. For the psychologist who is interested in the process of exerting control and its effects, how the person was making changes may be more important than the changes that were made. Disparate degrees of involvement might produce disparate degrees of control that would not be evident until future occasions. However, the two actors know it *now*. Consequently, there are disparate effects. As the nonlearner and the expert–learner passionately play "Chopsticks," the relations between piano and pianist are two entirely different affairs. At the beginning of the performance, they pose with piano in entirely different ways. The piano is a more distinguished, articulate piece of material for the worked self of the expert–learner than it is for the nonlearner, and as the performance goes on, the relation between piano and pianist that constitutes control is much more saturated for the expert–learner. The assertion that both pianists exerted the same degree of control on the basis of "comparable" performances of "Chopsticks" borders on the ridiculous.

The Deeper Issue

However, the outlined differences that distinguish mindlessness from mindful control are only symptoms of the crucial issue. A reading of those differences could leave the impression that human involvement is merely a method for getting in touch with structure or reality that is inherent in the world; that the natural environment (i.e., untouched by human hands) is a fixed arrangement of distinctive elements that interact in regular ways to produce "new" outcomes; that this arrangement offers definite measures of control for any who are familiar with the character of that organization and how it responds to manipulation; that humans have at their fingertips a number of ways for becoming familiar with nature's character, including description provided by others who in their work have exposed the contour of the natural world; but, that experience provides humans with the surest and most intimate path for revealing the organization of the environment; that this allows for human control through intervention in those organized ways by redirecting the naturally progressing environment; and, therefore, that experience is the surest way for informing one's self about a part of the world if one wishes to exercise control over that part.

However, there is something misleading about all of this. Involvements do not *reveal* the conditions and distinctions of the composed environment that are "found" to be relevant in order to change the world this way rather than let it go that way. Human involvement *produces* the conditions and distinctions that are humanly relevant. The human body is the cutting edge that carves the material world for meaningful human purposes, and it cuts both ways—"inward" and "outward." One of our species might forge ahead into the material of the world and find, through involvement with the material for certain purposes, that the material is best suited to a human purpose by doing it this way rather than that way. But one should not take the description given by this person as an indication of the fact that the difference was always there patiently waiting to be found. Nor should one assume that the person who forged ahead is the same one who returns with a report for us. The words of the report verify that it is a changed person who speaks to us. Description, though, can be a way for heading into experience. It can initiate the involvement of the person, and only through involved experience does the self change.

The fact that the world was decomposed (for certain purposes) does not dictate that the material was composed in the beginning. The mountain that Mallory climbed up is not composed of the same parts as the mountain that Yuichiro Miura skied down. Of course, the mountain is there. But the whole mountain does not assume a recognizable form of parts until a human approaches with purpose in mind. The deepening involvement of the human brings forth a more distinguished, articulate form of parts and a changed self-as-controller. After the fact, we can see the achievement that stands for the effort to control the material.

But one should not take the description as an indication that this is the way things finally are. Description is only a respite where, in holding the material still, one displays the product of ongoing involvement. It is a necessary respite if one is to tell others. If one mistakenly takes this respite to signify that the material has been mastered for control once and for all, then the process of mindless "control" (wherein control is given up) has begun. To the degree that the future does not resemble the past, future mindless involvement spells trouble. And the same goes for those others who take the description given by the person during the respite as an indication of the way things finally are. Once is not for all. Once you begin, you are always in the middle. No thing (or class of things) can be finally defined. New purposes might be generated tomorrow that would qualify some of those "same" objects while disqualifying others in the class. Control, then, refers to the fluctuating relation between self and material that define each other—more finely etching each other with each involvement. The self might demonstrate that control by effecting a certain change in the material (e.g., playing "Chopsticks" or driving a car). If one is to study the process of control and the effects of its exercise, one must have a measure not only of *what* was done but of *how* it was done. Capturing the latter calls for a more clever experimental design because it is not as visible as the former.

ISSUES IN RESEARCH

The Psychologist's Use of Used Structures

Experiments in psychology usually follow a procedure whereby the subject is "exposed" to a set of material arrangements that affords (from the experimenter's perspective) a "definite" measure of control. The measure of actual control that subjects are given is directly tied to the amount of change

the environment allows the subjects to effect. The form of parts tha\
tute the experimental situation allows for a certain degree of cor\
response to the subjects' intervention. All subjects in a particular con\
are scheduled to produce the same amount of change in light of their intervention. Consequently, all are invested with the same amount of control.
Subjects are expected to act on the basis of having that definite measure of
control. Experimenters then look at the effects of that exercised control.
Often, they infer from the subjects' responses that the subjects perceive
themselves to have one measure of control when the environment "actually" offered another measure of control.

However, it is only from the "privileged" position of the experimenter
that this disparity between actual control and perceived control is evident.
The experimenter "knows" how much "control" is available because he or
she had put the parts of the whole experiment together. He or she "knows"
the regular relation of the elements in the experiment and how much they
will bend in response to the subjects' manipulation. In that light, the experimenter views the subjects' involvement as a way for the subject to find out
the measure of control that the environment independently offers. After a
number of trials, actual control should be finally defined for the subject. If
this does not occur, then there must be some error in judgment on the
subject's part. This might be due to the distortions that "subjective" involvement and experience sometimes produce. However, according to our
new formulation, the manipulation of control involves the manipulation of
mindful versus mindless engagement in the activity, that is, encouraging the
making of distinctions or encouraging the use of made distinctions.

In some of our recent work, we have induced different levels of mindlessness–mindfulness or involvement by varying the degree of familiarity
subjects have with the material in question (Langer, Blank, & Chanowitz,
1978; Langer & Imber, 1980; Langer & Weinman, Note 1), by exploiting distinctions that have historically become commonplace in our culture (Langer & Newman, 1979), and by encouraging or discouraging the
maintenance of rigid categorical distinctions that were implied in information previously made available to subjects (Chanowitz & Langer, Note 2).

A brief description of each of these series of studies should help illustrate the point. In a study by Langer et al. (1978), subjects were presented
with information that was either structurally familiar or novel and semantically
sound or senseless. Equivalent responding to semantically sound and senseless information within familiar structure revealed mindless information processing. For example, because requests are typically followed by reasons,
requests without reasons should occasion mindfulness. In Study 1, requests
were made of subjects about to use a copying machine: (a) "Excuse me, may
I use the Xerox machine." (b) "Excuse me, may I use the Xerox machine

TABLE 5.1
Proportion of Subjects Who Agreed to Let the Experimenter Use the Copying Machine

	Reason		
Favor	No information	Placebic information	Sufficient information
Small	.60	.93	.94
n	15	15	16
Big	.24	.24	.42
n	25	25	24

because I want to make copies." (c) "Excuse me, may I use the Xerox machine because I'm in a rush." Structurally the last two requests are similar, whereas semantically the first two are similar. (What else would one do with a copying machine except make copies!) Table 5.1 shows that unless the request was very effortful (20 versus 5 pages to be copied), mindlessness was the rule. Therefore, if people are thinking about what is being said to them, there should be similar rates of compliance for the first two requests.

In the first of two studies by Langer and Imber (1980), vulnerability to labels connoting inferiority was assessed as a function of amount of practice on a task. Subjects had either no practice, moderate practice, or were overpracticed on the task. It was hypothesized that with practice a structure emerges that obfuscates the individual components of a task. If environmental events, like the impositon of a negative label, lead one to question one's competence, then those groups for whom the task components are not readily available (the no practice and overpracticed groups) should perform poorly because they would have difficulty hurrying through the steps of the task to provide evidence of their competence. Table 5.2 bears out the predicted curvilinear relationship between practice and vulnerability to labels. Further support for this interpretation was found in a second study where the components of an overlearned task were made salient for half of the sub-

TABLE 5.2
Mean Number of Errors Made in Postlabel Coding Task ($n = 14$ per cell)

	Label		
	Assistant	No-label	Boss
No practice	$5.35^{*}_{a_1}$	2.36_b	2.00_b
Moderate practice	1.64_b	1.93_b	1.50_b
Over practice	4.93_{a_2}	1.07_b	1.14_b

[*] Cells bearing different subscripts are significantly different from each other: a_1 differs from b cells at $p < .001$; a_2 differs from b cells at $p < .01$.

jects. As many be seen in Table 5.3, the original effect was replicated in the condition similar to the overpracticed group in the first study, and the salience manipulation prevented the debilitation in the components-salient group.

In a series of studies by Langer and Weinman (Note 1), subjects also were given familiar or unfamiliar material. However, now confidence judgments were taken along with performance measures. In the first study, subjects read a very familiar nursery rhyme or a semantically, stylistically, linguistically similar novel rhyme. Although much more confident of understanding the familiar, all measures indicated greater understanding and involvement with the latter. In the second study, subjects read what seemed to be familiar or unfamiliar sentences from cards. Although quite confident of reading the familiar cards correctly (e.g., "Mary had a a little lamb"), they were almost unanimously incorrect, whereas they were less confident but more often correct with the novel stimuli (e.g., "Mary had sexy a a little lamb"). Finally, in the third study, subjects were encouraged not to think before speaking about a novel or familiar issue. Results indicated that instructions to think resulted in a less well-articulated speech for the familiar issue but improved performance for the novel group.

Langer and Newman (1979) assessed whether familiar cues planted by experimenters result in mindless task performance by subjects. Using the Asch (1946)/Kelly (1950) paradigm, subjects were led to believe that a speaker they were about to hear was warm (cold), industrious, critical, practical, and determined. After the speaker finished talking, subjects completed bipolar adjective scales assessing the speaker and then were tested on recall of the speech. As predicted, (see Table 5.4), subjects who were mindless with respect to this information were more likely to confirm the Asch–Kelly prediction than to disconfirm it, whereas there was no difference for mindful subjects.

Finally, in a study by Chanowitz and Langer (Note 2), subjects were led to believe that the incidence in the general population of a certain disorder for which they were being tested was either 10% or 80%. Furthermore, half of

TABLE 5.3
Mean Number of Postlabel Proofreading Errors Correctly Located ($n = 12$ per cell)

Experimental condition	Label		
	Assistant	No-label	Boss
Components-salient	14.33_a [*]	13.99_a	14.41_a
Components-nonsalient	8.92_b	13.00_a	17.42_c

[*] Cells bearing different subscripts are significantly different from each other: b differs from all other cells at $p < .005$; c differs from all a cells at $p < .05$.

TABLE 5.4
Mean Bipolar Adjective Scale Scores[a]

	Mindless	Mindful
Warm	20.10	17.38
Cold	15.45	16.83

[a]Higher numbers indicate more positive evaluations.

each group was instructed to think about what it would be like to have the disorder. Because it was unlikely that the 10% group would have the disorder and because they were not encouraged to mindfully interact with the no instructions group, information about symptoms of the disorder that followed was irrelevant. This was expected to result in mindless information processing where the relationship between disorder and symptoms would be uncritically accepted. All subjects then discovered that they had the disorder. Follow-up tests were given that required skills that would be lacking in individuals so afflicted. Table 5.5 shows that there was strong support for the hypothesis. Relative to the groups for whom mindfulness was encouraged, the 10%–no instructions group performed less than half as well.

In this research we have demonstrated that, in sustaining mindlessness in subjects as they were engaged in activities that were seemingly identical to actions where "control" is exercised, subjects were actually exercising less control. The diminished control of mindless subjects who were going through the motions of control led to wasted effort (Study 3 in Langer et al. [1978]; vulnerability to negative external circumstances [Langer & Imber, 1980]; misplaced confidence [Langer & Weinman, Note 1]; inarticulate speech [Langer & Weinman, Note 1]; poor listener comprehension [Langer & Newman, 1979]; and the rigid and maladaptive use of initially irrelevant information, resulting in performance decrements [Chanowitz & Langer, Note 2]. These debilitations were avoided when subjects were mindful, (see Langer, 1978; Langer, in press b). This body of research that points to a qualitative difference between mindlessness and mindfulness provides

TABLE 5.5
Mean Scores on Follow-up Field Dependence Test[a]

Instructions	Incidence of disorder		
	10%	80%	No treatment control group
Think	23.06	22.19	
No think	13.31	21.25	20.29

[a]Higher numbers indicate better performance.

strong support for the idea that the study of control is not the study of *outcomes,* but rather the study of *process.* Other research can be interpreted in this light.[3]

Indeed, the course of the typical psychological experiment in the domain of control can be interpreted from this new perspective; that is, the notion of "actual" control based on outcomes seems justified only from the static position of the observing experimenter, who sees the situation as a form of distinct parts and who sees the amount of change those parts allow as tantamount to the actual control available. But the subject might not initially see *those* parts. In fact, the subject might take the experimental situation as an example of situations that occur in the natural world. In that case, the subject takes it to be his or her project to formulate the parts of that whole which can be endlessly refined in order to produce desired outcomes more of the time than has been the case in the past. In the course of each trial the subject is involved in trying to figure out the factors that produced the desired outcome on this trial but that *did not* on another trial. On each trial, the subject entertains a scheme of parts or factors whose manipulation will lead to the desired outcome. In being involved in the thick of things on each trial, the experienced course of success or failure informs the subjects that the way he or she decomposed the situation this time is more or less efficacious. Concomitantly, each trial builds up the notion of self-as-controller. The subject treats the sample of trials that the experiment offers as a sample for involvement in which he or she can get a feel for the character of the situation. The experimenter (for whom the notion of "actual control" is a sensible concept) treats the sample as a population that defines the character of the situation.

"Perceived" control, then, defines the actual relation between self and material as it is developing—developing to what the experimenter considers "actual" control or, perhaps, beyond it. "Actual" control is a nonsensical concept for the one who can always do better and be better as one becomes more involved.

In a manner of speaking, then, if we were to highlight the disparity

[3]A case in point is research conducted and reported by Alloy and Abramson (1979) and how their conclusions could be reinterpreted by applying this perspective. In a series of experiments, depressed and nondepressed subjects were exposed to experimental procedures that embodied states of noncontingency. Subjects were then asked to judge degree of contingency. Depressed subjects were found to accurately diagnose noncontingency. Nondepressed subjects were found to display the illusion of control—they consistently overestimated the degree of contingency. Applying this perspective, however, we could assert that *both* groups of subjects are accurate in their assessments. The nondepressed subjects are investing a greater degree of involvement than are the depressed subjects, and consequently, they (i.e., nondepressed subjects) *actually* have a greater measure of control available than do the uninvolved, depressed subjects. Unfortunately, the experimenters are siding with the disinterested party.

between the assessments of subject and experimenter, it would be appropriate to reverse the nomenclature; that is, the experimenter's grasp of the situation could be referred to as "perceived control" and the subjects' grasp could be referred to as "actual control." The subjects' assessment takes into account the differential contribution to control that differential involvement produces. That differential might be more clearly visible in *future* ("postexperimental") efforts to control. On the other hand, the experimenter's assessment unilaterally attributes the same measure of control to all subjects who have gone through the motions of effecting "identical" changes in the material world during the initial phases of the experimental session.

Similarly, the experimenter's characterizations of subjects' judgments of contingency as "inaccurate" or "biased" (and of subjects' efforts to control as "irrational")—when subjects' actions in the latter phases of experiments do not "conform" to the information provided in the initial phases—are unjustified. The substance of that characterization relies on a peculiar perception of the experimental situation that is available only from the experimenter's privileged position. It sees the experimental situation as being composed of a set of unchanging parts. It sees that situation as offering a definite measure of control regardless of who approaches or how they become involved. It treats involvement (and the changing character of the person that experience produces) as a spurious variable that is not intrinsically related to the measure of control that is generated in a situation. If change in the person is considered at all, it is considered as an *effect* of the exercise of control rather than as an intrinsic element in the exercise of control. The subjects' involvement in the initial phases of the experiment is only a way of "finding out" how much control the detached situation offers the subject.

Yet, this perspective contradicts what we know of the way control is assumed in the natural world over a period of time. Control is not something we *possess*. It is some way that we *are*. Consider what this perspective would imply if *we* attempted to make sense of baseball games. This perspective implies that baseball fans are motivated to purchase tickets for the game merely because they are curious to find out the final outcome of the game. They could wait outside the stadium for the exiting fans who would tell them the score, or they could wait for the evening news to find out the score. But, the best and quickest way of finding out the score is to be in the stadium as the game unfolds. It takes only a moment of imagining yourself in the baseball stands and reconstituting the experience of watching an exciting game in order to see that this account does not capture the spirit of the fan's excitement.

The absurdity of the experimenter's current position becomes apparent through a baseball game analogy. In the same way that a subject is seen as attempting to reveal preprogrammed contingencies, the players' actions would be seen as being directed at revealing an outcome—discovery of a score that existed at the beginning of the game. Players would be seen as playing out their roles in the rush to find out the conclusion of the game. But if the players did not show up, there would not be a score. And *how* they show up in part determines the score. This perspective obscures the view of the players' actions as efforts to *produce* an outcome, while it reinforces the view of the players' actions as efforts to reveal an outcome. But the fans are excited because they are witnessing the (creative) production of an outcome, not the revelation of (mechanical) reproduction of a predetermined outcome. The players are involved in fabricating a game. They are not revealing a prefabricated game.

When we speak of the players' control in that game situation, we refer as much to the players' stance for involvement as we do to the possiblities for change that the environment offers. The strongest exercise of that control presumes and preserves the unity of self and environment. It is only after the fact that we are capable of referring to the distinctive changes in self or environment that are demonstrations of exercised control. From this perspective, the exercise itself is indescribable because description relies on the distinctness of self and environment. But the strongest version of exercised control relies on the indivisible unity of self and environment.

Of course, there are other ways for baseball players to be involved with the game. The players could be operating under the assumption that the game is "fixed"; that is, they could believe that they are involved in reproducing a predetermined outcome. In that case, the players are exercising less control, regardless of whether or not that game is in fact fixed. And it has its effects. The player might not try as hard under these circumstances to catch a ground ball, allowing it to go through the infield for a base hit. It certainly has its effect on the players. For psychologists who are involved in assessing the effects of control on humans, it is as important to know *how* the players are involved in the game as it is to know whether or not they successfully make the play. But, if attention is focused only on the number of successful versus unsuccessful plays as a measure of the amount of control that the players exercise, we get a misleading picture, and sometimes, we get puzzling results. The measure of exercised control is as much a function of involvement as it is a function of successful change in the material world.

With involving experience, one assumes more and more control over a particular domain in the material world. Consequently, one becomes more and more successful at achieving desired outcomes. By the same token, with that involving experience, the self that is effecting desired outcomes in the exercise of control is also altered. The alterations in self are not as easy to see as the changes that are being effected in the material world during the exercise of control, but they are there, and they provide some of the available clues for sorting out the type of involvement the actor invoked during the exercise of control. The experimenter who refuses to recognize that involvement is a major factor during the exercise of control cannot see that there are conceptually distinguishable forms of involvement. In that light, the experimenter is oblivious to the distinguishable measures of control that were exercised on the basis of distinctive forms of involvement. However, the varying character of involved self is a vital ingredient that must be taken into consideration when trying to compute the amount of control that is *actually* exercised by the subject in any experimental situation.

An Improvement for Experimental Procedures

The exercise of control, then, is a whole situation (or, from the perspective of the actor, a whole experience) that cannot faithfully be fully reproduced as a number of parts or measures, whether that attempt at reproduction takes place in a laboratory or in a retrospective conversation among friends. However, as psychologists intent on observation, we can *heuristically* fragment that whole situation into a set of parts that best captures its spirit.

This perspective relies on the notion that in the laboratory we are involved in the process of imperfect reconstruction. It belies the traditional notion that we give exactly the same amount of control to all subjects by putting all of them through the same motions. But it does allow for the possibility of incorporating new elements in the experimental procedure that will make visible and account for other parts of the indivisibly whole experience when we, as psychologists, become aware of them. Thus, we must incorporate procedures in experiments on control that make visible and measure the subjects' involvement. These measures, along with the degree of materially effected change, would provide a more accurate assement of the amount of actual control that subjects exercise—a more accurate assessment of control than would be available if we relied exclusively on changes effected in the environment. Earlier in this article reference was made to five ways in which mindless involvement would produce effects that are distinguishable from the produced effects of mindful involvement: *(a)* the relative capacity to perceive during, rather than after, a sequenced activity that something foreign to the sequence is intruding; *(b)* the relative capacity to recognize the character of that foreign element and, accordingly, to adjust the fixed sequence in order to continue achieving desired outcomes; *(c)* the degree to which the environment that is controlled and the self that is controlling are seen as labile or rigid; *(d)* the degree to which the self-as-agent within a sphere of activity does or does not change as a result of continued activity in that particular sphere; and *(e)* the generalized affective and emotional consequences that ensue for the person as a result of continued activity. The inclusion of procedures in the experimental design that measure the effects on one or more of these given dimensions (some are obviously easier to incorporate than others) would provide some notion of the character and degree of the subject's involvement. Together with the degree of change effected in the environment, this would provide a more accurate assessment of the measure of control exercised by the subject.

By the same token, it should be clear that the "structure" (as laid out by the experimenter) of an experimental environment might be constructed so as to encourage one form of involvement rather than another. In fact, we can look at the data of some completed experiments for evidence that would bear on the ideas herein advanced. Do distinctive environmental structures provide distinctive experimental results? Hypothetically, then, this could be attributed to distinctive degrees of involvement (and, thereby, control) that the structure encouraged.

As the subject becomes involved in assuming control during the initial phases of the experiment, we can conceptually distinguish between two ways in which the subject proceeds. It becomes crucial to recognize whether the subject is involved in formulating parts or whether he or she is relying on formed parts while in the process of assuming control in the experiment. This might account for some of the disparity (or lack thereof) between the responses of subjects in the latter phases of the experiment that reflect the degree of control they "perceive" themselves to have, and the responses that the subjects should display if they had accurately assessed how much control they "actually" (form the experimenter's perspective) had. The design of the experimental environment in which control is assumed plays a part in the stance that subjects take. Of course, greater involvement (and the accompanying experience) does not dictate a disparity between "actual" and "perceived" control. It only allows for its possibility.

This might provide a plausible reconciliation of the contradictory findings, for example, between judgments of contingency based on summary data versus those based on data presented to subjects trial-by-trial that were found by Jenkins and Ward (1965) and Ward and Jenkins (1965). When the data for a number of trials are presented in summary forms, the whole (as the experimenter intends them) is clear to the subject. But in a trial-by-trial presentation, as the subject becomes involved in fathoming what is going on, he or she develops his or her own scheme, which might not coincide with the experimenter's.

It is important, then, to recognize that involving experience is an integral part of the control process, and the later demonstration of effecting intended changes in the material is but another *part* of the control process. As control is assumed, both aspects must be studied to see how they contribute to the subsequent effects of having control. Studies on the illusion of control (Ayeroff & Abelson, 1976; Langer, 1975; Langer, 1978b; Langer & Roth, 1976; Wortman, 1975) focus on the effects of involving experience on control when, in fact, outcomes in the world are not being redirected by the subjects' actions. For example, in one study in her illusion of control series, Langer varied passive involvement (i.e., thinking) in a lottery by encouraging high-involvement subjects to think about the lottery on several occasions or only once. Results revealed significantly more control for the high-involvement subjects than for low-involvement subjects. It is comparable to the rigged version of the aforementioned baseball game, in which the player has *not* gotten wind of the fixed character. One can thereby study how the self-as-controller accumulates with the accretion of involvement while the environment remains neither encouraging or discouraging. The subjects are making nothing happen. But how can a self, intent on control, look for nothing? On each involving trial, the subject is looking for factors that might influence the production of outcomes. That intentional, involving stance precludes the understanding that "factors" do not determine the outcome because there is a self involved in looking for the factors. That understanding would rely on a detached osition by the subject which the experimenter is not inviting when he or she asks the subject-qua-human to participate.

The Question of Contingency
and the Question of Its Character

An extension of this line of reasoning might shed some interesting light on experimental findings that have been offered as evidence that subjects have difficulty concluding that there is no relation between two elements when "in fact" there is no relation (Chapman, 1967; Chapman & Chapman, 1969; Hamilton & Gifford, 1976; Jennings, Amabile, & Ross, 1980; Smedslund, 1963; Kahneman & Tversky, 1973); that is, when subjects are exposed to a series of instances in which the presence versus absence of two elements is manipulated (and the presence of one element is not contingent on the presence of the other), subjects are incapable of detecting that state of noncontingency. This "bias" to perceive contingency (where "in fact" there is noncontingency) has been taken to indicate a defect that is intrinsic to human cognitive functioning. Even statisticians who are familiar with the concept of contingency display biases when they serve as subjects (Tversky & Kahneman, 1971). Consider, however, that the effort to ascertain a noncontingent relation between two elements relies on rigid, stable definitions for those elements as a prerequisite for the initiation of that effort. Concurrently, it encourages the observer to maintain a detached position as she or he records the appearance of the phenomenon in question, so as to preserve the sharp definition of those elements. Contrast this effort with the effort where contingency is presumed between two (ambiguously defined) elements and one is involved in ascertaining the *character* of that contingent relation. Under these circumstances, it is precisely the form of those elements that is at issue. Insofar as one is involved in determining the form of those elements, one is precluded from entertaining the possiblity of noncontingency, because entertaining that possibility relies on *already formed* elements. These two efforts invite radically different notions of self in relation to the phenomenon.

Perhaps the radical distinction between these two efforts can be clarified by imagining that we are trying to understand the occurrence of a heretofore unexplained phenomenon. There is a radical distinction to be drawn between a project (A) which seeks to ascertain that the occurrence of this phenomenon is randomly generated and a second project (B) which presumes that unknown-but-knowable factors produce the occurrence and seeks to ascertain what those factors are.[4] Project A relies on sharp definitions of the phenomenon and all other elements that surround its occurrence. Given these sharp categorical distinctions, the project is an essentially manipulative enterprise that seeks to determine whether or not there is an unreasonably high co-occurence of any other elements in the field with the phenomenon in question. The continued work of that determination (whether it concludes random generation or it detects a significant correlation) relies on preserving those sharp categorical distinctions, and it calls for a detached self that is capable of manipulating without violating those categorical boundaries.

On the other hand, Project B is essentially a creative, productive enterprise. It is the form of the phenomenon that is in question and the categorical distinctions that are at issue. As we name factors that promote the phenomenon's occurrence, by the same token, we are revising the defined form of the phenomenon itself. This project calls for an individual self that is itself altered as it assumes knowledge of the heretofore unknown. Conceptually, the two projects rely on radically distinctive frames of reference and self. Each relies on a conceptually distinct characterization of the "unknown." Yet, how is one to know beforehand in which way to treat the unknown as one seeks to investigate a phenomenon of interest? It is a *decision* that must be made (wittingly or unwittingly) beforehand and one that can later be revised. However, when subjects are invited to become involved in determining the relation between elements, they are busy defining the form of the elements. It is no wonder then that they "cannot" see noncontingency. That

[4]The use of the term "chance-determined" is an indication of the hybrid reasoning that occurs so often in everyday life and in psychological research. Chance does not determine. Rather chance characterizes a method for generating events.

sight would rely on formed elements. The inability of subjects to detect noncontingency is not a technical defect intrinsic to human cognitive function; it is the product of assumptions that are made as humans engage with material.

From a common sense point of view, the assertion that the incapacity to detect noncontingency represents a defect in human cognitive function is altogether puzzling. After all, how does one go about looking for "nothing"? And what does "nothing" look like when it is found? The conclusion of nothing can only be directed in characterizing the relation among predefined elements. However, this assertion of "bias" is even more puzzling when it comes from experimental psychologists. Why should we expect subjects to assert noncontingency? We all know that the null hypothesis cannot be *proven*. And even the attempt to *reject* the null hypothesis relies on sharply defined operational variables.

Reviewing the Literature

On some level, the name given to the phenomenon of the *illusion* of control can be misunderstood. It can foster the impression that this is an ephemeral version of control that has no relation to instances where control is actually exercised, where noncontingency is taken for contingency. It may be an illusion from the observer's perspective, but it is clearly not from the actor's point of view. The actor's involvement is the important part of the process of realizing control. It is just as important as that part of the process that we usually focus on; that is, effecting change in material on the basis of intended manipulations. They both contribute to the substantiation of self-as-controller and the articulation of the environment-to-be-controlled. Together they consitute the in flux relation of control that can be verified by examining, in stasis, effected changes in the world or in the self. That we can only assess *demonstrations* of control is dictated by the fact that we must stand apart from the object as we describe it. However, we can better understand control by devising measures that assess both what is done and how it was done during the exercise of control. Without a measure of involvement, we cannot recognize that effecting change in the world without its correspondent involvement in a deficient version of control.

Without deepening involvement on the actor's part, the effecting of change relies on preformed categories. The actor relates to the material from a detached position. To the degree that we find ourselves reforming these categories, to that degree we find ourselves becoming involved. Intuitively, then, we can clarify some of the conceptual distinctions that are used in control research. The exercise of Machiavellianism by the subject is characterized by manipulation of preformed categories. That exercise sustains a detached, rigidly formed, unchanging self-as-actor. That manipulation in the interest of achieving desired outcomes can be referred to as power. The exercise of control by the subject is characterized by forming (or re-forming) categories. That exercise sustains a changing self-as-actor as more knowledge is assumed. As observers, if we focus our attention on the relative success that the actor has had in achieving desired outcomes that were announced at the onset of activity, then we have no way of knowing whether those outcomes were achieved through the exercise of manipulativeness or creativeness. As with the earlier example of *Guernica,* we are faced with the problem of distinguishing between the *Guernica* that Picasso creatively produced and the *Guernica* that another manipulatively "produced." As psychologists who are concerned with the effects on humans of such activities, it is of paramount importance to distinguish between these forms of activities. Measures that indicate how the person is involved during the course of the activity are therefore vital.

Given this perspective, the distinction between powerlessness and helplessness becomes clearer. The failure of an attempted exercise of power (where one manipulates preformed categories that retain rigidity while reaching for desired outcomes) leads to a feeling of powerlessness. The failure of an attempted exercise of control (where one works to create categories that will aid in achieving desired outcomes) leads to a feeling of helplessness. Both are products of an environment that is unyielding to the actor's efforts. Both have points of reference in the person and in the environment. During the activity that will produce either helplessness or powerlessness, those points are constituents of an indivisible whole. For observers after the activity, these points are inevitably fragments that are pieced together as accurately as possible in order to capture the spirit of the earlier episode. It becomes clearer then why rage follows the discovery of powerlessness and why apathy follows the discovery of helplessness. Both originate in the discovery of the environment's unyielding character. During the exercise of power, the self is not at risk because the self maintains a rigidity that corresponds with the rigidly formed, categorical nature of the environment that is manipulated. During the exercise of control, however, the sef is at risk because its status as agent is informed by its capacity to create formulations of the environment in productive terms. The rage and apathy are, in fact, indications of how the subjects were involved with the environment in the effort to produce outcomes as they found those outcomes not forthcoming. Given this understanding, it is not surprising, for example, that a prison resident experiences rage as a notion of self-as-schemer is cultured, whereas a nursing home resident becomes apathetic as a notion of self loses viability. Thus, paradoxically, one's self has a better chance of surviving in a prison (albeit, in a damaged state) than in a nursing home (Langer, in press a).

Consider how a detailed application of this perspective would effect any one variable used in control research. For example, previously we could not see that there was more than one way to characterize the behavior that has been referred to as "reactance." Consider the experimenter who shifts the contingencies during the course of an experiment in order to "take" control away from the subject. In focusing on the effects produced by that limitation, the experimenter observes more active behavior that is taken to reflect a continued (if not increased) sense of control on the subject's part. The subject is seen to increase efforts of control. This is commonly taken to mean that the subject considers the experimenter's actions to be a threat. In the response of "reactance," the subject is irrationally determined to reassert and display the measure of control that she or he *does* have over the material despite the reduced control. Those behaviors are seen as a stubborn reaction to the experimenter's threat to the subject's freedom (Brehm, 1966; Wicklund, 1974). However, there is another equally plausible way to interpret the subject's behavior. If the subject is thoroughly involved in the course of the experiment, then it takes time to discover the shift of contingencies and appreciate its implications. The continuing involvement after the shift could be seen as, first, the process of discovering that the factors which produce the outcome have changed and, then, the process of getting a handle on the newly introduced factors so as to produce again those desired outcomes. It is, in fact, in this situation as it occurs in the natural world that we are reassured of our control and *increase* that control. Suppose, for example, one is involved in putting screws in the wall and all of a sudden the screwdriver is missing. One looks for something else to take the screwdriver's place. One recognizes that it is not the screwdriver that is important, but rather, it is the useful composition of properties that it has for getting the screw in the wall which is important. One finds and uses a knife to put the screw in the wall. In so doing, one recognizes that she or he has a handle on the factors that compose the act of putting the screw in the wall. In fact, control over screws has been *increased,* and the self-as-controller has been revitalized. However, it takes time and increased involvement during that time to find another way to produce the desired outcome in the light of new factors.

Thus, when the subject is confronted by the experimenter's limiting shifts of contingency, we can conceptually distinguish between two forms of response on the subject's part. The subject can respond rebelliously in light of the experimenter's threat to his or her freedom, or the subject can respond curiously, looking for a better way to achieve the outcome in light of the newly introduced factors. It depends on how the subject is involved. But without a measure for involvement, these two responses appear to be the same. Furthermore, by the experimenter's disregard for the factor of involvement, she or he cannot see how involvement in one way or the other produced the distinctive responses that seem to be the same.

A similar issue is at hand when we confront the controversy of statistical versus clinical prediction and the relative efficacy of each form of measure in the effort to control. Statistical assessments rely on formed parts, whereas clinical assessments focus on the forming of those parts. On a reduced level, this problem is parallel to that of the student who we rejected from graduate school. The student is dissatisfied with the fact that the admissions committee considered only the grades achieved during the undergraduate career. Feeling that she or he was treated unfairly, the student insists on a interview by the committee because she or he *knows* that the grades do not accurately reflect the quality of the work that was done. The description, in parts, of the activity does not do justice to the whole activity. The student wants to tell more. The whole is greater than the sum of its parts. The committee, however, feels they have enough evidence for making a judgment. The fact that the whole is *other* than the sum of its parts is lost in the dynamics of this argument. The grades say nothing at all about how the student was exercising control on the way to producing those grades. We need an entirely different measure for that assessment. The effort to produce an adequate formulation of that measure in particular situations requires that the observer become more involved. The inclusion of that measure might reveal that certain students with lower grades have more promise than other students with higher grades, just as some subjects in our experiments with poorer outcomes might be shown to have experienced more control then those who achieved materially greater outcomes. Without the recognized need for an entirely different set of measures, the argument focuses on whether the committee needs more or less of the same sort of information about the student in order to make a judgment. Those measures do not capture *how* they are doing it. Thus, for ourselves as researchers, the task is not to gather "more" data from our subjects. Instead, we should gather "other" data—data that will show more of what the subject knows.

REFERENCE NOTES

1. Langer, E., & Weinman, C. *Mindlessness, confidence and accuracy.* Prepublication manuscript, Harvard University, 1979.
2. Chanowitz, B., & Langer, E. *Premature cognitive commitment.* Prepublication manuscript, Harvard University, 1979.

6

On the Distinction between Anxiety and Depression: Perceived Control, Certainty, and Probability of Goal Attainment

JUDY GARBER
SUZANNE M. MILLER
LYN Y. ABRAMSON

INTRODUCTION

Anxiety and depression have captured the interest of researchers and clinicians alike. Historically, these two syndromes have been viewed as distinct diagnostic entities (e.g., DSM II, DSM III). Despite the nosological distinction, however, considerable overlap exists between the two syndromes with respect to manifest symptomatology and hypothesized etiology (Costello & Comrey, 1967; Grinker & Nunnally, 1968).

Clinically, some psychiatric nosologists (Lewis, 1966; Mapother, 1926) and personality theorists (Eysenck, 1960) have argued that the two states are phenomenologically indistinguishable because they share similar sets of symptoms. Psychometrically, anxiety and depression can be distinguished on a group basis such that pooled data from the clinical categories will yield group differences on a variety of measures. However, the distribution is unimodal, and there is considerable overlap between the two groups (Costello & Comrey, 1967; Kerr, Schapira, Roth, & Garside, 1970; Roth, Gurney, Garside, & Kerr, 1972). Experimentally, there has been a general trend toward the use of a unidimensional construct such as "stress" or "arousal" that embraces both anxiety and depression (e.g., Appley & Trumbell, 1967;

131

Duffy, 1941). Finally, at the theoretical level, similar cognitive processes have been invoked to explain both syndromes. Two such theoretical process are the perceived probability of the occurrence of an outcome and the perceived controllability of the outcome. Thus, it may be that no clear distinction can be made between the syndromes of anxiety and depression.

The goal of this chapter is to clarify the nature of the relationship between anxiety and depression. Toward this end we (a) examine clinical, experimental, and genetic evidence relevant to distinguishing between anxiety and depression; (b) review the major theories of anxiety and depression and compare the underlying cognitive processes invoked to explain each syndrome; and (c) propose a theoretical resolution which utilizes the concepts of perceived control, certainty, and probability of an undesirable outcome to distinguish between anxiety and depression.

EMPIRICAL DISTINCTIONS

Clinical Evidence

The symptoms of both anxiety and depression are well known and have been described since antiquity. Today, many investigators believe that each state is best viewed as a complex syndrome embracing a family of symptoms, no one of which is necessary for the disorder (e.g., Beck, 1967; Lazarus & Opton, 1966; Seligman, 1975). Neither phenomenon can be exhausted by any single definition. We consider the two states to be hypothetical constructs which are characterized by a number of converging response components or symptoms. It is useful to distinguish among four components of each affective state: emotional, behavioral, cognitive, and somatic symptoms (Beck, 1967).

Clinical evidence shows that it is not uncommon for patients to simultaneously manifest symptoms of both anxiety and depression. For example, in a group of patients diagnosed as anxiety neurotics, half of the patients were found to have secondary depressive disorder (Woodruff, Guze, & Clayton, 1972). In contrast to the other anxiety neurotics, these patients showed symptoms of fatigue, anorexia, and suicidal thoughts. Similarly, several investigators have identified a subtype of depression which is characterized by the presence of anxiety-type symptomatology (Overall, Hollister, Johnson, & Pennington, 1966; Paykel, 1971, 1972). Patients in this group displayed only moderate depression but showed feelings of anxiety, somatic agitation, fatigue, depersonalization, and obsessiveness. Using the typology of Overall et al. (1966), Raskin (1974) found that approximately half of a large sample of depressed patients fell into the anxious subtype. This group responded well to antianxiety pharmacological agents, such as minor tranquilizers, whereas other subtypes, such as retarded depressives, responded better to antidepressants (Raskin, 1974). Finally, attempts to differentiate the syndromes on the basis of psychometric indices have also been somewhat unsuccessful. In a general psychiatric population, both inpatients (Mendels, Weinstein, & Cochrane, 1972) and outpatients (Kellner, Simpson, & Winslow, 1972) tend to score high on various self-report measures of both syndromes.

Despite this apparent overlap between the two syndromes, however, results of several clinical studies have shown that it *is* possible to reliably discriminate between the two syndromes on the basis of certain symptom patterns. Table 6.1 summarizes these results according to the various components of each syndrome.

Affective Component

Studies of both inpatients (Roth et al., 1972), and outpatients (Derogatis, Lipman, Covi, & Rickels, 1972; Prusoff & Klerman, 1974), have revealed that feelings of sadness and despondency are severe and persistent among depressives but are more mild and episodic among anxious patients. In addition, depressives alone manifest diurnal variation of sad mood (Roth et al., 1972). In contrast to the foregoing, feelings of tension and panic are severe and persistent among anxious patients, whereas these same feelings are milder and more episodic among depressives. Some evidence also suggests that anxiety is accompanied by increased tearfulness (Prusoff & Klerman, 1974) and irritability (Derogatis et al., 1972), although other evidence suggests that crying (Derogatis et al., 1972) and irritability (Roth et al., 1972) occur equally as often in depression as in anxiety.

Behavioral Component

The behavioral component is indexed mainly by measures reflecting changes in activity level.[1] In general, depression tends to have a de-energizing effect on behavior, leading to lowered activity and decreased initiation of voluntary responses. Thus, depressives typically are less responsive and take little interest in things around them; they feel low in energy or slowed down, and show behavioral retardation. They also show a desire to escape, and a reduced motivation to continue living (Derogatis et al., 1972; Prusoff & Klerman, 1972; Roth et al., 1972). The equivalent deficits are saliently absent in anxiety. Instead, there is some indication that anxious individuals are behaviorally more active, and there tends to be an increase in the incidence

[1]The change in activity level is frequently explained in terms of motivation. However, this change is not *necessarily* a result of changes in motivation. It is equally as likely that the behavioral effects are a result of cognitive or physiological processes. In order to avoid confusion, we choose to refer to this component of the syndrome as behavioral rather than motivational.

TABLE 6.1
Summary from the Clinical Literature of Affective, Behavioral, Somatic, and Cognitive Symptoms That are Unique to Depression, Unique to Anxiety, and Which Overlap Both States

	Unique to depression	Unique to anxiety	Overlap both states
Affective symptoms	Persistent and severe feelings of sadness Diurnal variation of mood	Persistent and severe feelings of tension and panic	Crying Irritability
Behavioral symptoms	Lowered activity Behavioral retardation Lack of response initiation Lack of interest and energy Suicidal thoughts[a]	Increased activity Behavioral agitation	
Somatic symptoms	Decreased SNS[a] arousal Poor appetite Reduced sexual desire	Increased SNS arousal Somatic discomfort	Initial insomnia Restless sleep
Cognitive symptoms	Feelings of hopelessness and helplessness Self-blame and guilt Self-criticism Indecision	Repetitive rumination and thoughts Lowered self-confidence and insecurity Cognitive disorganization	Ruminations and worry Self-doubt

[a]Sympathetic nervous system

of panic attacks (Roth et al., 1972). In the case of agitated depression, of course, one is likely to find an increase in disorganized activity, despite the decreased interest in the things around them.

Somatic Component

Consistent with the behavioral evidence, depressives alone appear to be somatically hyporeactive, reporting poor appetite and reduced sexual desires (Derogatis et al., 1972; Prusoff & Klerman, 1974). Anxious patients, on the other hand, report increased pains, dizziness, sweating, and cardiovascular upset, whereas depressives generally do not (Prusoff & Klerman, 1974; Roth et al., 1972). However, both groups suffer equally from initial insomnia and sleep disturbance (Roth et al., 1972).

This evidence receives further corroboration from studies using actual physiological measures obtained from patients who have been classified as anxious or depressed on the basis of a psychiatric interview. Although researchers have investigated a range of autonomic responses (respiratory, electrocortical, etc.), we limit our review to electrodermal, cardiovascular, and muscular responses because they provide the most conclusive data. (See also Lader, 1975, and Lader and Noble, 1975, for a complete review.)

Studies of anxious patients show that they have increased arousal of the sympathetic branch of the autonomic nervous system. Such increased arousal means that the body's resources are mobilized for flight or fight activity. For the electrodermal system, the anxious group shows increased basal skin conductance level (Howe, 1958; Lader & Wing, 1966, 1969), a higher rate of nonspecific skin conductance responses (Goldstein, 1965; Kelly, Brown, & Shaffer, 1970; Lader, 1967; Lader & Wing, 1966, 1969; Malmo, 1966), slower habituation to specific stimuli (Lader, 1967; Lader & Wing, 1966, 1969; Stewart, Winokur, Stern, Guze, Pfeiffer, & Horning), and less extinction (Howe, 1958; Stewart et al., 1959). For the cardiovascular system, the anxious group shows increased basal pulse rate and heart rate (Goldstein, 1965; Kelley et al., 1970; Kelly & Walter, 1968, 1969; Lader & Wing, 1966; White & Gilden, 1937; Wishner, 1953; versus Jurko, Jost, & Hill, 1952; Malmo & Shagass, 1949), and increased basal forearm blood flow (Kelly et al., 1970; Kelly & Walter, 1968, 1969). Finally, muscular tension is generally elevated in anxious patients (Goldstein, 1965; Malmo & Shagass, 1949; Malmo, Shagass, & Davis, 1951), although the recording site may be critical (Martin, 1956; Sainsbury & Gibson, 1954).

Results of studies with depressed patients tend to be somewhat more inconsistent. However, the picture becomes clearer when patients are grouped into agitated depressives (those who show overt signs of excessive anxiety) and nonagitated or retarded depressives (those who are overtly underactive or nonreactive). Lader and Wing (1969), for example, found that agitated depressives had higher tonic skin conductance levels, more nonspecific skin conductance responses, and more arousal to specific stimuli than did normals. A reverse pattern emerged for the retarded group; that is, they showed lower tonic skin conductance levels, fewer nonspecific skin conductance responses, and less arousal to specific stimuli than did normals. This work has recently been replicated by Noble and Lader (1971). On the other hand, Dawson, Schell, and Catania (1977) and Kelly et al. (1970) failed to obtain these results, although sample differences may account for the inconsistency.

On the cardiovascular level, heart rate is greater in agitated depressives than in normals. Nonagitated and retarded depressives tend to show equivalent or slightly lower cardiovascular levels than do normals (Dawson et al., 1977; Lader & Wing, 1969; Kelly & Walter, 1968, 1969). Finally, muscular tension levels are often increased in depressives as compared to normal controls (Whatmore & Ellis, 1959), and this again may be due to the presence of agitation in some of the patients (Noble & Lader, 1971). Overall, then, a somatic "hierarchy" emerges, with anxiety neurotics at the top end of the activation dimension, followed by agitated depressives, normals, and finally, retarded depressives.

Cognitive Component

The cognitive manifestations of depression include a number of diverse phenomena. Most notably, depressives tend to exhibit a negative view of themselves, their world, and their future (Beck, 1967). Other symptoms such as guilt, low self-esteem, and indecisiveness are also apparent (Beck, 1967; Derogatis et al., 1972; Prusoff & Klerman, 1976; Roth et al., 1972). Thus, depressives experience dominant feelings of hopelessness and helplessness on the one hand, and feelings of self-blame and self-criticism on the other hand. Such thoughts are less prominent in anxiety. Alternatively, in anxiety, repetitive thoughts about danger and impending disaster (Beck, 1976), persistent feelings of dread, panic, and insecurity (Kolb, 1973), and cognitive disorganization (Derogatis et al., 1972; Roth et al. 1972) tend to predominate. Other studies, however, have shown that some of these symptoms, particularly the worry component, also occur in depression (Derogatis et al. 1972; Prusoff & Klerman, 1974).

In sum, as can be seen from Table 6.1, the clinical syndromes of anxiety and depression each are characterized by a unique symptom pattern. Typically, anxiety involves a pattern of hyperactivation. The anxious patient feels subjectively tense, behaviorally agitated, somatically labile, and cognitively panicky. In contrast, depression appears to involve a pattern of hypoactivation: The depressed individual is subjectively sad, behaviorally retarded, somatically quiescent, and cognitively hopeless and helpless. These are, of course, only the *classical* patterns of symptoms that characterize each syndrome. We have already mentioned that there is considerable overlap between the two syndromes. Moreover, it is often difficult to distinguish between them in individuals who simultaneously manifest both syndromes.

It is noteworthy that symptoms of anxiety are more common among depressed patients than are symptoms of depression among anxious patients. For example, Prusoff and Klerman (1974) found that for depressives, symptoms of depression were more severe than were symptoms of anxiety, and for anxious patients, symptoms of anxiety were more severe than were symptoms of depression, although the absolute level of impairment on symptoms of anxiety was similar for both anxious and depressed patients. More simply stated, both groups showed an equally high level of anxiety, whereas only the depressed group showed the high level of depression. Moreover, Roth et al. (1972) found that there was a tendency for the anxious patients in their sample to get more depressed over time; there was no corresponding tendency for the depressed patients to get more anxious over time. Interestingly, however, Beck (Note 1) has noted that depressed individuals tend to show increased anxiety as they are recovering from an episode of depression.

Level of depression also has been used in the differential diagnosis and treatment of the two syndromes. Downing and Rickles (1974) investigated a group of patients with a diagnosis of mixed anxiety and depression in an attempt to determine why some patients received anxiolytics (antianxiety drugs), whereas others were treated with antidepressants. They found that clinicians rated the two groups very differently, particularly with regard to level of depression. Patients receiving antidepressants were rated as having significantly higher levels of depression than were patients receiving the anxiolytic medication. These patients were rated as having more anxiety than were patients receiving antidepressants, although not significantly so. Moreover, patients treated with anxiolytic medication were rated as having a relatively higher level of anxiety than depression, although the difference was not very great. In contrast, patients treated with antidepressants were rated as having a higher level of depression than anxiety, and the difference in severity of symptoms was very striking. This suggests that when symptoms of depression become more salient and more severe, the patient is labeled depressed rather than anxious and is treated with an antidepressant.

The fact that symptoms of anxiety appear to be more pervasive than symptoms of depression is also consistent with data obtained from nonclinical populations. Several investigators have noted that in a population of college students it is extremely difficult, if not impossible, to identify a group high in depression but low in anxiety, although it is somewhat easier to identify a group high in anxiety and low in depression (Craighead, in press; Miller, Seligman, & Kurlander, 1975). The greater occurrence of symptoms of anxiety suggests that anxiety may be more easily activated than depression and may be associated with less overall impairment.

Thus, the clinical evidence suggests that there are certain patterns of symptoms which typically characterize the individual syndromes of anxiety and depression. However, these symptoms are by no means fixed, nor are they mutually exlusive. The simultaneous occurrence of both syndromes in one individual is not uncommon. In such cases it is often the severity of the symptoms associated with each symdrome which contributes to decisions about differential diagnosis and treatment.

Experimental Evidence

The experimental evidence differentiating anxiety and depression is even less conclusive than the clinical evidence. This appears to be a result, in part, of the emphasis on a unitary construct such as stress or distress; that is, experimenters typically have focused on how various experimental manipulations affect an individual's level of stress "as a whole" rather than delineate different kinds of stress responses. Nonetheless, some distinguishing features have been noted, and these data are summarized in Table 6.2.

Affective Component

Zuckerman and his colleagues (Zuckerman & Lubin, 1965; Zuckerman, Lubin, & Robins, 1965) reported that individuals who rate themselves as feeling tense and apprehensive also tend to rate themselves as feeling sad and despondent. Moreover, untreated control subjects who score high in anxiety on the Multiple Affect Adjective Checklist (Zuckerman et al., 1965) similarly score high in depression (Miller & Grant, Note 2). In addition, exposure to aversive events such as uncontrollable noise produces increases in self-ratings of both mood states (Gatchel, Paulus, & Maples, 1975; Gatchel & Proctor, 1976; Miller & Seligman, 1976). Thus, paralleling the results found in clinical populations, it appears that feelings of anxiety and depression can, and do, coexist in normal populations.

Unfortunately, methodological inadequacies detract from the theoretical value of these findings. On Zuckerman's Multiple Affect Adjective Checklist (MAACL), a frequently used self-report measure of affect, subjects are presented with a list of adjectives describing anxiety, depression, and hostility, and are instructed to check those adjectives that describe how they feel "at this moment." The nonspecificity of these instructions renders it impossible to determine whether individuals are feeling anxious or depressed about the same or different events, and whether these feelings occur simultaneously or sequentially. So, for example, in the case of uncontrollable noise, subjects may feel anxious and/or depressed with respect to the noise per se, the fact that it is uncontrollable, or that it is unpredictable.

TABLE 6.2
Summary from the Experimental Literature of Affective, Behavioral, Somatic, and Cognitive Symptoms That Are Unique to Depression, Unique to Anxiety, and Which Overlap Both States

	Unique to depression	Unique to anxiety	Overlap both states
Affective symptoms	Feelings of sadness	Feelings of anxiety	Feelings of depression and anxiety
Behavioral symptoms	Decreased initiation of aversively motivated voluntary responses Behavioral disruption due to passivity	Increased initiation of aversively motivated voluntary responses Behavioral disruption due to disorganization	Decreased initiation of appetitively motivated voluntary responses Behavioral disruption
Somatic symptoms	Decreased SNS arousal	Increased arousal	
Cognitive symptoms	Failure to expect future response–reinforcement contingencies Themes of personal loss and failure Negative distortions Internal attributions for failure Recall negative events	Anxious overconcern and self-preoccupation Self-deprecatory statements Ruminations about inadequacies	Ruminations and overconcern about personal adequacy

Behavioral Component

In a review of psychological deficits in depression, Miller (1975) con-cluded that depressives differ from nondepressives on a wide variety of behavioral tasks. Psychomotor retardation, in particular, repeatedly has been found to be characteristic of depression (Friedman, 1964). Furthermore, Lewinsohn and his colleagues (Lewinsohn & Graf, 1973; Lewinsohn & Libet, 1972; Lewinsohn & MacPhillamy, 1974; have found that depressed indi-viduals tend to engage in relatively fewer activites in general and an even fewer number of pleasant or rewarding activities than do nondepressed individuals. Finally, Seligman and his colleagues (Klein, Fencil-Morse, & Seligman, 1976; Klein & Seligman, 1976; Miller & Seligman, 1975) have reported that depressed college students and students made "helpless" by exposure to uncontrollable events fail to escape or avoid aversive stimuli and show debilitated anagram performance and discrimination learning.

In the case of anxiety, there is considerable evidence that chronically anxious individuals and inviduals made anxious or fearful in the laboratory appear to be motivated to perform instrumental responses that avoid or escape aversive stimulation (Geer, Davison, & Gatchel, 1970; Miller, 1979a; Miller, Note 3; Rothbart & Mellinger, 1972; Szpiler & Epstein, 1976). More-over, anxiety can have a facilitative effect on general learning and perfor-mance (Spielberger, Goldstein, & Dahlstrom, 1958). For example, Wortman and Brehm (1975) have suggested that when an individual expects control, exposure to negative outcomes intially produces "reactance" or increased motivation to execute controlling responses. However, once an individual becomes convinced that no control is available, exposure to negative out-comes produces "helplessness" and a decreased motivation to execute con-trolling responses.

It should be noted that there are cases in which anxiety appears to have a *de-energizing* effect on behavior. For example, although anxiety facilitates the performance of aversively motivated responses, it can interfere with the performance of appetitively motivated responses. This effect is illustrated in the classical Conditioned Emotional Response (CER) paradigm of Estes and Skinner (1941), where an uncontrollable fear-evoking stimulus (CS) is pre-sented to an organism who has been trained to bar-press for reward, such as food or water. The degree of response suppression supposedly gives some indication of the strength of fear evoked by the CS. Such procedures, however, do not clearly discriminate between an organism who has been "im-mobilized" with fear and anxiety, and an organism who is genuinely "pas-sive" as a result of helplessness or depression. Measures of other response components, such as degree of somatic reactivity, are needed to help identi-fy the relevant emotional state (see also Rescorla & Solomon, 1967).

Anxiety also can have a disruptive effect on performance when the organism becomes "overmotivated" in the face of intensely aversive stimulation. This effect is illustrated by the famous inverted U-shaped arousal curve, where performance is held to be optimal in the middle range of the arousal continuum (Duffy, 1941; 1962; Yerkes & Dodson, 1908). So, for example, high-anxious individuals show poorer serial learning (Sarason, 1972) and recall (Spielberger et al., 1958) under stressful conditions than do low-anxious individuals. Again, care must be taken to distinguish between behavioral disruption due to anxiety-generated disorganization and that due to depression-generated passivity.

Somatic Component

There is substantial evidence that subjects exposed to stressful laboratory (Hodges, 1968; Hodges & Spielberger, 1968; Katkin, 1964, 1965) and natural-life anxiety situations (Epstein, 1972) respond with increased autonomic activity (sympathetic nervous system), especially as indexed by electrodermal and cardiovascular measures. Evidence on other autonomic measures, such as muscle tension, respiration rate, etc., is less compelling.

Recently, attempts have been made to measure the autonomic correlates of experimentally induced depression. Individuals made helpless by exposure to uncontrollable aversive events show a decrement in some aspects of sympathetic nervous system arousal (i.e., on tonic skin conductance level and habituation of specific skin conductance responses) (Gatchel, McKinney, & Koebernick, 1977; Gatchel & Proctor, 1976). Instructions to "think sad thoughts" have been shown to produce increases in dysphoric mood and in the physiological concomittants in clinical depressives (Teasdale & Bancroft, 1977). Similarly, changes in physiological processes have been found following covert rehearsal of affectively valenced self-referential statements (May & Johnson, 1973; Rimm & Litvak, 1969; Rogers & Craighead, 1977; Russell & Brandsma, 1974). Shaw (Note 4) found that visualizing depressive fantasies led to reduced arousal, as measured by galvanic skin response, a finding consistent with studies documenting lower indices of arousal for depressed versus nondepressed psychiatric patients (Lader & Noble, 1975).

Studies comparing nonclinical populations of individuals who are chronically high on ratings of anxiety with those who are chronically high on ratings of depression have been relatively rare. Few studies have directly compared an anxious nondepressed group with a depressed nonanxious group on physiological measures. Rather, typically an anxious- or depressed-only group is selected and then compared with a nonanxious or nondepressed control group, respectively. For anxiety, some studies have shown that high anxiety is accompanied by an increase in sympathetic nervous system arousal

(Becker & Matteson, 1961; Bitterman & Holtzman, 1952; Fenz & Dronsejko, 1969), although other studies have failed to find a difference between high- and low-anxious groups on measures of arousal (Katkin, 1965; Katkin & McCubbin, 1965; Koepke & Pibram, 1966). For depression, the available evidence is somewhat limited and similarly ambiguous (Gatchel et al., 1977; Lewinsohn, Lobitz, & Wilson, 1973; McCarron, 1973). For more definitive results, the responses of anxious and depressed individuals should be directly compared within the same study.

Cognitive Component

The cognitive component of depression is characterized in terms of both what and how depressed individuals think. Depressives have been found to differ from nondepressives in their manifest dream content, reporting themes of personal loss and failure (Beck & Hurvich, 1959; Beck & Ward, 1961; Hauri, 1976), and in their greater tendency to identify with the victimized rather than the victimizing on a pictorial projective device (Beck, 1961). On a multiple-choice measure of expectancy, Weintraub, Segal, and Beck (1974) found that the tendency to endorse negatively distorted outcomes correlated significantly with ratings of negative affect. Similarly, Hammen and Krantz (1976) found that depressed female college students were significantly more likely than were matched controls to endorse a negatively distorted interpretation of various hypothetical situations.

Measures of the symptom of depressed affect have been found to correlate significantly with self-ratings of pessimism and negative self-concept (Vatz, Winig, & Beck, Note 5), whereas measures of the syndrome of depression on the Beck Depression Inventory (Beck, Ward, Mendelson, Mock, & Erbaugh, 1961) correlate significantly with various depressogenic attitude clusters on the Jones Irrational Belief Test (Jones, 1968). Finally, two recently constructed measures, the Automatic Thoughts Questionnaire (Hollon & Kendall, Note 6), a measure of experienced cognitive content, and the Dysfunctional Attitudes Scale (Weissman & Beck, Note 7), a measure of irrational beliefs specific to depression, have been found to correlate significantly with measures of depression.

The cognitive processes that have most recently been found to be associated with depression are attributions about the causes of events (see Abramson, Seligman, and Teasdale, 1978, for a review). A number of investigators (Klein et al., 1976; Kuiper, 1978; Rizley, 1978; Seligman, Abramson, Semmel & von Baeyer, 1979) have found that depressives are particularly likely to attribute negative outcomes (e.g., failure) to internal factors (e.g., personal incompetence). Other investigators (DeMonbreum & Craighead, 1977; Nelson & Craighead, 1977; Wener & Rehm, 1975) have found that relative to nondepressives, depressed people tend to underestimate the amount of reinforcement they receive. They suggest that this apparent nonresponsiveness to reinforcement is a result of distorting cognitive activity.

Seligman and his colleagues (Klein & Seligman, 1976; Miller & Seligman, 1973, 1976) have noted differences between depressed and nondepressed subjects in their expectancies of success following feedback on chance and skill tasks. Depressed subjects tend to change their expectancies less after performance feedback on a skill task than do nondepressed subjects. Moreover, this tendency is relatively specific to depression, for anxious subjects (Miller et al., 1975) as well as carefully diagnosed schizophrenics (Abramson, Garber, Edwards, & Seligman, 1978) show changes in expectancy on chance and skill tasks similar to that of normal controls.

Seligman (1975) also has argued that depressives have trouble learning that their responses produce outcomes and, therefore, fail to recognize contingencies when they experience them. For example, depressed and helpless individuals have difficulty learning that there is a pattern for solving anagrams, even after they have correctly solved a given anagram (Hiroto & Seligman, 1975; Miller & Seligman, 1976). Similarly, depressed subjects fail to escape noise in a shuttlebox task, even after trials on which they successfully have turned off the noise (Klein & Seligman, 1976).

Finally, several studies have indicated that memory functions of depressives differ from those of nondepressives. Lishman and his associates (Lishman, 1972; Lloyd & Lishman, 1975) found that depressed subjects were more likely to recall negative events than were nondepressives. Isen, Shalker, Clark, and Karp (1978) found that individuals made depressed in the laboratory similarly showed increases in recall of negatively toned materials.

In anxiety, there is a considerable literature which documents the ruminative or worry component of the syndrome (see Wine, 1971, for a review). In an earlier review, Sarason (1960) cited a number of studies that provided evidence that high-anxious subjects are "more self-deprecatory, more self-preoccupied, and generally less content with themselves than subjects lower in the distribution of anxiety scales [p. 404]." When normals are involved in a test-taking situation, they tend to focus on the task at hand. Anxious subjects, on the other hand, show excessive concern with their performance; they dwell on the consequences of their failure; they are preoccupied with thoughts of how well or how poorly they are doing; and they ruminate about their own inadequacies relative to those around them (Ganzer, 1968; Mandler & Watson, 1966; Marlett & Watson, 1968; Neale & Katahn, 1968). Mandler and Watson (1966), for example, administered a series of digit symbol tasks to subjects low and high in anxiety as assessed by the Test Anxiety Questionnaire (Sarason, 1958). On the posttask questionnaire subjects were asked, "How often during the testing did you find yourself thinking how well or how badly you seemed to be doing [p. 276]?" On a

10-point rating scale, high-test-anxious subjects indicated markedly greater occurrence of such thoooghts than did the low-test-anxious group. Marlett and Watson (1968) reported a similar result, as did Neale and Katahn (1968), who, in a partial replication of this study, reported identical results on this questionnaire item. Similarly, Metalsky and Abramson (Note 8) found that anxious students exhibited an attributional style similar to that of depressives: They attributed bad outcomes to internal, stable, and global factors.

In summary, it can be seen from Table 6.2 that the experimental data are fairly consistent with the clinical evidence in showing a pattern of affective, behavioral, somatic, and cognitive hypoactivation for depression, and an opposite pattern of hyperactivation for anxiety. It is also apparent, however, that there is a great deal of overlap between the two syndromes. For example, there is a tendency for individuals to react affectively with both anxiety and depression when exposed to uncontrollable aversive events. Moreover, individuals who are chronically anxious or chronically depressed tend to show similar behavioral and cognitive deficits. There is a need for more direct comparisons of anxious and depressed individuals on the same measures within the same study.

Genetic Evidence

The genetic evidence is briefly reviewed here in an attempt to provide additional clarity in our understanding of the distinction between anxiety and depression. Unfortunately, the existing evidence raises more questions than it answers. This is due, in part, to the problems of differential diagnosis that were mentioned previously.

While the data seem to suggest that there are significant genetic factors involved in anxiety neurosis and psychotic depression (particularly bipolar affective disorders), the same does not appear to be true of neurotic depression (see DeRubeis, Note 9 for a discussion of this issue). Evidence for the genetic basis of affective disorders has been provided by family (Angst, 1966; Gershon, Mark, Cohen, Belison, Baron, & Knobe, 1975; Perris, 1966; Winokur, Clayton, & Reich 1964), twin (Bertelson, Harvald, & Hauge, 1977; Kallman, 1954; Rosanoff, Handy & Plesset, 1935), and most recently adoption (Mendlewicz & Rainer, 1977) studies. In general, the results strongly support the importance of genetic factors in the transmission of affective disorders.

Early pedigree studies on morbidity risks in families of manic-depressives showed that first-degree relatives of probands have a much higher risk for affective illness than that of the general population (cf. Zerbin-Rudin, 1967). More recent investigations using Leonhard's (1959) division of affective illness into bipolar and unipolar types have found that the overall risks for affective disorder in relatives are usually, but not invariably, found to be higher when the proband illness is bipolar than when it is unipolar (Angst, 1966; Perris, 1966). In addition, twin studies similarly have contributed supporting evidence by showing that the concordance rate for monozygotic (MZ) twins tends to be significantly higher than the rate for dizygotic (DZ) pairs (Bertelson et al., 1977; Price, 1968; Zerbin-Rudin, 1967). Thus, there is fairly convincing evidence of the genetic basis of major affective disorders, particularly those diagnosed as psychotic or bipolar.

Compared to the literature on the genetics of psychotic depression, however, there is a paucity of research on genetic factors in neurotic depression. In fact, there are only three studies that bear directly on this questtion. An early family study by Majer (1941, reported in Stenstedt, 1966) provides only limited information because of the low number of probands. The expectancy of affective disorders among the first-degree relatives was reported at only 4.5%, thus casting doubt on genetic factors in the occurrence of neurotic depression in the probands.

A second, much more extensive study reported by Stenstedt (1966) found a lifetime expectancy of 4.8%, a figure very close to that mentioned earlier in Majer's (1941) work. All affective disorders in the first-degree relatives of probands were considered together, however, because it was felt that making discriminations between "neurotic" and "psychotic" on a retrospective basis would be difficult. Thus, Stenstedt's (1966) results are not specific to neurotic depression.

The third study of the genetics of neurotic depression, known as the Maudsley Twin Study, was conducted by Shields and Slater (1966, reported in Price, 1968) and similarly found little support for genetic factors in neurotic depression. None of the MZ nor the DZ twin probands diagnosed "depressive reaction" had co-twins who were concordant for "depressive reaction." Thus, these findings argue against the notion that this disorder is heritable and are in essential agreement with those reported in the previously mentioned studies.

Whereas there is a lack of evidence supporting genetic components in neurotic depression, such is not the case with the anxiety neuroses. The results of three family studies (Brown, 1942; Cohen, 1951; McInnes, 1937) indicate that anxiety neurosis is found significantly more often in the first-degree relatives of anxiety neurotics than in controls. In addition, there are two twin studies that provide further support for the genetic basis of anxiety. Shields and Slater (1966) found concordance for anxiety neurosis in 7 of 17 MZ twins, but in only 1 of 28 DZ twins, clearly supporting a genetic hypothesis. A second twin study (Braconi, 1961), which was summarized and reanalyzed in Slater and Shields (1969), found perfect concordance in the co-twins of his 10 MZ twins, whereas only 3 of 8 DZ co-twins were concordant.

Although the literature is somewhat limited, the results of the existing studies support the hypothesis that there is a significant genetic loading for anxiety neurosis and psychotic depression, but there is no significant genetic loading for neurotic depression. This conclusion raises a real question concerning whether the syndromes of neurotic anxiety and neurotic depression, as well as the syndromes of psychotic and neurotic depression, are unitary constructs with common underlying etiologies, or two separate and distinct phenomena with different etiologies. However, considering the limitations of the genetic studies conducted thus far, particularly the small sample sizes, and the problems with differential diagnosis, we can conclude only that the syndromes of anxiety and depression can be distinguished on the basis of the degree to which genetic factors contribute to each disorder.

In sum, it appears that the existing literature suggests that even though the syndromes of anxiety and depression have their own typical patterns of symptoms associated with them, there is considerable overlap between them. Clinically, it is not uncommon for one individual to experience both syndromes simultaneously, although not always to the same degree. Experimentally, similar laboratory procedures produce symptoms of both anxiety and depression. Moreover, psychometrically identified anxious and depressed subjects respond similarly to the same experimental manipulations. Despite this apparent overlap clinically and experimentally, however, the genetic evidence seems to suggest that the syndromes are quite different in terms of their etiology. How can we account for the similarities and differences between the syndromes of anxiety and depression? In the following section, the various theories of each disorder will be examined in an attempt to address this question further.

THEORETICAL DISTINCTIONS

Uncontrollability, Uncertainty, and the Probability of the Outcome

Many different theoretical accounts of both anxiety and depression exist (e.g., Fischer, 1970; Friedman & Katz, 1974). Although each theory has a somewhat different focus than the next, at least two key concepts figure prominently in the etiological frameworks for both emotional syndromes. The constructs of certainty and controllability have been used in one form or another by several theorists to explain the syndromes of anxiety and/or depression. For example, some researchers have related anxiety to perceived uncertainty about the occurrence of bad outcomes (Epstein, 1972; Lazarus & Averill, 1972), whereas others have related anxiety to the perceived uncontrollability of bad outcomes (Mandler, 1972; Mandler & Watson, 1966). Similarly, some theorists hypothesize that depression results when the perceived occurrence of a bad outcome is certain (Beck, 1967; Melges & Bowlby, 1969), whereas others argue that depression is linked to perceived uncontrollability (Bibring, 1953; Seligman, 1975). Consistent with this overlap in theoretical accounts is the fact that the twin operations of both certainty and controllability have been used in the experimental laboratory to produce both anxiety and depression. Individuals exposed to uncontrollable bad outcomes subsequently become both helpless and depressed (Klein & Seligman, 1976; Miller & Seligman, 1976) and show increased anxiety and tension (Gatchel et al., 1975). Uncertain bad outcomes also induce subsequent depression (Miller, 1979b, 1980) and anxiety and tension (Miller, in press; Note 3).

What, then, is the relationship between uncertainty and uncontrollability on the one hand, and anxiety and depression on the other? Why are certainty and controllability thought to play such major roles in producing both anxiety and depression? One reason for this apparent overlap and confusion in the literature is the absence of clear and precise definitions, as well as the failure to recognize that the three major dimensions of perceived certainty, probability, and controllability are not independent of each other. The definition of uncontrollability used here is similar to that of Seligman (1975): An outcome is uncontrollable for a person when its occurrence is independent of the person's responses. In other words, the probability of the outcome's occurrence is the same regardless of what responses the person makes. It is worth noting, therefore, that the concept of control is dependent on the concept of probability.

By *probability* of outcome, we are referring to the perceived probability rather than to the actual, objective probability. Moreover, when making judgments about control, an individual needs to consider two different probabilities with respect to any one outcome. He or she may estimate *(a)* the probability of the outcome occurring if no response is made; and *(b)* the probability of the outcome occurring if he or she does respond. These are two independent estimates. Together they produce *certainty,* which is the perceived net probability of the outcome's occurrence; that is, the certainty or uncertainty of an outcome's occurrence is a conjoint function of the perceived probability of the outcome, given a response and given no response. Table 6.3 illustrates several possible combinations of these various beliefs about controllability and probability.

In Table 6.3, the X axis depicts the person's beliefs about the probability of a bad outcome, given that he or she makes the best response in his or her repertoire, $P(BO)/R$. These probabilities range from zero to one. The Y axis depicts the person's beliefs about the probability of this bad outcome, given that he or she makes no response, $P(BO)/\bar{R}$. These probabilities also range from zero to one. Although both axes represent *continuua,* we have divided

TABLE 6.3
Possible Combinations of Various Beliefs about Controllability and Probability

Momentary belief about the probability of a bad outcome given no response	Momentary belief about the probability of a bad outcome, given your best response		
	$P(BO)R = 0$	$0 < P(BO)|R < 1$	$P(BO)|R = 1$
$P(BO)|\overline{R} = 0$	A Uncontrollable, certain, Probability = 0	D Controllable, uncertain, Probability = intermediate/R or Probability = 0/$\overline{R}$	G Controllable, certain, Probability = 1/R or Probability = 0/$\overline{R}$
$0 < P(BO)|\overline{R} < 1$	B Controllable, uncertain, Probability = 0/R or Probability = intermediate/$\overline{R}$	E Uncontrollable, uncertain, Probability = intermediate/R or Probability = intermediate/$\overline{R}$	H Controllable, uncertain, Probability = 1/R or Probability = intermediate/$\overline{R}$
$P(BO)|\overline{R} = 1$	C Controllable, certain, Probability = 0/R or Probability = 1/$\overline{R}$	F Controllable, uncertain, Probability = intermediate/R or Probability = 1/$\overline{R}$	I Uncontrollable, certain, Probability = 1

them into thirds for the purpose of exposition. For any cell in the table we can specify (a) whether or not the person believes he or she has control over the outcome; (b) the person's estimate of the net probability of the outcome's occurrence; and (c) the person's certainty about whether or not the outcome will occur, which is based on this net probability. For example, in Cell A, the person believes that if he or she makes no response, the probability of the bad outcome occurring is zero, and if he or she makes the best response, the probability of the bad outcome occurring is also zero. Therefore, the person in Cell A believes he or she has no control over the outcome, believes the net probability of the bad outcome occurring is zero (assuming he or she makes the best response), and is completely certain about whether or not the bad outcome will occur (in this case, it will definitely not occur).

An example of a case of uncertainty is Cell B. In this case, the individual's estimate of the probability of the bad outcome occurring is zero if he or she responds and between zero and one if he or she does not respond. The individual has some control because there is a differential probability if he or she responds or not, although he or she is uncertain whether the outcome will occur. There is uncertainty, for if the individual does not respond, the outcome has a chance of occurring, with a probability somewhere between zero and one.

In addition to clarifying the relationship between controllability and certainty, Table 6.3 also analyzes the terms "helplessness" and "hopelessness." Only in Cells A, E, and I does the individual believe that the outcome is independent of his or her responses. Therefore, these are the three cases in the table where the individual perceives him or herself to be helpless. In Cells A and E, however, the perceived probability of the bad outcome's occurrence is at least less than one (Cell E) or is zero (Cell A), and so the individual can still be hopeful, or even certain, respectively, that the bad outcome will not occur. In Cell I, on the other hand, the individual is both helpless and hopeless, because the bad outcome is certain to occur and no response (not even not responding) will prevent it; that is, the perceived probability of the bad outcome's occurrence is one. Thus, although three cells represent helplessness, Cell I alone represents hopelessness. It is also worth noting that a belief in helplessness may be a necessary, although not sufficient, component of the belief in hopelessness. In other words, if an individual believes that the probability of the bad outcome occurring is the same whether or not he or she responds (helplessness) *and* that this probability is a *certain* one, then the individual is also hopeless. Both the belief in helplessness and an estimated probability for the bad outcome of one may be the necessary and sufficient conditions for hopelessness. As long as the individual believes that the probability of a bad outcome is less than one, irrespective of his or her perceived helplessness, the person is not hopeless. Thus, it is possible to be helpless without being hopeless, but it is not possible to be hopeless without simultaneously being helpless.

Four additional points should be mentioned in order to clarify the framework outlined in Table 6.3. First, the valence of the outcome referred to in Table 6.3 is negative. By "bad outcome" we are referring to either the absence or loss of a highly desirable outcome or to the occurrence of a highly aversive outcome. We as easily could have used "good outcome," which would have referred to the presence of a desirable outcome or to the absence of an undesirable or aversive outcome. In this case, Table 6.3 would have looked essentially the same, although reversed. For the ease of exposition, however, we will refer here only to "bad outcomes."

A second point to be clarified is what is meant by "highly desirable." For example, we feel that winning $1,000,000 in a lottery, is a "highly desirable" outcome, even though we believe that this has a very low probability and is uncontrollable (once we buy the ticket). Yet, we typically will not feel severely and persistently sad or anxious upon realizing this. Some notion, like Klinger's (1975) "current concerns" or the concept of "importance" (e.g. Roth & Kubal, 1975) is needed to supplement our account. In Table 6.3, therefore, we are referring only to highly desirable outcomes that are currently "on our minds," "in the realm of possibility," "important to us now," and so on. One simple definition of "importance" is that the individual believes that the outcome has (or had at some previous time) a probability greater than zero, and that if it were to occur, it would have major ramifications (either quantitatively or qualitatively) for the individual.

The third point concerns the definition of "certainty" used here. According to Webster's (1947) dictionary, "certain" is defined as "fixed, sure, inevitable, or unquestionable." It does not specify, however, "certain" with respect to *what*. In the literature, definitions of certainty and predictability typically have focused on various classes of information regarding future events such as: *what* the nature of the event will be, *when* and *where* it will happen, *whether* or not it will occur, *what can be done* about it, and what the *consequences* of the event may be (Epstein, 1972; Hollon, Note 10; Miller & Grant, Note 2) Individuals may also be uncertain about their estimates of the probabilities that are combined to produce "certainty" as it is used here. The present discussion primarily focuses on the aspect of certainty that is concerned with *whether* or not a particular outcome is likely to occur. While we agree that uncertainty and ambiguity are major components, if not the "hallmarks," of anxiety (Lazarus & Averill, 1972), we will only emphasize the uncertainty of *whether* a highly undesirable outcome will occur in our attempt to explain the distinction between the syndromes of anxiety and depression.

Finally, we will not use Table 6.3 to present a new theory of depression or anxiety. Rather, we will attempt to highlight the similarities and differences between these syndromes and to propose a unified formulation in terms of the etiological mechanisms of perceived controllability, probability, and certainty in order to explain these similarities and differences. These mechanisms have been used by a number of other theorists, and in the following section of the paper we will examine the prominent theories of first, depression, and then, anxiety, with regard to their reliance on the dimensions of controllability, certainty, and probability of occurrence of a bad outcome.

Theories of Depression

Psychoanalytic View

Freud (1917/1957) took the similarity of symptoms in depression (melancholia) and mourning as a point of departure in formulating the basic psychoanalytic view of depression. In brief, Freud argued that the environmental cause of both depression and mourning was the same: loss of a loved person or loss of some abstraction that has taken the place of a loved one, such as liberty or some ideal. In this view, only the symptom of lowered self-esteem distinguishes between the two affective states. Whereas people in simple mourning do not show loss of self-esteem, depressed people do. To account for the presence of lowered self-esteem in depression, Freud argued that if a person has strong oral dependencies from childhood and suffers the loss of a loved one, then he becomes angry. Because the premorbid depressive often has identified with the loved one, he turns the anger inward on himself. Consequently, the depressive espouses a low opinion of himself because he is so angry with the loved object for abandoning him and views the loved object as despicable.

More recently, Fenichel (1945) has extended the psychoanalytic view and has argued that depression resembles an addiction. In Fenichel's view, the premorbid depressive depends on the opinions others have of him to regulate his self-esteem. When "narcissistic" supplies such as love are not forthcoming from others, such a person loses his self-esteem and becomes depressed.

In summary, psychoanlytic views of depression are outcome-oriented. People show the symptoms of depression when bad outcomes occur. Although the psychoanalytic view can account for lowered self-esteem and sad affect in depression, it has more difficulty accounting for the negative cognitive set and inhibition of voluntary responding associated with depression. Let us examine Table 6.3 and see in which cells depression should occur according to the psychoanalytic view. The psychoanalytic view rests on people's beliefs about the probabilities of outcomes, and issues of control and certainty do not figure largely. Thus, all cells in which the net probability of a bad outcome's occurrence is high regardless of its controllability should be associated with depression; that is, psychoanalytic theory predicts that depression should occur in Cell I.

Neo-Freudian View

While early psychoanalytic theories of depression did not emphasize cognitive processes in the disorder, later developments in ego psychology (e.g., Bibring, 1953; Lichtenberg, 1957) gave primary importance to cognitive factors in causing depression. Bibring (1953) argued that when people come to believe they are helpless to attain aspirations, they develop the symptoms of depression. The cognition of helplessness was hypothesized to lead to decreased voluntary responding because the person believes that responding is useless. Similarly sad affect and lowered self-esteem follow from the belief that one cannot attain narcissistically charged goals. Finally, depressives' views that they are helpless are reflected in their beliefs that their actions are doomed to failure. Thus, in Bibring's view, all of the symptoms of depression follow from the cognition of helplessness about narcissistically charged goals. Although the neo-Freudian theory of depression accounts for the relation among the symptoms of depression better than does the older view, it is difficult to evaluate because some of its postulates are not well specified. For example, does the theory require that to become depressed, people believe not only that they are helpless but also that they will not attain desired outcomes? If it is the uncontrollability of bad outcomes that is crucial for depression, then depression should occur in Cells, A, E, and I. If, on the other hand, both lack of control and failure to attain desired outcomes are necessary for depression, then depression will ocur only in Cell I. Recent theorists (see later discussion) have attempted to be more precise in specifying the relationship between the belief that one's responses do not influence outcomes and the syndrome of depression.

Reinforcement Views

Interestingly, contemporary reinforcement views of depression bear some resemblance to early psychoanalytic views. The reinforcement views of depression regard the disorder as a reduction in activity that occurs when accustomed rewards are withdrawn (Ferster, 1965; Lazarus, 1968; Lewinsohn, 1974; Skinner, 1953). The laboratory paradigm of extinction of instrumental responding provides a model of the disorder. The depressive's failure to initiate responses is seen as similar to the lowered probability of a laboratory organism's response when that response is no longer followed by rewards. Lewinsohn (1974), the most recent proponent of a reinforcement view of depression, argued that a vicious cycle occurs in depression. Initially, infrequent rewards for responses serve to reduce the activity of the depressive. The reduced activity of the depressive, in turn, leads to even fewer rewards in the future. According to Lewinsohn, three major factors determine the number of rewards a person receives. First, the individual's personal characteristics such as age and attractiveness to others influence the number of rewards the individual receives. A second factor limiting the number of rewards a person receives is the availability of rewards in the particular environment. For example, few rewards may be available to anyone in the concentration camp setting. Finally, the person's own repertoire of behaviors, such as vocational skills, influences the number of rewards he or she receives.

The reinforcement view is outcome-oriented and noncognitive. By virtue of its disregard of cognition, it makes *no* prediction about which cells in Table 6.3 are associated with depression. Instead, it specifies that whenever a person receives a low rate of rewards, he or she will become depressed. The person's beliefs about control, probabilities of outcomes, and certainty are not relevant to whether or not he or she will become depressed. Although such reinforcement views explain retarded initiation of responding in depression by making an analogy to the extinction paradigm, they do not account for the affective symptoms, cognitive symptoms, and lowered self-esteem associate with depression.

Hopelessness View

Hopelessness theories of depression (e.g., Arieti, 1959; Melges & Bowlby, 1969) have evolved from clinical observations of depressed patients. In brief, hopelessness theories characterize depressives as very pessimistic about attaining their goals. These theorists argue that failure to attain desired outcomes in the present is not sufficient for depression; rather, people must believe they will not attain such goals in the future as well in order to become depressed. Thus, hopelessness theories of depression characterize the disorder as future-oriented. Although Beck (1967) has focused on features of self-blame and heightened responsibility for failure in depression, he also regards hopelessness as a core symptom. Similar to the psychoanalytic and reinforcement views, hopelessness theories of depression are outcome-oriented. However, hopelessness views strongly emphasize the role of cognition in depression. Hopelessness theories of depression, then, specify that depression should occur in Cell I of Table 6.3 because the person believes the probability of a bad outcome occurring is 1. While hopelessness theories of depression easily explain the sad affect associated with the syndrome, they do not explain the cognitive and motivational features of the disorder nor the depressive's negative view of him or herself.

Helplessness Model

Seligman and his colleagues (Seligman, 1975; Seligman, Klein, & Miller, 1976) originally proposed that the laboratory phenomenon of learned helplessness provides a model of human depression. In this view, the expectation that outcomes are independent of one's responses is sufficient for the motivational, cognitive, and affective components of depression. The motivational deficit in depression consists of retarded initiation of voluntary responses and is reflected in passivity, intellectual slowness, and social impairment. The logic of the helplessness hypothesis is that if people expect that their responses will not affect some outcome, then they will be less likely to make such responses. According to this model of depression, depressives have a negative cognitive set incorporating the belief that their actions are doomed to failure. This cognitive set also is hypothesized to result from the belief in response–outcome independence. Finally, although it proposes no mechanism, the helplessness hypothesis states that belief in response–outcome independence is sufficient for sad affect.

According to the original helplessness hypothesis, depression should occur in Cells A, E, and I because in these cells the person believes the outcome of interest is uncontrollable. The original hypothesis makes the interesting prediction that people will display the symptoms of depression even when they are certain a bad outcome will not occur if they believe the occurrence of this outcome is beyond their control (Cell A). Unlike outcome-oriented theories of depression, then, the learned helplessness model emphasizes the controllability rather than the occurrence of bad outcomes in the etiology of depression.

Recently, a number of investigators have pointed to shortcomings in the original learned helplessness model of depression. For example, the original hypothesis cannot deduce lowered self-esteem as a symptom of depression (Abramson, Seligman, & Teasdale, 1978; Blaney, 1977). In addition, the original hypothesis cannot explain variations in the generality and chronicity of depressive symptoms (Abramson et al., 1978). In response to these criticisms, Abramson et al. (1978) proposed a reformulation of the helplessness hypothesis based on attribution theory. According to the reformulated hypothesis, the kinds of causal attributions people make for lack of control influence whether their helplessness will entail low self-esteem and whether their helplessness will generalize across situations and time. Attributing lack of control to internal factors leads to lowered self-esteem, whereas attributing lack of control to external factors does not. Furthermore, attributing lack of control to stable factors should lead to helplessness deficits extended across time, and attributing lack of control to global factors should lead to wide generalization of helplessness deficits across situations. Alternatively, attributing lack of control to unstable, specific factors should lead to short-lived, situation-specific helplessness deficits. Finally, contrary to the original helplessness hypothesis, Abramson et al. (1978) assert that depressed affect occurs only in cases in which individuals receive, or anticipate that they will receive, uncontrollable bad outcomes. In addition, the depressed affect associated with the occurrence of bad outcomes will be greater when individuals attribute their lack of control over the bad outcome to internal rather than external factors.

It is important to emphasize that unlike the original hypothesis, the reformulated helplessness hypothesis deduces that the symptoms of depression will not necessarily covary in a one-to-one fashion. In other words, the reformulation predicts that the cognitive and motivational symptoms of depression will occur in Cells A, E, and I, with the generality and chronicity of these symptoms depending on the person's belief about the globality and stability of the cause of uncontrollability. Depressed affect, on the other hand, is predicted to occur only in Cell I. Note, the depressed affect will be greatest when the person makes an internal attribution for lack of control. Finally, lowered self-esteem will occur in Cells A, E, and I whenever the person makes an internal attribution for lack of control, but not when the person makes an external attribution for lack of control.

Unlike many other theories of depression, the reformulated learned helplessness hypothesis of depression emphasizes that depression is a syndrome made up of various components which have different etiologies. According to the reformulation, depressed affect is outcome-related. Self-esteem, on the other hand, depends on whether or not people attribute their lack of control to internal factors. Finally, the expectation that one's own responses do not control outcomes is sufficient for the motivational and cognitive deficits in depression. The generality and chronicity of motivational and cognitive deficits are modulated by people's beliefs about the globality and stability of the cause of uncontrollability. It is well known among clinicians that an individual does not always manifest all of the symptoms of depression. Beck (1967), for example, speaks of depressives who do not display sad affect yet display the other symptoms of depression. An important advantage of the reformulated hypothesis is that it can account for cases of depression that do not incorporate all of the symptoms of the syndrome. According to the reformulation, Beck's depressive, who does not display sad affect, is a person in either Cell A or E who, perhaps, makes an internal attribution for his or her lack of control but believes that although a bad outcome is uncontrollable, it is unlikely to occur.

Theories of Anxiety

Psychoanalytic View

According to Freud (1926/1959) anxiety is an affective state character-ized by specific unpleasurable quality, efferent, or discharge phenomena and the perception of these phenomena. Thus, anxiety consists of affective, physiological, and cognitive (perceptual) components, respectively.

Freud's views on the origins of anxiety changed considerably over time. In the early formulation a sharp distinction was made between neurotic and realistic anxiety. Whereas realistic anxiety, or fear, was assumed to be caused by the perception of real danger, neurotic anxiety was considered to be the consequence of an inadequate discharge of libidinal energy. Moreover, neurotic anxiety was believed to be a *consequence* of *un*successful repres sion (psychoneurosis), or the consequence of sexual excitement without adequate gratification (actual neurosis). Neurotic anxiety was believed to play no part, per se, in psychic conflict or in any successful repression; it was believed to appear only when repression failed. Thus, in the original formulation repression was considered to be a necessary but insufficient condition for neurotic anxiety.

In the later version of the theory, Freud (1926/1959) made a number of changes with respect to the notion of dammed-up libido and repression. The idea that libido could be transformed into anxiety was abandoned, and the relationship between anxiety and repression was reversed. Whereas in the original theory repression preceded anxiety and anxiety was believed to appear only if repression failed, in the new theory, anxiety preceded repres-sion and, indeed, was considered to be the prime *motive* for repression. Thus, anxiety was considered to play an essential role in psychic conflict and to precede and motivate repression, whether or not repression then proved to be successful. Finally, the causal distinction between neurotic anxiety and real fear was abandoned, and the anxiety associated with the instinctual drives was related to several typical danger situations.

Thus, according to the psychoanalytic view, anxiety is not transformed libido, but rather it is the reaction to an anticipated danger. The anticipated danger, which is learned early in life, is the loss of the loved object and the resulting helplessness arising from the nongratification of needs. The ego, as it develops, acquires the capacity to react with anxiety to a danger situation, thus "signalling" the possible advent of a danger situation. In other words, the ego learns or gradually becomes able to react with anxiety to danger or to the anticipation of it.

The psychoanalytic formulation suggests that anxiety is the reaction to the anticipation of a danger, where danger is defined as "powerlessness," or the lack of control of the gratification of needs. When individuals anticipate or experience danger, they perceive the probability of an undesirable outcome to be greater than zero, and they become anxious. It is not clear, however, whether this anticipated undesirable outcome is always perceived to be uncontrollable. If so, then this view predicts anxiety in Cells E and I of Table 3. If the perception of uncontrollability is not necessary and it is simply the anticipation or experience of danger which produces anxiety, then it will result in Cells F and H as well.[2]

Neo-Freudian View

The essential difference between the Neo-Freudian and Freudian schools lies in the degree of importance that they attach to environmental influences for the development of anxiety. Both schools concede that constitutional hereditary factors exercise an influence, but in the Neo-Freudian view (Adler, 1927; Fromm, 1941; Horney, 1937; Sullivan, 1953), "it is above all the environment which lays . . . the seeds of subsequent neurosis [Wyss, 1966, p. 517]." Anxiety is socially produced; individuals are made anxious by the conditions under which they live.

According to Sullivan (1953), anxiety is the experience of unpalatable tension that results from real or imaginary threats to one's security. It is elicited by the experienced disapproval and/or condemnation by significant others. It expresses the individual's anticipation or actual sense of being a failure. Sullivan argues that anxiety "temporarily cuts the individual off from his necessary environment and renders him helpless [Fischer, 1970, p. 34]." In large amounts it reduces the efficiency of the individual in satisfying his or her needs, disturbs interpersonal relations, and produces confusion in thinking. Anxiety varies in intensity depending upon the seriousness of the threat and the effectiveness of the security operations that the person has at his or her command.

In addition to the affective and physiological components of anxiety, the Neo-Freudian view also accounts for the cognitive and behavioral disruptions that often accompany the disorder. Particularly noteworthy is Sullivan's description of "selective inattention" as one of the security operations

---

[2]Anxiety is not predicted to occur in Cell A because there is zero probability that the undesirable event will occur. In Cells C and G the probability of the event is also certain not to occur as long as the individual responds or does not respond, respectively. Under these circumstances, the individual would not experience anxiety because he or she neither anticipates nor experiences the bad event.

employed to avoid coming to grips with the fundamental meaning of "I am not an adequate human being." The concept of uncontrollability does not figure prominently in the Neo-Freudian view of anxiety, although it may contribute to the individual's sense of being a failure. The certainty of the outcome does not seem to be a distinguishing feature because *either* the anticipation *or* the actual sense of being a failure will produce anxiety. The view tends to be primarily outcome-oriented, in that individuals show the symptoms of anxiety when they receive disapproval and/or condemnation from significant others. Thus, in Table 6.3, all cells in which the net proba- bility of the occurrence of a bad outcome is greater than zero should be associated with anxiety; that is, Cells E, F, H, and I.

Learning Theory

The early learning theories of anxiety (Dollard & Miller, 1950; Mowrer, 1939) were attempts to directly translate the fundamental principles of psy- choanalytic theory into the conceptual framework of a stimulus–response learning system. However, whereas psychoanalytic writers explicity differ- entiated between fear and anxiety, this distinction became more blurred among learning theorists. Dollard and Miller (1950) argued that although anxiety and fear are not exactly equitable, the former is a particular form of the latter.

Neobehaviorists, struggling with orthodox Hullian dogma, originally conceptualized Pavlovian fear-conditioning in terms of drive–reduction (Mill- er, 1951; Mowrer, 1939). The essential features of this learned-drive con- ception were that anxiety: *(a)* is learned; *(b)* can serve to motivate trial and error behavior; and *(c)* its reduction reinforces the learning of new habits. Later, learning theorists shifted to the view that temporal contiguity alone, and not drive reduction, was the essential factor in the acquisition of condi- tioned fear. They argued that fear is a conditioned response to pain and that when an organism experiences pain in a particular situation, stimuli present during the experence tend thereafter to elicit the emotional, physiological, and avoidance tendencies that were initially elicited by the pain. In other words, anticipatory reactions of pain occur in response to stimuli that were present during the experience of pain, and it is these conditioned or antici- patory reactions that are defined as fear or anxiety.

Thus, learning theories of fear and anxiety can account for the affective, behavioral, and physiological components of anxiety. However, this learn- ing explanation is explicit noncognitive and therefore makes no hypotheses about the notions of perceived controllability, certainty, or probability of outcomes, nor any predictions about which cells in Table 6.3 are associated with anxiety. It simply states that when individuals encounter a stimulus previously associated with pain, they will react with anxiety. Their accompanying cognitions cannot be explained by this view. Because Table 6.3 specifically addresses cognitive factors, the learning view of anxiety is not represented here.

Hopelessness Theory

Stotland (1969) postulated a theory of hope that delineates a number of propositions concerning the relation between the perceived probability and the importance of obtaining a goal, and the subsequent emotional and behavioral effects. "Hope" is defined as an expectation of greater than zero of achieving a goal. The degree of hopefulness is the level of this expectation or the person's perceived probability of achieving a goal.

According to Stotland, "The lower an organism's perceived probability of obtaining a goal and the greater the importance of that goal, the more will the organism experience anxiety [1969, p. 9]." While Stotland acknowledges Mandler's (Mandler & Watson, 1966) suggestion that blockage of an individual's sequence of responses is anxiety-producing, Stotland proposes further that any event that is perceived to reduce the expectation of goal attainment will tend to increase anxiety. Moreover, the importance of the goal also contributes to the amount of anxiety experienced, such that anxiety will increase with the rising importance of a goal with a low probability of attainment.

Anxiety is defined by Stotland as a negative subjective state as well as a state of physiological arousal. In addition to the affective and physiological characteristics that define anxiety, there is a motivational component that produces subsequent behavior effects. Stotland proposes that individuals are motivated to escape and avoid anxiety, and the greater the anxiety, the greater the motivation to act. In an attempt to reduce anxiety, the individual can either raise the expectation of attaining the goal or lower the importance of the unattainable goal. According to Stotland, however, if the individual lowers the importance of the goal, he or she then tends to become depressed. Thus, anxiety is a function of a low probability of attaining an important goal, whereas depression is a result of lowering the importance of a nonobtainable but previously desirable goal. As the probability of obtaining the goal increases somewhat, it is no longer necessary to devalue the goal; so depression lifts, although the probability remains low enough to produce anxiety.

Thus, the hopelessness theory of anxiety primarily emphasizes the probability of goal attainment. Individuals show the affective, behavioral, cognitive, and somatic symptoms of anxiety when they perceive that the probability of attaining an important goal is low. Controllability is only important in terms of its effect on the probability of goal attainment. Although lack of control may be one means by which the probability of obtaining the desired goal is reduced, it is not a necessary condition for anxiety. Thus, Stotland's hopelessness theory predicts anxiety in all cells in which the net probability of obtaining the desired goal could be low; that is, in Cells E, F, H, and I.

Helplessness Theory

Mandler (Kessen & Mandler, 1961; Mandler, 1964, 1972) proposed a theory of anxiety which emphasized the role of physiological mechanisms and their relation to the psychological state of helplessness. He suggested that a state of discomfort, unease, or distress are fundamental to anxiety, with no "necessary relation to a specific antecedent event" (Mandler, 1972, p. 368). Following Schacter's (1966) notion that emotional states are generated by visceral states and their cognitive assessment, Mandler argued that one particular set of cognitive and environmental conditions that may turn arousal into the emotion known as anxiety is the general state of helplessness. Helplessness occurs when there is an unavailability of task- or situation-relevant behavior. "In a state of arousal, the organism who has no behavior available to him, who continues to seek situationally or cognitively appropriate behavior, is helpless and also may consider himself, in terms of the common language, as being in a state of anxiety [Mandler, 1972, p. 369]."

Mandler emphasizes the interruption of plans or behaviors as a condition that frequently leads to a state of helplessness. When an organized sequence of behavior or an organized plan is interrupted such that the individual is unable to complete the plan either behaviorally or cognitively, he or she is in a state of arousal. In such cases where interruption leads to arousal and no appropriate behavior is available either to substitute for the original plan or to find alternate ways to the original goal, the individual then is in a state of anxiety. Thus, according to Mandler, interruption is a sufficient condition for arousal and the emotion of anxiety to occur, although it is certainly not necessary.

One additional point that Mander makes is that the extreme case of helplessness and the reaction to it lead to the state of hopelessness. Whereas helplessness is an immediate reaction to the situation and somewhat stimulus-bound, hopelessness is a more generalized feeling of not knowing what to do in any situation. Moreover, this state of hopelessness typically leads to lowered self-esteem and eventually to depression. Helplessness, on the other hand, produces the symptoms of physiological arousal, the affective experience of anxiety, and the subsequent disruption of organized behavior.

Mandler does not explicitly address the notion of control, although his meaning of helplessness is compatible with the definition of uncontrollability used here. It appears, then, that Mandler would predict a state of anxiety in all cases where the individual is unable to control the desired outcome (which for Mandler would be the completion of plan or behavioral sequence); that is, in Cells A, E, and I. The certainty and perceived probability of the outcome itself are not relevant here.

A second helplessness view of anxiety has been proposed by Lazarus and his colleagues (Averill, Opton, & Lazarus, 1969; Lazarus, 1966, 1968; Lazarus & Averill, 1972; Lazarus, Averill, & Opton, 1970; Lazarus & Opton, 1966). This view suggests that emotions are "a complex syndrome of loosely intertwined component reactions. Their unity or organization derives from the cognitive processes of appraisal which mediate between situational and dispositional (personal) antecedents and the subsequent response [Lazarus & Averill, 1972, p. 244]." There are three formal kinds of appraisal processes: (a) primary appraisal of the threat; (b) secondary appraisal of coping alternatives; and (c) reappraisal based on the flow of events and reflections.

Lazarus defines anxiety as an emotion based on the appraisal of threat which entails symbolic, anticipatory, and uncertain elements. Anxiety results when cognitive systems no longer enable a person to relate meaningfully to the world about him or her, and may be accompanied by behavioral and physiological manifestations. The symbolic nature of the appraisal means that the threats which produce anxiety are not concrete, immediate events, but rather, are related to ideas, concepts, values, or cognitive systems to which the person is heavily committed. When the individual finds that his or her system of interpretive schemata is not adequate for the situation, he or she becomes anxious. Moreover, anxiety is anticipatory, not simply as an apprehension of future happenings, but also as a failure to comprehend events occurring in the present. Finally, uncertainty in terms of the ambiguity of the threat results in anxiety since there is no clear action tendency possible. There is uncertainty not only with respect to the exact nature of the threat (primary appraisal), but also concerning what might be done about it (secondary appraisal).

Thus, when an event cannot be interpreted or given meaning, and it cannot be dealt with, there is a kind of helplessness. While anticipation allows for preparation, and hence the possibility of control, the increase in uncertainty causes the individual to be more apprehensive about the future, and therefore helpless with respect to available coping alternatives. This view of helplessness emphasizes both uncertainty and uncontrollability in the production of anxiety. When individuals are uncertain about the symbolic meaning of events, as well as what to do about them, they become anxious. Thus, according to this model, Lazarus would predict that Cell E would produce anxiety.

Comparison between Theories of Anxiety and Depression

The previous discussion was not meant to be an exhaustive review of all theories of anxiety and depression. Rather, it attempted to provide a brief overview of how each of the major theories accounts for the various components of the disorders and to focus on the role of the critical variables of interest here—perceived control, certainty, and probability of outcome—with respect to each of the theories discussed. Because most of the theories do not incorporate these exact concepts, however, some extension and interpretation was necessary in order to fit them into Table 6.3 and to make comparisons across theories.[3] Such a comparison indicates that the various theories have used similar concepts, although frequently in different ways, to explain both the syndrome of anxiety and depression.

There was considerable agreement among three theories of anxiety with respect to the "probability of outcome." Anxiety was predicted to occur in Cells E, F, H, and I of Table 6.3 by psychoanalytic, neo-Freudian, and hopelessness theories. These theories are outcome-oriented and suggest that when an individual perceives the probability of an *undesirable* outcome to be greater than zero, he or she will be anxious. Moreover, all of the theories of anxiety reviewed here predicted anxiety in Cell E, although the explanations differ, with some emphasizing the probability and others emphasizing uncontrollability.

With respect to depression, the theories generally agree that cell I would result in depression, although again some theories (e.g., Freudian, hopelessness) emphasize the high probability of a bad outcome, whereas others (e.g., helplessness) emphasize uncontrollability as the critical etiological variable. Thus, although there is general agreement among anxiety theorists that Cell E will produce anxiety and general agreement among depression theorists that Cell I will produce depression, there is less consensus about the mechanism producing these syndromes. Does hopelessness *or* helplessness produce anxiety? depression? The lack of clear definitions, and the confounding between these two factors have contributed to the confusion associated with them. This will be discussed in greater detail in the following section.

A second area of confusion is evident when we compare across anxiety and depression theories. It appears that the various theories predict that Cells E and I will produce *both* anxiety and depression. Is it possible for the same etiological factors to simultaneously produce two distinct syndromes in the same individual? How is it that the ambiguous probability of an undesirable outcome (uncertainty) *or* the perceived lack of control (helplessness) will produce both anxiety and depression? For example, Seligman (1975) and Bibring (1953) have argued that uncontrollability leads to depression, whereas Mandler (1972) and Lazarus and Averill (1972) have suggested that uncontrollability leads to anxiety.

In sum, an examination of theories of anxiety and depression with respect to the variables of control, certainty, and probability has revealed

[3]The learning theory of anxiety and the reinforcement theory of depression were included here because they are both important theories in their own right. However, they clearly do not fit into Table 6.3, for these theories are explicitly noncognitive.

two areas of confusion. Using Table 6.3 as a guide, it appears that: (a) there are different explanations for the same syndrome found in a particular cell; and (b) the different syndromes are explained by the same etiological factors. The remaining section will attempt to resolve these discrepancies.

THE DISTINCTION BETWEEN
ANXIETY AND DEPRESSION

The general trend that emerges from the foregoing review is that the various theories agree that anxiety occurs in Cell E, whereas depression occurs in Cell I. As discussed previously, the concepts of helplessness and hopelessness—defined in terms of controllability, certainty, and probability of the outcome—are the proposed mechanisms of greatest etiological significance. In the case of anxiety, which occurs in Cell E, the individual believes that the probability of an undesirable outcome given a response is equal to the probability of the outcome given no response, and he or she believes that the probability of this outcome lies somewhere between zero and one. In the case of depression, which occurs in Cell I, the individual similarly believes that the probability of the undesirable outcome is independent of his or her responses, but that the probability of the undesirable outcome is a fairly certain 1.0. Thus, whereas anxiety is characterized by helplessness and uncertainty with respect to the outcome, depression is characterized by helplessness and hopelessness.

It is evident from this particular formulation that the syndromes of anxiety and depression share a belief in uncontrollability, although they differ with respect to the perceived probability of the outcome. Thus, helplessness is equally a part of both syndromes (at least for Cells E and I) and may be an important defining component. In the case of anxiety, however, the belief in uncontrollability is not a necessary defining feature of the syndrome. Rather, it is the uncertainty about the outcome that produces the anxiety. Helplessness is only important to the extent that it increases the uncertainty about the outcome. In the extreme example of Cell E, the individual believes that the probability of the outcome is intermediate whether or not he or she responds. This is the case of the greatest anxiety because it is the maximum case of uncertainty; that is, both the probability of the outcome given a response and the probability of the outcome given no response are ambiguous. Anxiety also occurs in Cells F and H, although to a lesser degree because in each case one of the two probabilities is certain. For example, in Cell F, individuals believe that the probability of the outcome if they respond is uncertain, falling somewhere between zero and one, while they believe that the probability of the outcome if they do not respond is certainly zero.

This is still considered a case of anxiety, although relative to Cell E there will be less anxiety because there is less uncertainty.

According to the present view, then, although helplessness is not a necessary feature of all cases of anxiety, it may significantly increase the intensity of the syndrome. In the case of depression, helplessness plays a somewhat more complex role. The original formulation of the learned help-lessness model of depression (Seligman, 1974, 1975) focused primarily on the importance of the uncontrollablility of the outcome and gave little atten-tion to the valence of the outcome. Situations involving noncontingent posi-tive reinforcement were considered analoguous, in terms of uncontrollability, to situations involving noncontingent aversive stimulation; in both cases there is nothing the individual can do to affect the outcome. Seligman (1975) noted the similarities of these situations and speculated that "not only trau-ma occurring independently of responses, but noncontingent positive events can produce helplessness and depression [p. 98]."

The more recent reformulation of the learned helplessness model (Abram-son, Garber, & Seligman, 1980; Abramson et al., 1978) has altered this view somewhat and states that "only those cases in which the expectation of response–outcome independence is about the loss of a highly desired out-come or about the occurrence of a highly aversive outcome are sufficient for the emotional component of depression [Abramson et al., 1978, p. 65]." Because it is the expectation of both an uncontrollable *and* undesirable out-come that produces depressed mood, it is impossible to clearly separate the effects of uncontrollability from the effects of the bad outcome, per se, on this symptom. Abramson et al. (1978) argued that *both* beliefs are necessary to account for *all* of the various components of the symdrome (i.e., cognitive, motivational, affective).

Although the present view essentially agrees with the reformulation's (Abramson et al. 1978) emphasis on the undesirability of the outcome, we suggest further that it is the perceived *probability* of this undesirable out-come which is crucial for producing the emotional component. It is not simply the expectation of an uncontrollable, undesirable outcome which produces sadness, but rather it is the expectation that this undesirable event is highly likely to occur which is crucial. This view is considerably more outcome-oriented than either the original (Seligman, 1975) or the reformulated (Abramson et al., 1978) models of learned helplessness.

So, for example, consider the case of an individual who believes that getting an important job is uncontrollable; that is, his or her responses do not make a difference in getting the job. Rather, getting the job depends on the mood of the employer. According to our view, if the person believes that the probability of his or her getting the job is one (e.g., employer is in a good mood), he or she will be neither depressed nor anxious, even though the outcome is uncontrollable. Alternatively, if the individual believes that the probability of the outcome is between zero and one (e.g., the employer may or may not be in a good mood), he or she will be anxious. Finally, if the person believes that the probability of the outcome is zero (e.g., the employer is in a bad mood), he or she will be depressed. Thus, in all these cases the outcome is uncontrollable because the individual's responses have no effect on the outcome. The affect is determined by the person's perceived probability of attaining the desired outcome—the job—and not by how much control he or she has. There are, of course, cases where for some individuals the desired outcome is, in fact, having control. This being the case in the foregoing example, the individual would be depressed, regardless of the perceived probability of getting the job. The individual would be depressed as a result of not obtaining the goal of *having control* over getting the job. It is probably the case that in the real world having control is often a desired outcome in itself, particularly in cases related to one's sense of efficacy in the world. Thus, in such cases individuals would be depressed with respect to the goal of having control if they believed the probability of this outcome to be zero.

It is the emphasis on the perceived probability of obtaining a desired outcome—the degree of hopelessness—which is proposed as the major factor distinguishing anxiety from depression; that is, when individuals expect that their responses are independent of an undesirable outcome *and* that the probability of this outcome is certain (approximately equal to one), they will be depressed, whereas when they perceive the probability of the outcome to be more uncertain, they will be anxious.

This view is somewhat different from Seligman's (1975) earlier suggestion that anxiety occurs when an individual is uncertain about controllability, whereas depression results when an individual is "convinced that the threat is utterly uncontrollable [p. 93]." The present view suggests that it is the certainty of one's hopelessness—that is, the perceived probability of the outcome—rather than the certainty of one's helplessness that distinguishes anxiety from depression.

We suggest, further, that a belief in uncontrollability that is at times common to both anxiety and depression (e.g., Cells E and I) may account for some of the existing confusion in the literature regarding both theories of etiology and clinical descriptions of symptomatology. For example, the decreased initiation of voluntary responses common to both anxiety and depression may result from the shared belief that the desired outcome is independent of one's responses. Moreover, when this is a belief in personal helplessness as opposed to universal helplessness (see Abramson et al, 1978), the cognitive symptoms of ruminations and overconcern about personal inadequacies may result. Thus, it appears that it is the belief in helplessness, defined in terms of response–outcome independence, that may account for the overlap in the symptoms characterizing the syndromes of anxiety and depression, whereas it is the belief in hopelessness, defined in terms of the probability of the outcome, that may account for the differences between these syndromes.

The symptoms that are uniquely associated with each syndrome described earlier in Tables 6.1 and 6.2 also may be explained in terms of the etiological constructs of controllability, certainty, and probability of the outcome outlined in Table 6.3. In the case of depression, for example, sad mood is outcome-related and will occur in Cell I. Alternatively, deficits in initiating responses, lowered self-esteem, as well as negative expectations about one's ability to control future events result from the belief in one's own helplessness and thus will occur in Cells A, E, and I. There is considerably less experimental evidence relating cognitions of controllability, certainty, and probabilities to the physiological and vegetative symptoms of depression. Decreased sympathetic nervous system functions have been found to be associated with helplessness and therefore would be expected to occur in Cells A, E, and I. We can only speculate, however, that the vegetative symptoms such as sleeping and eating disturbances are associated with helplessness only when it is accompanied by hopelessness—Cell I.[4]

The symptoms of anxiety are not derived as easily from Table 6.3. The cells seem to differ more with respect to the intensity and type of anxiety and are characterized by somewhat different cognitions. Cell E, discussed previously, results in the most intense and most characteristic syndrome of anxiety with all of its affective, behavioral, somatic, and cognitive accompaniments. It is characterized by the belief in uncontrollability and therefore results in behavioral disruption, leading to deficits in response–initiation and poor task performance. Cognitive manifestations include ruminations about self-worth and lowered self-confidence. As a result of the perceived helplessness, there is the greatest overlap between the symptoms of anxiety found in Cell E and the symptoms of depression found in Cell I.

Cell F typifies what may be called "normal" anxiety. This is the case where individuals believe that if they make their best response, the outcome has a probability of occurring between zero and one, but if they do not respond, the probability of the bad outcome occurring is one. For example, if an unemployed individual goes on a job interview, there is a chance (probability > 0) that he or she will get the job. If, however, the individual does not go out on the interview, the probability of remaining unemployed

---

[4]Although the present view emphasizes the role of cognitive variables, such as the belief in helplessness and hopelessness, in the etiology of depression and anxiety, it recognizes that other factors, including physiological states, chemical depletions, heredity, hormonal states, and so on, may produce these syndromes in the absence of such beliefs.

is one. This is an example of a situation in which if a person tries, there is a chance the person will get what he or she wants, but if the person does not try, there is no chance that the desired outcome will occur. Because many life situations fit the specifications of Cell F, we all experience some anxiety, at least the affective symptom of anxiety, some of the time.

In summary, using the concepts of control, certainty, and probability of desired outcomes, it is possible to predict the various symptoms comprising the syndromes of anxiety and depression. We have suggested that the belief in helplessness accounts for the similarity between the syndromes and that differential probability estimates account for the differences. One final question to be addressed is: How is it that the syndromes of anxiety and depression can occur simultaneously within the same individual? Are the syndromes of anxiety and depression compatible according to the theoretical formulation described here? It appears from Table 6.3 that anxiety and depression are distinguishable points on a common continuum and that an individual is in either one state *or* the other depending upon the perceived probability of the desired outcome. We suggest, however, that it is possible for an individual to simultaneously experience both anxiety and depression. This may result from either: *(a)* rapid vascillations in the estimated probability of the outcome; or *(b)* simultaneous probability estimates of different outcomes.

In the first case, because probability estimates are subjective and are not typically based on verifiable facts, they are subject to rapid changes based strictly on personal belief. So, at one moment an individual may believe that the probability of the outcome is between zero and one and therefore feel anxious, whereas at the next moment he or she may believe that the probability of the outcome is zero, and therefore feel depressed. Although this does not account for the actual simultaneous experience of both anxiety and depression, it does explain the *apparent* co-occurrence in some individuals.

The second, and more convincing, explanation for the simultaneous occurrence of anxiety and depression is that the individual is making probability estimates about *different* outcomes. So, for example, an individual may be anxious because he or she believes that the probability of getting an important job is between zero and one, but is depressed because he or she believes that the probability of developing a meaningful heterosexual relationship is zero. In this case, the syndromes develop fairly independently and are dependent on the perceived probabilities of the different outcomes.

It is also possible for an individual to feel depressed with respect to one outcome and anxious about its particular ramifications. For example, while an individual may be depressed as a result of estimating that the probability of getting a job is zero, he or she may be anxious about whether or not he or she will be able to pay the bills. Here, the syndromes develop with respect to different outcomes, although the anxiety is a consequence of the ramifications of the first outcome.

Finally, an individual may be concerned about only one particular outcome, but may be anxious and depressed about different aspects of it. As mentioned previously, it is the question of *whether* an outcome will occur and the estimated probabilities that distinguish anxiety from depression. There are other questions, however, that are also likely to produce anxiety. These are: what will occur, when will it occur, how will the individual handle it, and what will the consequences be? For example, it is possible for individuals to be depressed because they believe that a tornado will definitely occur, but to be anxious about when it will happen and what the damage will be.

Thus, it seems logically possible for an individual to simultaneously experience both anxiety and depression. There is a need for further research, however, to demonstrate empirically the parameters of the various conditions that have been outlined here.

SUMMARY AND CONCLUSIONS

This chapter addressed the question concerning the similarities and differences between the syndromes of anxiety and depression. A review of the clinical and experimental evidence revealed patterns of symptoms that characterize each syndrome, although there was considerable overlap between them. The genetic evidence suggests that the syndromes appear to differ with respect to the contribution of genetic factors to each disorder. However, the genetic conclusions are tentative due to problems of differential diagnosis and small sample sizes. The review of the various theories of depression and anxiety revealed that although similar constructs are used to explain these syndromes, there is a need for greater clarity in terms of their definitions.

We have attempted to provide some clarity by outlining a theoretical formulation that encompasses many of the etiological mechanisms suggested by the earlier theorists. Using the concepts of perceived controllability, certainty, and the probability of desired outcomes, we have argued that a belief in helplessness characterizes both syndromes of anxiety and depression, whereas differential beliefs in hopelessness (probability of the outcome) distinguish the two syndromes. The symptoms of each syndrome that are shared by both (e.g., behavioral disruption and lowered self-confidence) are a result of the belief in helplessness. The symptoms that differentiate them (e.g., passivity and suicidal ideation) are a result of different probability estimates.

In order to test these hypotheses, however, further work is necessary in the area of classification and differential diagnosis. We have attempted here to distinguish between psychologically caused disorders, which in the past came under the rubric of "neurotic" anxiety and depression. Since the development of DSM III, however, the classification of "neurotic" has become obsolete. There is a need for new research that uses the current diagnostic categories including the bipolar and nonbipolar affective disorders, as well as anxiety and the various specific phobias. Such research should directly compare, within the same study, the affective, behavioral, cognitive, and somatic symptoms of individuals who have received these various diagnoses.

Finally, a need also exists for prospective, longitudinal studies that observe individuals before, during, and after an episode of anxiety or depression. In such studies, the individual's beliefs about control, certainty, and probability should be assessed. The results of these studies would provide evidence (either confirmatory or disconfirmatory) of the hypotheses concerning the similarities and differences between anxiety and depression that were outlined in this chapter.

REFERENCE NOTES

1. Beck, A.T. Personal communication, April 6, 1979.
2. Miller, S.M. & Grant, R.P. *Predictability and human stress: Evidence, theory, and conceptual clarification.* Unpublished manuscript, University of Pennsylvania, 1978.
3. Miller, S.M. *Monitors versus blunters: Validation of a questionnaire to assess two different styles of coping with stress.* Unpublished manuscript, University of Pennsylvania, 1979.
4. Shaw, B.F. *Subjective and physiological responses to depression inducing stimuli.* Paper presented at the Annual Meeting of the Canadian Psychological Association, Victoria, British Columbia, 1972.
5. Vatz, K.A., Winig, H.R., & Beck, A.T. *Pessimism and a sense of future time constriction as cognitive distortions in depression.* Unpublished manuscript, University of Pennsylvania, 1969.
6. Hollon, S.D. & Kendall, P.C. *Cognitive self-statements in depression: Development of an Automatic Thoughts Questionnaire.* Unpublished manuscript, University of Minnesota, 1978.
7. Weissman, A.N. & Beck, A.T. *Development and validation of the Dysfunctional Attitude Scale: A preliminary investigation.* Paper presented at the Annual Meeting of the Educational Research Association, Toronto, Ontario, 1978.
8. Metalsky, G.I. & Abramson, L.Y. *Attributional styles in depression and test anxiety.* Unpublished manuscript, State University of New York at Stony Brook, 1979.
9. DeRubeis, R.J. *Behavior genetic and nosological issues in the distinction between depressive neurosis and anxiety neuroses.* Unpublished manuscript, University of Minnesota, 1979.
10. Hollon, S.D. *Prediction, control, and subsequent stress: An expectancy-based theory.* Unpublished manuscript, Florida State University, 1977.

II

CONCEPTUAL APPLICATIONS

7

A Cognitive–Expectancy Theory of
Therapy for Helplessness and Depression

STEVEN D. HOLLON
JUDY GARBER

INTRODUCTION

Treatment research is typically atheoretical and pragmatic. To the practicing clinician, it is often more important to know whether something works than to know how it works. Drawing on Bandura's (1977a) distinction between mechanism and manipulation, interest in the *processes* that underlie change often develops in the aftermath of the serendipitous discovery of those *procedures* that produce change. Witness the order of development of Freud's dynamic theory, which followed the observed efficacy of Breuer's "talking cure," or the articulation of amine theory in depression (cf. Schildkraut, 1965), which followed the accidental discovery of the antidepressant medications.

Basic research, on the other hand, has typically focused on those theoretical mechanisms involved in the etiology of a disorder—an emphasis on process rather than procedure and on induction rather than remediation. Helplessness theory (Seligman, 1975) and the reformulated helplessness theory (Abramson, Seligman, & Teasdale, 1978; Abramson, Garber, & Seligman, Chapter 1 of this volume) are essentially process models of etiology and, as such, can provide guides to the development of process models of

173

HUMAN HELPLESSNESS

remediation. Although they ought not be contradicted by the results of outcome research, the theories themselves do not speak directly to the processes or the procedures involved in therapy.

In this chapter, we present a cognitive–expectancy theory of the process of change in clinical depression. We argue that a strategy that focuses on identifying and explicitly testing those negative expectations typically held by depressed individuals provides the most powerful, most expedient mode of clinical intervention.

In a recent article, Akiskal and McKinney (1975) suggested that there exists a biochemical "final common pathway" in depression. Any of several processes (e.g., environmental, cognitive, behavioral, biological) were seen as sufficient to initiate a causal chain of events leading to a common biological process. This biological process produces the full syndrome of clinical depressin, which, once triggered, takes on a life of its own.

We are postulating a cognitive "final common pathway," one in which negative expectations for the near and distant future play the central role. Although any of several different processes may serve to produce negative expectations—such as perceptions of lack of control, negative views of the self, deficits in obtained reinforcements, or disturbances in neurotransmitter balances in the limbic system—those negative expectations become the mediators of the full syndrome of depression. Although any of several different sets of etiological factors are seen as *sufficient* to produce negative expectations, those negative expectations are seen as *necessary* antecedents of the full depressive syndrome.

Helplessness (Seligman, 1975) and reformulated helplessness (Abramson et al., 1978, and Chapter 1 of this volume), as essentially etiological models, may detail the ways in which some people become depressed. In our development of a cognitive-expectancy theory of change, we focus on an exposition of a *process* model of change, one which is consistent with, although neither directly deducible from nor ultimately dependent on, the validity of either the original or the reformulated helplessness models. This cognitive–expectancy model is also compatible with Beck's larger cognitive model (Beck, 1967, 1976). It represents not so much a departure from as an elaboration on Beck's theory by specifying what we believe to be the most efficient sequences of procedures for effecting rapid and long-lasting change in depression. In fact, our formulation has been guided by our experience with Beck's cognitive therapy (Beck, 1964, 1967, 1970). We have sought to explain the processes of change manipulated by those procedures that comprise the cognitive–behavioral interventions.

The theoretical significance of the model lies in its attempt to specify the nature and sequence of those processes involved in the reduction of syndrome depression. Processes central to the remediation of a disorder need not be isomorphic with those processes central to its etiology. Many causal events either alter the nature of the organism in some permanent way or follow a definite temporal sequence (Hollon & Beck, 1979). We will argue that both types of processes may occur in depression and that the most effective interventions are those that teach compensatory cognitive–behavioral strategies. These strategies focus on expectations (an end process in the reformulated helplessness theory) rather than on attributions, even though the latter may have indeed preceded the expectational aberrations in the initial causal chain leading to the episode of depression.

The practical significance of the cognitive–expectancy theory lies in its potential to guide the application of existing therapeutic procedures (e.g., see Beck, Rush, Shaw, & Emery, 1979), and to encourage the development of new, sharply focused intervention techniques. In this chapter, we first present the cognitive-expectancy theory and examine its relationship to existing theories of etiology. We then evaluate the adequacy of the model vis-a-vis existing empirical outcome data. Finally, we conclude with a discussion of potential procedural innovations and practical implications that follow from such a model.

A COGNITIVE-EXPECTANCY THEORY

Cognitions and cognitive processes play a central role in the various cognitively oriented etiological theories of depression (cf. Beck, 1963; Seligman, 1975). Cognitive approaches to the treatment of depression (cf. Beck, 1964, 1967, 1970; Seligman, Note 1) have in common an emphasis on changing the depressed individual's beliefs and ways of processing information and suggest a variety of techniques for altering depressive symptomatology. Although these approaches agree on the general processes involved, they differ somewhat in terms of the specific focus and procedures utilized. The major issue for cognitive–behavioral interventions concerns specifying what procedures targeted at what processes provide the maximum change with respect to the magnitude, stability, and generality of change in depressive symptoms.

An overview of a cognitive–expectancy model is presented in Figure 7.1. The basic model, adapted from Hollon and Kendall (1979), presents a functional analysis of the interrelationships between antecedent stimulus events (Sd's), organismic variables including cognitions (Cog 1) and affective and autonomic reactions (Aff/Auto 1), voluntary motoric behaviors (R's), and consequent environmental events (S*'s). As in all cognitive theories, cognitions are seen as: (a) mediating behavioral responses to events; and (b) directly determining the nature and intensity of affective reactions (Mahoney,

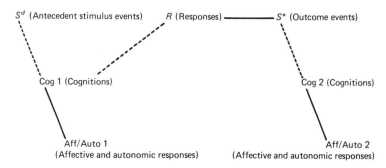

Figure 7.1. This is a graphic example of cognitive–behavioral functional analysis.

1977). Both classical and operant learning paradigms can be incorporated within this S-O-R framework, with the vertical dimension representing the classical paradigm and the horizontal dimension representing the operant paradigm. In both instances cognitions are viewed as playing a central mediational role (see Bandura, 1977b; Bolles, 1972; Grings, 1973; or Mahoney, 1977, for more detailed critiques of peripheralistic, as opposed to centrally mediated, learning theories). We have added the additional component of cognitive evaluations (Cog 2), with the attendant affective and autonomic components (Aff/Auto 2) following those responses (R's) that produce the consequent outcome events (S*'s).

Specific classes of cognitions are more likely to occur at different times. For example, in Figure 7.1, expectations will occur at Cog 1 and play a larger role in the maintenance and/or treatment of depression, whereas attributions of causality occur at Cog 2 and are more cental to the etiology of the disorder. Figure 7.2 presents a partitioning of what we regard as the major classes of cognitions central to depressive processes: perceptions, attributions, beliefs, values, and expectations. We assert that attributions of causality typically refer to events that have already occurred; expectations

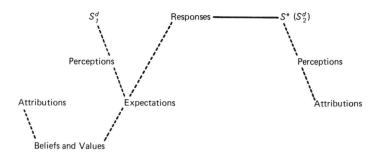

Figure 7.2. This diagram presents the organismic components of the S-O-R model.

refer to the subjective probabilities held regarding events in the near and distant future. Attributions may or may not contribute to the formulation of expectations, but it is the expectation which most directly produces the concurrent affect and subsequent behavior. As we shall describe in the sections to follow, expectations are seen as the *end point* of a cognitive causal chain. Although attributions may well play a major part in the initiation of an episode (and, perhaps, subsequent expectations), it is the expectation which is seen as most directly impacting key affective and behavioral processes.

A Taxonomy of Cognitive Processes

The distinction between expectations and attributions, based on each process's temporal relationship to external events, is crucial to our argument. It is this difference in temporality which, we argue, makes expectational processes the most *feasible* point of therapeutic intervention. In the sections to follow, we expand our discussion of the various classes of cognitions that comprise our taxonomy.

Perceptions

The first cognitive feature is the perception of the stimulus event (S_d). Perception includes identifying, discriminating, recognizing, and judging objects and events by means of sensory information. Perception, at some level, is, of course, essential for an event to have an impact on subsequent cognitions and behaviors. Furthermore, the recognition of contingencies between classes of events may be essential for learning. For example, people are not much affected by paired stimulation unless they recognize that the events are correlated (Brewer, 1974; Dawson & Furedy, 1976; Dulaney, 1968; Grings, 1973). When contingency awareness and conditioning are measured concurrently, predictive stimuli do not elicit anticipatory reactions until the point at which awareness is achieved. Alternatively, even in the absence of a specific objective event, the subjective perception of its occurrence may influence subsequent responses.

Many of the cognitive distortions identified by Beck (1963, 1967) as occurring in depressives are distortions in perception. *Arbitrary inference,* the process of drawing a conclusion that is contrary to the objective evidence in a situation, represents one such example. Other examples include *selective abstraction,* the drawing of an inference based on only part of the information available in a situation; *magnification,* the tendency to exaggerate the importance of an event; *minimization,* the tendency to underestimate the importance of positive events; and *all-or-none* thinking, the tendency to perceive situations in absolute terms.

Attributions

The second cognitive component involves the attributions made for events. Attributions are simply the causes one assigns to an event or, less important for our purposes, those characteristics ascribed to an individual or object (Heider, 1958; Jones & Davis, 1965; Kelly, 1967). Attributions are by no means necessary or automatic processes in the perception of events. An individual may or may not make an attribution in a given situation (Wortman & Dintzer, 1978). When individuals do make attributions, however, the attribution made can differentially influence subsequent cognitions, affects, and behaviors.

Recently, there has been increasing interest in the role of attributional processes in the etiology of depression (Abramson et al., 1978; Klein, Fencil-Morse, & Seligman, 1976; Kuiper, 1978; Metalsky & Abramson, in press; Rizley, 1978; Seligman, Abramson, Semmel, & von Baeyer, 1979). In general, these investigations find that depressives are more likely to make internal attributions for negative events (i.e., failure) and external attributions for positive events (i.e., success) than are nondepressives.

Beliefs

The third component of the model involves the beliefs held by the individual. Fishbein and Ajzen (1972) define beliefs as the subjective probability that an object has a particular characteristic.[1] Beliefs do not exist in isolation but are often associated with other beliefs in an organized system (Kihlstrom & Nasby, in press). The centrality of a belief, that is, its role in the individual's belief system, can be defined in terms of its degree of connectedness with other beliefs (Rokeach, 1968). For example, beliefs about one's own characteristics and capcities, the *self-concept,* may play a particularly central role in the individual's belief system.

Values

The fourth major component, values, represent important life goals or standards of behavior (Oskamp, 1977). Values are evaluative and represent relatively arbitrary preference hierarchies, either chosen or acquired, by an individual.

Expectations

The fifth and, for our purposes, major component of this model is the expectation. With the growing emphasis on cognitive views of behavior, the concept of expectancy is assuming an increasingly prominent place in con-

---

[1]Of course, attributions and expectations can be defined as specific types of beliefs. Attributions can be defined as the subjective probability that an event had a specific cause. Expectations can be defined as the subjective probability that an event will occur.

temporary psychological throught (Bandura, 1977a; Bolles, 1972; Heneman & Schwab, 1972; Irwin, 1971). An expectancy is a propositional statement about the anticipated nature of events. It is a person's subjective estimate that a given event is likely to occur.

Bandura (1977a) suggested that there are two important types of expectancies: (a) an outcome expectancy, which is a person's estimate that a given behavior will lead to certain outcomes; and (b) an efficacy expectancy, which is the conviction that one can successfully execute the behavior required to produce the outcome. These two types of expectancies correspond to the distinction between universal and personal helplessness suggested by Abramson et al. (1978). In addition to expectancies about controllability—responses lead to outcomes—one can also have expectancies about predictability—stimulus events (CS) signal the occurrence of other stimulus events (UCS). The notion of controllability typically has implications for motivation and behavior, whereas predictability has implications for affect.

Cognitive representations of future outcomes generate current motivators of behavior. The expectation that responding in a certain way will result in anticipated benefits or avert future difficulties may help produce a particular behavior (Bolles, 1972). The expectation of reinforcement is seen as motivating the associated behavior. Thus, behavior is largely controlled by voluntary, decisional processes that are influenced by response–outcome (R-S*) expectancies, whereas affect tends to be more automatic and autonomic and may be more influenced by event–outcome (Sd-S*) expectancies.

The Acquisition of Cognitions

According to Bandura's (1977a) social learning analysis, expectations develop from four major sources of information: performance accomplishments, vicarious experiences, verbal persuasion, and physiological states. Cognitive events are induced and altered most readily by experiences of mastery arising from successful performances. The strength of one's self-efficacy expectancy determines the amount of effort and persistence in the behavior. A meaningful expectancy analysis, therefore, requires a detailed assessment of the magnitude, generality, and strength of the expectations, measured with the same precision used to assess changes in behavior.

Both beliefs and values are generally considered to be learned. A variety of factors can operate in the acquisition process. Direct personal experiences, parental influence, peer and reference group norms, and mass media influences may all play a role. There is some evidence that attributional styles that are stable over time vary across individuals (Seligman et al., 1979), although it is not clear how these tendencies are acquired. The processes behind individual differences in cognitive styles are particularly poorly understood. For example, although Beck's cognitive model clearly describes distinct depressive styles in perception, no clear statement regarding the acquisition of these styles has been proposed.

It is likely that the different classes of cognitions influence one another reciprocally over time. The literature on perceptual defnese (Brown, 1961) suggests that values or hedonic relevance factors influence the nature of the perceptual process. Beliefs appear to be particularly stable over time, and it is likely that preexisting beliefs play a major role in both perceptual and attributional processes.

The discussion thus far has described the architecture of a cognitive system for depression. The various components of cognition are hypothetical constructs: an attribution represents the way things were; a belief represents the way things are; and an expectancy represents the way things will be. These processes are basically automatic habits of thought of which the individual is not always totally aware at the time, although if asked he or she may be able to produce them. None of these cognitions is necessarily a veridical reflection of reality, but instead represent the individual's perception of reality. Moreover, the certainty with which the individual maintains these beliefs determines the magnitude, stability, and strength of his or her subsequent responses, both behavioral and affective.

Thus, the current framework is a cognitively mediated model rather than a simple S-R model and is consistent with Bandura's (1977a) self-efficacy theory, Beck's (1967) cognitive schema, Bower's (1978) information processing theory, Ellis' (1962) A-B-C model, and Seligman's learned helplessness model (1975). The direction of causality among the various components is interactional rather than unidirectional, with each component having an effect on the others. Of course, any specific cognition can be influenced only by antecedent cognitions, and any given cognition can only influence subsequent cognitions. A careful recognition of the temporal dimension in interactive processes can help clarify the nature of the causal process.

In any given situation, depending on their particular cognitive structures, individuals may differ in the way they extract and combine information from the environment. Beck (1967) referred to this cognitive structure as a schema. A schema can be defined as a "complex pattern, inferred as having been imprinted in the organism's structure by experiences that combine with the properties of the presented stimulus object or of the presented idea to determine how the object or idea is to be perceived and conceptualized [English & English, 1958, p. 258]." It is the mode by which the environment is screened, coded, evaluated, and organized into relevant psychological facets. Moreover, even in the absence of immediate environmental stimulation, schemata can channel thought processes. The schemata pattern the stream of associations and ruminations as well as the cognitive responses to external stimuli.

Among the various components of the cognitive schemata, beliefs tend to be the most stable over time. Beliefs play significant roles in the way information is processed. How we organize information tends to influence how we organize subsequent input. There is a kind of self-fulfilling prophesy or confirmation bias (Snyder, Tanke, & Berscheid, 1977) that affects the process of assimilation and accommodation of new information. The focus of attention, attributions, and memory for events are influenced by existing belief systems. In turn, attributions then serve to confirm or disconfirm the original beliefs. Similarly, expectancies about the future are influenced by both present beliefs and explanations of the past. It is the expectancies, however, which, mediated by motivation, most directly influence behavior and affect.

The schematic diagrams presented in Figures 7.1 and 7.2. represent the typical sequence of events, cognitions, and responses in the development of depression. When an event is perceived to occur, an attribution that both influences, and is influenced by, the existing belief system may be made. This leads to the formulation of an expectancy about future action and events that then determines the response (both motoric and affective). Following the response, a new event (outcome or S*) may occur, which again may be followed by an attribution, and so on. Thus, although some attributions precede expectations, any given attribution for an event follows that event, whereas expectations about that event preceded the event and, hence, the attribution.

Expectancies are not necessarily tied to attributions for previous events and may be influenced instead by a variety of other factors that intervene between an original attribution and a later expectancy. For example, new experiences or new information about the past event or future consequences can alter the expectancy that logically might have followed from the original attribution. This hypothesized time lapse between attributions at Cog 1 and expectancies at Cog 2 has important immplications for subsequent responses.

The end result of the sequence of cognitions are behavioral, emotional physiological, as well as additional cognitive, responses. With respect to depression, specifically, these include such symptoms as dysphoric mood, passivity, low self-esteem, pessimism, and guilt. These various symptoms may result from the various cognitive components. For example, self-esteem is hypothesized to depend on the attributions made for events, with internal attributions for negative events leading to low self-esteem (Abramson et al., 1978). It is the expectancy of not obtaining desirable outcomes, however, that produces such symptoms as behavioral passivity, lack of motivation, and pessimism. The magnitude and certainty of these negative expectations about near and distant events produce the dysphoric mood that defines the syndrome. It is hypothesized here that negative expectations about the future produce much of the depressive symptomatology, and therefore, the cognitive-expectancy model of intervention suggests that the major focus of the process and procedure of therapy should be on expectations.

A COGNITIVE– EXPECTANCY THEORY OF INTERVENTION

The cognitive–expectancy theory is not intended to be a unique theoretical formulation of the etiology of depression. With regard to theory, the model overlaps with the general cognitive models of Bandura, Bower, and Ellis, and with the more specific models of depression by Beck and Seligman. Rather, the present model is an attempt to generate a theory of therapy for depression, one which is compatible with existing theories of etiology but which incorporates existing evidence regarding the efficacy of various intervention procedures into a coherent model of change. It provides a component analysis of cognitive and behavioral change processes in order to determine the most efficient and powerful procedures for producing change.

Because the cognitive–expectancy model is interactive, altering any one of the components of cognition should, in turn, alter the other components. The goal of any intervention is, of course, the eventual amelioration of undesirable symptomatology (i.e., dysphoria, lack of energy, anhedonia, hopelessness). The potency of intervening at various points in the model should be evaluated in terms of the magnitude, stability, and generality of change of these various symptoms. According to the S-O-R model, simply changing the environment (Sd-S*) or the behaviors (R) is not a sufficiently powerful intervention, particularly with respect to stability over time, or generality across situations, of the symptoms.[2] This has been a consistent criticism of strict behavior modification programs based on peripheral S-R learning models (cf. Bandura, 1977b; Beck, 1970; Hollon & Kendall, 1979; Mahoney, 1977). Although these approaches may alter behavior in the laboratory, where the reinforcement contingencies are explicit and powerful, once the individual is away from the laboratory and the external reinforcers, the behavioral improvements disappear rapidly. As a result of these failures, clinicians and researchers alike have begun to examine the role of cognitions in behavior change. Cognitive theorists have stopped asking whether they should intervene at the level of cognition or behavior and have begun to ask which cognitive processes are most important. Should interventions be made at the level of perception, attribution, belief, value, or expectation?

---

[2]The term "simply" here refers to the restriction of intervention technique, not the ease with which those techniques can be accomplished. Important external reinforcers are frequently beyond the therapist's direct control, particularly when clients are adults seen in a noninstitutional setting—the modal depressed client.

We will argue that the most efficient point of intervention is that which stands at the end, rather than at the beginning, of the presumed causal chain. Specifically, those interventions that most directly impact on expectations, rather than perceptions, attributions, beliefs, or values, ought to produce the most rapid and the powerful change.

Onset of an Episode

Let us provide an example of this model in action. As shown in Figure 7.3, an individual competes for a job with several others (Sd), engages in various activities (e.g. submitting a resume, going to an interview (R's), and does not receive the position (S*). The individual can then make any of several attributions for not getting the job. According to the reformulated helplessness model, if the individual makes a global, stable, internal *attribution* (e.g., "I am incompetent"), he or she is most likely to become depressed over the event. So far, we have described the *onset* of an episode of depression and have done so largely by recourse to an attributional mechanism. Also note that one component of the attribution, specifically, *stability,* involves a temporal component. It is likely that the characteristic (incompetence) seen as causal to the disappointing outcome will remain constant over time, remaining a factor in future situations. When an individual *thinks about* a stable characteristic interfering with obtaining desired outcomes in the *future,* that individual is generating an *expectation* about the future. An individual may well make an attribution to some stable characteristic without considering the implications of that stability. For example,

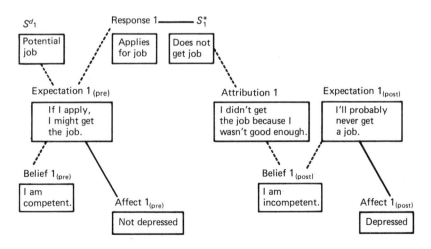

Figure 7.3. This diagram traces the onset of an episode of depression in terms of the model.

an individual can make an attribution to stable factors without necessarily generating an expectation (e.g., "I didn't get the job because I am incompetent"), but as soon as the individual considers the implications of that attribution (e.g., "Because I am incompetent, I will never get another job"), he or she is, by definition, generating an expectation. We will argue later that one essential difference between sadness (or normal grief) and depression (or melancholia) is the generation of negative expectations. The individual who does not get a job is sad, the individual who believes he or she will never get a job is depressed.

We have now generated an episode of depression in accordance with the reformulated helplessness model. The individual has experienced an undesirable outcome (it as easily could have been the loss of an important relationship) and has attributed that outcome to an internal, stable, global cause—his or her own incompetence. The individual's belief prior to this sequence, that he or she was generally competent, has been altered such that he or she now holds a belief in personal incompetence. The generality of the attributed causal factor leads to the expectation of nonsuccess across disparate situations, and the stability factor of the attribution makes it likely that the individual will generate expectations of subsequent nonsuccess in future endeavors. Given this constellation, the affect is one of profound dysphoria.

Maintenance of the Episode

We now move into the maintenance phase of the episode. As depicted in Figure 7.4, the already depressed individual enters the next situation convinced of his or her own incompetence. Upon encountering the stimulus of a second potential job opening, the belief in personal incompetence is likely to lead to the formulation of a negative expectation, namely that, even if he or she tries, he or she still will not get the job. Note that we are not dealing directly with an attribution for a past event at this point, we are dealing with an expectation generated from a belief generated by an earlier attribution. The relevant expectation concerns the *events to come,* and the relevant attribution concerns the *events that have occurred.* The relevant belief has served as the unit of cognition that has stayed stable over time from the first to the second situation; after being altered in the first situation from one of competence to one of incompetence, it has bridged the temporal gap between the prior attribution and the current expectation. Note that the prior attribution, in a sense, has led to the current expectation. Hence, prior attributions at times may cause subsequent expectations.

The individual, now expecting not to succeed even if he or she engages in the appropriate behaviors, does not apply for the job. The individual's

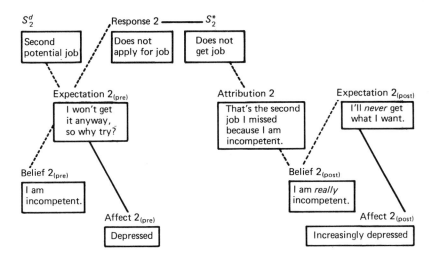

Figure 7.4. This diagram illustrates the next phase of the model—maintenance of an episode of depression.

nonactivity guarantees nonsuccess; one does not get jobs when one does not apply for them. Note that the individual's negative expectation has had two consequences: *(a)* he or she has not acted in a potentially adaptive fashion; and *(b)* he or she has experienced an increase in dysphoria even prior to the time for action and prior to the time when the actual event (obtaining or not obtaining the job) could possibly have occurred. These two consequences represent, respectively, the behavioral and affective consequences of negative expectations. The individual is passive, and, prior to the actual point of nongratification, the individual grieves for the loss. This capacity of humans to anticipate loss or disappointment and to respond affectively in advance of that event represents a major distinction between cognitive (or cognitive–behavioral) and strictly behavioral theories of depression.

Note also that we have not postulated any deficit or distortion in the individual's sytem of values. The individual need not have any desire to fail or desire to suffer; he or she need have no retroflected anger against the self to cathart nor any guilt to expiate. It is only necessary that the individual *expect* that he or she cannot do something that he or she values greatly. As hypothesized in the reformulated helplessness model, it may even be the case that the greater the value (importance) of the goal, the more severe the dysphoria over its perceived nonobtainability. This emphasis on disruptions in the expectational side of the expectancy–value theory of motivation (Heckhausen, 1967; Lewin, 1935) rather than on distortions in values or desires represents a major distinction between cognitive (or cognitive–behavioral) and traditional dynamic theories of depression.[3]

There is a third, essentially cognitive, consequence resulting from this expectancy-mediated passivity; that is, the depressed individual, by not acting, confirms his or her own negative expectation. He or she does not get the desired job. The attribution, if one is made, is similar to that made for the precipitating event—specifically, "Again, I have failed to obtain a job *because* I am incompetent." The effect is to provide yet another piece of evidence to support the belief that one is incompetent. The individual does not have to *want* to believe in his or her own lack of ability; he or she may even *wish* that it were not so. But it would be a very dysfunctional organism, indeed, which could not perceive what seem to be the facts in the situations—two job possibilities and two instances of failure. The problem, of course, lies with the errors in thinking based on the inaccurate attributions, although from the individual's point of view the problem lies in a deficit in his or ability to get a job. The individual has engaged in an instance of *self-fulfilling prophecy;* he or she has acted in accordance with an inaccurate belief (by not trying for the job) in such a way as to generate evidence that seems to confirm that initial belief. The individual has not acted irrationally; rather, the individual has acted rationally given an inaccurate premise. We shall return to this point later.

Reversal of the Episode

At this point, the individual is depressed; he or she is without a job and is convinced of his or her own incompetence. This is the point in the sequence of events at which the individual is most likely to consult a professional therapist. What is the referral question? Typically, the individual approaches the therapist for help in reducing the symptoms of depression: the negative affect, sense of personal helplessness and/or hopelessness, behavioral lethargy, motivational difficulties, and vegetative symptoms that comprise the syndrome of depression (Beck, 1967). The individual typically leaves

[3]There is, of course, a wide range of dynamic theories of depression, several moving beyond Freud's classic retroflected anger model (Freud, 1917). Recent revisions by Jacobson (1971) and Arieti and Bemporad (1978), for example, rely heavily on ego mechanisms, which are, in part, related to expectational processes. Bibring's (1953) formulation of depression, although still retaining a place for unconscious, repressed motivational aberrations, emphasized the role of the conscious perception of hopelessness in the etiology of depression and served as an important point of departure for subsequent, nondynamic cognitive formulations. Even though we see little justification for retaining a role for unconscious motivational processes, we are struck by the increasing tendency of revisionist dynamic theorists to incorporate expectational mechanisms in their theories.

unchallenged the belief in his or her own inability; the therapist is asked to help the client feel better despite the perceived deficits or to provide skills to overcome those deficits rather than to explore the validity of this perception.

Figure 7.5 presents a schematic diagram that depicts the optimal point of intervention from the perspective of a cognitive-expectancy theory. Paralleling the maintenance phase of the episode in Figure 7.4, the client enters the situation convinced of his or her own incompetence. Presented with a third possible job opportunity, the client generates the following expectation: "I won't get the job anyway, so why try?". At this point, the therapist directly intervenes, remarking, "How can you be sure? Although you don't know for sure that you won't get the job, you do know that if you don't try, you can't get the job." The emphasis is on altering the patient's expectation, or at least on questioning the certainty with which the client holds that expectation. Assuming, as the reformulated helplessness model does, that the initial attribution to incompetence was incorrect, the client should have some greater than zero probability of success, *if the necessary behaviors are emitted.* Once the behaviors are emitted and once some one or more successful outcomes are experienced, the client begins to be confronted with

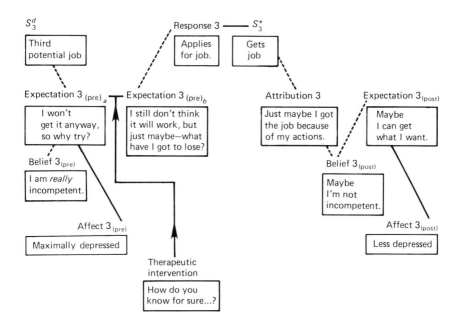

Figure 7.5. This graphic representation shows a reversal of an episode of depression at the optimal point of intervention.

evidence that is inconsistent with his or her belief in personal incompetence, the belief held when entering the situation. To the extent that those beliefs can be questioned and to the extent that subsequent expectations can be altered (e.g., "Maybe it's not totally hopeless"), the patient experiences a lessening of depression.[4]

Alternative Points of Intervention

Why not begin by attempting to alter the patient's initial attributions, if, according to Abramson et al. (1978), attributions are assumed to be central to the onset of the episode and to the subsequent alteration of self-concept and generation of negative expectations. We are not arguing that this should not be attempted; rather, we suggest that it is less likely to be effective. Discussions of previous events and the attributions made in their wake are necessarily post hoc; the therapist was not present to observe the sequence of events. Our experience has been that clients are typically skeptical of explanations that are more benign than those they have generated for an event. Although they would like to believe the therapist's rationale, most people share the common-sense notion that reexplanations of past events are, no matter how persuasive, essentially unconfirmable. Efforts directed at changing attributions essentially are focused on the past; by their very nature, attributions cannot be tested in any rigorous, prospective fashion *unless one specifically formulates expectations about events to come.* Just as for the scientist, for whom theory change proceeds most powerfully when hypotheses are confirmed or disconfirmed by actual observations, so too are individuals' beliefs most amenable to change on the basis of prospective disconfirmation rather than on the basis of simple reexplanation.

Bandura (1977a) has presented data that suggest that the use of enactive procedures provides the most powerful means of producing cognitive change. We would concur and point out that an initial emphasis on testing expectations forces the client and therapist to utilize enactive procedures in the course of therapy. The reexplanation of causality, the heart of reattribution

---

[4]We would not want to imply that all negative perceptions or beliefs are inaccurate. Undesirable events do occur, and unpleasant expectations may, at times, be borne out. Reality-based depressions probably do occur, although it is important to distinguish conceptually between probable and necessary precipitants of depression. Probable precipitants are events and/or situations that most individuals would become depressed in response to if they occurred. These types of events clearly exist. Necessary precipitants are those events that guarantee that a depression must follow if those events occur. It is not clear that any such conditions exist. Probable precipitants may well interact with cognitive and/or biologic factors to produce the resultant variability in susceptibility observed.

techniques (Beck et al., 1979), does not. Therein lies the central difference between an expectational and an attributional focus of intervention.

Evidence for the Theory

What evidence exists that speaks to this formulation? Actually, we are aware of little in the way of existing data that relates directly to our formulation. Bandura's work (Bandura, 1977a; Bandura, Adams, & Beyer, 1977) may be indirectly related. Focusing on change in approach behavior for snake phobics, Bandura and his colleagues compared modeling plus enactive contact, modeling alone, and a nonspecific control and found that the modeling plus enactive contact most powerfully altered both expectations and subsequent behavior. Furthermore, within each modality, changes in expectations proved to be a more powerful predictor of subsequent behavior than even previous behavior. This finding, although not relevant to the expectational versus attributional distinction, can be interpreted as supportive of the notion that an enactive exposure which tests expectations is a more powerful change technique than is the simple acquisition of information alone.

Is there any evidence that addresses the expectational versus attributional focus? Nisbett, Borgida, Crandall, and Reed (1976) have reported on attempts to alleviate mild depressions in ambulatory college students by means of reattribution therapy. The authors provided mildly depressed college students with normative information regarding weekly mood swings, namely, that some variability was normal and not an indication of psychopathology. The attributional manipulation had no observable effect on mood levels.

Dweck (1975) minimized the effects of failure in school children by manipulating the attributions made for those failures. However, in this instance, the intervention was at the same time as the occurrence of one precipitating event (a failure experience). We would not be at all surprised if an intervention that prevents an individual from making the initial misattribution served to *prevent* the onset of an episode of depression. Indeed, the potential capacity of the reformulated helplessness model to serve as a guide to the development of powerful *preventative* interventions may prove to be the greatest contribution made by the model. But, as we have described, those procedures that produce reversals in a phenomenon need not be isomorphic with those factors that produced it. In fact, a cognitive-expectancy model of intervention would argue that expectancy change procedures are preferred only when attempting to reverse dysphoria in an individual who is already depressed (the typical clinical situation), whereas an attributional focus would be preferred when attempting to forestall the onset of a depression. If our analysis of the causal chain of events is correct, then misattributions should play a central causal role in the etiology of negative expectations, and attribution therapy should play a central role in prevention. Alternatively, negative expectations play a major role in the maintenance of the syndrome (including the maintenance of negative affect), and expectational interventions should play a central role in the reversal of the phenomenon.

Klein and Seligman (1976) provided an additional set of observations that speak to the issue. Undergraduate college students were exposed to either solvable or unsolvable cognitive problems. Those subjects exposed to unsolvable problems were then given either solvable problems, a form of enactive exposure therapy, or no problems. Moreover, groups of mildly depressed college students also were given either the "therapy" treatment or not. Subsequent performance on a novel escape–avoidance task indicated that both groups given the "success" therapy, whether initially depressed or initially nondepressed but made "helpless" by exposure to the insolvable problems, showed no indication of performance deficits on the subsequent task. In this case, we may assume that the experience of success changed subjects' expectations about the ability of their responses to produce outcomes, and therefore averting the performance deficits typically associated with depression and helplessness.

Do clinically depressed individuals evidence patterns of change similar to those of analogue populations? Again, we are unaware of any direct evidence that speaks to this issue. Several studies are somewhat relevant, however. Loeb, Beck, and Diggory (1971) found that the experience of success on laboratory tasks increased optimism and enhanced performance among depressed outpatients. Such findings, of course, speak only to the notion that the actual disconfirmation of negative expectations via enactive exposure to success can enhance subsequent expectations and behaviors. It does not contrast expectational versus attributional modes of intervention.

Taylor and Marshall (1977) have provided such data. In the conext of a controlled clinical trial involving a quasi-analogue population (community volunteers for what was promoted as a therapy study), Taylor and Marshall contrasted a strictly cognitive, a strictly behavioral, and a combined cognitive–behavioral intervention. A fourth cell provided a waiting list control. Treatment was conducted in a six weekly, individual therapy sessions. Although the cognitive therapy did not consist solely of reattributional procedures, it relied heavily on such procedures. Change depended largely on the therapists' capacity to *persuade* the clients that they were not weak, incompetent, unlovable, etc. The procedures closely approximated those that comprise the heart of rational–emotive psychotherapy (Ellis, 1962; Ellis & Grieger, 1977; Ellis & Harper, 1975). The strictly behavioral approach relied heavily on the use of activity scheduling to ensure that clients experienced both pleasurable and mastery (success-producing) experiences. As such, the therapy relied heavily on enactive procedures without paying explicit attention to cognitive processes, either expectational or attributional. The combined cognitive–behavioral cell involved the use of both cognitive- and behavior-change procedures.

The results indicated that although both the strictly cognitive and the strictly behavioral cells outperformed the waiting list control, both single-focus modalities were outperformed by the combination of cognitive and enactive procedures. Shaw (1977) similarly found a combined cognitive–enactive approach superior to either a strictly enactive or a nonspecific modality, although both of these latter modalities proved superior to a waiting list control.

In recent reviews, Hollon (in press) and Hollon and Beck (1979) observed that in each separate study in which the combination of cognitive and enactive procedures was tested against alternative procedures, those cognitive–behavioral procedures proved superior to those alternative interventions. This finding was observed in the comparisons between cognitive–behavioral versus strictly cognitive procedures (Taylor & Marshall, 1977), versus strictly behavioral procedures (Shaw, 1977; Taylor & Marshall, 1977), versus systematic relaxation behavior therapy (McLean & Hakstian, 1979), versus nonspecific and/or dynamic interventions (Fuchs & Rehm, 1977; McLean & Hakstian, 1979; Shaw, 1977; Shipley & Fazio, 1973, studies I and II), and pharmacotherapy (McLean & Hakstian, 1979; Rush, Beck, Kovacs, & Hollon, 1977). These last two studies are particularly noteworthy, for traditional or dynamic psychotherapies have consistently fared poorly when compared to drugs (Covi, Lipman, Derogatis, Smith, & Pattison, 1974; Friedman, 1975; Klerman, DiMascio, Weissman, Prusoff, & Paykel, 1974). Although it is clear that pharmacotherapies (particularly the tricyclics, but also the monoamine oxidase inhibitors and, perhaps, lithium) are the current standard of efficacy in the treatment of clinical depression (Hollon & Beck, 1978) and are clearly more effective than traditional approaches, the superiority of cognitive–behavioral interventions to pharmacotherapy in the only two available completed trials is striking indeed. Two final studies deserve mention at this point. Hollon, Bedrosian, and Beck (Note 2) found that the addition of pharmacotherapy to cognitive–behavior therapy did not produce any greater change than did the cognitivie–behavior therapy alone, although both replicated the superior rates of change shown by the cognitive–behavioral intervention in Rush et al.'s 1977 comparison with drugs alone. Finally, Zeiss, Lewinsohn, and Munoz (1979) found no difference between strictly cognitive, strictly behavioral, and interpersonal approaches in treating outpatient community volunteers, essentially replicating Shaw's (1977) and Taylor and Marshall's (1977) findings of comparability between any of several *single* modality interventions.

All of these data are admittedly only indirectly relevant to our major thesis. They are, however, consistent; in controlled therapy outcome studies, combined cognitive–enactive procedures outperform strictly cognitive, strictly enactive, traditional dynamic, and even pharmacologic interventions. Available basic research findings, although again indirect, are also consistent with our formulation. Although strong data based on prospective tests of the hypothesis are clearly needed, the available data appear supportive of the cognitive–expectancy formulation.

ATTRIBUTIONAL VERSUS EXPECTATIONAL APPROACHES

Abramson et al. (1978) and Seligman (Note 1) have proposed a system of intervention based on the reformulated helplessness model. This system consists of four major components; (a) environmental enrichment; (b) personal control training; (c) resignation training; and (d) attributional retaining. We would argue that these procedures, when active, operate largely through expectancy–disconfirmation procedures.

Environmental enrichment, which Seligman defines in expectational terms as changing the estimated probability of the relevant event's occurrence, need not depend on cognitive processes. When it does, however, it relies largely on altering the individual's expectations of gratification or security in the near and distant future.

Personal control training, defined by Seligman as changing the individual's expectation from uncontrollabiility to controllability, may require skills training when deficits exist but, more typically, requires the remediation of the *perception* of deficit. As with the bulk of the helplessness remediation procedures, (e.g., Klein & Seligman, 1976), the reversal of the inaccurate *expectation* of noncontrol is seen as a key process in the treatment of depression.

Resignation training, defined as making highly preferred outcomes less preferred (or highly aversive outcomes less noxious), is seen by Seligman as resulting largely from challenging beliefs held about the *implications* of those events [e.g., "If I fail in anything, it means I'm unsuccessful" (Beck, 1976; Ellis, 1962]. Implications are by definition conditional expectations about the future. We would argue that prospective tests of these expectations may provide the most compelling means of disconfirming these beliefs.

Finally, attributional retraining refers to changing attributions for failure from internal, stable, global to external, unstable, specific, and changing attributions for success from external, unstable, specific to internal, stable, global. Although it is not *necessary* to focus on events in a prospective fashion (e.g., one could, for example, discuss the reasons for losing one's *last* job), we would argue that it is more powerful to do so (e.g., focusing on efforts to test the client's expectation that he or she could not get, or could not hold, the *next* job). In a sense, the cognitive–expectancy theory argues for testing, often via enactive procedures, expectations about the stability and globality components of the reformulated helplessness model's attributional style.

We would concur that attributional processes are central to the onset of the disorder but would argue that expectations play an equally large role in the maintenance of the disorder and that the explicit disconfirmation of those expectations provides the most efficient means of reversing all the various dysfunctional cognitive processes. Efforts at therapy require shifting one's frame of reference from processes of etiology to processes of intervention.

THEORIES OF ETIOLOGY AND THEORIES OF INTERVENTION

We have, in our formulation, operated on the assumption that the reformulated helplessness model adequately describes the etiology of depression. The evidence for this model has been presented elsewhere (Abramson et al., 1978, and Chapter 1 of this volume). It is important to note that the validity of the cognitive–expectancy model does not depend on the validity of reformulated helplessness or its applicability to any given type of depression (i.e., helplessness depressions). Just as the efficacy or lack of efficacy of a pharmacological intervention does not prove that a biological process did or did not produce a depression, neither does the success or lack of success of a cognitive–behavioral intervention prove or disprove a psychological formulation of etiology. However, treatment efficacy does speak directly to the validity of the model of intervention on which it is based. Treatments that have little, if any, direct impact on those factors that caused a disorder may well prove effective. Theories of intervention must be flexible enough to encompass effective interventions.

Psychoactive drugs appear to be active interventions in about 70% of all unselected primary depressives; cognitive–behavioral interventions in at least that many or more (Hollon, in press). Are we to assign a unique, unimodal process of etiology to account for those same disorders that appear to be responsive to multiple interventions? Perhaps, but it may be preferable for any model of intervention to be able to account for the apparent multiplicity of points of intervention in depression. What has yet to be determined is exactly what types of depression exist and which types of interventions are most likely to be effective with which types of the disorder. Our suspicion is that any of several points of intervention will prove possible for the majority

of individuals and that the most effective type of intervention may not necessarily be that which is most similar to those processes that initiated that
particular episode. Various pharmacologic approaches may well create an
impact on exactly those cognitive processes discussed in the preceding
section. The various cognitive–behavioral approaches may well influence
exactly those neural processes central to the biologic models.

We suggest that a cognitive–expectancy model represents a "final common pathway" for interventions in depression, one that may operate *in
relative independence of the specific nature of the etiological factors involved.* We prefer intervention procedures that focus on using enactive
procedures to disconfirm negative expectations because these procedures
represent the most effective means of nonpharmacological intervention, not
because they are tied to any specific model of etiology.

Elsewhere (Hollon, in press; Hollon & Beck, 1979) we have argued for
the necessity of discriminating between different parameters of change. For
example, the *magnitude* of the reduction of symptoms during an episode
may be more differentially affected than the *stability* of those changes over
time. Clearly, pharmacologic interventions, once discontinued, provide little protection against subsequent relapse or reoccurrence of the disorder.
Similarly, such relapses or reoccurrences are more likely to be forestalled by
cognitive–behavioral interventions for *some types of etiological processes
than for others.* Helplessness-based depressions, should they exist, are most
likely to be forestalled by cognitive learning-based interventions that alter
information processing styles. Genetically based biolgic depressions are less
likely to be prevented. Either type, or other types, of depression may well
prove amenable to any of the several types of interventions with respect to
the magnitude and rapidity of the reversal of symptomatology.

SUMMARY

We have described a cognitive–expectancy theory of therapy for depression. This theory of change holds that those procedures (typically some
combination of enactive and symbolic techniques) that most directly and
explicitly disconfirm negative expectations most rapidly and effectively reverse the negative affect, cognitive distortions, and behavioral passivity central to depression. The optimal model for the therapeutic relationship is one
of collaborative empiricism (Hollon & Beck, 1979), in which client and
therapist work together to test the client's beliefs.

The cognitive–expectancy theory of change is seen as compatible with,
although not dependent on, reformulated helplessness; if that model's attributional account of the etiology of depression is correct, the procedures

generated by a cognitive–expectancy theory of change should provide the optimal description of effective intervention. Specific emphasis on changing attributions is seen as being inefficient, because it requires altering beliefs about events that have already occurred in a post hoc fashion. Specific emphasis on testing those expectations that were, perhaps, generated by dysfunctional attributional styles permits the use of prospective, enactive hypothesis testing and serves as the most efficient means of altering existing belief systems or attributional styles. We believe that we have not presented a theory of change that breaks with the reformulated helplessness model. We have instead formulated a model of treatment that describes the most efficient procedures of intervention, if that reformulated helplessness model proves to be correct.

REFERENCE NOTES

1. Seligman, M. E. P. *Behavioral and cognitive therapy for depression from a learned help-lessness point of view.* Paper presented at the NIMH-sponsored conference "Research recommendations for the behavioral treatment of depression," L. P. Rehm, Chairperson, University of Pittsburgh, Pittsburgh, April 1979.
2. Hollon, S. D., Bedrosian, R., & Beck, A. T. *Combined cognitive–pharmacotherapy vs cognitive therapy alone in the treatment of depressed outpatients.* Paper presented at the Annual Meeting of the Society for Psychotherapy Research, Oxford, England, July 1979.

8

Learned Helplessness
and Intellectual Achievement[1]

CAROL S. DWECK
BARBARA G. LICHT

INTRODUCTION

Failure has dramatic effects on performance. For some children, these effects are positive ones: Effort is escalated, concentration is intensified, persistence is increased, strategy use becomes more sophisticated, and performance is enhanced. For other children, the effects are quite the reverse: Efforts are curtailed, strategies deteriorate, and performance is often severely disrupted. Indeed, these children often become incapable of solving the same problems they solved easily only shortly before. Although the behavior of these two groups of children differs markedly following failure, it looks remarkably similar before failure occurs. In all of our research on failure effects in achievement situations, we find that the two groups start out with virtually identical performance—that is, equivalent speed, accuracy, and sophistication of problem-solving strategies. They are also indistinguishable on standardized measures of intelligence. What distinguishes them are their cognitions about their successes and failures.

[1]The research reported here and the preparation of this chapter were supported in part by Grants MH 31667 from NIMH, NE G-00-3-00-88 from NIE, and ND 00244 from the U.S. Public Health Service.

197

In this chapter we will examine some of the causes and consequences of these cognitions and explore the implications of these disparate patterns for long-term intellectual–academic achievement. Specifically, we will ask: Which intellectual pursuits are *most* likely to be hampered by inability to cope with failure and which ones are *least* likely to? Indeed, in which areas might such children particularly excel? To answer this question we will analyze the task requirements in different intellectual–academic subject areas to determine what is demanded of the individual during acquisition and performance in each area. We will then compare these requirements to the cognitive–motivational characteristics of our two types of children. What we will propose is that certain patterns of achievement cognitions make an individual especially well-suited or ill-suited to achieve in particular areas.

HELPLESSNESS VERSUS MASTERY-ORIENTATION

Our research has shown that disparate responses to failure are associated with very different constellations of achievement cognitions—those characteristic of learned helplessness versus those characteristic of mastery-orientation.

Learned helplessness has been defined as the perception of independence between one's responses and the onset or termination of aversive events (Seligman & Maier, 1967). In achievement situations, then, helpless children would be characterized by cognitions that imply the inevitability or insurmountability of failure, whereas mastery-oriented children would be characterized by cognitions that imply that their successes are replicable and their mistakes rectifiable. Our initial research focused on attributions for failure as indicants of children's beliefs about the controllability of failure (e.g., Dweck, 1975; Dweck & Reppucci, 1973). For example, failure attributions to stable factors, such as lack of ability, suggest that the failure is likely to continue or recur, whereas failure attributions to less stable factors, such as insufficient effort, suggest that future success remains possible (Weiner, 1972, 1974). Briefly, these studies demonstrated that children who show deterioration of performance in the face of failure have a greater tendency to attribute their failures to stable factors and that those who show enhanced performance under failure tend to choose attributions to more variable factors. Moreover, Dweck (1975) demonstrated that a treatment that taught extremely helpless children to attribute their failures to a lack of effort (instead of to a lack of ability) led to great improvement in their reactions to failure. In fact, a number of the children receiving this treatment began to show performance after failure that was superior to their performance prior to failure.

When one directly assesses attributions (either via questionnaires or via probes within the experimental situation), as in this research, one has *ipso facto* defined the children as having failed by virtue of asking them to explain their failure(s). This raises several questions. Would children have perceived themselves to have failed at that point? If so, would they ordinarily make attributions for that failure? In other words, individuals may well differ in the point at which they define failure and in whether and when they seek to explain it. Past emphasis on solicited attributions raises other questions as well. What other achievement cognitions might figure prominently? When do they come into play? It is highly unlikely that the causes of failure are the only things children ponder as they experience achievement setbacks. For example, what about strategies for surmounting the failure? In response to these issues, Diener and Dweck (1978) employed a procedure that would enable children to tell them what their cognitions were as they occurred.

In two studies, the sophistication of problem-solving strategies was monitored as children performed a discrimination–learning task and went from success to failure. Both studies showed a rapid and marked decline in the maturity of helpless children's strategies with the onset of failure. Mastery-oriented children not only were able to maintain mature strategies over the failure trials, but a number of them actually began using more sophisticated strategies over the course of the failure trials. In the second of the two otherwise identical studies, the children were asked (after the sixth of eight success problems) to verbalize aloud as they performed the task. The instructions gave them license to reveal any of their thoughts, task-relevant or not—and they did.

On the two problems preceding the onset of failure, the two groups did not differ in the statements that emerged. Over the course of the failure trials, however, clear differences became obvious. Table 8.1 contains the distribution of the different types of verbalizations for helpless and mastery-oriented groups on the four failure trials. On the first of these trials, before "failure" became apparent, both groups continued to emit a considerable number of useful task strategy statements. As failure continued, however, helpless children began making causal attributions for failure—to a lack of ability (e.g., poor memory) or to a loss of ability (e.g., confusion). In addition, they began to express negative affect toward the task and a desire to withdraw from the situation, despite the fact that only moments before they were quite happy with it. Task-irrelevant statements also became quite numerous and may, in fact, have represented attempts to escape from the task cognitively, because it was not possible to do so physically.

In marked contrast, mastery-oriented children did not make attributions for the failures. Although they acknowledged that they were making "mistakes," there was little to indicate that they considered their present state to constitute "failure" or that they expected to remain in that state much longer.

TABLE 8.1

Number of Helpless and Master-Oriented Children with Verbalizations in Each Category[a]

Category of verbalizations	Group		$\chi^2 (df = 1)$	p
	Helpless	Mastery-oriented		
Useful task strategy	26	26	0	—
Ineffectual task strategy	14	2	12.27	.001
Attributions to lack or loss of ability	11	0	13.46	.001
Self-instructions	0	12	15.0	.001
Self-monitoring	0	25	42.86	.001
Statements of positive affect	2	10	6.0	.025
Statements of negative affect	20	1	26.46	.001
Statements of positive prognosis	0	19	27.8	.001
Solution-irrelevant statements	22	0	34.74	.001

[a] Adapted from Diener, C.I., & Dweck, C.S. An analysis of learned helplessness: Continuous changes in performance, strategy, and achievement cognitions following failure. *Journal of Personality and Social Psychology*, 1978, 36, p. 459. Copyright 1978 by the American Psychological Association. Adapted by permission.

Most of their statements indicated greater task involvement and increased orientation toward obtaining the solution. Specifically, they engaged in a good deal of self-instruction (e.g., reminding themselves to concentrate) as well as self-monitoring (e.g., checking to see that they were engaging in the behaviors that would facilitate performance). Moreover, a number of statements reflected increased positive affect toward the task (e.g., welcoming the challenge). Perhaps most striking was the unflagging positive prognosis— the expression of confidence and, in some cases, certainty that they would soon be back on the track. In their present situation, then, causal attributions would appear quite unnecessary. Regardless of the factor that led to their "mistakes," be it bad luck, insufficient effort, increased task difficulty, or lower ability than previously believed, intensifying one's efforts or varying one's problem-solving strategy would still appear to be a good route to success. Not until one has exhausted all avenues or until one has decided that the goal does not warrant a further expenditure of effort does it make sense for the mastery-oriented child to explain his or her failure, for not until then is there a failure to be explained.

Thus, the helpless and mastery-oriented children differ quite markedly in the constellation of achievement cognitions they entertain when they encounter difficulties. When failures occur, the cognitions of the helpless children reflect their tendency to dwell on the present, to dwell on the negative, and to seek an escape from the situation. The cognitions of the mastery-oriented children reflect their tendency to look toward the future, to emphasize the positive, and to invest their energies in actively pursuing solution-relevant strategies.[2]

Although the performance of helpless and mastery-oriented children is indistinguishable prior to failure, a number of findings suggested that their cognitions about those successes might differ (Diener & Dweck, 1978; Dweck, 1975; Dweck & Reppucci, 1973). For example, the verbalizations offered by the helpless children in the Diener and Dweck study implied either that their prior successes were forgotten or that they considered them to be irrelevant to their future successes. In contrast, the statements made by mastery-oriented children implied that their successes remained quite salient to them, that these successes documented their capabilities on the task and hence

---

[2]If mastery-oriented children do not tend to make attributions for the failures they encounter, then what can we say about attribution retraining as a means of getting helpless children to behave in a more mastery-oriented fashion? In other words, does it still seem like a reasonable strategy to teach helpless children to attribute their failures to variable factors like effort? Although this is ultimately an empirical question, it would appear to be necessary to rid seriously helpless children of their maladaptive attributions by such a direct method before they can effectively employ the more adaptive self-instructions and self-monitoring of the mastery-oriented child.

their ability to attain success once again. Dweck (1975) showed that extensive success did little to prevent debilitation when helpless children subsequently confronted failure. To the degree that helpless children acknowledge neither the extent nor the positive implications of their success, it will be less likely to serve as a buffer against the effects of failure. What is the nature of helpless/mastery-oriented differences in perceptions of success and when might these differences occur?

There are a number of differences that may exist. First, it could be the case that helpless and mastery-oriented children are quite similar in their perceptions of success while they are successful, but failure prompts a reappraisal. In other words, perhaps both groups view their successes as indicative of ability and as predictive of future success, but when failure occurs, the helpless children may reinterpret the successes as having been due to luck and not to skill. They may then see the failures as reflecting their true ability and as predicting future failure. Or, it may be that failure is simply so salient to the helpless child that it essentially obliterates the past successes. For example, following failure the number of successes may be substantially underestimated and the number of failures exaggerated.

Alternatively, there may be differences in the processing of successes as they occur. These might be differences in the tendency to see the current success as indicating high ability and a high probability of future success. There may be differences in how successful they think they are actually being—how many problems they believe they have solved and how they think their performance compares to that of others their age.

To assess which of these alternatives was the correct one, Diener and Dweck (in press) replicated their original study (without verbalizations) but asked children to make a series of judgments about their performance either just after a series of successes or after subsequent failures. The correct alternative turned out to be "all of the above." Helpless children seemed to seize all the available ways of discounting their successes.

After success, helpless children, compared to the mastery-oriented, underestimated the number of problems they had solved, were less likely to attribute their successes to ability, and tended to think other children would do better than they had done, even though they had solved every problem correctly. In line with this, they predicted poor future performance (e.g., an average of only 7.46 out of 15 correct if given more of the same kind of problems). Indeed, they did not seem to have experienced "success" at all. To compound this, after failure they overestimated the number of problems they failed to solve and, compared to the mastery-oriented children, further discounted their prior successes as reflecting ability. The mastery-oriented, in contrast, accurately recalled the number of successes, thought they were doing better than other children, saw their performance as indicative of ability, and expected their successes to continue unabated. (They predicted they would get an average of 13.43 correct if given 15 more problems.) Failure prompted little revision of this optimism for the mastery-oriented. Perhaps most striking was the fact that when children were asked whether they thought they could solve one of the original success problems if they forgot the answer and were given the problem over again, *all* of the mastery-oriented children thought they could. Only 65% of the helpless thought so.

In the same way that mastery-oriented children appear not to define themselves as failing when failures are programmed, helpless children do not appear to define themselves as succeeding when successes are programmed. In the same way that the mastery-oriented children look beyond the failed problems to ultimate success, the helpless children almost seem to look beyond their current successes to ultimate, if not imminent, failure. Thus, helpless children truly see themselves to be lacking in control—they do not believe they can reliably reproduce successes or overcome failures.

Given the characteristics of helpless children, on what kinds of intellectual tasks or in which academic areas would their performance be most impaired *or* most facilitated? Given the characteristics of the mastery-oriented children, what tasks and which areas would provide the best or poorest fit with their motivational tendencies? To begin to answer these questions, we will examine two groups of children (the two sexes) who typically display differences in helplessness versus mastery-orientation. We will then examine the two subject areas in which they evidence the most consistent differences in achievement: mathematical and verbal areas. We will show how the behaviors necessary for the pursuit of and success in mathematical areas are the very ones that the helpless children do not exhibit but the mastery-oriented do and how the characteristics of math learning and performance situations are ones that will be most aversive to the helpless child, but most attractive to the mastery-oriented. In a similar manner we will show how verbal learning and performance situations will fit most closely with the characteristics of helpless children, but more poorly with those of the mastery-oriented.

SEX DIFFERENCES IN LEARNED HELPLESSNESS

A good deal of research has shown girls to be more helpless than boys in achievement situations: They are more likely to condemn their abilities when they encounter difficulties and to show decreased persistence or impaired performance. Moreover, girls show lower expectancies of success than do boys across a wide variety of domains. For example, they often predict lower grades for themselves or poorer performance on novel experimental tasks. They also avoid tasks that pose a challenge or that test their skill (e.g., Butterfield, 1965; Crandall & Rabson, 1960; Dweck & Bush, 1976; Dweck & Gilliard, 1975; Dweck & Reppucci, 1973; Nicholls, 1975; Veroff, 1969). All of these effects have been found to occur even on tasks at which girls have clearly demonstrated their ability or in areas in which they have clearly out-performed boys. Boys, in contrast, do not tend to see failure feedback in academic settings as indicative of their competence; instead, they tend to view failure as stemming from controllable or variable factors, such as motivation or luck. They respond to such failure in the mastery-oriented manner—with improved performance or increased persistence—and they tend to select tasks that will provide a challenge. Furthermore, when they do succeed, boys are more likely to credit success to their abilities (Nicholls, 1975).

This sex difference is typically found with adult evaluators but does not seem to occur with peer evaluators. Indeed, Dweck and Bush (1976) found boys and not girls showing helplessness when peers delivered failure feedback. Therefore, it is not children's general histories of socialization in achievement situations that have taught boys and girls a stereotyped response to failure. Rather, it appears to be their specific experiences with specific classes of evaluators that determine how they interpret and respond to feedback. Although the greater helplessness of girls is not generalized to all evaluators, the fact remains that throughout children's academic careers the major evaluators of their work are adults. It is thus of great importance to determine precisely what aspects of adult–child interactions lead to helplessness or mastery-orientation.

Even a cursory glance at grade school classrooms should be sufficient to convince one that girls' helplessness does not stem from teachers' negative stereotypes of them or their abilities. Research amply supports the view that girls are the ones who are favored by teachers on almost every count and are the ones who shine academically over this period. Girls consistently receive higher grades than boys (McCandless, Roberts, & Starnes, 1972), outscore boys on tests of reading achievement (Asher & Markell, 1974), receive less criticism from teachers (see Brophy & Good, 1974), and are perceived by teachers to be the possessors of the superior intellectual and personal virtues (Coopersmith, 1967; Digman, 1963; Stevenson, Hale, Klein, & Miller, 1968). Moreover, girls themselves believe that teachers consider them to be smarter and harder working and that teachers like girls better (Dweck, Goetz, & Strauss, in press). The roots of girls' helplessness must lie, then, in more subtle aspects of adult–child evaluative interactions. We therefore analyzed the pattern of evaluative feedback given by grade school teachers to boys and girls in their classes (Dweck, Davidson, Nelson & Enna, 1978).

The focus was on teachers' use of negative feedback: its frequency relative to positive feedback, its typical referents, the specificity of its use, and the teachers' attributions that accompanied their feedback. One would expect that negative feedback would not be interpreted by boys as indicating a lack of ability if the teacher is habitually more negative than positive toward them, if the negative feedback is often addressed to nonintellectual aspects of behavior, and if the teacher attributes failures to a lack of motivation. If a teacher is generally negative toward a boy, he can question the objectivity of the teacher's evaluations of his work and can plausibly attribute failure feedback to the teacher's bias. (cf. Enzle, Hansen & Lowe, 1975; see Kelley, 1971). If negative feedback to boys is used frequently for various nonintellectual referents, it is likely to lose its meaning as a clear assessment of the intellectual quality of boys' work (cf. Cairns, 1970; Eisenberger, Kaplan, & Singer, 1974; Warren & Cairns, 1972). In addition, if teachers explicitly attribute boys' failures to a lack of motivation, boys will learn that failures need not detract from their perception of their competence.

One would expect that negative feedback *would* be seen by girls as suggesting a lack of ability if the teacher is typically quite positive toward them, if the teacher uses negative feedback with a high degree of specificity to indicate intellectual inadequacies in their work, and if the teacher fails to provide other explanations, such as lack of motivation, for their intellectual failures.

To examine these hypotheses, trained observers coded every instance of evaluative feedback that fourth- and fifth-grade children received from their teachers during academic subjects. The observers noted whether the feedback was positive or negative and noted the type of behavior to which the feedback referred: *(a)* intellectual aspects of academic work (e.g., correctness of answers, quality of ideas); *(b)* nonintellectual aspects of academic work (e.g., neatness); or *(c)* conduct. In addition, they recorded the explicit attributions that teachers made for children's successes and failures.

Boys and girls did not differ in the absolute frequency of feedback they received for intellectual aspects of their work or in the proportion of this feedback that was positive or negative. In other words, the two sexes were quite similar in actual success and failure feedback for intellectual matters. However, when one places this feedback within the context of all feedback, dramatic differences emerge. First, boys received a great deal more negative feedback overall. Moreover, the negative feedback for boys was used more diffusely to indicate a variety of referents, making it more ambiguous with regard to the intellectual quality of their academic performance. In fact, a greater proportion of boys' negative feedback was given for conduct and nonintellectual performance (67.5%) than for the intellectual aspects of their work (32.5%).

Even if one looks only at work-related feedback and not at conduct, a surprisingly large percentage of negative feedback for boys' work—45.6%—was addressed to its nonintellectual features. The fact that nearly half of the criticism teachers gave boys for their *work* was unrelated to its intellectual quality is particularly noteworthy. Intellectual and nonintellectual aspects of work usually occur simultaneously, and if negative feedback is used with nearly equal frequency for both, then on a given occasion when the referent is not specified (e.g., on report cards), the basis of the evaluation or the referent of the feedback may be highly ambiguous. Indeed, there were several instances in which, following the delivery of a correct answer, boys were given no feedback for the correctness but were criticized for nonintellectual aspects of their performance. This never occurred for girls and highlights the ambiguity of work-related criticism of a reflection of boys' intellectual competence.

When one looks at explicit attributions made by teachers for their students' intellectual failures, again, a striking difference between the sexes is evident: Teachers attributed boys' failures to a lack of motivation eight times as often as they did girls' failures.

Examining the whole picture, then, one can see that when a boy receives failure feedback from a teacher, he can easily view it as unrelated to his behavior. Instead, he can view it as reflecting the teacher's attitude toward him. If he does view the feedback as reflecting on his work, he can view the feedback as being based on an evaluation of its nonintellectual components and as unrelated to its intellectual adequacy. Finally, if he does view the feedback as indicating an intellectually deficient performance, he can attribute it to a lack of motivation. In short, boys learn a variety of ways to interpret the negative evaluations they receive—interpretations that allow them to maintain a belief in their ability to succeed despite the occurrence of failure. Even if a teacher's bias poses a serious and somewhat long-lasting obstacle to success, a teacher's reign is of limited duration, and confidence in one's abilities should lead to a rebound in expectancy of success with new teachers in future years.

In contrast to boys, relatively little of the negative feedback given to girls referred to conduct or to nonintellectual aspects of performance. The vast majority of their work-related criticism (88.2%) was aimed specifically at intellectual features of the work. This specificity in the use of negatives implies that girls will be less apt to view criticism as an evaluation of nonintellectual matters. This pattern of feedback, in conjunction with the fact that they received more overall praise than did boys, also implies that girls will be less likely to view criticism as resulting from teacher bias. Furthermore, because both teachers and girls view girls as being highly motivated, attributions of failure to lack of motivation become implausible. Thus, girls are led to conclude (or allowed to conclude) that negative feedback represents an objective evluation of their work and has direct implications for their competence. Many of girls' failures or errors, of course, are not the result of a lack of ability. Nonetheless, to the extent that they take them to be signs of incompetence, they will be less likely to persist in trying to obtain solutions to difficult problems or to try alternative strategies in the face of failure.

In sum, the pattern of negative feedback given to boys and girls makes it far more likely that girls will view such feedback as a valid index of their intellectual abilities. The patterns of positive feedback given to the two sexes were not as discrepant. Nevertheless, they suggested that praise is more likely to serve as a valid indicant of intellectual competence for boys than for girls.

One may wonder to what extent teacher feedback practices determine sex differences in responses to feedback or to what extent the feedback practices simply represent teachers' reactions to preexisting differences between the two sexes. To examine whether the patterns of feedback can actually cause boys' and girls' divergent interpretations of failure, the contingencies of negative feedback observed in the classroom were programmed in an experimental situation (Dweck et al., 1978).

In this study, children worked on a task at which they succeeded on some trials and failed on others. Children in one group received negative feedback that was based sometimes on intellectual quality of performance (correctness) and sometimes on nonintellectual aspects (neatness), just as boys receive in the classroom. Other children received negative feedback that was based exclusively on intellectual quality of performance, similar to what girls receive in the classroom. All children then performed a second task, failed on the first few trials, and received failure feedback of an unspecified basis from the same experimenter. The question was whether children would interpret that feedback differently as a function of their prior feedback from that evaluator. The results showed that children, regardless of their sex, who experienced the contingencies that boys experienced in the classroom did not interpret subsequent failure feedback as indicative of their level of ability. Children of both sexes who received the pattern of feedback girls received in the classroom overwhelmingly attributed subsequent negative feedback to a lack of ability. These findings clearly indicate that teachers' feedback practices can indeed have direct consequences for children's interpretations of their failures.

Sex Differences in the Generalization of Failure Effects

Not only are girls more debilitated by failure but they are also more likely to show generalization of these effects to new situations. Some of our recent research (Dweck et al., in press) indicates that following failure girls' expectancies of success are less resilient: They show less recovery in response to situational changes that should prompt optimism. It also suggests that even when girls do express confidence about their future performance, that confidence is more fragile and may dissipate with situational changes that for boys tend to lead to heightened confidence.

When one considers boys' and girls' differing interpretations of failure (and of success), one would predict different patterns of generalization for them. Specifically, if boys tend to attribute failures to evaluator bias more than girls do, then they would be more likely than girls to greet a new teacher with renewed optimism for success in that area. If girls attribute their failures in a given subject to a lack of ability, a new teacher should do little to raise their hopes as long as the ability area remains similar. In fact, if girls attribute their successes to a *positive* teacher bias (the teacher liked them, was nice, graded leniently, etc.), then their confidence should fall with the advent of a new teacher. It was noted previously that girls have been found to display consistently lower expectancies of success than do boys. One would predict that the discrepancy between the two sexes in their expectancy of academic success would be greatest at the start of a school year. When beginning a new grade or entering a new school, children confront new teachers but similar academic subjects. At that time boys' successes in these academic subjects should be most salient to them because they have been indicative of ability; however, girls' failures should be most salient to them because they have been seen as the more valid index of their competence. In addition, as indicated, a new teacher should signal to boys a new chance for success and should prompt renewed effort; however, it should signal to girls the possible disruption of their successes.

A field study and an experimental laboratory study were conducted to test these predictions about the generalization of failure effects for boys and girls (Dweck et al., in press) In the field study, the course of children's expectancies for their academic performance over the school year was examined. In the laboratory analogue, changes in the task and the evaluator were programmed following failure, and recovery of expectancies was monitored.

The results from the field study showed that when children were asked to predict how well they would do on their upcoming report cards, the hypothesized pattern was obtained. Before their first report cards, boys expected to do significantly better than girls expected to do, both on an absolute expectancy measure (a 1–10 scale ranging from "I don't think I'll do very well" to "I think I'll do very well") and on a relative expectancy measure (ranging from "I think most everyone will do better than me" to "I think I will be one of the best in the class"); both on specific measures in each subject area and on a general measure. This occurred even though the boys had received significantly lower grades than did the girls the previous year and were to do so again on their report cards in the current year.

Although this discrepancy in expectancy disappeared by the second report card period, girls still did not exhibit higher expectancies than did boys, which is what veridical perceptions on both of their parts would yield.

It is interesting to note that when children were asked to commit themselves to actual grades by filling out facsimiles of the report cards they were shortly to receive, the results were quite different. Under these circumstances girls did indeed assign themselves higher grades than did boys. It may well be that when children are forced to attend to the concrete data they have at their disposal (e.g., test scores) in order to compute their grades, the reality of boys' and girls' relative performance holds sway. When children are asked for less concrete, more "impressionistic" estimates, boys' and girls' tendencies to weigh their successes and failures differentially seem to dominate. It appears likely, however, that the more impressionistic perceptions are the ones children will tend to generate spontaneously and, therefore, are the ones that will more often influence children's behavior in achievement situations.

The results from the experimental study also confirmed the notion that children's interpretations of their outcomes are related to generalization to novel situations. For example, boys' expectancies of success following failure recovered significantly more than did girls' when a new evaluator was introduced. An expected finding, however, was the fact that when both the task at which children failed and the evaluator for that task were changed, boys showed complete recovery of their success expectancies (i.e., to pre-failure levels), but girls did not. In other words, girls appeared to carry over failure effects to what was largely a new situation. Although several interpretations are plausible, it is possible that when girls blame their abilities for failure, they blame an ability that transcends the task at hand (see also Abramson, Seligman, & Teasdale, 1978). In other words, they may apply a general label to their perceived incompetence, and this label will then mediate the generalization of the failure effects across situations—the more general the label, the wider the generalization.

LEARNED HELPLESSNESS AND
TASK CHARACTERISTICS

We have seen that girls and boys have different characteristic ways of dealing with positive and negative outcomes. They interpret their successes and failures differently and have different views of the implications for their abilities. They may indeed have different criteria for defining success and failure given a series of outcomes. They make different predictions about future outcomes even when their prior outcomes are not discrepant. They differ in the persistence of their attempts to solve a difficult problem, in the quality of their performance after failure, and in their task choices after they encounter difficulty. What implications might these tendencies have for children's success in or pursuit of different academic areas? Academic tasks certainly vary in the degree to which persistence in the face of difficulty is necessary for success. Academic areas vary in the degree to which persistence is necessary throughout the school years for the mastery of new concepts and skills. In view of the different tendencies of boys and girls, one would predict differential debilitation and facilitiation depending on the characteristics of the area in question. We will begin by examining those characteristics that would be least desirable for girls, but not boys, and then focus on those characteristics that would have the reverse properties. As we will see, it is the mathematical areas that have the qualities least suited to girls, and it is the verbal areas that have the qualities least suited to boys.[3]

First, given girls' maladaptive response to failure, one would expect them to perform most poorly in those subject areas where failures are the most likely to occur. Each failure provides girls with another opportunity to conclude they lack ability. If girls then blame an intellectual ability that goes beyond the particular task at hand, the negative effects of failure may generalize to all tasks perceived to fall into the same ability area, resulting in: (a) decreased persistence in the face of difficulties; (b) avoidance of the area if that option is available; and (c) perhaps interference with the acquisition of new material in that area. In contrast, given boys' tendency to view difficult tasks as posing a challenge, a moderate probability of failure in a particular subject area may serve to increase the attractiveness of the area for them.

In line with the above analysis, one would also predict girls to be more adversely affected in areas where the mistakes that do occur are highly salient. Children will not always realize when they have erred or performed in a less than adequate way. To the degree that even minor errors are made obvious to the children, girls' motivation and performance may suffer. If, however, deviations from perfect performance may suffer. If, however, deviations from perfect performance are not likely to be noted, girls' maladaptive failure attributions would not be called forth even if errors have been made.

A third characteristic that would differentially affect boys and girls is the extent to which one can compensate for perceived intellectual inadequacies by doing well on some other aspect of the same task. That is, if a child fails to perform well on one component of a task (e.g., developing imaginative ideas for a composition), can he or she decrease the probability of an overall task failure (e.g., low grade on a whole paper) by performing well on some other aspect of the same task (e.g., grammar, spelling, organization of ideas, penmanship)? If this opportunity is not available in a particular subject area,

[3]Although our analysis is framed in terms of sex differences, the differential predictions made for girls versus boys would apply as well to helpless versus mastery-oriented children within each sex.

then any perceived inadequacies that girls may have in that area, however small, should create a good deal of concern for them. An opportunity to compensate for intellectual weaknesses, however, would be less important to boys because they are less likely to view themselves as having any intellectual weaknesses. They would also be less concerned about guarding against future failures because those failures would not be taken as a sign of low competence.

Another prediction arising from a consideration of children's attributional tendencies is that girls' impairment by failure will be heightened in subject areas where failure feedback is most plausibly seen as reflecting on ability, such as areas with little feedback for nonintellectual aspects of performance. In other words, although girls quite readily conclude that they lack ability when they receive failure feedback, this conclusion might be reached even more readily in areas characterized by an emphasis on intellectual correctness and a deemphasis of nonintellectual matters. Boys, however, given their feedback history with teachers, would not tend to see either kind of feedback as implying insufficient ability and should therefore not be adversely affected in the same way as are girls. Indeed, one might even predict the opposite for boys. Boys might show impaired motivation in areas where intellectually irrelevant skills are seen as important, since boys both value thes skills considerably less than girls do and value them considerably less than intellectual skills (Dweck et al., in press).

In accord with our analysis, one can specify an additional task characteristic that might impair boys' performance, but not girls'. Boys would be expected to show decreased motivation in areas where the criterion for success is ambiguous and teachers' prejudices can enter into judgments of performance. Boys receive more negative feedback than do girls for conduct and other nonintellectual matters and tend to view teachers as somewhat biased against them (Dweck & Bush, 1976; Dweck et al., 1978). Therefore, to the extent that evaluative feedback in an area is seen as influenced by such biases, boys may tend to view failures in that area as being beyond their control. Girls, on the other hand, accurately perceived teachers as positively inclined toward them. As a result, they should not anticipate failures stemming from teachers' biases but perhaps might even favor situations where teachers' attitudes can influence evaluations.

Mathematical versus Verbal Areas:
Acquisition, Performance, and Feedback

If one analyzes the different academic areas as they are learned over the school years, mathematics emerges as an area possessing those characteristics that should be most debilitating and least attractive to girls, but appealing for boys. More of the verbal areas, on the other hand, appear to have the characteristics that would be most appealing to girls and that would facilitiate their performance but not boys'. This is not intended to imply that every aspect of all mathematical tasks will facilitate boys and debilitate girls or that all verbal tasks provide a better fit with girls' tendencies than with boys'. However, the majority of tasks in each of the two areas does tend to favor one sex to a considerable degree. Even when specific verbal tasks possess characteristics that are debilitating to girls, they almost always possess at least one of the characteristics that is facilitating, unlike most math tasks. Similarly, when a math task has characteristics that are unfavorable to boys, it also possesses ones that are favorable.

It is well known that females perform as well as or better than males in verbal areas (Anastasi, 1958; Donlon, Ekstrom, & Lockheed, Note 1; Maccoby, 1966; Maccoby & Jacklin, 1974), but that males outperform females in mathematical achievement (Donlon et al., Note 1; Ekstrom, Donlon, & Lockheed, Note 2; Fennema & Sherman, 1977; Flanagan, Davis, Daily, Shaycoft, Orr, Goldberg, & Neyman, 1964; Fox, 1976; Hilton & Berglund, 1974; Maccoby & Jacklin, 1974). In early elementary school, girls show equivalent math performance (Maccoby & Jacklin, 1974), but boys begin to surpass them beginning in adolescence, and this difference increases over the course of the school years (Flanagan et al., 1964; Hilton & Berglund, 1974; Maccoby & Jacklin, 1974).

It should be noted that although sex differences in mathematics achievement do not emerge until adolescence, we are proposing that the underpinnings lie in the elementary school years, when sex differences in achievement orientations become pronounced. The differences in actual achievement may not occur until the later years because: (a) as explained later, the conceptual leaps between units become greater and provide more failure opportunities; (b) the problems themselves become more difficult and require more complex strategy formulation and other behaviors that are particularly disrupted by helplessness; and (c) it is not until later that girls have the option of avoiding math. Furthermore, one might argue that given girls' higher achievement scores in verbal areas, their higher grades in school, and their greater motivation in the elementary school years, the fact that they are not ahead of boys in mathematics achievement might be an indicant of early debilitation.

A number of alternative explanations have been offered to account for sex differences in achievement, particularly males' superiority in math. Perhaps the most typical explanation involves the notion that math is stereotyped as a male domain (Fennema, Note 3; Fox, Note 4). Girls are assumed to learn this and to lower their expectations accordingly. Teachers are assumed to exacerbate the situation by continually communicating the stereotyped expectation to girls. Certainly sex-role stereotyping of achievement domains can exert powerful influences on behavior, particularly in the later school years when these academic stereotypes become more pronounced. However, our analysis suggests that other factors are critical. Let us examine, then, these other factors that can account for the sex differences in question. Toward this end, mathematical and verbal areas will be contrasted along the dimensions identified earlier as likely to differentially affect males and females. It will be shown how children's achievement-related orientations can interact with the performance requirements of academic tasks to determine their actual achievement. Indeed, as we will suggest later, it may be this very process that led to the stereotyping of the areas in the first place.

Probability of Failure

Regardless of one's intellectual capabilities, one is more likely to experience failure or encounter difficulties in mathematical than in verbal areas. After the fundamental verbal skills—reading, spelling, vocabulary—have been acquired, increments in difficulty tend to be gradual. Rarely is the child ever again confronted in school with a new unit for which he or she feels totally unprepared or for which a completely new set of concepts, skills, or strategies must be mastered. In learning to read, spell, or define a new word, one employs basically the same processes one has employed in the past. The new material is essentially assimilated into an existing body of knowledge, and so a careful application of this knowledge should, in most cases, be sufficient to avoid failure.

With math, however, a new unit may involve totally new concepts, and the relevance of past learning in math may not be evident. New units in math often entail large, sudden, qualitative changes as, for example, when one goes from arithmetic to algebra to geometry to calculus and so on. Young children may even fail to realize the relationship between addition and multiplication or between multiplication and division. As a result, children may experience considerable confusion whenever they begin a new unit in math, and this confusion may, like failure, lead girls to entertain doubts about their abilities, doubts that may not be dispelled by subsequent mastery of the unit.

It is not only the case that new units in verbal areas can be related more easily to old units, but material presented in verbal areas can also be related more easily to "reality." Language, after all, is designed to describe one's everyday world and to enable one to communicate about it. It is, of necessity, anchored to experience. Mathematical concepts, however, are often far removed from one's actual life experiences. When, for example, does one experience a square root or an imaginary number or two simultaneous equations? One has few experiences to which one can tie such concepts in order to make them more comprehensible. This increases further the probability that the child will experience confusion, the probability that the confusion will be of a greater magnitude, and the probability that the child will not be able to extricate himself or herself from that confusion by appealing to other knowledge. This becomes increasingly the case as one moves through school and as mathematical operations become more and more remote from one's reality.

Thus, the nature of the acquisition process in mathematics provides repeated opportunities for initial failures and for girls to conclude that they lack ability. As indicated earlier, failures may lead girls to consider themselves lacking in an intellectual ability that goes beyond the particular task on which they failed. In this way, a girl may transfer a failure experience from, for example, geometry to algebra by applying the general label "math" to her perceived deficit, even though the two areas may involve different skills. All subsequent stumblings on any type of math task will confirm these suspicions of generalized incompetence. In addition, once a girl perceives herself to lack general mathematical ability, the problem may be amplified by the fact that each new math course has a different label and contains operations with strange, new names—implying that the specific skills acquired in the old units are no longer relevant and will not help her through the new material. Therefore, girls should be more likely than boys to drop out of math as soon as the option becomes available, even if they have objectively done well in previous math courses. Sherman and Fennema (1977) present data to suggest that girls are in fact more likely than boys of comparable ability to discontinue math. This is in contrast to verbal areas where inferences of incompetence will have been less likely and where previously acquired knowledge should still seem relevant for most tasks. In writing more advanced compositions or reading more difficult books, for instance, one continues to rely on previously acquired knowledge of grammar, spelling, vocabulary, and the like.

In summary, the greater probability of failures in math allows girls to infer that they lack mathematical ability, to generalize this inference across tasks, and perhaps, to anticipate future incompetence where none currently exists. Because boys are inclined to focus on their successes and not on their failures, the ease with which failure effects and inferences of low ability can be generalized should have far less impact.

Salience of Failure

Although the greater likelihood of failure in math than in verbal areas should have debilitating effects on girls, it is, of course, not an error per se that triggers their maladaptive failure attributions. Rather it is girls' perception or belief that they have erred, perhaps combined with the knowledge that an evaluator has recognized or emphasized the mistake. It is only when errors are noted by the child or made salient by an evaluator that one would expect them to have disruptive effects on girls' performance. Boys, because of their mastery-orientation in the face of failure, should not be adversely affected by the salience of their errors.

Errors in math are likely to be more salient than errors in verbal areas. For example, consider the evaluative feedback that teachers are apt to give. One would expect teachers to correct even minor errors when tasks have a clear criterion of correctness, as they do in math, but not when the criterion of correctness is vague, as is often the case in verbal areas. In math, there is almost always one and only one correct answer. The teacher need not make fine discriminations to know that a child has erred on a math problem and, furthermore, will feel compelled to correct even the smallest error because it will lead to an incorrect answer. In many verbal areas, however, perfection is difficult to define, and so the criterion for correctness is considerably less precise. A teacher may feel that the way a child has defined a word or written an essay is "good enough," and errors may go uncorrected or even unnoticed. There are certainly some verbal tasks, such as spelling, for which the criterion of correctness is as unambiguous as it is in math. However, an unambiguous criterion for correctness appears to be the rule in math and somewhat more of an exception in verbal areas. This is particularly the case as one advances through the school years and verbal areas become more and more saturated with tasks like essay writing and less focused on tasks like spelling.

Since the greater salience of errors should be debilitating to girls and aversive to them, one would expect them to respond more favorably to tasks on which the criterion of correctness is somewhat imprecise. On such tasks they would seldom have to confront the bald certainty of failure. Of course, one might argue that the clarity of the correctness criteria in math should also make one's *successes* more salient. Although this may be true, it would not have a compensatory effect for girls since they tend not to see their successes as reflecting ability or as predictive of future outcomes. Boys, who view their successes, not their failures, as the more predictive of future outcomes, are the ones who should benefit from the increased salience of success that accompanies clear correctness criteria. Indeed, for reasons to be discussed later, one might expect boys to perform more poorly on tasks for which the criterion of correctness is ambiguous.

Compensation for Perceived Inadequacies

Thus far we have proposed that the greater frequency and salience of errors in math make it more likely that girls will infer low ability in math than in verbal areas. Carrying this a step further, it appears likely that a perceived deficit in math will have a more debilitating effect on girls than will a perceived deficit in verbal areas. More specifically, perceived inadequacies should be more disruptive when one sees little chance to compensate for them, as is more likely in math. On verbal tasks there are many opportunities to compensate for one's perceived inadequacies by performing well on some other components of the same task, thereby preventing an overall task failure. Suppose, for example, that one were having difficulty coming up with an imaginative idea for an essay. One could reasonably improve one's grade on the essay by excelling on other aspects of the task. For example, in the nonintellectual realm, a child can take special care to have neat hand-writing and to adhere to the proper format. There are also more intellectual components of the task that could serve as the focus of the child's compen-satory efforts, such as grammar or clarity of expression. In math, however, it is more difficult to identify sets of clearly different skills that enter into the performance of a task. Therefore, if one lacks the knowledge necessary for the solution of a given problem or set of problems, it would be difficult to figure out how to still achieve a commendable level of overall performance. This is not to suggest that one cannot receive "partial credit" for a math problem, but simply that compensating for the absence of one skill by increasing attention to another is not as readily applicable to math tasks.

In the same vein, verbal tasks make it easier for evaluators to buffer their failure feedback by allowing them simultaneously to deliver compensatory praise. For example, an evaluator can soften a negative comment about sentence structure by pointing out that although the grammar was incorrect, the ideas the child was attempting to express were excellent.

In later years, the more verbal areas allow an additional avenue for avoiding failure, one that is not provided by math. This might be termed the "fudge factor." That is, in areas other than math (indeed, in any area where the mode of expression is verbal), one can attempt to camouflage one's ignorance by formulating something that resembles a legitimate answer. For example, suppose an individual has studied for an exam in an area where responses are verbal, and finds that he or she does not know the answer to one or more questions on the exam. That individual, having access to the body of knowledge that he or she has studied, may develop several lines of reasoning that seem related to the question and may, in fact, concoct an answer that appears respectable. If the criteria of correctness are rather subjective, then the student may receive a fair amount of credit for the answer. It may even be the case, on occasion, that the correct answer will appear among the student's offerings.

In math, where one must usually solve a problem, the opportunities for fudging are more limited. One cannot easily raise related issues derived either from the course or from outside experience. One cannot use the politician's ploy of reinterpreting the question and then answering it. Indeed the student may have no option but to leave the answer blank. In short, one cannot display one's body of knowledge, but rather must apply the proper mathematical operations in the proper way. Even on multiple-choice tests, a similar discrepancy between math and more verbal areas remains. In the verbal areas one is in a better position to make "educated guesses," to examine the alternatives, and to judge which appears to be most plausible. In math, if one cannot work the problem, how can one assess the relative merits of the choices?

Interpretation of Failure Feedback

The evaluative feedback in mathematical and verbal areas is likely to differ in ways that will occasion different causal attributions, with girls being more debilitated by their attributions in math and boys being debilitated in verbal areas. As we have noted, girls' tendency to view failure feedback as a condemnation of their ability makes them more likely to show impairment in areas where failure feedback is most easily interpreted as reflecting on ability. Boys, however, should show debilitation and avoidance in areas where the feedback is most plausibly seen as reflecting a teacher's negative subjective judgments. What kind of negative feedback, then, would be most readily interpreted as reflecting ability and what kind would most readily be seen as reflecting teacher biases? There are two characteristics that appear to be particularly important. The first involves the degree to which responses are evaluated against an objective criterion. Feedback for answers that have a highly subjective criterion of correctness might plausibly be seen as reflecting the teacher's biases, whereas feedback referring to whether or not an objective criterion of success has been met is less likely to be interpreted in this way. As discussed earlier, verbal tasks are much more likely than math tasks to have subjective criteria of success, particularly tasks such as writing essays, defining words, or reporting on books. Math, on the other hand, requires problem solving of a prescribed nature that can yield only one correct answer. A correct solution in math will be recognized regardless of the teachers' opinion of the student—the child will be treated fairly in that the feedback will be commensurate with the product.

The second characteristic that is particularly important in determining the types of attributions children will make is the relative porportion of the evaluator's feedback that refers to intellectually relevant versus intellectually irrelevant aspects of performance. Previous research has shown that lack of ability is a more plausible attribution for failure the more the evaluator's feedback refers to intellectual aspects of the child's work (Dweck et al., 1978). Considering the nature of most math and verbal areas, it is likely that less feedback of a nonintellectual nature is given in math than in verbal areas. If a child obtains the correct solution to a math problem, other considerations clearly become secondary. However, even if a child writes a brilliant composition, it may still be important that it be neat and in proper form. If feedback for math contains fewer intellectually irrelevant comments, this means that negative feedback is even more likely than usual to be taken by girls as a sign of low competence. Boys, on the other hand, would be expected to welcome the emphasis on exclusively intellectual feedback because this should provide some relief from the negative feedback for nonintellectual skills they typically receive and because they value tests of skills that the nonintellectual work does not provide (Dweck et al., 1978). In math, then, boys need not be concerned with the nonintellectual domain in which they do poorly and in which they have little desire to exert effort (Dweck et al., in press).

In summary, the criteria of correctness on mathematical tasks are clearly more objective, and the focus of evaluation on mathematical tasks is more likely to be on intellectual aspects of performance. Subjective evaluations of correctness and evaluations of nonintellectual aspects of work are more likely in verbal areas. These factors make math better adapted to the achievement orientations of boys and verbal areas better adapted to those of girls.

Susceptibility to Disruption

We have thus far examined a number of factors in mathematical areas that promote girls' maladaptive failure attributions. Even if such attributions were equally likely to occur in math and verbal areas, would their impact on subsequent task performance necessarily be the same in both areas? When one analyzes the performance requirements on mathematical versus verbal tasks, it appears that the very behavior necessary for good performance on math tasks is that which is particularly disrupted by helplessness. First, success on many mathematical tasks requires that in the face of difficulty one sustain concentration and maintain a sophisticated problem-solving strategy. Moreover, one must retain flexibility of strategy use, discarding ineffective strategies, selecting reasonable alternatives, and evaluating their efficacy. The ability to perform these behaviors in the face of difficulty becomes more and more important as one goes on in math and as problems require greater ingenuity and perseverance. Verbal areas generally do not involve a lengthy problem-solving period throughout which strategies must be maintained. As the research described at the outset amply demonstrated, the concentration and strategy use of helpless children decline dramatically when they encounter failure. Furthermore, given the low criteria helpless children appear to have for defining themselves as having failed, it may well be the case that the long presolution period that is *necessary* on difficult problems is viewed as evidence of incompetence, as a sign of impending, if not already present, failure. Mastery-oriented children typically display their best performance when a task calls for the surmounting of obstacles. Thus, girls' greater helplessness would be a particular liability in mathematical areas, and boys' greater mastery-orientation a particular asset.

The mathematical tasks in which boys have been found especially to excel are those that appear to involve visual–spatial skills (Maccoby & Jacklin, 1974). Biologically based theories (e.g., differences in brain lateralization) are often invoked to explain this sex difference. Also invoked are socialization explanations involving boys' greater experience with toys and games that develop spatial skills. However, the difference can also be readily understood in terms of the issues discussed here. When one considers the nature of the problem-solving process on visual–spatial tasks, it is clear that it is a process that is highly susceptible to interference. The ability to perform nonverbal mental operations requires a mind that is cleared of all else, combined with completely unbroken concentration. The kinds of cognitions that helpless children typically entertain in such achievement situations would prove hopelessly disruptive.

SUMMARY AND CONCLUSION

We have examined the compatibility of different subject areas with different achievement orientations and have found mathematics and helplessness to be incompatible. Helpless children attribute their failures to lack of ability and show performance impairment under failure. Failures in math are more probable, more salient, and more difficult to compensate for than failures in verbal areas. The feedback in math makes failures appear more reflective of low ability, and when this occurs, math performance is more susceptible to disruption. Let us explore some implications of this analysis.

As noted earlier, the most typical explanation of sex differences in mathematical and verbal areas involves the notion that children are responding to the stereotyping of math as "masculine" and verbal areas as more "feminine." This argument, however, raises a fundamental question. Why were math and verbal areas steretotyped in the first place? Perhaps the most common response would be that the skills required to learn mathematical tasks are the ones in which males are traditionally thought to excel, whereas the skills required for verbal tasks are the ones in which females are thought to excel. Yet an examination of math and verbal areas reveals a most interesting point—the acquisition and performance requirements of math can just as plausibly be viewed as stereotypically female, and those of verbal tasks can easily be seen as stereotypically male. In writing essays, for example, one must take many initially poorly-formed and abstract ideas and organize them into a clear, coherent, convincing communication. One must be able to distinguish the relevant from the irrelevant, developing the former and suppressing the latter. To do this well, one must be both *logical* and *lucid*. These abilities have been viewed as stereotypically masculine. Mathematical tasks, on the other hand, appear to require a great deal of attention to fine details. After all, a small miscalculation on a math problem will result in an answer that is entirely wrong. To do well one must be careful and methodical —skills in which females are traditionally seen to shine. One could continue in this vein to illustrate that if one had fewer preconceived notions, math could just as easily be viewed as requiring "feminine" talents and verbal areas as requiring "masculine" ones. Why then should math be viewed as a male domain? Our analysis raises an intriguing possibility. Perhaps what is usually seen as the "chicken" is really the "egg." Perhaps it is actually girls' avoidance of math and their poorer performance (because of the incompatibility of girls' achievement orientations with the requirements of mathematics) that has led, in part, to the labeling of mathematics as "male." In other words, what is usually viewed as the consequence of the stereotype may in fact have been one of its causes.

In our analysis, we have presented a general characterization of mathematical and verbal areas. However, the analysis could easily be applied within each area. The tasks within each area can be categorized along the relevant dimensions—for example, the degree to which new concepts must be acquired, the ease with which new learning can be related to prior learning, the objectivity of the correctness criteria, the importance of nonintellectual aspects of performance, the extent to which the requisite cognitive processes are susceptible to disruption. One would then predict differential performance for helpless and mastery-oriented children, depending on the degree to which a given task resembled our "prototypical" math task or our "prototypical" verbal task along these dimensions. Areas other than math and verbal ones could, of course, be subjected to similar analyses.

In our discussion we have concentrated on the grade-school years because these years appear to be critical in the formation of the achievement orientations of interest. However, some important factors may undergo changes in subsequent years. First, conduct and nonintellectual aspects of performance are expected to become increasingly peripheral. As a result, teachers' feedback patterns will change, and the interpretations of teachers' feedback, in turn, will change. Specifically, attributions of failure to teacher bias against boys become less compelling, and attributions to ability may become more likely. Second, as students are given more and more freedom over the school years to determine their own courses of study, students should, in line with our analysis, vary in the type of course they tend to select. Some will concentrate on courses with "math-like" characteristics and others on more "verbal" courses. With this divergence will come differential experience with different types of feedback (e.g., based on objective versus more subjective criteria). This would mean, for example, that those who concentrate on math courses will receive more feedback that can be seen as reflecting directly on their ability. Moreover, as students determine their own academic programs, lack of motivation becomes a less likely explanation for one's failures. How might these changes affect an individual's achievement tendencies? For example, might some of the mastery-oriented children begin to tend more toward helplessness in the face of these changes?

In conclusion, the determinants of achievement have long been of great interest but in many ways have remained a mystery. The present analysis provides a means of understanding some of the factors that determine an individual's choice of one achievement area over another and that influence performance in those areas.

REFERENCE NOTES

1. Donlon, T. F., Ekstrom, R. B., & Lockheed, M. Comparing the sexes on achievement items of varying content. Paper presented at the meeting of the American Psychological Association, Washington, D.C., September 1976.
2. Ekstrom, R. B., Donlon, T. F., & Lockheed, M. E. The effect of sex-biased content in achievement test performance. Paper presented at the meeting of the American educational Research Association. San Francisco, Calif., April 21, 1976.
3. Fennema, E. Influences of selected cognitive, affective, and educational variables on sex-related differences in mathematics learning and studying. Paper prepared for the National Institute of Education under grant number P-76-0274, 1976.
4. Fox, L. H. The effects of sex-role socialization on mathematics participation and achievement. Paper prepared for Education and Work Group, Career Awareness Division of National Institute of Education, December 1976.

9

Helplessness and the
Coronary-Prone Personality[1]

DAVID C. GLASS
CHARLES S. CARVER

INTRODUCTION

Coronary heart disease is a major cause of death in this country. Its most common forms are myocardial infarction (heart attack) and angina pectoris (a painful and debilitating constriction in the chest). Coronary heart disease results from damage to the coronary arteries. Such arterial damage is termed coronary artery disease or atherosclerosis (Friedberg, 1966) or, less technically, hardening of the arteries.

Data from various epidemiologic studies (e.g., Brand, Rosenman, Scholtz, & Friedman, 1976; Dawber & Kannel, 1961) indicate that the following specific factors are associated with high risk of coronary heart disease: (a) aging; (b) sex (i.e., being male rather than female); (c) elevated levels of cholesterol and related fats in the blood; (d) hypertension; (e) heavy cigarette smoking; (f) diabetes mellitus; (g) parental history of heart disease; (h) obesity; and (i) physical inactivity. The likelihood of heart disease increases when the number of risk factors increases. Nevertheless, the best combination of these factors still fails to identify most new cases of the disease

[1]The research reported in this chapter was made possible by grants to David C. Glass from the National Science Foundation and the Hogg Foundation for Mental Health.

223

(Jenkins, 1971). The majority of cardiac patients do not have excessive levels of serum cholesterol; only a small number are hypertensive; and even fewer are diabetic. Moreover, there is considerable controversy surrounding some of the risk factors themselves (Friedman, 1969). It is by no means clear, for example, that obesity directly increases the risk of heart disease, as is commonly believed.

These limitations in current medical knowledge argue for the need to broaden the search for contributing causes of cardiovascular disease. It is significant in this light that there is now a sizable body of research intended to determine what psychological factors enhance the risk of developing cardiac disorders (Jenkins, 1971; Jenkins, 1976). Two promising variables have been identified in recent years—psychological stress and the Type A coronary-prone behavior pattern.

PSYCHOLOGICAL STRESS

Stress has been defined as an internal state that occurs when an individual confronts a threat to his or her physical and/or psychic well-being (Lazarus, 1966). Implicit in this definition is the assumption that the internal state can be inferred by physiological, self-report, and overt behavioral measurements—for example, increased or decreased heart rate, inability to concentrate, or impaired interpersonal relations.

Stressful life events, including job dissatisfactions, economic frustration, and excessive work and responsibility, all appear related to the risk of coronary disease (House, 1975; Jenkins, 1971). The jobs of people at high risk generally entail a high degree of responsibility for others, work overloads, and role conflicts, among other stresses. Unhappiness in nonoccupational areas such as marital and family relations has also been implicated in the occurrence of coronary disease, and acute stressors over which the individual has little control—for example, the sudden death of a spouse—have been correlated with the subsequent onset of cardiac disorders in the surviving spouse (e.g., Parkes, Benjamin, & Fitzgerald, 1969).

To the extent that stress plays a role in pathogenesis of cardiovascular disease, its contribution probably occurs by affecting the physiological and neurohumoral mechanisms involved in the initiation and development of atherosclerotic plaques and/or sustained elevations in blood pressure. Recent research suggests what some of these physiological and neurohumoral mechanisms are (see Eliot, 1974; Friedman, 1969; Rosenman & Friedman, 1974). They include increases in cholesterol; accleration of the rate of damage to the intime (inner layer) of the coronary arteries over time; and facilitation of the aggregation of blood platelets (i.e., substances found in the blood that are important in coagulation), which are then incorporated into arterial plaques and contribute to narrowing of the coronary vessels and subsequent myocardial infarction. As an illustration of this physiological mediation, consider research that documents an association between cholesterol level in the blood and stressful life events. In this research, tax accountants were found to have significantly higher serum cholesterol levels during the first two weeks in April (prior to the April 15 tax deadline) than during the months of February and March, and their average cholesterol level fell sharply after April 15 (Friedman, Rosenman, & Carroll, 1958). These findings have been replicated several times, using a variety of procedures for inducing stress (see Rosenman & Friedman, 1974, for a summary of these studies).

Stress may also contribute to coronary disease through the body's nonspecific reactions to aversive stimulation. It is widely agreed that such stimulation leads to discharge of the sympathetic nervous system and related hormones such as adrenalin and noradrenalin (see, for example, Mason, 1972). These hormonal substances, collectively termed catecholamines, are secreted from the adrenal medulla and, in the case of noradrenalin, from sympathetic nerve endings as well. There is evidence that catecholamines may have special significance in the development of coronary disease. It is well known that these neurohomoral substances elevate blood pressure, and some research indicates that adrenalin and noradrenalin can accelerate the rate of arterial damage and indeed induce myocardial lesions (e.g., Raab, Stark, MacMillan, & Gigee, 1961; Raab, Chaplin, & Bajusz, 1964). Catecholamines also potentiate the aggregation of blood platelets, and the release of platelet contents is considered to be an important factor in atherogenesis as well as in the genesis of thrombosis (Ardlie, Glew, & Schwartz, 1966; Duguid, 1946; Theorell, 1974). It follows from this that any psychological agent that increases catecholamines in the blood may be a potential pathogen for cardiovascular function. Thus, since psychological stressors enhance the release of adrenalin and noradrenalin, stress may be related to coronary disease because of its generalized effects on the sympathetic nervous system and adrenal medulla.

TYPE A BEHAVIOR PATTERN

A second psychological factor in coronary heart disease is the Type A behavior pattern. The Type A pattern consists of three principal components: competitive achievement striving, a sense of time urgency, and aggressiveness, although the assumption that this set of predispositions is fully integrated in a given individual remains to be demonstrated. Pattern A has been linked to the occurrence of coronary disease in a number of studies. For example, research has shown that Type A men had more than twice the rate of heart disease as Type B men (defined by relative absence of A-type characteristics) during an 8½ year follow-up period (Rosenman, Brand, Jenkins, Friedman, Straus, & Wurm, 1975). This was true even when adjustments were made for traditional risk factors like cigarette smoking, serum cholesterol, and hypertension. Thus, the predictive relationship of Pattern A to coronary disease cannot be totally explained away by the presence of other risk factors; Pattern A exerts an independent pathogenic influence. Indeed, other research (Jenkins, Zyzanski, & Rosenman, 1976) has found that an objective measure of this behavior pattern was the strongest single predictor of recurring heart attacks, based on a set of predictor variables that included cigarette smoking and serum cholesterol level. There is also evidence indicating an association between atherosclerosis and Pattern A, with Type A patients showing a greater degree of occlusion than Type B's (e.g., Zyzanski, Jenkins, Ryan, Flessas, & Everist, 1976; Blumenthal et al., Note 1).

Despite the independent contribution of Pattern A to the occurrence of coronary disease, its influence may be mediated in part by certain of the traditional risk factors. For example, some studies indicate that fully developed Type A individuals over 35 years of age have significantly higher serum cholesterol levels than do Type B's (Friedman & Rosenman, 1959). Similar differences have been reported for other fats and related substances in the blood (e.g., Rosenman & Friedman, 1974). In fact, greater serum cholesterol concentrations have been observed in extreme Type A's, as compared to extreme Type B's, among subjects as young as 19 years of age (Glass, 1977).

There is little evidence of a relationship between hypertension and Pattern A (e.g., Shekelle, Schoenberger, & Stamler, 1976), although one study indicated that elevated diastolic blood pressure enhanced the risk of coronary disease only when the elevation occurred in Type A men (Rosenman, Friedman, Straus, Wurm, Jenkins, & Messinger, 1966). On the other hand, laboratory experiments have shown that Pattern A traits such as hostility—at least when induced by acute frustration manipulations—produce episodic rises in both systolic and diastolic blood pressure (McGin, Harburg, Julius, & McLeod, 1964). In addition, a very recent paper reports that Type A's responded to a reaction–time task with greater increases in both systolic blood pressure and heart rate than did Type B's (Dembroski, MacDougall, & Shields, 1977). These findings suggest the possibility that future research may yet uncover subtle associations between the behavior pattern and increased blood pressure.

As in the case of stress, the relation of Pattern A to coronary disease may be mediated by the sympathetic–adrenal medullary system. Support for this hypothesis comes from a number of sources, including the finding that, compared to Type B's, Type A men show less decrease in platelet aggregation in response to noradrenalin after stressful treadmill exercises (Simpson, Olewine, Jenkins, Ramsey, Zyzanski, Thomas, & Hames, 1974). Other studies indicate that bloodclotting of Type A's is hastened during periods of stress more so than is true of Type B's (Rosenman & Friedman, 1974). Of greater significance, perhaps, is the finding that A's exhibit elevated plasma levels of noradrenalin immediately before, during, and after a stressful competitive situation to a greater degree than do B's (Friedman, Byers, Diamant, & Rosenman, 1975). Simpson et al. (1974) also showed that physically fit Type A's have the largest increase in noradrenalin immediately after a treadmill test, whereas the less fit among the B's exhibited the lowest increase in noradrenalin. In addition, there is evidence that extreme Type A's excrete considerably more noradrenalin in their urine during active working hours than do Type B's (e.g., Friedman, St. George, Byers, & Rosenman, 1960).

Measuring the A and B Behavior Patterns

Classification of subjects as Type A or Type B[2] is customarily based on a standardized stress-inducing interview (Friedman, 1969; Jenkins, Rosenman, & Friedman, 1968). The subject is asked questions dealing with the intensity of his ambitions, competitiveness, time urgency, and hostile feelings. Although the content of a subject's answers is certainly an important determinant of the classification of his behavior pattern, the manner and tone in which he answers are given somewhat more weight in making a diagnosis. For example, Type A's use explosive vocal intonations more than do Type B's. Indeed, a recent study has shown that an index of volume of voice and speed of speech yields substantial agreement in classification (87%) with the more standard technique that utilizes content as well as vocal stylistics (Schucker & Jacobs, 1977).

Another approach to behavior pattern classification is based on a self-administered questionnaire called the JAS, or the Jenkins Activity Survey for Health Prediction (Jenkins, Rosenman, & Zyzanski, 1972). It consists of a series of items such as the following: (a) "How would your wife (or closest friend) rate you?" where "Definitely hard-driving and competitive" is an

[2]Descriptions of Type A and Type B individuals represent extremes of a bipolar continuum that is probably normally distributed in the United States. Indeed, diagnoses based on the interview are typically made on a four-point scale: fully developed A's, incompletely developed A's, incompletely developed B's, and fully developed B's. Therefore, it is probably more accurate to speak of Pattern A and Pattern B than Type A and Type B, as we are not really dealing with a typology. For ease of exposition, however, the terms Type and Pattern are used interchangeably here.

extreme Pattern A response and "Definitely relaxed and easy going" is a Pattern B response; and *(b)* "Do you ever set deadlines or quotas for yourself at work or at home?" where "Yes, once per week or more often" is a Pattern A response and "No" and "Yes, but only occasionally" are Pattern B responses. The JAS provides a continuous distribution of A–B scale scores.

The JAS has recently been modified for use with college students (Glass, 1977). Most of the research to be described here used this student version. Subjects typically were classified as A's or B's by division at the median of a large distribution of JAS scores obtained from male college students over a 3-year period. In some experiments, however, subjects were deliberately selected from the extremes (e.g., upper and lower thirds) of the JAS distribution. Use of the two approaches to classification produced similar patterns of results, although not surprisingly the effects were usually somewhat stronger with extreme A's and B's.

Pattern A, as previously discussed, can be defined and measured reliably. It has good validity for predicting coronary disease. There is even evidence regarding some of the mechanisms by which Pattern A contributes to cardiovascular pathology. Despite these data, there was until recently virtually no systematic evidence that Type A's do indeed exhibit excessive achievement striving, time urgency, and hostility. About 6 years ago, a program of research was begun, to elucidate the interplay of Pattern A and psychological stress in the production of coronary disease. Empirical documentation of the assumed characteristics of Pattern A was taken as the first order of business (see Glass, 1977, for a complete report of the research). These behavioral characteristics were investigated through controlled procedures that are familiar to experimental psychologists.

Construct Validation Studies of Pattern A

In both laboratory and field settings, research showed Type A's to be achievement-oriented people who work at near maximum capacity relative to B's. For example, college-age A's attempted reliably more arithmetic problems than did B's on a test in which all subjects were told that there was no time limit for completion (Burnam, Pennebaker, & Glass, 1975). When the arithmetic test was administered with an explicit 5-minute deadline, the difference between A's and B's disappeared, due largely to the increased performance of the B's. Type A subjects worked at about the same elevated level, irrespective of the presence or absence of a deadline.

Other research indicates that achievement striving is also evident in the day-to-day activities of Type A's. For example, college student A's earned reliably more academic honors than did their Type B counterparts. Moreover, when asked about their "plans after college," approximately 60% of the

A's said they would "go on to graduate or professional school," whereas 70% of the B's said, "go to work, get a job." Still other studies indicate that although Pattern A itself does not show a significant heritability estimate (Rosenman, Rahe, Borhani, & Feinleib, 1975), the behavior pattern correlates about .50 with activity level, as measured by standard temperament scales. Because activity level does have a reliable heritability coefficient (Matthews & Krantz, 1976; Rosenman et al., 1975), it may be that the hard-driving and achievement-oriented behavior of Pattern A reflects a more basic genetic predisposition to be active. Another, perhaps more likely, possibility is that Pattern A behaviors are taken on by persons whose genetic make-up renders them susceptible to shaping in the direction of that hard-driving behavioral style (see Butensky, Faralli, Heebner, & Waldron, 1976; Glass, 1977).

The preceding set of findings calls to mind the description of the Type A as a person who believes that with sufficient effort he can overcome any obstacle (e.g., Friedman, 1969). This thought led to the speculation that relative to B's, A's might suppress performance-threatening subjective states in order to achieve task mastery. An example of such a potentially debilitating state is fatigue. Would Type A's suppress fatigue in order to persist at a tiring but challenging task?

The paradigm chosen to investigate this question (Carver, Coleman, & Glass, 1976) was designed to produce veridical feelings of fatigue. In it, subjects were required to walk continuously on a motorized treadmill at increasingly sharp angles of incline (see Balke, 1954; Balke, Grillo, Konecci, & Luft, 1954). Type A and Type B subjects completed this treadmill test while rating their fatigue on an 11-point scale at 2-minute intervals. Each subject also completed a running test designed to assess maximum aerobic capacity, that is, the person's maximum rate of oxygen consumption. Each subject's walking performance subsequently was scored as a proportion of his maximum capacity.

Physical characteristics (e.g., percentage of body fat) of Type A and Type B subjects were essentially the same. But Pattern A subjects reached an oxygen absorption rate on the walking treadmill test equal to 91.4% of their maximum capacities, whereas Pattern B subjects reached an average rate equal to only 82.8% of their capacities. It thus would appear that A's worked at levels closer to the limits of their endurance than did B's. Even as they did so, A's expressed less overall fatigue than did B's (means = 6.2 and 5.2, $p <$ .04). Indeed, Type A's rated their fatigue as significantly lower than did Type B's on each of the last four ratings made prior to termination of the walking treadmill test. Subsequent research (Matthews & Brunson, 1979) suggests that these findings reflect an active suppression of awareness of the intrusive fatigue symptoms.

As previously suggested, this tendency toward fatigue suppression may be understood in terms of the achievement orientation of Pattern A. Denial or suppression of fatigue has instrumental value: It aids in the Type A's struggle for attainment of desired goals—in this case, superior treadmill performance. The acknowledgement of fatigue, on the other hand, might interfere with successful task mastery—a situation that A's could not easily tolerate.

Another difference between Type A's and B's is the presence of a sense of time urgency. Experimentation indicates that A's become impatient with delay and report that a time interval of 1 minute elapses reliably sooner than Type B's (Burnam et al., 1975). The arousal of impatience has behavioral consequences as well. For example, Type A's have been shown to do more poorly than Type B's on a task that required a delayed response (Glass, Snyder, & Hollis, 1974). Because this task provides differential reinforcement of low rates of responding, it is typically abbreviated as "DRL." On the DRL task, the subject must wait during a fixed time interval before responding; any premature response resets the time relationship, and the subject does not obtain reinforcement. The DRL task is quite difficult and can be mastered only with considerable patience. Type A subjects' reinforcement scores were significantly lower on this test than those of Type B subjects (medians = 66.5 and 77.6, $p < .05$). More detailed analysis revealed that A's performed more poorly because they were unable to wait long enough after receiving reinforcement before responding again. Behavioral observations also confirmed the impatience of A's with delayed responding. Approximately 48% of the A's but only 12% of the B's displayed tense and hyperactive movements during their DRL sessions.

Lengthy intervals between trials on other kinds of tasks—for example, reaction time (RT) procedures—might also be expected to arouse impatience in A's, with resultant restless behavior and distraction. If such activity diverted attention away from the task at hand, it would cause the Type A individual to respond more slowly than his Type B counterpart when the cue for response eventually appeared. To test this reasoning, performance on a complex RT task was assessed in a study in which intertrial intervals were either short (1.5 seconds) or relatively long (random intervals ranging from 4 to 9 seconds). Speed of response was measured as the mean latency over the 48 trials.

Analysis of the latency scores revealed that B's were indeed faster than A's when intertrial intervals were long (means = 445.7 and 484.8 milliseconds), whereas A's reacted slightly more quickly than B's when intervals were short (means = 382.9 and 394.8 milliseconds). The statistical interaction in these data ($p < .06$) provides additional validation for the time urgency component of Pattern A: Type A's reacted more slowly when conditions placed a premium on patience than when such delays were not imposed. By contrast, Type B's show similar reaction times irrespective of the length of the intervals between trials.

A third major facet of Pattern A is hostility and aggressiveness. Carver and Glass (1978) conducted two experiments to examine this behavioral tendency. The first study tested the idea that, relative to B's, A's would react with enhanced aggressiveness toward another person who denigrated their efforts to perform a difficult task. Accordingly, some subjects were harassed by a confederate while attempting to solve a very difficult puzzle ("instigation" condition). An opportunity was later given to subjects to administer ostensible electric shocks to the harassing individual (cf. Buss, 1961). Subjects assigned to a control condition participated only in the shock phase of the study. In comparison to the control treatment, the instigation procedure aroused substantial aggression ($p < .01$). The principal source of this main effect was the amount of shock delivered by Type A subjects. That is, individual contrasts revealed that instigated A's delivered higher levels of shock than did their control group counterparts ($p < .01$). On the other hand, Type B's given the instigation treatment did not shock at a reliably higher level than did control group B's ($p > .30$). The overall interaction effect in the analysis of variance did not achieve an acceptable level of statistical significance ($p > .15$); nevertheless, the contrasts indicate that A's are not uniformly more aggressive than B's. Rather, they become so in response to a specific set of arousing circumstances.

This finding subsequently was replicated (Carver & Glass, 1978, study 2) in an experiment that also provided additional information regarding antecedents of differences in aggression between A's and B's. This second experiment included a "frustration" condition, in which subjects failed at the puzzle but were not harassed by the confederate. Analysis of shock means from this study revealed that the most reliable difference between Pattern A and Pattern B individuals occurred in the frustration condition ($p < .03$). Type A's were very nearly as aggressive after having been frustrated as they were when they had been exposed to the full instigation procedure; Type B's, in contrast, responded to the frustration with a slight (nonsignificant) decrease in aggression. Thus, an interpersonal provocation apparently is not required to elicit aggression from the Type A; a task frustration by itself is sufficiently challenging to evoke that response. Type B's, however, are indifferent to the frustration.

INTERPLAY OF STRESS AND PATTERN A

The research on Pattern A described thus far can be viewed from three different perspectives. The studies provide systematic documentation for the three behavioral components of Pattern A. In so doing, the research also provides evidence for the validity of the measures used to classify subjects as A's or B's. Finally, these results may also be examined from a conceptual point of view. Such an analysis would seem to provide insight both into the motivational dynamics of Pattern A and into the relationship between this behavior pattern and psychological stress. This approach may have far-reaching implications. In particular, consideration of these issues may suggest mechanisms by which Pattern A adversely affects the cardiovascular system.

An examination of the validity studies as a group reveals an apparent commonality among the many specific empirical findings. To recapitulate: compared to B's, Type A's work hard to succeed, suppress subjective states (e.g., fatigue) that might interfere with task performance, exhibit rapid pacing of their activities, and express hostility after being frustrated and harassed in their efforts at task completion. At the crux of all of these behavioral effects, we would submit, is an attempt by the Type A to assert control over environmental demands and requirements. Moreover, it is also likely that these demands involve at least minimal stress, for the possibilities of failure and loss of esteem were inherent in most of the experimental situations used in the validation studies. The coronary-prone behavior pattern thus might be described as a characteristic style of responding to environmental stressors that threaten the individual's sense of control (cf. Glass & Singer, 1972). The Type A is engaged in a continual struggle for control, whereas the Type B is relatively free of such concerns and, hence, is free of Pattern A traits.

The concept of control may be defined in terms of perceptions of contingencies. If a person perceives a contingency between his behaviors and an outcome, that is, if he believes that his behaviors determine that outcome, the outcome is considered controllable. By contrast, if a person believes that his actions do not influence an outcome, the outcome is uncontrollable. Stressors can be either controllable or uncontrollable. A controllable stressor is a potentially harmful stimulus that can be avoided by appropriate instrumental responses. An uncontrollable stressor is a harmful stimulus that the person can neither escape nor avoid.

Responses to Uncontrollable Stress

The initial reaction of Type A's to an uncontrollable stressor may be termed *hyper-responsiveness,* because it is assumed to reflect an effort to assert control over the stimulus. In comparison to B's, A's display increased motivation—at least initially—to master stressful situations that they perceive as potentially uncontrollable. An important question is whether this heightened motivation generalizes across tasks. If so, after having been briefly exposed to an uncontrollable stress (for example, a few trials of inescapable noise stimulation), the Type A would be expected to exert greater efforts than the Type B to master a subsequent task in an attempt to reestablish a sense of control.

Such enhanced motivation, of course, may facilitate or disrupt later performance, depending upon the nature of the task. Consider the reaction time (RT) study previously described, which used long intertrial intervals. Pattern A subjects, it will be recalled, showed longer latencies of response than did Pattern B subjects, presumably because of their inability to sustain the patience needed to remain alert during the relatively long waiting period. Assuming that uncontrollable stress enhances the motivation of A's, shorter response latencies might be expected if the same long-interval RT task were administered after exposure to inescapable compared to escapable noise. In other words, after being threatened with loss of control, A's might be expected to contain their impatience in order to perform well, thereby reasserting control. This should result in relatively faster RT responses among A's, following the uncontrollable stressor. Type B's, in contrast, should show less improvement after an experience with uncontrollability, for they are assumed to be less responsive to the incentive of environmental control.

The foregoing line of thought was tested in the following manner. Twenty Type A's and 20 Type B's were exposed to 12 bursts of 100-decibel noise.[3] Half the A's and half the B's in the study were randomly assigned to a pre-treatment in which they were able to escape from each of the noise bursts by appropriate lever-pressing responses (escape condition). The other half of the subjects were unable to terminate the sound (no escape condition). The test phase of the study, which immediately followed the noise pretreatment, consisted of an RT task with long intertrial intervals. The major dependent measure consisted of response latencies (in msec) averaged across RT trials.

The escape–no escape noise pretreatment proved to be successful in inducing differential perceptions of lack of control. In a postexperimental questionnaire, subjects were asked, "How much control did you feel you had over the termination of the noise?", where 7 = "completely in control" and 1 = "no control at all." The mean for subjects in the escape condition was 4.8, and for those in no escape, 1.7, the difference being highly significant ($p < .001$).

The response–latency results are presented in Figure 9.1. The reliable interaction between behavior pattern and type of pretreatment ($p < .005$) confirmed initial expectations: A's are normally slower than B's on this

---

[3]This amount of stimulation was selected as constituting a brief exposure to an uncontrollable stressor because research that will be discussed later indicated that more prolonged exposure (e.g., 35 noise bursts) produces learned helplessness rather than facilitation effects (see also Hiroto, 1974).

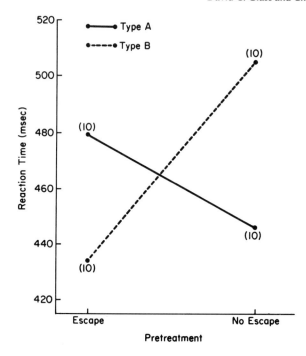

Figure 9.1. Mean reaction times of Type A's and Type B's for 47 trials on the choice reaction time task, after pretreatment with escapable or inescapable noise. (Group sizes are in parentheses.)

particular RT task; the interpolation of an escapable pretreatment was not expected to alter this difference, and it did not. However, the threat inherent in exposure to uncontrollable noise appears to have motivated Type A subjects in the no escape condition to respond more rapidly to the RT signal light, despite the lengthy waiting period. Type B's, in contrast, may have experienced a decrement in motivation, because their RT performance was impaired by prior experience with uncontrollability.

These results were conceptually replicated in an experiment that induced perceived lack of control by random positive and negative reinforcements (i.e., "correct" or "incorrect" evaluations) for attempts to solve two cognitive tasks (see Hiroto & Seligman, 1975). Noncontingent reinforcement of this kind implies that the probability of being correct is independent of the subject's responses; hence the procedure is tantamount to inducing perceived uncontrollability (see Seligman, 1975). Controllability perceptions were induced among other subjects by giving them contingent reinforcement for their attempts to solve the tasks. That is, these subjects were told "correct" when their answers were correct and "incorrect" when their answers were wrong. The effect of these pretreatments was measured on a subsequent DRL task. Recall that Type A's do more poorly on DRL than do Type B's (see earlier discussion). To the extent that uncontrollable pretreatment enhances their motivation to succeed, however, we might expect better performance from A's than from B's after such a pretreatment.

The results of this study are shown in Figure 9.2. It is readily apparent that the interaction $(p < .02)$ is remarkably similar to the one depicted in Figure 9.1, except that a delayed response is correct here, whereas a fast response was correct in the first study. This replication shows, then, that As' performance was enhanced after exposure to uncontrollable stress, even though such behavior appears to require suppression of As' customary impatience with a DRL task.

Findings of these two studies, taken together, support the inference that had been made from the validity studies: Pattern A behavior emerges in the presence of perceived threats to environmental control. It would appear that

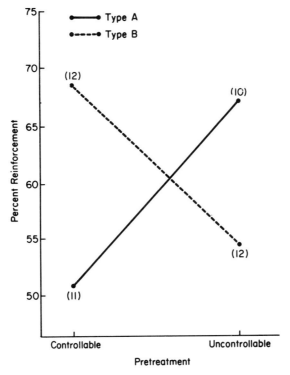

Figure 9.2. Percent reinforcement for Type A's and Type B's over the DRL session, after pretreatment with controllable (soluble) or uncontrollable (insoluble) reinforcement. (Group sizes are parentheses.)

Type A behavior is a strategy for coping with potentially uncontrollable stress; enhanced performance reflects an attempt to assert and maintain control after its loss has been threatened. This interpretation has received further support from experimentation using other techniques for inducing lack of control, including various partial reinforcement procedures that were perceived as differentially uncontrollable (see Glass, 1977).

Responses to Extended Exposure to Uncontrollable Stress

Enhanced responding aimed at asserting control over an uncontrollable stressor must prove ineffective in the long run, for extended exposure eventually leads to the perception that no relationship exists between responses and outcomes. The Type A individual might then be expected to give up efforts at control and to display *hyporesponsiveness* to uncontrollable events (see Wortman & Brehm, 1975), a giving-up pattern that has been termed "learned helplessness." Although B's may also experience helplessness under these circumstances, it is the A's who are likely to show greater hyporesponsiveness because of their tendency to experience loss of control as more threatening.

This hypothesis was first tested using Seligman's (1975) learned helplessness paradigm (Krantz, Glass & Snyder, 1974). Type A's and Type B's were exposed to a pretreatment consisting of either loud (105 decibels) or moderate (78 decibels) noise, in an effort to induce differential degrees of stress. Thirty-five, rather than 12, noise bursts were administered to each subject. Half the subjects within each stress–level condition were unable to escape from noise (no escape condition), whereas the other half could terminate the noise by manipulating rotary switches (escape condition). The test phase of the study used the same intensity of noise as had the first part of the experiment. However, all subjects could now escape, or even avoid, the noise by making appropriate responses with a shuttle box lever.

The dependent variables measured in the test phase of this study included the number of trials taken to achieve a criterion of three consecutive escape and/or avoidance responses (see Table 9.1). Analysis of variance conducted on this measure revealed an escape–no escape main effect ($p <$ .01), a stress level by A–B interaction ($p <$ .02), and a significant triple-order interaction ($p <$ .02). Subsequent contrasts indicated that Type A's in the no escape–high-stress condition took significantly more trials to learn the escape response than did A's in the escape–high-stress condition ($p <$ .05). Type B's in the escape and no escape groups did not differ under high-stress conditions. Just the opposite pattern occurred in conditions of moderate stress. Type B's given the no escape pretreatment took more trials to

TABLE 9.1
Mean Number of Trials to Criterion for Escape and/or Avoidance Learning[a]

	Escape	No escape
High stress, Pattern A	6.3 (n = 9)	12.7 (n = 9)
High stress, Pattern B	7.2 (n = 6)	8.7 (n = 6)
Moderate stress, Pattern A	7.7 (n = 7)	8.5 (n = 6)
Moderate stress, Pattern B	9.0 (n = 8)	20.0 (n = 9)

[a]Comparisons between cell means were conducted using the error-mean-square from a three-way analysis of variance. These comparisons revealed a number of significant differences ($p < .05$ or better), including those between the following cell means: (a) 12.7 and 6.3; (b) 20.1 and 9.0; (c) 20.1 and 8.7; (d) 20.1 and 8.5. The differences between (a) 12.7 and 8.5, (b) 9.0 and 7.2, and (c) 7.7 and 6.3 were not statistically significant ($ps > .20$).

reach criterion than did B's given the escapable pretreatment ($p < .05$), whereas there was no difference between A's in the escape and no escape groups.

These results were somewhat surprising. The initial prediction had been only for an interaction between behavior pattern and the pretreatment manipulation of controllability (see Krantz et al., 1974). However, the data suggest a more complex relationship, in which stress level somehow mediates the reactions of A's and B's to extended exposure to uncontrollable stress. A seemingly obvious interpretation would be that A's experience more arousal than do B's, but the A–B variable failed to show reliable associations with either electrodermal or self-report measures of arousal collected during and immediately after the pretreatment phase of the study. It is always possible that differences were present but went undetected because of insufficient and/or incorrect sampling of physiological channels. On the other hand, additional studies conducted by the authors have been unsuccessful in producing A–B differences in heart-rate and finger-vaso-constriction responses to stressful stimulation. We cannot dismiss the possibility of an arousal interpretation; A's have, after all, been found to respond to the challenge of experimental tasks with greater increases in systolic blood pressure and heart rate than do their Type B counterparts (Dembroski et al., 1977). However, the physiological results from the experiment under discussion did not indicate the viability of an arousal explanation of the learned helplessness results. Therefore, a cognitive interpretation was proposed and explored in subsequent research.

This interpretation was as follows. If Type A's are more concerned than Type B's about maintaining environmental control, A's might be expected to distort or deny cues signifying absence of control when such cues do not compel attention. If Type A's thereby can minimize the fact that they are unable to control the situation, they thus may encode the fact of uncontrollability less effectively and, hence, fail to display learned helplessness in a subsequent task. This may have been what occurred in the Krantz et al. (1974) research among Type A's given relatively moderate inescapable noise. If, on the other hand, lack of control is highly salient—which should have been the case when the inescapable noise was loud enough to be aversive— A's should experience considerable difficulty in ignoring the absence of control. Perhaps A's exert heightened efforts at locating control-relevant cues, which should eventually lead to stronger certainty that nothing can be done to gain control. These expectations may then transfer from the pre-treatment to the test phase of the paradigm, where they appear as impaired learning of escape and avoidance responses.

Although this line of thought (cf. Schachter & Rodin, 1974) appears to fit the pattern of results obtained in the Krantz et al. helplessness experiment, the interpretation is obviously post hoc and requires independent verification. Accordingly a second study was done by Hollis and Glass (reported in Glass, 1977), which used a different manipulation of salience and a manipulation of uncontrollability that was based on noncontingency of reinforcements for task performance (see earlier discussion). In this study, there were four rather than two tasks, thereby extending the subjects' exposure to lack of control. Salience was manipulated by systematically varying the prominence of reinforcement—for example, by having some subjects keep detailed records of whether their responses were "correct" or "incorrect." This procedure made it relatively simple for a subject to see if there was a relationship between his answers and the reinforcements he received during the session. The effects of these manipulations of lack of control were assessed with an anagrams task that had been used in previous learned-helplessness research (Hiroto & Seligman, 1975). A major dependent measure was the number of trials needed to achieve an arbitrary criterion of three consecutive anagram solutions in less than 15 seconds each. (A more complete account of procedural and measurement details is contained in Glass, 1977, ch. 8.)

The results of this study corresponded to those of the Krantz et al. (1974) helplessness experiment. Indeed, comparison of the two sets of data revealed distinct similarities in the principal contrasts between experimental conditions. Type A's in this study showed greater helplessness (i.e., more trials to the anagrams criterion) after uncontrollable than controllable pretreatment, provided that the cues signifying lack of control were made salient ($p < .05$). When cues were low in salience, Type A's showed minimal evidence of helplessness ($p > .20$). Unlike the previous helplessness study, however, B's in the low-salience–uncontrollable condition took only marginally more trials to reach criterion than did comparable B's in the controllable condition ($p = .10$).

In summary, prolonged exposure to uncontrollable stress causes a giving-up response to replace the Type A's exaggerated attempts to control his environment, which had been the central feature of earlier findings. However, this vulnerability of A's to learned helplessness must be qualified by the degree of prominence or salience of cues signifying the uncontrollable nature of the stressor. That is, Type A's exhibit helplessness only under conditions of high salience. The case for these generalizations is strengthened by the range of conditions under which predicted effects have been observed, including various subject populations, different experimenters who were blind to the subject's A–B classification, and somewhat different techniques for inducing perceived lack of control.

CONTROL AND CORONARY HEART DISEASE

The helplessness results that have been reported above take on added significance when viewed in the light of recent work on the relationship between changes in an individual's life and the occurrence of disease. Early research in this area suggested that accumulated life events, whether positive or negative, had an impact on disease onset; the important factor, it was believed, was the total amount of change experienced (e.g., Holmes & Rahe, 1967). More recent studies indicate, however, that events must be negative in order to potentiate illness (e.g., Dohrenwend & Dohrenwend, 1974). Moreover, there is even some suggestion that it is the uncontrollability and helplessness induced by certain types of negative life changes that is critical in facilitating the onset of some diseases (cf. Paykel, 1974).

Events such as the death of a close friend, a sudden financial setback, and a loss in occupational prestige are all adverse occurrences that are not easily affected by our own actions. Such losses often lead to helplessness, depression, and a tendency to give up the attempt to cope with the environment (Seligman, 1975). It has been proposed (e.g., Engel, 1968; Schmale, 1972) that this kind of helplessness has a role in the pathogenesis of a variety of physical diseases, ranging from the common cold to cancer. Others (Greene, Goldstein, & Moss, 1972) have shown that sudden death is abnormally frequent among men who had been depressed for a week to several months prior to death (according to reports of next of kin). Although these data are certainly not conclusive, they do suggest the possibility that helplessness-inducing life events are precursors to coronary heart disease as well as to other diseases. Because so many disorders have been linked to uncontrollable life stressors, however, we must consider what other factor might interact with helplessness to produce coronary disease in particular. A reasonable possibility for investigation is that the Type A behavior pattern constitutes a predisposing condition that mediates the relationship between helplessness and cardiovascular pathology. The laboratory research described earlier indicates that extended experience with salient uncontrollable stressors results in helplessness among Type A's. By extrapolation, it seems plausible that the interaction of Pattern A and helplessness-inducing life events might be a precursor to clinical coronary disease.

The ideal test of this hypothesis would require a prospective study. That is, support gained from retrospective research might conceivably reflect a tendency for coronary cases to rationalize their illness in terms of hurrying and hard work and/or the stress of uncontrollable life events. Although practical considerations have made it impossible for us to do longitudinal research on this question thus far, one retrospective project has been conducted as an exploratory test of the foregoing reasoning. Hospitalized coronary patients and noncoronary controls were compared to each other in terms of their A–B scores and their recall of life events prior to disease onset. A 1-year period of life events was selected for assessment, because previous research has suggested that it is this period that is most relevant to clinical coronary disease (Theorell & Rahe, 1975).

Three samples were examined in this study: 45 patients in the coronary care unit of the Veterans Administration Hospital in Houston, Texas; 77 patients in the general-medical and psychiatric wards at the same hospital (the hospitalized control group); and 50 building-maintenance employees from the University of Texas at Austin campus (the healthy or nonhospitalized control group). All participants were males, aged 35 to 55, and the groups were frequency-matched in terms of social class, race, and religion.

Each subject completed the Jenkins Activity Survey and a modified version of the Schedule of Recent Experience, an instrument used in previous research on stressful life change (e.g., Holmes & Rahe, 1967). The latter measure asked the respondent to enumerate the occurrences of each of 47 life events during the 1-year period prior to hospitalization or, in the case of the healthy controls, prior to the time the questionnaire was completed. Before the study was conducted, a loss index was developed, consisting of 10 items that were agreed upon by three members of the research staff as reflecting stressful life events over which minimal control could be exerted. Examples are "death of a close family member," "being fired," and "large decline in financial status." Also constructed was a negative events index that contained 7 items designed to reflect life events that would be experienced as stressful but not necessarily as uncontrollable or helplessness-inducing losses. Items in this index included "detention in jail" and "large increase in number of arguments with spouse."

Analysis of the JAS data revealed that coronary patients had significantly higher Pattern A scores than did either the hospitalized or nonhospitalized controls ($ps < .01$). In addition, a reliably higher percentage of each patient group (coronaries and hospitalized noncoronaries) than healthy controls reported having experienced at least one loss in the previous year. In contrast, percentages for the negative events index did not differ among subject samples.

From these data, it would appear that helplessness-inducing life events—not just negative events—discriminate persons with illness from those without disease. Moreover, Pattern A seems to discriminate persons with coronary heart disease from those with other diseases, inasmuch as coronary patients had higher JAS scores than did either the hospitalized or the non-hospitalized control subjects. These findings are consistent with the reasoning previously presented: that an excess of life events involving loss of environmental control, when experienced by persons possessing the Type A behavioral style, may be specifically associated with coronary disease. Prospective research obviously is needed, however, to corroborate these findings.

A BIOBEHAVIORAL MODEL

The studies discussed above analyzed the relationship between Pattern A and uncontrollable stress. However, the long-range goal of research in this area is to show how these two variables interact to influence the development of coronary disease. The pursuit of this goal necessarily involves systematic examination of physiological and biochemical processes, for in the final analysis such processes must mediate the impact of behavior on cardiovascular pathology. The necessary research is only in its early stages; nevertheless, it is possible at this time to specify some of the possible mediating physiological mechanisms.

As was discussed earlier in this chapter, there is evidence that elevated levels of adrenalin and noradrenalin may potentiate the development of coronary disease. Because these two catecholamines are intimately related to autonomic nervous system discharge, it is not surprising that stress influences their relative presence in the blood. It is also recognized that active coping with a stressor leads to an increased discharge of noradrenalin, whereas adrenalin levels remain relatively unchanged during coping (e.g., Funkenstein, King, & Drolette, 1957; Weiss, Stone, & Harrell, 1970; Elmadjian, 1963). Other data indicate that, though adrenalin levels sometimes rise initially in response to stressful stimulation, they decline as the person's felt ability to master the disturbing stimuli increases (Frankenhaeuser, 1971). Finally, recent studies have also shown that severe depletion of brain norepinephrine in rats is often associated with helplessness and giving-up responses (e.g., Weiss, Glazer, & Pohorecky, 1976).

The following represents a tentative integration of these biochemical processes with the behavioral data reported earlier in this chapter. When a person perceives a threat to his sense of environmental control, he struggles to reestablish and maintain control. During this period of active coping efforts, we would expect concomitant elevations in circulating noradrenalin, though adrenalin levels should remain unchanged or perhaps even decline. As the realization develops that control has been lost, the person becomes passive and gives up. During this period, noradrenalin levels are likely to decline.

This behavioral sequence—efforts to exert control followed by giving up—is undoubtedly repeated over and over again during the life of an individual. It is entirely possible that the more frequently this cycle occurs, the more one's coronary arteries are affected by atherosclerotic disease. This extrapolation derives, in part, from results cited earlier suggesting that excessive elevations of catecholamines over time may serve as an intermediary process whereby stress leads to coronary pathology (see, e.g., Raab et al., 1964; Rosenman & Friedman, 1974). The extrapolation also derives from more speculative notions implicating the rise and fall of catecholamines and rapid shifts between sympathetic and parasympathetic activity in the etiology of coronary disease and sudden death (Engel, 1970; Richter, 1957). Also relevant here is research indicating that patients with coronary heart disease show substantially impaired parasympathetic regulation of heart rate (Eckberg, Drabinsky, & Braunwald, 1971).

How might Pattern A fit into this general picture? We noted earlier that Type A's seem to show enhanced platelet aggregation in response to noradrenalin, as compared to Type B's (Simpson et al., 1974). Moreover, at least three studies have indicated that A's display elevated noradrenalin reactions to stressful stimulation, whereas B's fail to show this responsiveness (Friedman et al., 1960; Friedman et al., 1975; Simpson et al., 1974). Given these findings, it might be argued that the atherogenetic processes previously described for people in general apply a forteriori to Type A's. In other words, persons possessing Pattern A characteristics experience the alternation of active coping and giving up more frequently and intensely than do persons with Pattern B characteristics. This assumption is not at all unreasonable: Recall that A's vigorously engage in efforts to master their environments; nevertheless, many human struggles end in failure and helplessness. To the extent that coronary disease is influenced by a cycle of hyperreactivity and hyporeactivity, the greater likelihood of the disease among A's than among B's might be accounted for by the cumulative effects of excessive rise and fall of catecholamines, released by the repetitive interplay of Pattern A and uncontrollable stress.

These speculations obviously do not tell the entire story—perhaps not even a significant portion of it. This general explanation has been offered only as a heuristic guide to future thinking and research. Coronary disease clearly must be regarded as having a multifaceted etiology. Some of the traditional risk factors (e.g., elevated serum cholesterol, cigarette smoking) will have to be incorporated into any complete analysis of the pathogenesis of the disease. However, it should be emphasized that a thorough knowledge of how psychological and physiological variables interact to produce coronary disease will add an important dimension to our understanding of its etiology. Though many theoretical questions remain to be answered, the behavioral research described in this chapter provides a partial basis for analysis of the coronary disease process.

REFERENCE NOTE

1. Blumenthal, J. A., Williams, R. B., Kong, Y., Thompson, L. W., Jenkins, C. D., & Rosenman, R. H. *Coronary-prone behavior and angiographically documented coronary disease.* Paper presented at the Annual Meeting of the American Psychosomatic Society, March 21, 1975, New Orleans.

10

Personality and Locus of Control[1]

HERBERT M. LEFCOURT

INTRODUCTION

Much of the research literature concerned with helplessness, perceived control, and causal attributions has derived from investigative procedures that involve only brief or momentary elicitations of causal perceptions. As this writer noted after reviewing several attribution studies (Lefcourt, Hogg, Struthers, & Holmes, 1975), most causual ascriptions have been obtained after subjects have performed on tasks that are no longer than 2–4 minutes in duration. Given the assumed importance of these research topics in providing leads to the comprehension of depression, affective experiences, and responses to stress, concern with the reliability and ecological validity of procedures employed in their study becomes warranted.

The focus on momentary processes has not been shaped solely by the substance or phenomena under investigation. Though experimental procedures often do necessitate the use of analog models and singular observations, a great influence in this direction also derives from the theoretical contributions of Walter Mischel. With his criticism of personality theorizing

[1]This chapter was compiled while the author was supported by Canada Council Grant No. 410-77-0342.

in which there is an absence of attention to the situational determinants of behavior, Mischel (1968) may have helped to discourage the sort of research that would endeavor to evaluate more generalized and stable characteristics of individuals. Consequently, in the literature on helplessness, for instance, the focus of most research is upon the creation of states of helplessness. On the other hand, little effort has been expended on the exploration of helplessness as an enduring quality of individuals.

Recently, several psychologists have attempted to redress the overzealous eschewing of concern with stable personality characteristics. Block (1977), for one, has reported on the reliability of inferred personality characteristics over several years duration, such that adult test scores and performances are found to be predictable from analogous measures obtained during early adolescence. Epstein (1977), likewise, has found high reliability for self-rated moods and affects as a function of the number of times that the self-ratings were obtained; that is, the greater were the number of mood assessments, the more highly were composite scores related to like scores obtained at other times. Given individuals, then, could be characterized as generally morose or buoyant with greater confidence than would have been possible if only single self-ratings had been available.

With this support for a return to the investigation of relatively stable characteristics (Magnussen & Endler, 1977), we may feel encouraged to examine helplessness as a personality characteristic or as a description of individuals that transcends situational specificity to some degree.

One construct that more readily allows for the investigation of helplessness as a personality characteristic is locus of control. Other cognate constructs such as personal causation (de Charms, 1968), alienation (Seeman, 1963), and hopelessness (Stotland, 1969), might be equally useful. However, the sheer weight of accummulated research with the locus of control construct makes its utility more likely when considering helplessness as a personality variable.

LOCUS OF CONTROL AS
A PERSONALITY CONSTRUCT

Description of the Construct

The term "locus of control" refers to a construct that originated from within Rotter's social learning theory (Rotter, Chance, & Phares, 1972). In social learning terminology, locus of control is a generalized expectancy pertaining to the connection between personal characteristics and/or actions and experienced outcomes. It develops as an abstraction from a number of specific encounters in which persons perceive the causal sequences occurring in their lives. For some individuals, many outcomes are experienced as dependent upon the effort expended in their pursuit. Such persons may come to believe that outcomes are generally contingent upon the work put into them, so that they are more apt to exert themselves when engaged in important tasks. On the other hand, individuals living in less responsive milieus may fail to perceive the connections between efforts and outcomes. In societies where nepotism, graft, and other inequitous procedures may dominate the economic scene, for example, success is probably perceived as being more a function of luck or "being related to the right people" than it is of effort or ability. Consequently, more time may be expended in prayer, gambling, or a search for succour than at instrumental acts that could help to create the desired ends.

When environments are extreme in terms of opportunity, we are less likely to ascribe such perceptions of response–outcome relationships to "personality." Rather, we are apt to discuss social constraints and opportunities with the assumption that behavior would change with alterations of environmental conditions. However, when the milieu is such that constraints are not all pervasive and obvious, then it becomes easier to speak of causal perceptions as personality characteristics or as relatively stable individual differences.

Locus of control, like helplessness, concerns the beliefs that individuals hold regarding the relationships between actions and outcomes. Whereas Seligman (1975) describes helplessness in terms of response–outcome independence, a generalized expectation of external control is defined as a pervasive belief that outcomes are not determinable by one's personal efforts. The converse, an internal locus of control, is the belief that outcomes are contingent upon actions. Within social learning theory it is possible to describe individuals as holding expectations that are more "internal" or "external" with regard to causation and thus to control.

Since the early introduction of the locus of control construct (Rotter, Seeman, & Liverant, 1962) and the Internal–External Control of Reinforcement Scale (I–E-Rotter, 1966), there have been innumerable studies reported that have served to demonstrate the construct validity of locus of control as a personality variable. Two recent books (Lefcourt, 1976; Phares, 1976) have attempted to summarize this burgeoning literature.

In general, persons who have described themselves as holding generalized expectancies of external control appear to behave in ways that are congruent with descriptions of helplessness. They are less likely to be active in the pursuit of information related to the state of their own well-being, are less likely to use information if it is available, and are less likely to express those positive affects that are associated with a state of well-being than are internals. As expressed by Lefcourt (1976):

> Where fatalism or external control beliefs are associated with apathy and with-drawal, the holding of internal control expectancies presages a connection between an individual's desires and his subsequent actions. As such, locus of control can be viewed as a mediator of involved commitment in life pursuits. If one feels helpless to effect important events, then resignation or at least benign indifference should become evident with fewer signs of concern, involvement and vitality]p. 152[.

Given these descriptions, which have been derived from a large body of empirical research, one could conclude that locus of control is an adequate personality equivalent of the states of helplessness that have been examined in laboratory research.

Difficulities and Complexities in the Use of the Locus of Control Construct

Recently, Rotter (1975) and Lefcourt (1976) have offered suggestions and criticisms with regard to the ways in which the locus of control construct has been put to use. As is often the case, when a construct is opera-tionalized by a simply administered assessment instrument, it will be used in ways that the test constructors never dreamed of. Correlations with a host of barely relevant dependent measures are reported, and a confusing network of associations result. In all, what emerges is a rather blurred picture of the construct that overlaps with seemingly similar but different concepts. In the case of locus of control, confusion sometimes arises from a blurring with needs for power, autonomy, and control as well as with other expectancy-like constructs such as hope.

Another source of confusion arises from terminology and language. When making use of abbreviated terms such as "internals" or "externals" for expedience in expression, it is simple to forget that such labels are descriptions of beliefs or expectancies and not of individuals per se. If we describe persons as internals, we are designating persons as members of a group who have expressed internal control expectancies about the particu-lar events sampled within given assessment devices. Depending on which realms of experience have been assessed, these individuals can be accurate-ly said to be internals only with regard to those particular realms. The most commonly used I–E scale has been Rotter's, which consists of 23 items that sample expectancies concerning achievement, affilation, business, and world affairs. Given the paucity of items in each area and the unsystematic sam-pling of areas, the scale is not to be thought of as powerful nor as a vehicle from which different scores may be adequately derived. The one useful score obtained from the scale is interpreted as a rough and general measure of locus of control. To label that person who scores in the external direction on Rotter'a scale an external is strictly a research convenience that is tolerable where errors of classification are relatively unimportant. Therefore, if one were to assume that high magnitude predictions can be made from I–E scores or that "personality types" can be inferred from such scores, the likelihood of disappointment would be high and would be increased by the degree to which criterion behavior diverged from the type of items sampled on the I–E scale. To express it concretely, one would have difficulty in accurately predicting affectional behaviors from I–E scores derived from items concerned with achievement, world affairs, etc.

The Limits of Locus of Control as a Predictive Construct

One of the earliest criticisms of the locus of control literature pertained to milieu constraints that alter the meaning of locus of control as a personality variable. Gurin, Gurin, Lao, & Beattie (1969) raised the issue that urban blacks would be foolish to consider their worlds as being personally controllable. In fact, they suggested that black persons who characterized themselves as internals were likely to be demoralized from holding themselves responsible for an inevitable number of defeats. Those criticisms raised an interesting question with regard to base rate experience. For individuals who are favored with success experiences, internal control expectancies could result in a sense of pride, positive affects, and assertive, striving behavior. However, for individuals who are more likely to experience setbacks and failures, an internal locus of control could result in depression, self-denigration, and a surrender of ambition.

In addition to this complication, there has been some disagreement pertaining to the ways in which locus of control relates to responses made in failure situations. Phares (1976) has contended that internals have greater difficulty in assimilating negative feedback, whereas Lefcourt (1976) has argued the reverse—that internals are less quick to draw generalizations about their inabilities than are externals and, consequently, should be better able to accept specific instances of failure.

It is apparent that issues are made more complex by the inclusion of other variables such as the incidence of success and failure experiences or the evaluations that persons have of those experiences. If individuals do not care about particular goal areas, then little value should be obtained with I–E measures in predicting behavior related to those goals. With regard to Gurin's concerns about poor urban blacks, it is questionable whether the areas described in Rotter's I–E scale would be of immediate importance to that sample. It is plausible that academic achievement is of lesser priority to urban black children than is success at getting along with peers. In a milieu where one's safety on the streets is at stake, the ability to win friends who can help to defend one in tight circumstances may be of greater salience than achievement-related behaviors. Likewise, belief in the ability to defend one's self in rough encounters may have as much impact upon daily behavior styles of ghetto dwellers as beliefs regarding academic competence may have for middle-class persons.

Naditch (Note 1) has demonstrated the importance of considering values in predictive formulae that include the locus of control variable. Only for subjects who represented the upper third in scores indicating interest or value for achievement, social competence, sports competence, etc., were locus of control scores predictive of relevant criteria. Thus, if a person were disinterested in sports, for instance, locus of control scores would be unrelated to indications of sports competence.

Another complication in the locus of control literature derives from the almost inevitable value judgments attached to either end of the continuum—internality being adjudged good, externality as bad.

Internal control expectancies about many aspects of our lives would be foolish and possible precursors of negative fates. The person who refuses to be led, helped, or consoled because he or she perceives him or herself as the only agent capable of handling crises such as cardiac arrest may find him or herself miserable or perhaps dead because of this failure to allow others a part in aiding his survival. As Gurin et al. (1969) noted, internal control expectancies among those who are obstructed by external constraints may be self-destructive.

Related to the aforementioned difficulty is the problem of veridicality. The attribution processes of severely disorganized persons diagnosed as paranoid or manic-depressive seem to bear little resemblance to reality. For the paranoid, others are viewed as the causes of one's distress at most times, although to outside observers, the claim may seem specious. Maniacal persons, on the other hand, may express grandiose visions of themselves and their capacities. All goals seem attainable through the efforts and character of a person in a manic state. Aside from these extremes, many individuals hold locus of control expectancies that are at odds with the "objective" judgments of others. Student radicals in the 1970s responded to Rotter's I–E scale with extreme scores in the external control direction. Such scores were belied by their daily efforts, which would scarcely have been undertaken if these students truly believed that efforts and outcomes were unrelated. Such discrepancies have led different investigators to become concerned about "defensive externality" on the one hand, and the content sampled in I–E scales on the other. As this writer has remarked, I–E scales rarely sample implausible, let alone impossible, events in questions about control. Thus, the "inappropriate internal" is not discriminable from the more realistic or veridical internal on most locus of control measures.

Finally, there is the problem of overgeneralization. Scales such as Rotter's assess "generalized expectancies" in the sense that they do not focus on singular goals or outcomes. However, most scales are far from exhaustive in sampling the range of possible reinforcements and experiences. Since outcome areas typically sampled are limited, as are the causal attributions included in most scales, it is foolish to assume that existing measures are true representations of generalized expectancies. Because of the shortcomings in many assessment devices some investigators have created scales that adequately sample particular attributes. Levenson (1973), for example, has created separate scales for assessing beliefs about internal control, powerful others, and chance as causal agents.

Given the complications involving locus of control research, we may now approach the issues of where, when, and in what ways locus of control retains its utility as a personality construct.

APPROPRIATE CONCERNS FOR THE USE
OF THE LOCUS OF CONTROL CONSTRUCT

Reinstating Locus of Control in
Social Learning Formulations

Specific versus Generalized Expectancies

In Rotter's social learning theory (Rotter et al., 1972), expectancies are differentiated between those that are specific to a given end, outcome, or event and those that are more abstract or of a higher order, transcending specific events. In Rotter's theorizing, specific expectancies take precedence in most situations in which persons have already had some experience. In familiar settings, tasks, or interactions, individuals will have established particular or specific expectancies regarding the causal chain between actions and outcomes. In novel situations, however, persons will more readily rely on their previous experiences for estimating likely outcomes.

Most of the research reported with locus of control has been of the generalized expectancy variety. With the exception of Crandall's work with academic achievement (Crandall, Katkovsky, & Crandall, 1965), the largest number of studies have employed general measures such as Rotter's I–E scale. It is to the credit of the construct and to its investigators that the research reported has been as robust as it has been. It is still reasonable to investigate correlates of locus of control with scales such as Rotter's if high magnitude relationships are not required. If, however, one has a specific criterion in mind, then an ideal strategy would be to construct a locus of control measure for that particular criterion. As will be discussed later in this chapter, several investigators have begun to develop such "tailor-made" devices. In this way the greater power of specific expectancies can be used to add to our knowledge of locus of control as a personality construct.

The Role of Values

In social learning theory, expectancies and reinforcement values interact, sharing equal status within predictive formulae. Given measures of subjects' concerns or values, locus of control measures that are specific to those concerns, and expectancies of success with regard to those concerns, it should be possible to obtain fairly high-magnitude predictions of goal-directed behavior. A field study by Jessor, Graves, Hanson, and Jessor (1968) demonstrated this kind of predictive power with the use of several interrelated expectancy and value measures.

The Constraints of Reality and Circumstances

To maintain external control expectancies when opportunities are available to act in one's behest seems a tragic waste. Such mistaken or situation-inappropriate externality resembles learned helplessness. Equally inappropriate is the maintenance of internal control expectancies in a nonresponsive or malevolent milieu. To survive the onslaughts of an oppressive system suggests heroism—the refusal to succumb to overwhelming nonresponse. However, such heroism or courage may not derive as much from an internal locus of causation as from stoicism or the hope that times will improve. According to concentration camp survivors (Des Pres, 1976), inmates did not actually believe that their survival was contingent upon their actions. Luck was viewed as the principle determinant of one's being spared on any given day. The basic quest was to hold out long enough so that luck would serve one until the war ended. To have believed that one's actions determined one's survival would have seemed bizarre.

In less extreme cases, such as work settings, homes, and marriages, there are many instances where given outcomes are simply not within one's sphere of competence. Work layoffs, interactions with oppressive employers when no alternative work is available, and certain familial difficulties are often beyond the ken and influence of individuals. Beliefs in external control that such persons hold with regard to their difficulties may prepare them to more readily accept advice and influence from other sources. A mistaken self-reliance when one's actual skills are limited could be as self-defeating as would be the helpless retreat of persons when opportunities for control are available.

Conclusion

Locus of control has proven to be a useful construct in predicting the manner in which persons confront challenges. However, there are limits within which locus of control may function as variable. The reinsertion of the construct into the schema from which it first developed should make it a more powerful and useful variable in predicting helpless behavior.

Current Directions in Locus of Control Research

Development of Goal-Specific Measures

A most encouraging development in recent years has been the construction of locus of control scales for assessing particular goals or life events. Both Kirscht (1972) and Wallston, Wallston, Kaplan, and Maides (1976) have created locus of control scales pertinent to health, and Reid and Ziegler (1977; in press) have constructed an I–E measure for the specific reinforcements valued by senior-citizen home residents.

This writer with his colleagues has been in the process of constructing and testing out a new instrument called the Multidimensional Multiattributional Causality Scale (MMCS) (Lefcourt, Von Baeyer, Ware, & Cox 1979). The scale is unique in that it is comprised of subsets of items derived from the more extensive attributional sources described by Weiner, Heckhausen, Meyer, and Cook (1972). Weiner et al. described two characteristics of causal attributions—the locus and the stability. Thus, four types of attributes are created: internal stable, internal unstable, external stable, and external unstable. Internal stable attributes, such as skill, talent, and intelligence, are contrasted with internal unstable attributes, such as moods, impulses, effort, motivation, etc. External stable attributes, on the other hand, are difficulty levels, the nature of the settings in which events occur, or the sorts of people surrounding one, whereas unstable external attributes are luck, accidents, weather, etc.

Our scales are composed of a balanced number of each set of these causal attributes, with six items in each subscale equally divided for successes and failures. Our scales allow for total locus of control scores with respect to particular goal areas at present affiliation and achievement as well as for locus of control scores with respect to failures versus success with respect to each goal.

In our research thus far we have obtained evidence of adequate reliabilities and some interesting validity data of pertinence to this chapter.

Some indications of discriminant validity have been obtained with regard to goal specificity. In an achievement-relevant task, where the testing procedure was designed to interfere with self-direction, persons who scored as internal for achievement were found to make more body movements indicative of tension than did those who were external for achievement. On the other hand, affiliation locus of control scores were minimally related to the criteria.

In another investigation concerned with social competence and responsiveness, the locus of control for affiliation measure proved to be more predictive than the achievement I–E scale. Subjects engaged in prearranged social interactions with fellow subjects. Topics of conversation were preselected by the experimenter and varied with regard to their personal nature. Each subject was rated in terms of self-disclosure while speaking and in terms of "acceptance" or "good listenership" when listening. Affiliation locus of control scores became significantly related to ratings of disclosure as the topics became more personal in nature. Achievement locus of control, in contrast, was unrelated to the social interaction criteria. The relationship proved to be even greater when the affiliation effort subscale was used. Self-disclosure and listening skills both were more characteristic of persons who attributed affilation outcomes to effort. Thus, the potential value of subscales is apparent.

Several subsequent studies have been conducted with equally interesting results, suggesting that the MMCS goal-specific scales possess discriminant validity. Let it suffice to state that with the construction of goal-specific locus of control scales it may prove possible to ascertain profiles of perceived competence and helplessness. To know that a person feels helpless to effect the events of his or her intimate–affection reinforcements but perceives him or herself to be competent to effect events at work or amid friends should allow for finer descriptions and suggestions for therapeutic interventions.

Likewise, in the exploration of concomitants of helplessness, such as depression, the value of scales such as the MMCS could prove high. Internal control expectancies for failures and external control expectancies for successes in some valued realms of reinforcement could prove to be more relevant to the development of episodic depression than internality or externality per se. Even though there is a need for empirical explorations to illuminate potential relationships, it is evident that more differentiated conceptions of locus of control should stimulate research pertaining to personality processes.

Reliable Correlates of Locus of Control

Among the research areas that have been reviewed by Lefcourt (1976) and Phares (1976), one that has been reliably associated with locus of control is that of assimilation of information. If people are not to succumb to the various travails that life offers them, they must, in some way, be prepared to meet those challenges. To seek out information in preparation for possible aversive events is the antithesis of passively accepting fate.

Strickland (1978, 1979) has summarized a literature implicating locus of control as a predictor of various health-related behaviors. From responses to warnings regarding the health hazards involved in smoking or the use of seat belts to minimize injuries incurred in automobile collisions to awareness of information regarding particular medical conditions, persons assessed as internal on I–E scales have been found to be more prepared for potentially aversive experiences.

Lefcourt (1979) has recently summarized a literature focused on locus of control as a mediator of responses to stress. Illustrating that chapter was the case study of a man who survived the aftermath of an air crash with relative aplomb. From a state of nearly complete incapacity, this man managed to recover many of his bodily functions through deliberate effort, information seeking, and self-administered therapy. The point of relevance to this chapter inheres in the reasons provided by this victim for his active pursuit of recovery. This man always viewed the responsibility for his life's events as potentially internal, and he would not happily eschew participation in any decisions that involved him. His participation included learning about and then undertaking painful exercises that helped to restore the use of his hands. In addition he worked at recovery-related tasks that helped him to avoid the demoralization that could have easily occurred as he anticipated a lengthy hospitalization and multiple surgery. Much as with the Bulman and Wortman (1977) accident victims, an internal locus of control and the more ready assimilation of information pertinent to the recovery process seemed to be prognostic of better coping with the hardships involved in the recuperative period.

Locus of Control and Affective States

In the foregoing section, an allusion was made to the demoralization that can occur with physical disability. Seligman (1975), Klinger (1977), and this writer (Lefcourt, 1976) have each discussed the impact of morale maintenance on recuperation and the greater likelihood of death with demoralization. In each, the implication has been drawn that demoralization is often associated with helplessness during encounters with aversive events. Where Seligman has experimentally produced depressive-like behavior, such as the passive acceptance of aversive stimulation, the locus of control literature contains reports of correlational evidence linking depression with an external locus of control.

Naditch, Gargan, and Michael (1975) found an interaction between locus of control scores and an index of discontent (the discrepancy between aspirations and achievement) in the prediction of depression scores obtained on the Cornell Medical Index. In this case, discontented persons who held external control expectancies were more likely to report depressive symptomotology than were internals or less discontented externals. In another report, Naditch (1974) found the same variables interacting in the prediction of hypertension.

Other investigations have reported the reliably obtained correlations between locus of control scores with measures indicating affect. Among them, one study deployed a goal-specific measure of locus of control concerning the valued goals for the target sample. Reid and Ziegler (1977; in press) created a measure of locus of control concerning the experiences judged to be important by residents of a senior citizens home. Items concerned the decision making regarding daily activities, the ability to determine if and when one would be visited, the ability to keep possessions where the resident desired, etc. Internality regarding these ends was positively related to nurses' ratings of subjects' happiness and residents' self-ratings of contentment.

This finding parallels that of Langer and Rodin's study (1976) of nursing home residents in which one group was encouraged to assume some responsibility for their daily activity. Those residents who were so encouraged and who had responsibility for the care of a plant were found to show improvement as compared to a "nonresponsible" group on assessed "alertness, active participation, and a general sense of well-being."

These two studies accentuate the reliability of the assumed linkage between responsibility or internal locus of control and positive affect states. The divergent procedures for observing the impact of locus of control give greater credence to the locus of control–affect connection which was most dramatically demonstrated in the clinical study reported by Melges and Weisz (1971). In that study, persons who had attempted to commit suicide were asked to reconstruct their state of mind immediately prior to their suicide attempt. Increases in suicidal ideation were associated with changes in locus of control scores, the greater externality occurring with increased despair.

Conclusion

In each of the aforementioned research areas there is considerable ongoing activity. Much stimulation for research derives from the development of more differentiated conceptions of locus of control, the assimilation of information generated by investigators of attribution processes, and the use of locus of control in conjunction with other relevant variables for predicting given criteria. Despite the restructuring of the construct and the creation of new assessment tools, the relationships with criteria such as information assimilation, action taking, and morale have remained robust, supporting the optimism of investigators with interests concerning the locus of control construct.

FUTURE POSSIBILITIES FOR RESEARCH WITH LOCUS OF CONTROL

The need for a refining of the locus of control construct has become apparent in recent years. New measures for assessing the construct based on more specific goals and attributions have been created, and research has drawn attention to various criteria associated with locus of control. In a symposium focused on perceived control and depression (Strickland, Note 2) more questions were raised than answered with regard to the ways in which depression and locus of control are related. One conjecture offered by this writer was that depression would seem to be more likely among persons who believed that positive outcomes occur noncontingently but that negative outcomes are contingent upon their actions. Little in the way of personal relevance could then be derived from positive events, and self-concepts would more readily be affected by failures and unhappy experiences. The imbalance between attributions for successes and failures could be diagnostic of depression and other difficulties as was indicated in the research by Ducette, Wolk, and Soucar (1972). This portrayal of depression bears similarity to that advanced by Beck (1967).

Whereas the concern with active striving and goal pursuit was more evident in earlier locus of control research, a more recent trend has been to explore the role of locus of control as a mediator of responses to negative events. Some investigators such as Gregory (1978) have found locus of control to be relevant only to avoidance behavior and that only feelings of control for negative events were related to attribution statements subsequent to performance feedback. With the additional stimulation of research on helplessness before aversive events by Seligman (1975), and on the perception of control as a mediator of stress by Glass and Singer (1972), this trend may be comprehensible.

Learned helplessness has been induced most often through having subjects experience severe noncontingent aversive stimulation. For canine subjects, this entails prevention of routine escape responses during the administration of shock. To find parallels of such training among humans requires some ingenuity and translation. The research of Hetherington (1972; Note 3), which examines the repercussions of parental death or divorce, and that of Murphy and Moriarity (1976), which focuses on how early life events can accont for greater or lesser vulnerability to stress in later childhood, offer some analogs to the learned helplessness paradigm: Children who suffer upsets and traumas when they are too young to cope with those events are found to exhibit certain behavioral deficits in later childhood and adolescence. These deficits, in turn, allow us to infer the development of an external locus of control or helplessness with regard to the specific areas in which such children had been traumatized. This linkage between early traumatic events and later assessments of locus or control have begun to be assessed with measures deriving from epidemiological studies of health. Bryant and Trockel (1976), for example, have found that affectively significant life stresses recalled from the preschool era are related to highly external control orientations in adulthood. Similar findings have emerged from our research with the MMCS. Davies (Note 4) found that affectively significant stresses recalled from the preschool era produced an $r = -.52, p < .001$, $N = 44$, with ability attributions for affiliation. The more the recall of early stresses, the less likely were subjects to ascribe cause for affiliation outcomes to personal abilities and skills. This relationship was most marked for females for whom $r = -.72, p < .001, N = 20$. Other attributes were similarly but less dramatically related to early experiences. That affiliation rather than achievement ability scores were more highly related to the recall of early stresses pertaining to social relations such as death, separations, or strife within the family supports the current advocacy of goal-specific measures in locus of control research.

SUMMARY

Locus of control research has paralleled and complemented investigations with learned helplessness, attribution processes, and the perception of causation. The focus of locus of control research is more often on the perception of control as a relatively stable characteristic of individuals and represents an abstraction made by individuals as to their likelihood of being able to effect particular outcomes. As we have noted, there are difficulties within the literature which hopefully will not detract from the interest that has been so high. Visible are the future directions of locus control research which will blend with research that is concerned with attribution processes, coping strategies, information processing, and utilization. Given such blends and crosscurrents, locus of control research should continue to enrich the literature that is helping to elucidate those processes that underlie vitality and depression.

REFERENCE NOTES

1. Naditch, M.P. *Putting value back into expectancy value theory.* Paper presented at the Eastern Psychological Association Convention, Washington, D.C., April, 1973.
2. Strickland, B.R. (Chairperson) *Perceived control and human depression.* Symposium presented at the Eastern Psychological Association Convention, Boston, April, 1977.
3. Hetherington, E.M. *Beyond father absence: conceptualization of effects of divorce.* Paper presented at the Society for Research in Child Development, Denver, April, 1975.
4. Davies, K. *The relationship between early life stresses and locus of control.* Unpublished honor's thesis, University of Waterloo, 1977.

11

Aging and Control[1]

RICHARD SCHULZ

INTRODUCTION

Most people would agree that growing old and dying are at best trying experiences. Although researchers and writers increasingly emphasize the positive aspects of old age, there is compelling behavioral evidence that, at least in Western society, old age and death are things to be avoided and delayed for as long as possible. The reasons for this predominantly negative view of growing old and dying are almost too obvious to mention. Aging is characterized by losses in almost every domain important for an individual's view of him or herself. Almost everyone experiences declines in physical and psychological functioning as one approaches the sixth, seventh, and eighth decades of life. Some declines can be compensated for by the use of external aids such as eyeglasses and hearing aids or by strategy shifts such as greater cautiousness. However, although these compensatory mechanisms might make an aged person functionally equivalent to a younger person, their very need underscores the reality of the deficits. The impact of each

[1]The research reported in this chapter was supported in part by a grant from the National Institute on Aging, AG 00525.

specific deficit may in fact be minor, but the combined effect of many losses may induce feelings of lack of control and helplessness.

Now available are large quantities of observational and correlational research documenting that lack of personal autonomy may account for some of the negative effects observed among the aged in general and the institutionalized aged in particular (Schulz, 1976; Schulz, 1978; Schulz & Brenner, 1977). For example, the available data strongly suggest that a sense of personal control in old age may have powerful effects on an individual's physical and psychological well-being. In a recent review and analysis of the literature on relocation of the aged, Schulz and Brenner (1977) presented a theoretical model that stressed the importance of control and predictability as medidators of relocation outcomes. Briefly, they argue that the response to the stress of relocation is largely determined by: (a) the perceived controllability and predictability of the events surrounding a move; and (b) differences in environmental controllability between pre- and post-relocation environments. Support for this model is found in numerous relocation studies (see Schulz & Brenner, 1977). Available findings indicate that: (a) the greater the choice the individual has in being relocated, the less negative the effects of relocation, (b) the more predictable the new environment is, the less negative the effects of relocation; and finally (c) decreases in environmental controllability are associated with negative outcomes, whereas increases in controllability are associated with positive outcomes.

An analysis of the literature on heart attack and kidney transplant patients (Krantz & Schulz, 1980; Schulz, 1978) and terminal cancer patients (Schulz, 1976; Schulz, 1978) also suggests that patients' feelings of control over important outcomes may determine their physical prognosis as well as their psychological reactions to the disease. For example, Eisendrath (1969) and McKegney and Lange (1971) point out that feelings of personal control are important determinants of kidney patients' physical well-being and their adjustment to hemodialysis. Simlarly, Verwoerdt and Elmore (1967) and LeShan (1961) suggest that response to cancer treatments and the probability of survival are related to the amount of perceived control individuals feel they have over their lives. Patients with more perceived control tend to respond better to treatment and tend to live longer. In sum, two psychological variables, predictability and control, appear to play an important role in mediating health-related outcomes in stressful situations.

Although there are abundant data available implicating the importance of control and predictability as determinants of health-related outcomes, these data have been derived primarily from correlational studies. It is not clear from an inspection of this literature whether a sense of control is an antecedent or a consequence of the individual's physical status. Furthermore, because none of the research was specifically designed to test a control model, it is often necessary to make assumptions about the details of some studies in order to apply a control model. Given the post hoc nature of such an analysis and the fact that this research is primarily correlational, it is necessary to carry out controlled experiments before the importance of control and predictability can be substantiated. Several such experiments have been completed recently.

Schulz (1976) hypothesized that some of the characteristics frequently observed among the institutionalized aged, such as feelings of depression and helplessness as well as accelerated physical decline, are at least, in part, attributable to loss of control and decreased environmental predictability. A field experiment in which institutionalized aged were randomly assigned to one of four conditions was carried out to assess the effects of increased control and predictability upon the physical and psychological well-being of the aged.

Individuals in three of the four conditions were visted by college undergraduates under varying contingencies, whereas persons in the fourth condition were not visited and served as a baseline comparison group. Subjects in the control condition could determine both the frequency and duration of visits they received. To assess the effects of predictability, a second group of subjects (Predict) was informed when they would be visited and how long the visitor would stay, but they had no control over these details. A third group (Random) was visited on a random schedule. Holding amount of visitation and the quality of interaction constant across the three groups, strong support was found for the hypothesis that predictable positive events have a powerful positive impact upon the well-being of the institutionalized aged. In addition to demonstrating the importance of control and predictability as mediators of health-related outcomes among the aged, this experiment also served to demonstrate that weil-controlled and ethical experiments can be carried out in applied settings.

This study was followed by a conceptually similar experiment carried out by Langer and Rodin (1976). In their study, an intervention designed to encourage elderly nursing home residents to feel more control and responsibility for day-to-day events was used. One group of residents was exposed to a talk delivered by the hospital administrator emphasizing their responsibility for themselves. A second group heard a communication that stressed the staff's responsibility for them as patients. These communications were bolstered by offering to subjects in the experimental group plants that they could tend, whereas residents in the comparison group were given plants that were watered by the staff.

The results of this study indicated that residents in the responsibility-induced group became more active and reported feeling happier than did the comparison group of residents who were encouraged to feel that the staff would take care of them and try to make them happy. Patients in the responsibility-induced group also showed significant improvement in alertness and increased participation in nursing home activities. Although the results of the Langer and Rodin (1976) experiment must remain somewhat clouded because the experimenters failed to run a critical no treatment control group, their data do point to control, in this case operationalized in terms of responsibility, as a determinant of important outcomes for the institutionalized aged.

Taken together, the studies by Schulz (1976) and Langer and Rodin (1976) demonstrate that: (a) increasing environmental control has a positive impact on the physical and psychological status of the institutionalized aged; (b) this effect is obtainable with very different operationalizations of the conceptual variable control; and (c) introducing predictable positive events into the lives of the aged also has a positive impact on their health and psychological status. Although these findings provide some important answers to questions regarding the psychology of growing old, they raise several other questions as well. First, the subject populations used by both Schulz (1976) and Langer and Rodin (1976) were of relatively high socioeconomic status. We need to ask, therefore, to what extent to the obtained data on the importance of predictability and control apply only to high socioeconomic status populations residing in the better institutional facilities available to the aged? Second, how do the interventions used in these experiments interact with the individual differences of subjects who participate in them? Ideally, it should be possible to eventually identify those subjects who need and would benefit most from control-enhancing interventions. And third, given the extensive short-term impact of these interventions, what are the long-term effects of participating in such research? Some answer to these questions have been obtained from research carried out recently and will be discussed next.

GENERALITY OF EFFECT ACROSS
DIFFERENT POPULATIONS

A recently completed experiment (Krantz & Schulz, 1980) was carried out to address the generality of the predictability effect by using a low socioeconomic status population and to test one aspect of the relocation model proposed by Schulz and Brenner (1977). It was hypthesized that enhancing the predictability of an institutional environment for new admissions to a long-term care facility for the aged would facilitate adaptation and decrease some of the physical and psychological deficits typically associated with relocation.

Psychologically alert old persons recently admitted to a long-term care facility were randomly assigned to one of three treatment conditions. One-third of the subjects were exposed to a treatment designed to enhance the predictability of the new environment. Subjects in this condition (Relevant Information) received an individualized orientation program that included detailed information about schedules and routines within the hospital, facilities and services available to them, their location within the institution, and directions on how to get to different areas of the hospital. Clearly, such information should make the environment more predictable for these persons.

In order to control for the effects of increased attention given the Relevant Information group, individuals assigned to a second group (Irrelevant Information) were given the same amount of personal attention but did not receive information designed to make their environments more predictable. These patients were told about the facilities within the hospital that were irrelevant to their functioning, such as the bakery and laundry. A third group (No Treatment) received treatment as usual, which included a short orientation to the hospital provided by the social services staff.

Data assessing patients' level of activity and their physical and psychological status were collected from patients before and after the interventions were completed and from the nursing staff after the interventions were completed. In addition, past history and trait information were collected from each subject to determine how the interventions might interact with individual differences. It was expected that the Relevant Information group would be superior on indicators of health and psychological status to the Irrelevant Information and No Treatment groups. It was further hypothesized that simply paying attention to the recently institutionalized aged may be beneficial; thus, it was expected also that the Irrelevant Information group would fare better than the No Treatment group.

At the completion of the intervention, all subjects were asked to indicate whether or not they felt they had improved in physical and emotional health since their arrival at Kane and since the beginning of the manipulations. Subjects in the Relevant Information group were more likely to say their emotional health had improved since their arrival than were persons in the No Treatment group. Subjects in the Relevant Information group were more likely to say that their physical health had improved in the last two weeks than were the No Treatment group subjects.

A similar pattern of results was obtained when nurses were asked to rate each person on health status and zest for life. The Relevant Information group was perceived to be healthier than the No Treatment group, and both the Relevant and Irrelevant Information groups were judged to be superior to the No Treatment group on ratings obtained on the "zest for life" scale.

Finally, subjects in the Relevant Information group participated in more activites requiring physical effort than did persons assigned to the No Treatment group.

These data are consistent with the findings reported earlier (Schulz, 1976), showing that predictable positive events have a powerful positive impact on the well-being of the institutionalized aged. Although the results are similar, this study differed from the earlier experiment in two important respects. First, predictability was operationalized in very different ways. Schulz (1976) manipulated the predictability of a specific positive event. The present study focused on the impact of generally increasing the predictability of a new environment. Second, the subject populations differed significantly in the two experiments. Schulz's (1976) population was comprised of highly educated and high socioeconomic status aged persons. In contrast, subjects in the present study had little education and were of primarily low socioeconomic status. The similarity of results in the two studies suggests that predictability is an important mediator of well-being among the aged regardless of the particular situation or population characteristics.

Because it was impossible in this setting to provide predictability-enhancing information without at the same time increasing the amount of attention paid to the subjects, it was deemed important to run a control condition where subjects received the attention but not the relevant information. This was the reason for including the Irrelevant Information group. Subjects in this condition were given the same amount of personal attention but did not receive information designed to make their environments more predictable. With the exception of one dependent measure, the data for this group fall between the Relevant Information and No Treatment groups. Subjects in the Irrelevant Information group were consistently superior to individuals in the No Treatment group on indicators of activity and health and psychological status, although these differences were not statistically reliable. However, subjects in the Irrelevant Information condition were significantly more likely to say that their physical health had improved in the last two weeks than were persons in the No Treatment condition.

What can we conclude about the impact of increased attention on the well-being of the institutionalized aged? The pattern of results clearly indicates that increased attention has small but consistent positive effects. This conclusion is further supported by the fact that the Relevant Information group, although significantly superior to the No Treatment group on many indicators, did not differ significantly from the Irrelevant Information group. It is likely that the superiority of the Relevant Information group represents the combined effects of increased attention and increased predictability.

These findings have important implications for those involved in the delivery and evaluation of intervention programs for the aged. To the extent that a researcher is interested in evaluating the effects of a specific intervention, it is necessary to include conditions that allow the researchers to separate the impact of a specific therapeutic procedure from such confounding factors as increased attention. Too often intervention programs for the elderly are implemented and then evaluated without running such control conditions.

INDIVIDUAL DIFFERENCES

The second question raised earlier was "How do the interventions used in these experiments interact with individual difference variables?" One goal of the Krantz & Schulz (1980) study previously described was to determine how specific personality variables mediate institutional adaptation in general and to understand how these variables interact with the interventions used. In that study measures of three personality variables—depression, self-esteem, and feelings of control—were collected as part of the initial interview. Subjects were classified as high, medium, or low on each variable depending on whether they agreed or disagreed with items from the MAGI personality Inventory (Schoenfield, 1972). The differences, which will be reported later, although substantial, did not reach statistical significance because of the small number of subjects in each condition.

Regardless of which condition a subject was assigned to, persons with high self-esteem or those who felt they had control over their lives were more likely to participate in activities and were rated as healthier by the nurses. Level of depression at the initial interview was not related to any of the outcome measures when the data for all three experimental conditions were combined. However, level of depression did interact with treatment conditions. Subjects in the Irrelevant and Relevant Information groups who were initially not depressed or only minimally depressed participated in more activities than did those who were depressed or those who were not depressed but in the No Treatment condition. In addition, persons in the Relevant Information condition who were initially not depressed were more likely to feel better emotionally at the end of the study than were persons who were either initially depressed or not depressed but in the No Treatment or Irrelevant Information conditions.

Individual differences were also examined as possible predictors of health status and zest for life at the completion of the Schulz (1976) study. Analysis of these data revealed that persons who were more aggressive, less introverted, felt good both physically and psychologically, and who experienced an increase in environmental control or predictability were highest on indicators of health status and zest for life at the conclusion of the study.

The small number of subjects in both studies precludes drawing any firm conclusion, although the similarity of the results of the two studies is compelling. The implication of these results is that persons with high self-esteem, who feel they have some control over their world (high internals), or persons who are not depressed can benefit greatly from interventions that make their environments more predictable or controllable. Although we must wait for the results of a predictive study to test this individual difference model, the available data raise several important questions. For example, is there a threshold level of individual functioning below which any intervention will have little or no impact? Clearly, persons who do not have the cognitive capacity to comprehend verbal instructions are not likely to benefit from the types of interventions used in these studies. But such subjects have been intentionally excluded from the completed studies. There appear to be no large cognitive ability differences between subjects who improve as a result of the intervention and those who do not, although this has not been directly tested. At this point, perhaps the best distinction that can be made between those who improve and those who do not is that the former have higher expectations for a predictable and controllable world.

LONG-TERM PARTICIPATION EFFECTS

The final question raised concerns the long-term effects of participating in these experiments. Even though subjects exposed to predictability or control-enhancing interventions exhibited large positive effects at the completion of these studies, it is important to know whether or not these gains persisted over time. For example, it may be that these gains are dependent on the presence of the experimenter and quickly dissipate after a study is terminated. Alternatively, these interventions may permanently alter subjects' ability to cope with institutional environments and hence facilitate functioning on a long-term basis. Data addressing this issue are now available from two follow-up studies. Rodin and Langer (1977) collected health and psychological status data 18 months after their study was completed and found that subjects in the responsibility-induced condition showed higher health and activity patterns, and mood and sociability did not decline as greatly when compared to the staff-support comparison group. They concluded that decline in the aged can be slowed or, with a stronger intervention, perhaps even reversed by manipulations which provide an increased sense of effectance in the institutionalized elderly.

A second follow-up study was recently completed by Schulz & Hanusa (1978) on subjects who participated in the Schulz (1976) experiment. Data were collected at 24, 30, and 42 months after the experiment was terminated. The activities director of the retirement home, who was personally familiar with all the participants in the study but blind to the conditions subjects were in, provided a variety of ratings for each subject. Our discussion here will focus on two nine-point Likert-type scales assessing "health status" and "zest for life." The end points of the "health status" scale were labeled "in perfect health" and "extremely ill" and the end points for the "zest for life" scale were labeled "extremely enthusiastic about life" and "completely hopeless." Identical scales had been completed by the same activities director at the completion of the original experiment.

In general, the results of this study indicated that the effects of the particular interventions used were temporary. Persons who had previously improved in psychological and health status when an important positive event was made either predictable or controllable for them exhibited significant declines after the study was terminated. These findings stand in sharp contrast to the follow-up results obtained by Rodin and Langer (1977) described previously. The pattern of results observed for the predict and control groups in the present study raises important theoretical and ethical issues.

Theoretical Issues

Viewed from a theoretical perspective, these data are consistent with an attributional analysis of learned helplessness recently proposed by Abramson, Seligman, and Teasdale (1978). According to this analysis, persons generate reasons for their ability to control outcomes, and these reasons can be classified along three othogonal dimensions. Whereas two of these dimensions (internal–external, stable–unstable) have been frequently used by attribution theorists (e.g., Weiner, 1974), the third (global–specific) is introduced as a new dimension by the authors. Thus, internal causes stem from the individual, and external causes from the environment; stable factors are long-lived and recurrent, whereas unstable factors are short-lived and intermittent. Finally, global factors occur across situations, whereas specific factors are unique to a particular context. The authors further suggest that each type of attribution has specific consequences for the individual: Attributions to internal–external factors should affect self-esteem; attribution to stable–unstable factors should determine the long-term consequences of a particular experience; and attributions to global–specific factors should determine the extent to which individuals will generalize a particular experience to other situations.

Although there is no direct evidence indicating the types of attributions made by individuals in either the Langer and Rodin (1976) or Schulz (1976) studies, the long-term effects in each study can be understood from an attributional perspective. It is likely that the intervention used by Langer and Rodin altered subject's self-attributions regarding their ability to control outcomes in an institutional environment. More specifically, the communication delivered to the experimental group emphasizing their responsibility for themselves and their outcomes probably encouraged subjects to make internal, stable, and global attributions (e.g., "I control important outcomes because I am responsible and competent, and this should not change as long as I am here"), and as predicted, the gains evidenced by the experimental group persisted over time.

On the other hand, when increased control is attributed to unstable factors, the long-term impact of such an intervention should be temporary. The results of the present follow-up study are consistent with this analysis. The intervention used by Schulz probably caused subjects to make external, unstable, specific attributions (e.g., "I can control one outcome"; "I can do this because someone is allowing me to do it," and "I can do it only for a specific period of time"). Feelings of control in this situation are dependent on the presence of an external agent and should not persist once that agent is removed.

Because the attributional patterns generated in the two studies may be different on all three dimensions, it is difficult to conclude with certainty that the stability dimension alone accounts for the long-term differences between the two studies, although the Abramson et al., model would suggest that this is the case.

A second possible explanation for the declines exhibited by subjects in the present study is that their expectations for a predictable and/or controllable environment were violated by the termination of the study. Subject's expectations for controlling or predicting important events in their lives may have been raised by the intervention used and then abruptly violated when the study terminated and experimenters and visitors disappeared. This analysis suggests that the declines might have been avoided had we provided substitute predictable or controllable events.

Ethical Issues

From an ethical perspective, the critical question raised by this research is, "Did the termination of the study actually harm the participants?". Although subjects in the enhanced groups did drop below baseline on both indicators, the analysis showed that they were reliably below baseline on only one indicator at one point in time. This is suggestive but hardly compelling. Nevertheless, we might ask, what factors might account for such negative effects?

The interventions accomplished two things. First, they resulted in strong personal attachments between the subject and visitor. Second, they raised expectations for a predictable and controllable environment. Any harm attributable to the termination of the study could be due to either of these causes.

The fact that the nature of the relationships did not differ across experimental groups (e.g., persons in the random group enjoyed the visits just as much as persons in the predict and control groups) and the fact that the random group did not exhibit the same declines found for the predict and control groups suggest that the severing of personal attachments was not the primary cause for the decline. Furthermore, it was anticipated when the study was initiated that the termination of the visits might upset the participants. As a result, several precautions were taken: (a), subjects were informed that the college visitors would return to their homes for summer vacation; (b), visitors were not suddenly withdrawn at the end of the study—the visits continued after the initial follow-up data were collected and terminated gradually at the end of the semester; and (c), visitors were encouraged to keep in touch with subjects whenever strong attachments had developed.

The intent of these precautions was to alleviate the potential stress of severing strong attachments. The fact that the random group suffered no declines when the study was terminated suggests that these precautions served their purpose. Hindsight suggests that had we provided a substitute predictable or controllable positive event, the declines exhibited by the predict and control groups might also have been avoided. Whether or not these results could or should have been anticipated is debatable, but they do contain several important lessons for researchers engaged in methodologically similar approaches to this topic (see Schulz & Hanusa, 1978, for a detailed discussion of this).

FUTURE RESEARCH

The research completed as part of our program has provided information regarding the impact of control- and predictability-enhancing intervention on the institutionalized aged, the long-term effects of these interventions, the generality of the effect across widely divergent populations, and the relationship between these interventions and individual differences of subjects. In addition, research now in progress is aimed at investigating the relationship between competence and control. Although these findings provide some important answers to questions regarding social–psychological aspects of aging, they raise several new questions as well.

Competence and Control

One persistent theme in much of the completed research is that the intervention used may not only affect perception of environmental control but may also enhance feelings of comptence. Thus, both Schulz (1976) and Langer and Rodin (1976) suggested that their control manipulation may have made subjects feel generally more competent. The control-enhancing message used by Langer and Rodin (1976), for example, explicitly stated that subjects were responsible for making some important decisions regarding their lives, implying that they were competent enough to make these decisions. We might ask, therefore, what is the relationship between competence and control?

Existing laboratory research (Dweck & Repucci, 1973; Hiroto, 1974; Hanusa & Schulz, 1977) suggests that lack of control is most devastating when it carries with it broad implications of the individual's self-worth. Conversely, manipulations that increase control and at the same time elevate feelings of competence should have greater and a longer lasting positive impact than control-enhancing interventions that do not affect competence attributions. This may account for the differences in long-term effects found by Rodin and Langer (1977) and Schulz and Hanusa (1978). It is likely that the responsibility intervention used by Langer and Rodin (1976) encouraged subjects to make positive self-attributions, where Schulz's (1976) intervention did little to cause subjects to change their overall self-concept. Given this analysis, one would expect the impact of the responsibility-enhancing intervention to persist over time.

Aged individuals may be especially susceptible to competence-enhancing interventions because of the decline in physical and psychological functioning typically associated with aging. Schaie and Schaie (1977), for example, have suggested that an aged person's functioning "could be enhanced if negative feelings about adequacy and perceived value were modified [p. 715]." Similarly, Kuypers and Bengtson (1973) suggest that the social breakdown of the elderly, a process whereby the elderly person is defined as and eventually views him or herself as incompetent, can be counteracted by interventions that enhance feelings of competence in three areas: social-role performance, adaptive capacity and personal feelings of mastery, and inner control. Kuypers and Bengtson make specific suggestions for accomplishing these goals, but to date there are no experimental demonstrations documenting the effects of competence-enhancing interventions among the aged.

Understanding Psychological Determinants of Health Outcomes

Several studies have demonstrated that control- and predictability-enhancing interventions can positively affect an individual's health status (Schulz, 1976; Langer and Rodin, 1976; Krantz & Schulz, 1980). The value of these findings could be greatly enhanced if we understood more precisely what accounts for this effect.

Two types of explanations are possible in accounting for the process through which psychological interventions are translated into physical outcomes. One, predictability- and control-enhancing interventions, may change the individual's behavior in health-related areas. He or she may follow his or her diet more closely, be more diligent in taking prescription medicine, do better in adhering to physician's advice, and so on. Two, predictability- and control-enhancing interventions may directly affect a large variety of internal physiological states, including biogenic amine lvels in the brain. Support for the latter hypothesis is found in numerous laboratory studies. For example, Reim, Glass, and Singer (1971) found that subjects given perceived control over the termination of adversive noise exhibited significantly less autonomic reactivity (vasconstriction) than did subjects for whom the noise was unpredictable. Similarly, Geer and Maisel (1972) found that subjects given control over aversive stimuli exhibited lower galvanic skin response reactivity than did simlar subjects who did not have control. Finally, Weiss (1970; 1971; 1972) and Adler (1971) have investigated the physiological consequences of helplessness in rats. In a series of studies they have demonstrated that the amount of gastric ulceraction and weight loss in rats is significantly reduced when a stressor such as electric shock is made either predictable or controllable. Perhaps of even greater significance is the association between catecholamine levels in the central nervous system and psychological state. Rats able to avoid and escape shock showed an increase in the level of brain norepinephrine, whereas helpless animals showed a decrease in norepinephrine. High levels of norepinephrine are thought to be important in mediating active, assertive responses, whereas depletion of norepinephrine is viewed by some (see Schildkraut & Kety, 1967; Coppen, 1968; Mendels, Stern, & Frazer, 1976) as a factor in depression in humans. Weiss (1972) speculated, "It may well be that the causal sequence leading from helplessness to behavioral depression depends on biochemical changes in the central nervous system such as changes in norepinephrine. This would indicate that depressed behavior can be perpetuated in a vicious circle—the inability to cope alters neural biochemistry, which further accentuates depression, increasing the inability to cope, which further alters neural biochemistry and so on [p. 113]."

These findings are suggestive, but it should be remembered that there are important differences between an institutional environment and laboratory stress simulations. Probably the most important of these is the duration and intensity of the stressors found in the two situations. In the laboratory, researchers typically use one type of stressor for short durations and at high intensities. In an institutional environment, the stressors are many; they are less intense and longer lasting. Whether control- and predictability-enhancing interventions are translated into similar physiological mechanisms in these very different situations remains to be seen.

No attempt has been made thus far to closely monitor either the health-relevant behaviors or physiological indicators of subjects participating in long-term control experiments. However, some researchers have monitored peripheral catecholamine levels in workers exposed to working conditions characterized by lack of control. Frankenhaeuser (1976) assessed adrenaline and noradrenaline levels in saw mill workers differing in the amount of control they had in their work setting. Adrenaline excretions were consistently higher in the group with little control, and both adrenaline and noradrenaline levels were higher at the end of the day for the low-control group when compared to the group that had more control or when compared to baseline levels assessed during nonworking hours. Interview data and health records indicated that persons with little control were unable to relax after work and evidenced higher rates of a variety of psychosomatic symptoms including high blood pressure, gastrointestinal disorders, back pain, headache, and unspecified nervous disorders. These data are correlational and should be viewed cautiously; however, the consistency between these findings and laboratory data showing that increased control in stressful situations reduced catecholamine secretions suggests that there may be a direct link between feelings of control and peripheral catecholamine levels in humans.

Two types of data should help us explain how feelings of control or predictability affect health status. The behavior change hypothesis can be tested by collected detailed health-relevant information from study participants and the medical staff. Persons who have control may be more motivated to find out about their health status, follow a drug regimen and doctor's orders more closely, eat better, and so on. Internal state information, including catecholamine levels, could be collected by doing blood and urine assays and perhaps by attaching telemetry devices that broadcast blood pressure and heart rate. Even without these more sophisticated methods, useful information should be obtainable from medical charts of patients.

Impact of Significant Others

The focus of the completed research in this area has thus far been on enhancing feelings of control and predictability in the institutionalized aged individual. We have paid little attention to the significant others in the aged person's life and the extent to which they contribute to his or her well-being. The significant others in the institutionalized person's life include two types of individuals: (a) the caretaking staff, including primarily nurses and doctors; and (b) friends and relatives who may or, as is sometimes the case, may not interact with the patient on a regular basis.

How might significant others affect the institutionalized person's well-being? In addition to having to deal with the constraints of an institutional environment, the aged individual may receive a variety of feedback indicating that he or she is an undesirable or stigmatized individual. The individual frequently experiences physical avoidance from the medical staff. This has been documented in the literature on the behavior of physicians and nurses toward the seriously ill elderly (Livingston & Zimet, 1965; Glaser & Strauss, 1965; Kastenbaum & Aisenberg, 1972; Perlman, Stotsky, & Dominick, 1969), and is further documented by the low staff morale and high turnover rates often found in institutions for the aged.

The frequency of visits from family members typically declines a few weeks after an individual has been admitted to a long-term care facility. When visits do occur, the aged individuals may receive mixed messages from his or her friends and relatives. The visitors may communicate the obligatory nature of the visit, avoid discussion of sensitive topics, or provide conflicting verbal and nonverbal cues. A frustrated visitor may at times exhibit negative outbursts, which lead to guilt feelings that cause further withdrawal from the aged individual. The net result of such interactions is that the aged individual often feels rejected and his or her well-being is adversely affected.

What accounts for such behaviors on the part of the medical staff and friends and relatives? Because the motivations behind these acts is too varied and complex to be fully discussed here (see Wortman & Dunkel-Schetter, 1979, for a detailed discussion of motivational factors), we will focus primarily on control-related factors that might account for these behaviors.

The avoidance behavior of physicians may be attributable in part to medical training that emphasizes an interaction style between physician and patient described by Lief and Fox (1963) as "detached concern." The medical student is advised to be empathic and involved with the patient but, above all, to remain objective. In addition, the specifics of medical training are usually focused on saving lives and restoring health to the exclusion of dealing with patients who may never be completely well again or who may be terminal. As a consequence the medical staff may associate the institutionalized sick elderly patient with failure and disappointment. Friends and relatives likewise may be frustrated by their inability to positively affect the aged individual's physical status. In short, both staff and friends may come to feel helpless about their ability to make positive contributions to the aged person's well-being. More specifically, they come to feel helpless about their ability to control the most important of all outcomes for the aged individual: his or her health and survival. The inability to control important outcomes may affect the individual's motivation to control less critical but, nevertheless, important outcomes.

Stotland (1969) has suggested that persons have hierarchies of outcomes that they feel capable of controlling. When control over one item in the hierarchy is removed, the individual ceases to exercise control over those items that fall below the critical item on the hierarchy. This model may be useful in understanding some of the behavior of significant others toward the elderly. The individual who interacts with the institutionalized aged may have the following types of cognitions: "If I can't effect any control over the real important aspects of this person's life (i.e., his or her physical status), what good does it do to exercise control and affect the less important aspects of his or her life (i.e., psychological status)." In short, those outcomes over which significant others may have control are perceived as trivial, and consequently, control ceases to be exercised. The net result is avoidance of the institutionalized individual at a time when he or she is in great need of support.

CONCLUSION

There is more to aging than institutionalization. In fact, only a small proportion (5%) of those over 65 years of age live in institutions, although a much larger proportion of the aged will spend some time in institutions before their death. The emphasis in this chapter has been on control as it applies to the institutionalization process and to the institutionalized aged. Why the emphasis on the institutionalized aged? In part, our choice is dictated by convenience. Institutional environments are relatively convenient settings for studying nonstudent subjects. Problems of attrition are minimal, and institutionalized aged persons are typically eager to participate in research programs that appear to embellish their lives a bit.

But institutional settings are important for theoretical reasons as well.

The transition to institutional settings can be viewed as a natural control-relevant intervention that simulates in miniature broader social–psychological aspects of aging. The transition provides unique opportunities for studying control phenomena in a population underoing rapid and severe changes in their ability to exercise control. In sum, our approach should be useful in gaining greater understanding of aging on a much broader scale, and it should provide insights into the effects of institutionalization on persons of all ages.

12

Coping with Undesirable Life Events[1]

ROXANE L. SILVER
CAMILLE B. WORTMAN

INTRODUCTION

At some point, most people encounter stressful events that can have a major impact on the course and direction of their lives. They or those they love may be confronted with a disabling accident, serious illness, death, or violent crime. How do people respond to such outcomes? Over the past several decades, theorists and researchers from a variety of disciplines have devoted attention to this issue. In this chapter, we draw from these sources to address several questions that we believe to be central to the coping process: Are there any reactions such as shock, anger, or depression that are universally experienced when people encounter an aversive life event? Do persons who encounter life crises that are as different as physical disability and loss of a spouse show any similarities in response? Do people progress through an orderly sequence of stages as they attempt to cope with the outcome? Is it true that with time, people accept or recover from their crisis and move on to the next stage in their lives? Finally, what *is* successful adjustment to an aversive life event?

[1]Support for the research and writing of this chapter was provided by National Science Foundation Grant BNS78-04743 to the second author.

279

Past Research in Social Psychology

As social psychologists, we began our investigation of these questions by considering the empirical research in our own field. Over the past two decades, this discipline has devoted a great deal of attention to understanding reactions to outcomes that are stressful or unpleasant. With some exceptions (e. g., Bulman & Wortman, 1977; Janis, 1958; Johnson & Leventhal, 1974; Langer, Janis, & Wolfer, 1975), the majority of these studies have been conducted in laboratory settings. Subjects have been exposed to a variety of mildly aversive outcomes such as electric shocks, noise bursts, or failure at problem-solving tasks. Although these studies have been conducted by investigators from many different theoretical orientations, they have focused primarily on two distinct issues. The first concerns specific factors that may reduce a person's subjective distress when an aversive event is encountered, such as whether the stressful event is predictable or controllable (e.g., Geer, Davison, & Gatchel, 1970; Pervin, 1963), or whether preparatory information is provided (e.g., Lanzetta & Driscoll, 1966; Staub & Kellet, 1976). A second issue concerns the conditions under which exposure to unpleasant outcomes results in undesirable aftereffects. Most of these latter studies have been designed to test predictions from the learned helplessness model developed by Seligman and his colleagues (see, e.g., Hiroto & Seligman, 1975), which predicts that exposure to uncontrollable stressors will result in subsequent cognitive and motivational deficits (see also Glass & Singer, 1972).

As this research has begun to accumulate, many investigators have become disillusioned with the laboratory paradigm as a vehicle for providing useful information about reactions to negative life events (see, e.g., Blaney, 1977; Bulman & Wortman, 1977; Lazarus & Launier, 1978; Roth, 1980; Wortman & Brehm, 1975). Despite the experimental control afforded by a laboratory approach, surprisingly few replicable findings have emerged, and a number of basic questions remain unanswered. For example, although it is commonly assumed that predictability and perceived control reduce th aversiveness of stressful outcomes, the research evidence on this question is inconsistent (Averill, 1973; Wortman, 1976). It is also not clear when exposure to uncontrollable outcomes will result in renewed determination to overcome one's obstacles and thus facilitate performance, and when it will result in feelings of helplessness, passivity and subsequent performance decrements. (See Dweck & Wortman, 1980; Miller & Norman, 1979; or Wortman & Dintzer, 1978, for a more detailed discussion of this issue.)

Moreover, there are fundamental differences between stressors encountered in the laboratory and most aversive life events that may limit the generalizability of results from laboratory paradigms (Wortman, Abbey, Holland, Silver, & Janoff-Bulman, 1980). Obviously, these outcomes differ in magnitude, as well as in the length of time that a person is confronted with the consequences (Lazarus & Launier, 1978). Coping responses that are effective for minor, transitory stressors may have little impact on prolonged or severe distress. Human subjects' guidelines require that laboratory stressors be delivered with the subject's explicit consent, and subjects are generally provided with a "cover story" or rationale for any distress they are asked to endure. In contrast, undesirable life events often happen without foreknowledge, and frequently occur for no apparent purpose or reason (Bulman & Wortman, 1977). For all of these reasons, there is some question as to the applicability of the laboratory approach to understanding real world reactions.

Plan of the Chapter

Because of the problems inherent in applying laboratory research in our own discipline to the issue of how people respond to undesirable life events, we felt it was important to broaden our focus by examining data collected in natural settings. We have considered the limited work in social psychology, and have also turned to related disciplines such as medicine, clinical psychology, psychiatry, sociology, and social work. In each of these areas we have examined a number of articles, books, and book chapters on reactions to specific life crises, including acute, chronic, and life-threatening illness, physical disability, separation, bereavement and criminal victimization. Some of these works have proposed theoretical models of the coping process; others report empirical findings; still others consist primarily of impressions from interview data or clinical practice. Not surprisingly, the majority of these studies lack the methodological rigor that characterize most of the laboratory experiments on reactions to distress. Considered together, however, they suggest some preliminary answers to questions concerning reactions to undesirable life events.

In the remainder of the chapter we draw from these works in an attempt to examine how people cope with life crises. By "coping" we are referring to any and all responses made by an individual who encounters a potentially harmful outcome. In addition to overt behaviors, we would include cognitions (e.g., "I'm not really sick"), emotional reactions (e.g., anger, depression) and physiological responses (e.g., nausea, sleep disturbances). The particular means of coping employed by an individual may alleviate the problem or reduce the resulting distress, and may thus be considered effective coping. However, coping responses may also exacerbate the problem or may become problems themselves (e.g., alcohol or drug abuse). Our use of the term "coping" is somewhat broader than that employed by most other theorists and researchers in this area, who often restrict its use to problem-solving efforts utilized by individuals to master or overcome a potentially threatening situation. (See Haan, 1977; Lazarus & Launier, 1978; and Lipowski, 1970, for critical discussion of the coping construct, and Chodoff, Friedman, & Hamburg, 1964; Friedman, Chodoff, Mason, & Hamburg, 1963; and White, 1974, for alternative definitions of the concept.)

In the discussion to follow, we have focused exclusively on how individuals cope with aversive life events of serious magnitude. We have not discussed the process of adjustment to life transitions, such as adolescence, marriage, parenting, and the aging process. We have also limited ourselves to outcomes that are caused, at least in part, by factors that the individual was unable to influence. For example, some of the outcomes we have considered (e.g., cancer, accidents, rape) may stem partially from the individual's own behavior (e.g., smoking cigarettes, driving too fast, returning home late at night) and partially from external or uncontrollable factors (e.g., genetic predisposition, drunk drivers, poorly lit streets). We have not considered distress brought about primarily by the respondent's own behavior, such as that resulting from a suicide attempt or drug abuse; or outcomes associated with voluntary behaviors, such as the choice of a specific career (see Mechanic, 1962).

Because we feel that inquiries regarding reactions to aversive life events should be theory-based, we begin by examining five theoretical formulations proposed in this area (Abramson, Seligman, & Teasdale, 1978; Klinger, 1975, 1977; Lazarus & Launier, 1978; Shontz, 1965, 1975; Wortman & Brehm, 1975). In so doing, our interest is not in validating any specific model, but rather in highlighting some of the critical issues that surround theoretical development in this field. These models help to illustrate some promising directions for subsequent theoretical work, as well as some of the conceptual difficulties that remain to be resolved.

An interesting feature of these and other theories that have been advanced on coping is that they share some common assumptions about the adjustment process—assumptions that are also widely held by practitioners and the lay public. It is commonly believed that there are universal reactions, such as shock or depression, that occur in response to crisis situations; that people go through stages of emotional response as they cope with an undesirable life event; and that the crisis is ultimately resolved. A careful examination of the available research data, however, suggests that each of these assumptions may be unwarranted. We consider a great deal of evidence indicating that people react to crises with considerable variability, and that they may recover less quickly or completely than they or others expect. Current theoretical frameworks afford little help in accounting for this variability or predicting effective adjustment. We therefore explore some conceptual variables not incorporated into prior theories that may influence the coping process. Finally, we discuss the implications of the rich and diverse findings in this field for future theoretical work, for subsequent research, and for the treatment of individuals confronted with undesirable life events.

PAST THEORETICAL APPROACHES

During the past several decades, many theoretical approaches have been proposed that have potential relevance for understanding reactions to undesirable life events (Caplan, 1964; Engel, 1962; French, Rodgers, & Cobb, 1974; Haan, 1963, 1969, 1977; Harrison, 1978; Holmes & Masuda, 1974; Kahn, 1964; Kaufman & Rosenblum, 1967; Moos & Tsu, 1977; Murphy & Moriarty, 1976; Pearlin & Schooler, 1978; Riss & Scalia, 1967; Schneirla, 1959; Selye, 1946, 1976; Solomon & Corbit, 1974; White, 1974). We feel that by examining theorists' attempts to conceptualize the nature of the coping process, one can gain a better understanding of the problems and issues involved. Because a review of each of these theories is clearly beyond the scope of this chapter, however, we have chosen to focus on a representative but diverse sample of theoretical formulations: Klinger's (1975, 1977) theory of commitment to and disengagement from incentives; Wortman and Brehm's (1975) integrative model; Seligman's learned helplessness approach (Abramson et al., 1978; Seligman, 1975); Shontz's (1965, 1975) theory of reaction to crisis; and Lazarus' taxonomy of coping responses (Lazarus, Note 1; Lazarus & Launier, 1978). These models represent a variety of theoretical orientations and research traditions, ranging from experimental psychology to clinical and health fields. We have limited our discussion to models which are broad enough to have relevance to a number of different life crises, as opposed to those which are specific to a particular aversive outcome (e.g., Kubler-Ross, 1969). These particular models were selected not because they are necessarily the most precise, the best developed, or the most influential, but because we feel that each provides unique insights about the issues involved in the coping process. In the following sections, we briefly describe each of these models, highlight the intriguing issues they raise, and critically examine their ability to predict reactions to undesirable life events.

Klinger's Incentive– Disengagement Theory

Klinger's (1975, 1977) major interest concerns how people become committed to and disengaged from various incentives or goals. Drawing from his clinical background, as well as many other areas in psychology, he argues that commitment to a goal influences a person's patterns of attention, information processing, and thought content. Klinger maintains that when an aversive life event removes or blocks a particular goal, individuals go through a process of disengagement in which their cognitions, feelings, and behaviors unfold in an orderly and predictable sequence.

According to this theory, a person initially responds to obstacles or to threatened loss of a goal with increased vigor. Efforts to achieve the goal may become more powerful and/or rapid, and concentration may become more intense. If these initial responses are unsuccessful in obtaining the incentive, however, the person becomes increasingly frustrated and angry, and his or her behavior becomes more stereotyped, primitive and often more aggressive. This phase may be characterized by disbelief or angry protest. After sustained but unsuccessful activity to achieve an outcome, however, individuals begin to abandon their pursuit. This phase of the cycle, called the "depression phase," is thought to be characterized by pessimism and apathy. Klinger argues that depression is a normal part of the process whereby individuals disengage themselves from incentives. As a person's commitment to the incentive slowly dissipates, so does the impulse to obtain it, and its influence on his or her thoughts and fantasies decreases as well. Over time, the incentive becomes a smaller and smaller part of the person's life, and he or she experiences longer and longer periods of pleasant feelings until recovery from the loss is complete.

According to Klinger (1977), people may be involved simultaneously in several incentive-disengagement cycles, which combine to determine their emotional state:

> Since every loss produces an incentive-disengagement cycle, and since losses are likely to be staggered over time, a person may be in different phases of more than one incentive-disengagement cycle at a time. . . . [Thus,] if several ventures turn sour at about the same time—a special friend left town abruptly, the soup burned, and one misplaced one's notes for writing a term paper—one is likely a little later to feel somewhat blue [p. 140].

This view implies that individuals who are attempting to cope with a major life crisis may be particularly vulnerable to the effects of additional problems. Conversely, people faced with a large number of other problems may be especially vulnerable to life crises.

Wortman and Brehm's Integrative Model

Although Wortman and Brehm (1975) were working on an entirely different set of problems, they developed a model with some similarities to Klinger's invigoration–depression sequence. As social psychologists, Wortman and Brehm were quite interested in how people respond when their freedom or control is taken away. Brehm (1966) had developed a theory of psychological reactance that suggested that when free behavior is restricted, people respond with feelings of hostility, anger, and enhanced motivation to obtain the outcome in question. This theoretical work, and the research supporting it, appeared to be inconsistent with the learned helplessness model (Seligman, 1975). This approach predicts that individuals who are exposed to uncontrollable outcomes become passive and depressed, and show subsequent motivational deficits and impairments in active problem-solving.

Wortman and Brehm were interested in developing an integrative model that would resolve the contradictions between these two formulations, and specify the precise conditions under which invigoration or depression would occur. Drawing from reactance theory, they maintained that the nature and intensity of an individual's response to an uncontrollable outcome would depend both on the expectation of control over the outcome, and the outcome's importance. The integrative model predicts that among individuals who expect to be able to influence an important outcome, exposure to loss of control results in enhanced motivation to obtain the outcome, and in aggressive and angry behaviors. However, expectations of control should diminish over time as people make repeated but unsuccessful attempts to change the situation. Once a person stops trying to alter the outcome, continued exposure to it should result in lowered motivation, passivity, and depression. Wortman and Brehm maintained that the greater the initial expectation of control, the more controlling behavior a person will show before giving up, and the more depressed he or she will become after giving up. They also argued that individuals who do not expect to be able to influence the outcome will become depressed without an initial period of invigoration. Wortman and Brehm's model is similar to Klinger's in that it proposes an invigoration–depression sequence of responses. Unlike Klinger, however, Wortman and Brehm do not assume that invigoration will generally precede depression. They have attempted to incorporate mediating variables which will determine whether invigoration or depression will occur, and how intense or long-lasting these responses will be.

The Learned Helplessness Approach

Like Wortman and Brehm's (1975) model, the learned helplessness model was originally developed to account for laboratory data on reactions to uncontrollable outcomes, rather than to explain reactions to life crises. Of course, the original helplessness model predates the theoretical statements of Klinger as well as Wortman and Brehm (Seligman, Maier, & Solomon, 1971). This approach had its origins in Seligman's work on Pavlovian fear conditioning with infrahuman species, where it was discovered that exposure to uncontrollable shocks resulted in subsequent passivity and performance deficits (Overmier & Seligman, 1967; Seligman & Maier, 1967). When investigators began testing the model on human subjects, however, the findings were inconsistent. Exposure to insoluble problems or uncontrollable noise bursts or shocks did not always result in passivity, performance decrements, or depressed mood as the model would predict (see Miller & Norman, 1979; or Roth, 1980, for reviews).

On the basis of these data, investigators began to speculate that helplessness effects may stem not from the uncontrollability of an aversive stimulus, but from the way in which the stimulus is interpreted by the subject (see Dweck & Wortman, 1980). In an attempt to address these and other criticisms of the original theory, Abramson et al. (1978) proposed a reformulated model. They argued that the nature of the helplessness effects depends on the attribution of causality that a person makes when confronted with an uncontrollable outcome. According to Abramson et al., attributions can be categorized according to three orthogonal dimensions: internality, stability, and globality. They predict that attributions to internal factors (e.g., "I'm stupid") are characterized by loss of self-esteem, while attributions to external factors (e.g., "These problems are impossible") are not. Attributions to stable factors (e.g., "I was mugged because the streets of New York are never safe") are hypothesized to produce greater subsequent performance deficits than attributions to unstable factors (e.g., "I was mugged because I was unlucky"). Attributions to global factors, or those which occur across many situations (e.g., "My business failed because I am completely incompetent") should lead to deficits which generalize further than attributions to more specific factors (e.g., "My business failed because it was in the wrong location"). Unlike the models described previously, the reformulated helplessness model focuses solely on passivity, depression, and performance decrements as responses to uncontrollable outcomes. The model predicts no invigoration effects, nor does it focus on changes in reactions over time.

Shontz's Theory of Reaction to Crisis

The same year that models by Klinger (1975) and Wortman and Brehm (1975) were published, a book appeared by Shontz (1975) on the psychological aspects of physical illness and disability (see also Shontz, 1965). In this book, Shontz drew from his experience in rehabilitation and health settings to delineate a general model of reaction to crisis. Like Klinger, as well as Wortman and Brehm, Shontz maintains that individuals go through a series of stages as they attempt to cope with an aversive outcome. However, the sequence he proposes is quite different from that outlined by the others. Unlike the theorists described previously, Shontz considers the ways in which individuals respond to and interpret information prior to the onset of a crisis. During this time, an effort is made to interpret any unusual symptoms as something benign or unthreatening. For example, a parent whose child is manifesting early signs of leukemia might regard the initial symptoms as evidence of a minor, transitory illness. As the symptoms or problems become more pressing, however, people realize that their existing patterns of adjustment are inadequate, and experience considerable anxiety and stress.

Once the inevitability of the crisis becomes clear, Shontz holds that a person's first reaction is one of shock. Shock is especially likely to be observed if the crisis occurs without warning, but occurs to some degree in virtually every crisis state. According to Shontz, this stage is characterized by a feeling of detachment and by a surprising efficiency of thought and action. Following the initial shock, an encounter phase occurs in which the individual begins to experience profound helplessness, disorganization and panic. During this phase, reality may seem overwhelming, and the individual may show an inability to plan, reason or engage in active problem-solving to improve the situation.

Because this period is so intense, individuals begin to manifest a type of avoidance that Shontz calls "retreat." During this phase, the individual may deny either the existence of the crisis or its serious implications. As time goes by, however, reality again imposes itself and the person learns that he or she cannot escape the implications of the outcome indefinitely. The individual then breaks down his or her defenses slowly in an attempt to deal with reality piece by piece. The most unique feature of Shontz's model is his view that the adaptive sequence is characterized by a continual shifting between encounter and retreat from crisis. Retreat provides a "base of operation from which forays into the future can be made and to which the person may withdraw for safety if they fail [1975, p. 172]."

Each time an individual begins to face reality, feelings of anxiety, frustration, and depression may occur. Shontz argues that such feelings are not necessarily maladaptive, but are necessary precursors to positive psychological growth. These cycles "occur progressively less frequently . . . until they become virtually unnoticeable when adaptation is complete [1975, p. 166]." A renewed sense of personal worth, a gradual lowering of anxiety, and an increase in feelings of satisfaction may be experienced as views of oneself and of the crisis become more stable.

Lazarus' Analysis of the Coping Process

Lazarus has been a major contributor to our understanding of the coping process for the past two decades. His earlier theoretical and empirical work (e.g., Lazarus, 1966; Lazarus & Alfert, 1964; Lazarus, Averill, & Opton,

1974; Speisman, Lazarus, Mordkoff, & Davison, 1964) has focused on how a person's cognitive appraisal of a stressful situation influences the emotional responses that are elicited, the coping strategies that are employed, and the ultimate success of a person's adjustment to the crisis. In his more recent papers, his emphasis has begun to shift toward the process of coping with undesirable life events of serious magnitude (Coyne & Lazarus, in press; Lazarus, Note 1; Lazarus & Launier, 1978).

Like Shontz, Lazarus is one of the few theorists to discuss how individuals respond to potentially harmful information before it has been defined as a crisis. He maintains that individuals appraise the significance of the situation for their well-being, as well as the coping responses at their disposal for dealing with the harm. In addition, Lazarus has recently suggested that an individual may appraise a potentially harmful situation as a threat and thus focus on the possible harm; or regard it as a challenge and focus on the potential for mastery or gain (Coyne & Lazarus, in press; Lazarus & Launier, 1978).

In their discussions of the coping process, most of the other theorists have focused on the conditions under which individuals will engage in direct actions to improve or change their stressful situations. Lazarus has considered several other kinds of coping strategies that he regards as equally important: inhibition of action (e.g., withholding insults or aggressive responses), information seeking (e.g., augmenting one's store of knowledge about a particular disease), and intrapsychic modes (e.g., denial or thinking calming thoughts). Lazarus has not provided a detailed analysis of the conditions under which each mode will be employed. However, he has noted that a high degree of uncertainty or ambiguity about a given outcome may result in decreased use of direct action and increased use of information seeking. If information is not available, the individual may resort to intrapsychic modes of coping. Intrapsychic modes may also be used if direct action has been unsuccessful and/or if harm has already occurred or is judged as inevitable (Lazarus & Launier, 1978). Finally, Lazarus has also emphasized that in addition to overcoming the crisis, coping responses may be directed toward controlling or regulating one's emotional reaction to the situation (see also Mechanic, 1962). For the most part, the other theorists have restricted their discussion to coping mechanisms directed toward the crisis itself.

IMPLICATIONS OF THE THEORIES

Because the aforementioned theorists represent diverse research traditions and focused their attention on a variety of problems and issues, we feel that each of them offers a valuable perspective on the coping process.

Some of the models reviewed are broad and general; others allow more specific predictions. Some were designed to account for serendipitous or contradictory laboratory findings; others are based more on clinical or practical experience. Some focus their attention on how individuals react to a single life crisis; others specifically discuss responses to outcomes that are repeated over time. In general, each theorist suggests an important aspect of the coping process that is unique to his or her model. In the following section, we explore an intriguing issue or point raised by each of these theoretical formulations and discuss their implications for coping research. We then examine the potential effectiveness of these models in predicting how individuals respond to an aversive life event.

Issues Raised by the Models

Klinger's Focus on Thoughts about the Crisis

While all of the theorists discussed previously have considered the role of cognitions in the coping process, Klinger (1975, 1977) has provided particular emphasis on the importance of thoughts about the crisis. He offers a cogent analysis of the effect of one's goals on the content of thoughts, fantasies, and dreams. For example, he suggests that immediately after a goal has been blocked, it completely dominates a person's thought content: "Very likely, this phenomenon accounts for the loss of 'perspective' often noted in people who have become embattled in pursuit of a blocked goal [1977, p. 144]." He argues that as the person recovers from the loss, it occupies less and less of his or her thoughts. Klinger also suggests that it may be possible to speed recovery by taking the person away from cues which are associated with the lost incentive.

An interesting issue addressed by Klinger, and also discussed briefly by Wortman and Brehm (1975), concerns the value of the lost goal. Both models predict that when a goal is initially blocked it becomes more attractive. But what happens to the evaluation of the loss over time? Do people gradually become indifferent to the lost object, or do they come to view it negatively? In an intriguing analysis, Klinger (1977) suggests that a person may develop feelings toward the goal that are highly ambivalent: "Whereas earlier the person wanted very much to achieve the incentive, he is now both attracted and repelled by it; and this ambivalence is so painful that he may avoid the very situations in which he can contemplate the incentive [p. 167]."

In our judgment, the question of how people evaluate the life crises that befall them has not received adequate attention from other theorists or researchers. When a person loses a spouse, for example, are the spouse's strengths and weaknesses judged objectively? Or does the spouse come to be idolized, as Engel (1964) suggests: "[The bereaved individual] finds it necessary to bring up, to think over, and to talk about memories of the dead person . . . until there has been erected in the mind an image of the dead person almost devoid of negative or undesirable features [p. 96]'' (see also Benson, McCubbin, Dahl, & Hunter, 1974; McCubbin, Hunter, & Metres, 1974b). How do these judgments influence a person's emotional reaction to the loss? Do these evaluations change over time? How are they related to effective long-term adjustment? Are people who become indifferent to a lost goal more likely to cope effectively than people who enhance the attractiveness of what they have lost?

Changes in Beliefs about Oneself and the World

Most of the models of life crises have explored reactions to a single undesirable event. A unique feature of the models proposed by Wortman and Brehm (1975) and by Abramson et al. (1978) is that they focus on reactions to repeated stressors. In the original laboratory research on which these models are based, subjects were exposed to several trials of uncontrollable stimulation. Both Seligman (1975) and Wortman and Brehm (1975) hypothesized that exposure to repeated uncontrollable outcomes alters people's beliefs about themselves and their ability to influence the environment. Such changes in underlying beliefs are not postulated by the other models. If they occur, these belief changes are likely to mediate whether a person's emotional and behavioral reactions will generalize to other settings.

Since the learned helplessness and integrative models were originally designed to account for the effects of a series of stressors, they may be particularly applicable to individuals who encounter a distressing experience several times. For example, do foster children become helpless if they are repeatedly uprooted? Do epileptics show invigoration and/or helplessness effects as they attempt to cope with recurrent uncontrollable seizures? At present it is unclear whether the predictions of these models are applicable to individuals who experience a single aversive life event. Nonetheless, the suggestion that such an outcome may change a person's enduring beliefs, and influence subsequent behavior, is an important one. To what extent does losing a spouse or being raped alter a person's beliefs about his or her ability to influence future outcomes, and thus influence subsequent persistence or passivity in the face of later goals? Under what conditions do the emotional reactions experienced by a bereaved person or a rape victim generalize to other areas of his or her life? By and large, other theorists have given no consideration to these important issues. In discussing invigoration effects, for example, Klinger maintains that feelings of anger and frustration will predominate. But are such feelings directed solely toward the blocked goal, or are these reactions manifested toward other factors in the environment?

What Behaviors Are Adaptive or Functional?

Unlike the other models reviewed, Shontz's (1965, 1975) theory was developed from his experience in health-care and rehabilitation settings. This orientation has led to a number of intriguing observations. For example, Shontz challenges the widely shared assumption that disabling accidents or serious illness invariably produce negative psychological effects. In Shontz's view, severe illness may not represent a crisis for all people; in fact, it may sometimes solve problems for a patient rather than create them. Some individuals may view their disease as a punishment for past sins, and, in so doing, may be able to alleviate destructive and oppressive feelings of guilt. For others, a disease may provide a welcome relief from stressful obligations and responsibilities. According to Shontz, health-care professionals must be sensitive to this possibility, and should avoid pressing patients to respond to crises that are not actually being experienced. (See Lipowski, 1970, for a similar analysis.)

Once a crisis occurs, Shontz maintains that individuals who fail to progress through the sequence of stages as he has delineated them are likely to have subsequent problems adjusting to their trauma. For example, if they retreat from the crisis too quickly, they may fail to assimilate any realistic information about their situation, and subsequent attempts to cope with the outcome may be hampered. But if they do not retreat fast enough and thus remain in a state of intense negative affect for too long, emotional and physical exhaustion can result. Regardless of one's adherence to Shontz's model, his suggestion that particular stages or responses may have functional value is intriguing. For the most part, the other theorists reviewed have not explored whether progression through particular stages is necessary. Must a person with a spinal cord injury experience depression if long-term adjustment is to occur, as some investigators have suggested (e.g., Dembo, Leviton, & Wright, 1956; Siller, 1969)? Does a bereaved person who initially becomes depressed, but later experiences intense anger, cope less effectively than a person who shows an invigoration–depression sequence?

Broadening Our View of Coping

Lazarus is unique among the theorists we have considered in his attention to the variety of coping responses that may be employed by individuals who encounter life crises. Other models we have reviewed have focused almost exclusively on when individuals will attempt to alter an aversive outcome, and when they will give up (Wortman & Brehm, 1975; Abramson et al., 1978). This question may be of central importance in understanding how individuals react to outcomes of limited duration and/or importance, such as noise bursts administered in a laboratory setting. However, the available evidence suggests that when the outcomes are serious or permanent, people engage in a wide variety of responses in addition to direct action (Burgess & Holmstrom, 1976, 1979; Chodoff et al., 1964; Hamburg, Hamburg, & DeGoza, 1953; Katz, Weiner, Gallagher, & Hellman, 1970; Sanders & Kardinal, 1977; Visotsky, Hamburg, Goss, & Lebovits, 1961). (For a discussion of the diversity of coping strategies that can be employed and potential techniques of measurement, see McCubbin, Dahl, Lester, Benson, & Robertson, 1976; Penman, 1979; Sidle, Moos, Adams, & Cady, 1969; Weisman, 1974, 1979.)

A second feature of Lazarus' work that we feel is of critical importance is his distinction between coping responses that alter the stressful situation itself, and those that are designed to alter the emotional response to the crisis. An intriguing point made by Lazarus is that under certain circumstances, individuals may achieve one of these coping functions at the expense of another. For example, a woman may reduce her distress by denying initial symptoms of breast cancer, thus delaying treatment and reducing her chances for a favorable outcome. In our judgment, responses that palliate one's emotional reactions should receive careful attention. Intense emotional distress is not only unpleasant, but may impede coping or problem-solving efforts (cf. Anderson, 1976), particularly if the task in question is complex in nature (Broadhurst, 1959). For all these reasons, coping responses that can reduce the respondent's level of emotional distress to a moderate level might be adaptive or functional. Moreover, in cases where direct actions can be undertaken to alter the outcome, behaviors that might superficially be judged as maladaptive (e.g., increased alcohol consumption) may be functional if they do not reduce the level of arousal to a point too low for optimum performance.

Predictive Power of the Models

In the previous section, we have highlighted some of the unique insights that have been suggested by the theoretical models described. How do these models fare in predictive power? The most general of the models we have reviewed is that of Lazarus, who has maintained that there is a continuous interplay among cognitions, emotions, and coping strategies in which each influences the other as the individual struggles with a particular outcome. Although his rich account of the coping process has provided numerous insights and broadened the way we look at coping, his model does not offer precise predictions regarding an individual's behavior in a single instance. As individuals begin to appraise the potentially harmful situation, for example, what antecedent factors will determine whether they will feel threatened, or whether they will regard the outcome as a challenge? Once the appraisal process has been completed, it is not clear which particular emotional reactions will predominate, or which coping mechanisms will be selected. Specifically how do these components of the coping process influence one another, and how do they relate to ultimate adjustment? As Lazarus himself acknowledges, his work represents more of a taxonomy of possible reactions to life crises than a formal model (Lazarus & Launier, 1978).

The models proposed by Shontz (1965, 1975) and Klinger (1975, 1977) are somewhat more specific in that each suggests that individuals progress through a particular sequence of stages as they attempt to cope with a crisis. In our judgment, however, neither of these theorists has given sufficient attention to specifying intervening variables that may affect the sequence. In Shontz's model, what factors determine the duration of particular phases such as encounter or retreat, or the length of the cycles that occur? Moreover, although Shontz clearly intends his model to be useful in understanding patient reactions, application is extremely difficult. Under what conditions should health care professionals conclude that the person is resisting a crisis that should be faced, and under what conditions should they conclude that the outcome does not constitute a crisis for the individual? Similarly, how is a health care professional to determine whether a person is remaining in a particular phase, such as retreat, for too long? Klinger has also noted that invigoration responses are sometimes absent, but provides no basis for predicting when this will occur. Do individuals respond with invigoration even when it is clear from the beginning that these responses will not be instrumental in altering the situation, such as when a spouse has died? In short, Klinger has given insufficient attention to specifying mediating variables that might affect the nature, course, or duration of the incentive-disengagement cycle or specific reactions that comprise the cycle.

A clear advantage of the models postulated by Wortman and Brehm (1975) and by Abramson et al. (1978) is that they have included mediating variables, and thus permit relatively precise predictions about reactions to life crises. Using the constructs of expectations of control and judged importance of the outcome, the Wortman and Brehm (1975) model makes clear predictions concerning when particular emotional reactions (anger or depression) will occur, and how intense such reactions will be. Similarly, by introducing subjects' attributions of causality as a mediating variable, the model proposed by Abramson et al. (1978) affords precise predictions regarding how long behavioral deficits will last and how far such deficits will generalize.

Unfortunately, there are other shortcomings associated with each of these models that limit their usefulness in understanding reactions to life crises. A major problem with the Abramson et al. (1978) model is that although the authors have argued that certain attributions are predictably followed by specific behavioral consequences, they have failed to specify the conditions under which a given attribution will be made. What determines whether a person facing a particular outcome (e.g., rape) will make internal, stable, and global attributions or external, unstable, and specific ones? Until the determinants of particular attributions can be delineated, the model will lack predictive power. (See Wortman & Dintzer, 1978, for a more detailed discussion of additional shortcomings of the reformulated model.)

One question that might be raised about Wortman and Brehm's (1975) model concerns their major variable, expectations of control. Unlike Abramson et al. (1978), Wortman and Brehm were precise about the antecedents of this variable, noting that expectations would be based on one's prior experience with the task, and/or one's observations of others' performance. This variable is relatively easy to operationalize and measure when dealing with such outcomes as failure on a problem-solving task. However, Wortman and Brehm (1975) did not explore how this variable might be extended to non-laboratory settings. Do people's reactions to outcomes like permanent paralysis or rape depend on their generalized expectations of control (Rotter, 1966) or on specific expectations associated with the accident or assault? Are emotional reactions and subsequent adjustment influenced primarily by expectations that the outcome could or should have been avoided, by expectations that the consequences can be altered or changed, or by expectations that the outcome can be prevented in the future?

An additional limitation of the models developed by Wortman and Brehm (1975) and by Abramson et al. (1978) is their narrowness, which may be a reflection of their original focus on animal and laboratory research. Wortman and Brehm focus only on invigoration and depression as reactions to uncontrollable outcomes. The reformulated helplessness model is narrower still, focusing solely on the reactions of helplessness and depression. These models have not incorporated other emotional reactions or coping mechanisms, and have devoted relatively little attention to the process by which individuals move from helplessness or depression to recovery or resolution.

In summary, we have attempted to highlight some of the difficulties associated with conceptual work in this area. Each of these theoretical formulations raises provocative questions about the coping process and suggests numerous hypotheses. However, the models fail to provide a clear basis for predicting which responses will predominate when life crises occur, how these responses influence one another, or which are associated with successful resolution of the crisis. Nonetheless, we feel that each model brings an important perspective to the problem, and suggests some desirable features that should be incorporated in subsequent theoretical work.

EMPIRICAL RESEARCH ON REACTIONS
TO UNDESIRABLE LIFE EVENTS

In the previous section we examined several theoretical models in order to illustrate specific problems and conceptual issues involved in the area of coping with life crises. In so doing, our purpose was not to validate any particular model, but rather to use the models as a springboard for subsequent discussion. At this point, we would like to move beyond the specific models to a consideration of the more general issues of the coping process that they raise. Despite their many differences, these and other models share some common assumptions. One such assumption concerns the existence of a general pattern or consensual response to life crises. Although there are differences from model to model, most have suggested that people respond to crises in specific, predictable ways (e.g., with shock, anger, or depression). Second, it is commonly assumed that individuals go through a series of stages over time in attempting to come to terms with an aversive life event. Of the theorists we have reviewed, Klinger, Shontz and Wortman and Brehm have proposed specific stage models, and this notion is quite popular among other theorists in the area. A third commonly held assumption is that individuals accept or resolve their crises. In fact, people are often expected to recover quite quickly, and thus move on to the next stage of their lives. In this section of the chapter, we examine the empirical evidence for each of these beliefs. We find that although these assumptions are widely shared by theorists and researchers in this area, there is little evidence to support any of them.

In the past, most critical discussions of research on undesirable life events have focused solely on studies within a particular type of life crisis. For example, critical reviews have appeared in such areas as physical illness and disability (McDaniel, 1976; Trieschmann, 1978), breast cancer (Meyerowitz, 1980), heart disease (Croog, Levine, & Lurie, 1968; Doehrman, 1977; Garrity, Note 2), and grief and bereavement (Schulz, 1978; Vachon, 1976). While such a narrow focus may enhance our understanding of a particular life crisis, it is not appropriate for assessing the validity of the broad theoretical assumptions we have delineated. Therefore, we have examined the research across several areas of victimization, including acute, chronic, and terminal illness, physical disability, separation, bereavement, and criminal victimization. In the discussion to follow, we consider what we believe to be the best empirical work in each area.

Is There a General Pattern or Consensual Response to Undesirable Life Events?

Most of the models we have reviewed suggest that individuals react to crises in predictable ways. Shontz (1965, 1975) has proposed, for example, that once the inevitability of a crisis is realized, virtually all individuals experience shock. According to Klinger (1975, 1977), people initially respond to crises with invigoration, anger, and aggression. Wortman and Brehm (1975) have also maintained that invigoration will occur when people believe they can alter the outcome. Depression figures prominently in all of the models except Shontz's, although the models make different predictions about precisely when it will occur. Are there any universal reactions, such as shock, anger, or depression, that occur in response to aversive life events?

It is difficult to evaluate the prevalence of an initial "shock" response, since investigators are not typically present or able to question respondents at the time the crisis is encountered. We have been able to locate only one report in which on-the-spot observations were made. Tyhurst (1951) conducted immediate observations of individuals who were involved in community disasters such as apartment-house fires or floods. He observed three distinct reactions. Many individuals appeared to react with shock, and showed many of the behaviors that Shontz described as characteristic of a "shock" phase: a "stunned" or "bewildered" reaction, "a definite restriction of the field of attention," "lack of awareness of any subjective feeling or emotion," and "automatic or reflex behavior" (p. 766). But a second group of survivors were "cool and collected" during the acute situation. A third group responded with feelings of overwhelming confusion and manifested such reactions as "paralyzing anxiety" or "hysterical crying." Although shock was the most prevalent reaction, it was clearly not universal.

In most of the other studies that have assessed reactions of shock, respondents have been questioned at some time after the crisis and asked to report retrospectively about their initial feelings. However, several investigators have interviewed rape victims shortly after the attack and have mentioned that shock or disbelief are sometimes experienced (see, e.g., Burgess & Holmstrom, 1974; Sutherland & Scherl, 1970). McCombie (1975) also asked rape victims to describe their feelings during and immediately after the assault. Although precise figures are not reported, she indicates that feelings of numbness or disbelief were second in frequency; fear was the most common emotion reported.

In a prospective study of 14 wives of cancer patients, Schmale (1971) reports that "the only uniformity of response in these subjects was the reaction [of] disbelief and shock [p. 166]" to both the diagnosis and to the actual death of their spouses. Friedman et al. (1963) suggested that all of the 46 parents they interviewed recalled a feeling of "shock" or of being "stunned" upon learning the terminal diagnosis of their child. In contrast, Parkes (1972) interviewed both widows and amputees approximately one month after they lost a spouse or a limb, and indicated that initial feelings of shock and numbness were retrospectively reported by only about 50% of the respondents. In a later study of reactions to bereavement (Parkes, 1975b), the specific percentage of subjects experiencing shock is not reported. However, the immediate reaction of disbelief was retrospectively described more frequently by individuals who had less than 2 weeks forewarning of the impending death of their spouse than by those who had more foreknowledge.

Variable results also emerge when we explore whether individuals respond initially to aversive outcomes with invigoration or anger (cf. Klinger, 1975, 1977; Wortman & Brehm, 1975). Studies of rape victims have reported that anger is a relatively rare reaction, at least during and immediately after the assault (McCombie, 1975; Notman & Nadelson, 1976). Only 10% of the 70 women interviewed by McCombie reported that they felt angry during the rape, and only 20% reported feeling angry immediately after the attack. Less than one-half of the cancer patients interviewed by Peck (1972) expressed anger at having cancer. Similarly, only 28% of the parents studied by Kupst and Schulman (Note 3) reacted with anger to the leukemia diagnosis of their child. Among the bereaved, Glick, Weiss, and Parkes (1974) report that approximately 3 to 4 weeks after the loss, one-third of the widows in their sample were rated by interviewers as showing feelings of hostility, and about 20% expressed anger toward their husbands for not having taken better care of themselves. In contrast, feelings of anger were relatively absent among the widowers in Glick et al.'s sample.

Both Klinger (1975, 1977) and Wortman and Brehm (1975) have suggested that feelings of invigoration may be directed toward recovering an incentive that is blocked or removed. An interesting question not addressed by these models is whether such reactions will occur even when there is no realistic hope of recovering the lost object, such as when a spouse has died. Although no percentages are reported, Parkes (1972) suggests that such behaviors sometimes occur among the bereaved. He argues that the urge to recover the lost relationship is manifested in several ways: "in restless scanning of the environment, in the strong perceptual set which the bereaved person develops for the lost person, in the tendency to misperceive and thus to identify strangers as being the one who is lost, in the tendency to return to places associated with the lost person [p. 345]." Cornwell, Nurcombe, and Stevens (1977) report similar findings from parents who have lost an infant to the Sudden Infant Death Syndrome. These researchers indicate that "Parents often wandered to the baby's room in search of the child. Their minds were attuned to perceptions of the baby [and they remained] primed to search for their lost baby for well over a year after its death [p. 657]." These data suggest that individuals' behaviors may be directed toward recovering a lost object even when the loss is irrevocable. However, it is not clear what evidence is required to convince a person that a loss is in fact permanent. Fully 8 weeks after losing a spouse, Glick et al. (1974) report that over one-half of the widows they interviewed, and about one-fifth of the widowers, reported believing that their spouse might actually return.

Even in cases where it is still possible to influence the outcome, however, it is by no means clear that anger is a universal response. A number of investigators have examined how children react to separations from their mothers, and have found their emotional reactions and behaviors to be highly variable. Some children show anger and/or increased activity, others show despair and/or immobility, others alternate between activity and immobility, and still others show no visible response of any sort (Heinicke, 1956; Heinicke & Westheimer, 1966; Maccoby & Feldman, 1972; Robertson & Robertson, 1971; Spitz, 1946).

Is depression commonly experienced following an undesirable life event? There is a fair amount of consensus that individuals experience feelings of sadness or depression soon after losing a spouse. Glick et al. (1974) report that 88% of the widows in their sample became sad and despairing. Similarly, Clayton, Desmarais, and Winokur (1968) found that 87% of the bereaved they interviewed reported experiencing sadness or depressed mood. These individuals showed considerable variability in the onset of their depression, however. While 41% became depressed for the first time during the bereavement period, 46% reported that they were depressed prior to the bereavement while their relative was ill, and 13% denied depressed mood at either time. The investigators report that neither the presence nor the onset of depression appeared to be related to such factors as the closeness of the relationship between the deceased and the respondent, or the length of time the relative had been ill prior to the death.

Several studies on psychological reactions to cancer have also found depression to be a prevalent response. Not surprisingly, however, the percentage of patients responding with depression varies from study to study. Peck (1972) indicated that 74% of the sample of cancer patients he interviewed appeared depressed. In contrast, Plumb and Holland (1977) studied 97 cancer patients with advanced disease and reported that almost all of these patients scored in the "non-depressed" range of the Beck Depression Inventory. Moreover, the patients were found to be significantly less depressed than physically healthy patients hospitalized for a suicide attempt. Maguire (1978) reports more variable data. Four months after a mastectomy, one woman in his sample was rated as severely depressed, 19 were thought to be moderately depressed, 24 were judged to exhibit minor depression, and 31 showed no evidence of depression. However, breast cancer patients were found to be significantly more depressed than a control group of patients who had had a biopsy that was not malignant. Taken as a whole, these and other studies (Achte & Vauhkonen, 1971; Craig & Abeloff, 1974; Hinton, 1963) suggest that depression is a common, but far from universal response to cancer, and that while cancer patients may show significantly more depression than normal controls, a sizable minority of patients show no evidence of depression in response to the diagnosis or treatment.

Studies of the initial reactions to rape suggest that feelings of depression are uncommon (Burgess & Holmstrom, 1974; McCombie, 1975). In contrast, fear or anxiety appear to be the most prevalent responses (McCombie, 1975), and such feelings as fear of being alone or fears of being followed, nightmares, and obsessional thoughts concerning the rape appear to be very common (Burgess & Holmstrom 1974; Sutherland & Scherl, 1970). Feelings of anxiety are also frequently observed among bereaved widows, with a majority reporting anxieties concerning their financial status or their occupation and fears about raising their children (Glick et al., 1974). In most studies of reactions to life-threatening illness, the frequency of patients experiencing anxiety appears to be as high or higher than the frequency of those experiencing depression (see, e.g., Achte & Vauhkonen, 1971; Chesser & Anderson, 1975; Hinton, 1963; Maguire, 1978; Peck, 1972). In Peck's (1972) study, for example, 49 of 50 cancer patients responded with feelings of anxiety and this anxiety was rated as severe in almost one-half those interviewed. Moreover, the available evidence suggests that such feelings may persist for a considerable period of time. Maguire (1978) reports almost identical percentages of patients experiencing moderate or severe anxiety at 4 months after a mastectomy and again at 1 year. In a longitudinal study of reactions to bereavement, Parkes (1975b) found that the number of persons exhibiting moderate or severe anxiety increased from 26% at the initial interview 3 to 4 weeks after the loss, to 44% at the final interview 2 to 4 years later.

Despite the relatively high prevalence of anxiety among individuals confronted with undesirable life events, this emotional reaction has not been discussed by other theorists in the area. Except for Shontz, who has noted that encounters with reality are accompanied by anxiety, this response has not received more than cursory attention from the theorists discussed earlier. The available evidence suggests that in subsequent theoretical work, the role of anxiety in the coping process should be explored more fully.

Taken as a whole, the empirical evidence suggests that there is little consensus concerning how individuals react to undesirable life events, and there is a great deal of variability across life crises. We have noted, for example, that depression is a very common reaction to bereavement, fairly typical of cancer patients, and relatively rare among rape victims, at least during the initial period following the attack. Perhaps even more noteworthy, however, is the variability of response that has been reported within a given type of life crisis. This was described very early in coping research by Hamburg et al. (1953), who studied the reactions of burn patients. They indicated that

> When a psychiatric observer enters a ward in which there are a number of severely burned patients, all in the acute phase (covered with bandages, receiving transfusions and so on), he is likely to be impressed by the varieties of behavior evident. One patient is crying, moaning, complaining, demanding that more be done for him; another appears completely comfortable and unconcerned; another appears intensely preoccupied and seems to make very little contact with the observer; still another appears sad and troubled but friendly, responding with a weak smile to any approach made to him; and so it goes from one bed to the next [pp. 2–3].

In fact, it appears that respondents show considerable variability not only in the particular emotional responses demonstrated, but in whether they exhibit any reaction at all. Following the death of a terminally ill child, Natterson and Knudson (1960) report that a majority of mothers they studied reacted with feelings of "calm sorrow and relief," while the others reacted "hysterically" (pp. 462–463). Similarly, Burgess and Holmstrom (1974) report that when interviewed within a few hours of a rape, about half of the women in their study showed an "expressive style," in which feelings were expressed through such behavior as crying, sobbing, smiling, restlessness, and tenseness. In sharp contrast, the remaining women exhibited a "controlled style, in which feelings were masked or hidden and a calm, composed, or subdued affect was seen [p. 982]."

The theoretical formulations discussed earlier do not contend that all individuals will respond identically to all aversive outcomes. Nonetheless, they clearly suggest that there will be some common reactions in response to undesirable life events. Unfortunately, current theories are of limited utility in explaining the extreme pattern of variability that is demonstrated by the empirical data.

Do People Go through Stages of Emotional Reactions in Response to an Undesirable Life Event?

The notion that individuals follow a predictable, orderly path of emotional response following a life crisis is a popular one. Although they each propose different patterns, three of the general theories described previously (Klinger, 1975, 1977; Shontz, 1965, 1975; Wortman & Brehm, 1975) contend that people will respond to an aversive outcome with a sequence of reactions, perhaps first with shock, then anger or invigoration, invariably depression, and ultimately recovery. Stage models of emotional response have also been proposed by theorists or clinicians for many specific life crises, including separation (Bowlby, 1960, 1973), physical disability (Gunther, 1969; Guttmann, 1976; Hohmann, 1975; Siller, 1969), bereavement or loss (Bowlby, 1961; Engel, 1962, 1964), criminal victimization (Symonds, 1975), and terminal illness (Nighswonger, 1971). Do the available empirical data support the existence of stages of response?

Several research reports have claimed to provide support for a stage model. Some investigators have conducted retrospective interviews and reported the existence of stages of response (Fitzgerald, 1970; Randall, Ewalt, & Blair, 1945). For example, Fitzgerald (1970) interviewed individuals who had been blind for at least a year and asked them to describe their immediate and present reactions to the disability. The author contends that subjects reported a four-phase reaction of disbelief, protest, depression, and recovery. However, such retrospective assessments are necessarily hampered by the limitations of memory and the problems of hindsight.

Other researchers have reported that they longitudinally studied victims of life crises and maintain that these individuals go through stages of emotional response. Perhaps the best known is the pattern described by Kubler-Ross (1969) for the terminally ill: denial, anger, bargaining, depression, and acceptance. Investigators have also reported stage models of response to many other types of undesirable life events, including cancer (Gullo, Cherico, & Shadick, 1974), chronic hemodialysis (Beard, 1969; Reichsman & Levy, 1972), open heart surgery (Dlin, Fischer, & Huddell, 1968), miscarriage (Zahourek & Jensen, 1973), rape (Sutherland & Scherl, 1970), spinal cord injury (Bray, 1978; Cohn, 1961; Weller & Miller, 1977a), and loss of a limb, a spouse (Parkes, 1972), or a child (Natterson & Knudson, 1960). Nonetheless, each of these reports is merely descriptive in nature, often subjective impressions of interview data, or simply anecdotal reports. Sample sizes are often small, methodology for assessment is unspecified, and details of interview technique are generally not provided. Since there has been apparently no standardized assessment of emotional reactions, the aforementioned reports cannot be considered evidence for the existence of stages of response.

A number of empirical investigations have made systematic assessments of emotional reactions at more than one point in time. Such studies have been conducted primarily among the dying (Hinton, 1963; Lieberman, 1965), cancer patients (Bard & Waxenberg, 1957; Craig & Abeloff, 1974; Maguire, Lee, Bevington, Kuchemann, Crabtree, & Cornell, 1978; Morris, Greer, & White, 1977; Sobel & Worden, 1979; Vachon, Note 4; Weisman, 1976) and the bereaved (Bornstein, Clayton, Halikas, Maurice, & Robins, 1973; Clayton et al., 1968). However, many of these reports do not discuss what percentage of respondents experience specific mood states or how these moods change over time (e.g., Bard & Waxenberg, 1957; Craig & Abeloff, 1974, Lieberman, 1965; Vachon, Note 4). Others repeatedly assess and report the incidence of such feelings as anxiety and depression, but do not discuss whether respondents move from one emotional state to another (e.g., Bornstein et al.,1973; Clayton et al., 1968; Hinton, 1963; Maguire et al., 1978; Morris et al., 1977). Some recent investigations have made frequent and repeated systematic assessments of several different emotional states (e.g., Sobel & Worden, 1979; Weisman, 1976). However, these researchers were apparently not interested in validating a stage model, and therefore do not report the frequency of emotional responses nor changes in emotional reactions over time.

Surprisingly, we have been unable to locate any studies that systematically measure several affective reactions and report their prevalence from one time point to the next. Nonetheless, a limited number of empirical reports do present data relevant to the stage concept (Dinardo, 1971; Glick et al., 1974; Kimball, 1969; McDaniel & Sexton, 1970). Although none of these studies were specifically designed to test the stage model, each has produced results that fail to conform to prevailing stage theories. For example, Dinardo (1971) conducted a systematic cross-sectional investigation of depression in a population of spinal cord injured patients who had been disabled between 0 and 15 months. He reported that the degree of depression experienced by his subjects was independent of the time that had elapsed since their injury. In a longitudinal investigation, McDaniel and Sexton (1970) studied 22 men who suffered a recent spinal cord injury and made assessments at four time points during their hospitalization and rehabilitation. Ratings by nurses, physical therapists, and occupational therapists indicated that levels of anxiety, depression, irritability, and the use of denial among these patients remained "relatively constant" over the entire period of study. In addition, anxiety and depression levels were found to be independent of staff ratings of patients' acceptance of their loss over time. It must be noted, however, that these data are reported as group means at each time point and there is no discussion of affective change within individual subjects.

Another study that provides data inconsistent with a stage model was conducted by Kimball (1969), who followed open heart surgical patients for approximately 15 months. He reports that responses during the preoperative period were highly variable, with some patients exhibiting denial, others showing depression, and still others reacting primarily with anxiety. Immediately following the operation, responses were again extremely variable.

Some patients appeared "euphoric": "They were radiant, confident, and demonstrated considerable bravado [p. 100]." Others showed a "catastrophic" reaction, laying immobile and behaving "as if they were afraid to move for fear of waking up to find themselves dead or severely mutilated [p. 100]." These differences emerged despite the fact that there were no significant group differences in the age of patients, the severity of their diseases, or the previous duration of their illnesses. The authors do note, however, that responses during the intermediate period of hospitalization were "roughly the same for all survivors regardless of their earlier or later responses [p. 101]." During this period, most patients experienced anxiety, then depression, and eventually a return to anxiety as plans for the future were formulated.

General stage models that have discussed anger and invigoration responses (e.g., Klinger, 1975, 1977; Wortman & Brehm, 1975) have maintained that if such reactions occur, they are likely to reach their maximum intensity fairly early in the process of adjustment to a loss. These models suggest that over time feelings of anger should be gradually replaced by feelings of depression. Few studies have reported a systematic and repeated assessment of respondent's feelings of anger. However, the data of Glick et al. (1974) suggest a different pattern. Interviewers in this study of the recently bereaved "felt that both men and women displayed increased anger toward family, friends, children, or others, as time went on [p. 266]." In fact, they maintained that 40% of the widows and 32% of the widowers displayed more anger at the second interview (conducted approximately 8 weeks after the loss) than they expressed approximately 3 weeks after their spouses' deaths.

As noted earlier, few investigators have made systematic efforts to validate some aspect of the stage model of response. In fact, we have been able to locate only one such study conducted with human subjects. In a sophisticated, comprehensive study, Lawson (1976) sought to test the assumption that spinal cord injured persons experience a period of depressive affect or grief in their psychological adjustment to the injury. Using a longitudinal approach, he took measures of depression 5 days per week on 10 patients for the entire length of their rehabilitation hospital stay, an average of 119 days. A multimethod assessment of depression included self-report, a behavioral measure, ratings by professional staff, and a psychoendocrine measure utilizing daily urinary output. His results indicated that there was no clear period of at least 1 week in which the dependent measures were consistently in the depressive range for any patient. Although other emotional reactions were not assessed in this investigation, its results suggest that all spinal cord injured patients do not experience a stage of depression during their adjustment to permanent paralysis.

Primate research on the effects of separation offer a large degree of experimental control in which to test a sequential pattern of response. Although perhaps limited in their generalizability to other aversive life events such as rape or chronic illness, several animal studies have been conducted to test Bowlby's (1973) model of protest–despair–detachment following separation. Although some of these primate investigations have found support for such a sequence following peer or maternal separation (Hinde, Spencer-Booth, & Bruce, 1966; Kaufman & Rosenblum, 1967; Schlottman & Seay, 1972; Seay, Hansen, & Harlow, 1962; Suomi & Harlow, 1975), the results have not always been consistent. Others have shown a mixed pattern of results or have not found any evidence of stages of response (Bowden & McKinney, 1972; Erwin, Mobaldi, & Mitchell, 1971; Jones & Clark, 1973; Kaplan, 1970; McKinney, Suomi, & Harlow, 1972; Preston, Baker, & Seay, 1970; Rosenblum & Kaufman, 1968). For example, Lewis, McKinney, Young, and Kraemer (1976) reported the results of five different studies of mother–infant separation in rhesus monkeys. While some animals showed a protest–despair response, some showed protest but not despair, others showed despair but not protest, and still others showed little behavioral response of any kind to the separation. In summarizing their findings, these authors concluded that the results "clearly do not support any unitary concept of a protest–despair response to mother–infant separation [p. 704]."

In summary, the limited data that are available do not appear to clearly fit a stage model of emotional response following life crises. In addition, the extreme pattern of variability that exists in response to aversive life events also does not support the notion of stages of response. In fact, it seems remarkable that there is no body of methodologically sophisticated research that has systematically assessed changes in emotional reactions over time and reported the existence of stages. We are not alone in questioning the validity of the stage concept (see, e.g., Schulz & Aderman, 1974; Trieschmann, 1978). However, it must be noted that there are numerous problems inherent in collecting data that are capable of testing a stage model. While it is desirable to assess respondents' emotional reactions soon after the crisis, it may be difficult to obtain cooperation at this time, and techniques used to enhance participation may raise serious ethical questions (see Wortman et al., 1980).

Since it is not clear from most theoretical formulations precisely how long a given stage will last or when a person will shift from one stage to another, it is also desirable to assess people's emotional reactions at several points in time. Moreover, within each time point it may be necessary to make more than one assessment in order to obtain a valid indication of a respondent's emotional reaction. As Lawson (1978) has demonstrated, hospitalized patients' moods may be strongly influenced by critical events that have happened that day, such as receiving a visit from a family member or a report from one's physician. Similarly, Bruhn, Thurman, Chandler, and Bruce (1970) report that environmental influences such as witnessing a fellow patient die in a cardiac intensive care unit can significantly influence one's level of anxiety.

Of course, frequent and repeated assessment of individuals experiencing distress may be burdensome to respondents and thereby result in increased attrition. Reactivity may also be a problem when repeated assessments are made. Finally, many investigations may take the form of unplanned therapeutic interventions. Does merely asking respondents about their trauma and emotional reactions affect their responses or alter the adjustment process? Do they become sensitized to the emotional reactions being assessed? This problem is particularly important in longitudinal studies, and a control group of individuals who are studied only at the final assessment point would be helpful in interpreting the results.

While difficult to implement, a daily, multifaceted assessment of affect, such as that conducted by Lawson (1976), is probably the closest test of a stage model of response on a population of individuals who have encountered a life crisis. However, it must be recognized that some theorists contend that people may experience more than one stage simultaneously, may move back and forth among the stages, and may skip certain stages completely (see, e.g., Klinger, 1975, 1977; Kubler-Ross, 1969). For this reason, such models are particularly difficult to test and/or to disconfirm. Future models must therefore be more precise concerning the exact pattern of reactions to be expected.

Do People Accept or Recover Following an Undesirable Life Event?

Almost without exception (see, e.g., Bray, 1978), every stage model we have examined has postulated a final stage of resolution which most victims of aversive life events are expected to achieve. This is the case for both the general theoretical formulations we have reviewed, as well as for those models which focus on a specific life crisis. Whether called recovery (Klinger, 1975, 1977) or acceptance (Kubler-Ross, 1969), it is commonly suggested that individuals will resolve their crisis, thus moving on to the next stage of their lives. This is assumed not only when the person encounters a single aversive event (e.g., rape, loss, permanent injury), but also in the face of one's own deteriorating physical condition, when the next stage would be death. Is this view supported by the empirical evidence which bears on the question?

On the contrary, among the dying it appears that many people do not approach death with the calm acceptance some authors have proposed. Plumb and Holland (1974) found little evidence for such an acceptance of death among the late adolescent/early adult group of terminally ill cancer patients they observed. In fact, they contend that such a state is a very difficult one for the young cancer patient to achieve. In their report of individuals who received fatal burns, Imbus and Zawacki (1977) observe that even "the most severely burned patient may speak of hope with his last breath [p. 308]." Hinton (1963) found depression prevalent in approximately 20 to 40% of the dying patients he prospectively studied during the last 8 weeks of their lives. This figure rose further in the last week or two before death, suggesting that for many patients, a state of acceptance was not reached. Moreover, in an analysis conducted after the death of chronically ill geriatric patients, Kastenbaum and Weisman (1972) report that approximately one-half did not passively accept their impending death, but rather "maintained their allegiance to life right up to the last possible moment [p. 216]."

It is difficult to postulate precisely how much time should elapse before recovery from a single traumatic life event. Yet an individual who has recovered would not be expected to experience a disrupted life style or extreme emotional distress after a rather lengthy period of time. Nonetheless, several studies on psychological reactions to mastectomy have found that many women show severe distress a year or more after surgery, even when the disease does not recur. For example, Maguire et al. (1978) found that 39% of the breast cancer patients they studied were still experiencing levels of anxiety or depression and/or sexual difficulties "serious enough . . . to warrant psychiatric help [p. 963]" 1 year after their mastectomy. In fact, these problems were significantly more prevalent than those in a matched control group of women with benign breast disease (see also Maguire, 1978). Similarly, Morris et al. (1977) found that 1 year after surgery, 30% of their breast cancer patients still appeared to be distressed by the operation and had "failed to adjust" (p. 2386). By the second year assessment only an additional 1% had improved further (see also Vachon, Note 4). Finally, Ray (1978) interviewed mastectomy patients 18 months to 5 years post surgery and found that they were more depressed and anxious than a control group of women who did not have the surgery. In fact, he reports that some women "felt considerable grief and resentment about their loss several years after the operation [p. 36]."

Investigators have found long-term negative effects from a trauma in other populations as well. Kaltreider, Wallace and Horowitz (1979) report that following a nonelective hysterectomy without resulting malignancy or with excellent future prognosis, almost 30% of the respondents were still experiencing stress symptoms including anxiety, depression, phobias, and obsessive thoughts 1 year after the operation. In a longitudinal study of bereaved widows, Vachon (Note 4) found that 38% of the respondents were experiencing a high level of distress after 1 year. Two years after the loss, she reports that one-quarter of her sample was still experiencing a level of psychological distress sufficient to warrant psychiatric assessment. Fifty percent of the bereaved interviewed by Schwab, Chalmers, Conroy, Farris, and Markush (1975) over a year after the loss of a relative were rated as still grieving intensely. Similarly, 81% of the widows studied by Marris (1958) did not consider themselves to be completely recovered from the death of their spouse, even though they had been widowed an average of 2 years at the time of the interview. Most of the previously reported research has assessed respondents' reactions to the crisis within the first few years. In a longitudinal study of recovery from rape, however, Burgess and Holmstrom (1978) found that 26% of the rape victims they followed still did not feel they had recovered from their assault 4–6 years later.

Engel (1962) has written that "Some people never completely dissipate the sense of loss of and their dependence on the lost object and they remain in a prolonged, even permanent stage of unresolved grief. They continue actively to miss the dead person, feeling sadness or crying at every memory or reminder, even years later [p. 280]." This has been perhaps most convincingly demonstrated in the study of bereaved widows and widowers conducted by Glick et al. (and reported in Parkes, 1975b). After 2–4 years, 24% of the sample felt that the death was not real, and that they would wake up and it would not be true. The same percentage expressed agreement with the statement "Down deep, I wouldn't care if I died tomorrow." In fact, on a combined assessment of a number of psychological, social and physical health measures, 30% of the bereaved studied were judged as showing a "bad outcome" 2–4 years after their spouses' deaths. Parkes (1972) has also reported that 63% of the amputees and 76% of the widows he interviewed "still felt disinclined to think of the future even a year after the loss [p. 344]." Finally, Shadish, Hickman, and Arrick (Note 5) obtained similar findings in a cross-sectional study of the reactions of spinal cord injured patients. Individuals disabled up to 38 years before the assessment indicated that they still think about the things they cannot do since their injury and "really miss" these things almost weekly.

Clearly, the evidence reviewed suggests that a simple expectation of acceptance or recovery from a serious life crisis is unwarranted for a large minority of people. Most studies find significant levels of distress or disorganization after a year, and those that have continued to follow their sample for a longer period of time have not typically found substantial improvement (Glick et al., 1974; Morris et al., 1977; Parkes, 1975b; Vachon, Note 4). Nonetheless, many researchers have stressed that for most victims of life crises, emotional distress is reduced and lives are reorganized with time. In emphasizing the number that do recover, however, we feel that others have not devoted enough attention to the sizable minority who do not. Of course, there are relatively few studies that have documented reactions to life crises several years after the event has occurred. Nevertheless, there is a clear suggestion from the available evidence that for many people acceptance or recovery is not apparent despite the passage of a long period of time.

Even when individuals appear to recover from an aversive life event, there is some limited evidence to suggest that feelings of severe distress and disorganization may emerge at a later date. Lindemann (1944) was the first to report such a delayed grief reaction. He maintained that these reactions often arise following "deliberate recall of circumstances surrounding the death or spontaneous occurrences in the patient's life" and may appear "after an interval which was not marked by any abnormal behavior or distress [p. 144]." Similarly, Burgess and Holmstrom (1974) identified a silent rape reaction in which unresolved feelings from an earlier assault can resurface years later. Notman and Nadelson (1976) contend that among rape victims, anxiety and depression may reemerge long after the rape has oc- curred, "often precipitated by seemingly unrelated events that in some small details bring back the original trauma [p. 412]." Among the bereaved, Bornstein and Clayton (1972) found that 67% of the widows and widowers they interviewed reported a mild or severe anniversary reaction to their loss. Similarly, Wiener, Gerber, Battin, and Arkin (1975) report that some bereavement symptoms "tend to recur at various times, precipitated by anniversaries, memories, meetings, geographical locale, etc. [p. 64]." Parkes (1970) suggests that during these times, "all the feelings of acute pining and sadness return and the bereaved person goes through, in miniature, another bereavement [p. 464]." In their study of the chronically ill, Reichsman and Levy (1972) report that long-term adaptation to maintenance hemodialysis was "marked by fluctuations in the patient's sense of emotional and physical well-being .... All patients experienced prolonged states of contentment alternating with episodes of depression of varying duration [p. 862]."

In conclusion, it is clear that prevailing notions of recovery need to be reconsidered. There is evidence that a substantial minority of individuals exhibit distress for a much longer period of time than would be commonly expected. There are also a number of indications that people continually reexperience the crisis for the rest of their lives. While some theorists have mentioned this possibility (e.g., Benner, Roskies, & Lazarus, 1980; Klinger, 1977), only Shontz's (1965, 1975) model can account for the slow, unsteady progress and subsequent distress that seems to occur. Unfortunately, none of the previously discussed models, including the one proposed by Shontz, are useful in identifying those individuals who are particularly likely to have difficulty in resolving their crisis successfully.

EXTENDING THE THEORETICAL MODELS

Our review of the available literature suggests that a great deal of variability exists in individual reactions to negative life events, both within a particular life crisis and across different crises. We have found little reliable evidence to indicate that people go through stages of emotional response following an undesirable life event. We have also reviewed substantial evidence suggesting that a large minority of victims of aversive life events experience distress or disorganization long after recovery might be expected. Current theoretical models of reactions to aversive outcomes cannot account for the variety of responses that appear. Variables that may mediate individual coping responses are clearly necessary to explain the diverse pattern of results. With few exceptions, however (cf. Abramson et al., 1978; Wortman & Brehm, 1975), most theorists have not incorporated any intervening variables into their models. Without such mediators, general theoretical models have limited utility in predicting reactions to undesirable life events.

As a result of our review of the literature, as well as our clinical experiences with people who have encountered life crises (see Wortman et al., 1980), a number of conceptual variables have emerged that may further our understanding of people's responses to stressful outcomes and increase our ability to predict the nature, sequence, duration, and intensity of their reactions. In this section of the chapter, we discuss some variables that we feel are especially promising for subsequent theoretical and empirical work. These include perceived social support, the opportunity for ventilation or free expression of feelings, the ability to find meaning in the crisis, and experience with other stressors. (For a discussion of additional variables see Wortman et al., 1980; Wortman & Dintzer, 1978.) With the exception of perceived social support, these variables have not been extensively researched. Therefore, we rely on the limited evidence that is available in the discussion to follow.

Perceived Social Support

In a recent survey concerning how Americans view their mental health (Veroff, Douvan, & Kulka, in press), respondents were asked to indicate whether they had encountered any life crises such as becoming ill, losing a job, or the death of a loved one, and if so, where they turned for help. These authors concluded that "informal support systems [family members, friends, and neighbors] are probably *the* critical way that people in the new generation have adopted to deal with their life problems [p. 19]." Does expecting and receiving support from family and friends influence people's emotional reactions to a crisis, or help them cope more effectively with the outcome and its ramifications?

A number of investigators have explored the issue of how interpersonal relationships influence people's responses to a variety of stressful events. Almost without exception, these studies have clearly demonstrated a relationship between perceived social support and effective adjustment. In a longitudinal study of reactions to job termination due to a plant closing, Cobb and Kasl (1977) report that social support from one's spouse, relatives, and friends reduced much of the distress associated with the loss. Among the physically disabled, support from the family has been associated with rehabilitation success both in the hospital and in the community (Kelman, Lowenthal, & Muller, 1966; Litman, 1962; Smits, 1974). In fact, it has been suggested that such support may be particularly critical for the most severely disabled (Kemp & Vash, 1971). The benefits of social support have also been demonstrated in a longitudinal study of 81 victims of rape (Burgess & Holmstrom, 1978). Among those women who were judged to have adequate social support, 45% reported 4 to 6 years later that they felt they had recovered from the rape within months; without support not one woman reported recovering within months. In fact, at the 4- to 6-year follow-up interview, 53% of the victims who did not have adequate social support still did not feel they had recovered from the attack.

Perceived support has also been shown to be associated with emotional adjustment among the bereaved. Depression evident 1 month following the death of a spouse was significantly correlated with fewer children whom the bereaved considered close and therefore able to provide support (Clayton, Halikas, & Maurice, 1972). Even after 13 months, the availability of supportive others still influenced the level of depression in this population (Bornstein et al.,1973). Similarly, the contribution of perceived support toward successful adjustment has been reported for the terminally ill (Carey, 1974) and for cancer patients (Jamison, Wellisch, & Pasnau, 1978; Weisman, 1976). In a comparison study, Vachon (Note 4) sought to explore the differing effects of social support on the cancer patient and the bereaved. In her 24-month longitudinal investigation of psychological adjustment to breast cancer and widowhood, she found that perceived lack of support was associated with high psychological distress for both groups of women. While lack of social support was most clearly associated with distress in the first year following bereavement, it appeared most important for breast cancer patients 1 to 2 years after diagnosis.

There is some evidence that perceived social support influences health status and physical well-being as well as psychological adjustment. In a prospective study of response to open heart surgery, Kimball (1969) reported that those patients who were classified as clinically depressed preoperatively "were characterized by a past, present, and projected future of weak or absent object relationships in terms of spouses, parents, children, and jobs [p. 103]." Despite the fact that there were no significant differences in the severity of their conditions, these same individuals were significantly more likely to be dead within 15 months of their surgery than others in the sample. Weisman and Worden (1975) report similar effects on survival rates of the cancer patients they studied. Maddison and Walker (1967) questioned widows 13 months after their loss, and asked them to report retrospectively on their perceived social support during the first 3 months of bereavement. According to the authors, widows who reported a bad health outcome at 13 months "perceived themselves as having many more unsatisfied needs in interpersonal exchanges during the bereavement crisis than did those with a good outcome [p. 1062]." Finally, adult asthmatics undergoing life changes of various kinds required less medication if they were receiving high levels of social support than if they were not (de Araujo, van Arsdel, Holmes, & Dudley, 1973).

On the basis of the aforementioned studies, many investigators have concluded that social support facilitates the coping process. Because of the correlational nature of this research, however, such a causal inference may be unwarranted. As Heller (1979) has noted, people who are poorly adjusted or in ill health may underestimate the amount of support available to them. It is also possible that coping and social support are causally related, but that one's coping or prognosis determines the amount of support available. There are also many reasons why others may be unwilling or unable to provide support for people who are extremely ill or coping poorly (Coates, Wortman, & Abbey, 1979; Wortman & Dunkel-Schetter, 1979, Note 6). Such individuals may unwittingly create discomfort in others by making them feel vulnerable to a similar fate. Interacting with people who are suffering can also produce feelings of awkwardness and inadequacy because there may be little that one can say or do to help.

Finally, it has been suggested that the very ill or poorly adjusted may lack social competence (Heller, 1979), and therefore drive others away by engaging in socially inappropriate behaviors (Maddison & Walker, 1967). In fact, Heller has suggested that deficits in social competence may "produce the poorer levels of adjustment reported for unsupported individuals, as well as accounting for the lower levels of support they receive [p. 375]." Many of these ambiguities could be resolved by longitudinal research which assessed available social support at one point in time and examined its ability to predict distress or physical deterioration at a later point.

A causal relationship between support and effective long-term adjustment could also be established by intervention studies in which participants are assigned to treatments which supplement the support available to them. In fact, many health-care professionals, suspecting the benefits of supportive interpersonal relationships for individuals in distress, have sought to augment existing social contacts with professional or peer support. Each of these interventions has produced positive psychological and/or medical benefits compared to control groups which received no treatment following cancer surgery (Bloom & Ross, Note 7; Ferlic, Goldman, & Kennedy, 1979), heart attack (Gruen, 1975), and bereavement (Gerber, Wiener, Battin, & Arkin, 1975; Parkes, 1975a; Raphael, 1977). Most of these interventions have been multifaceted, sometimes including psychotherapy and information as well as emotional support. For this reason, it is not clear which specific components of the supportive treatment were most important in producing the desired effect.

In recent years, investigators have moved away from considering social support as a unitary concept, and have attempted to increase the specificity of the term by identifying its components. One type of support involves the expression of positive affect (Kahn & Antonucci, in press); this may include information that one is cared for and loved, or that one is esteemed and respected (Cobb, 1976, 1979). A second distinct kind of support involves expressing agreement with, or acknowledgment of the appropriateness of a person's beliefs, interpretations, or feelings (Kahn, 1979; Kahn & Antonucci, in press; Walker, MacBride, & Vachon, 1977; Wortman & Dunkel-Schetter, 1979, Note 6). A third, closely related aspect of support involves encouraging the open expression of such beliefs and feelings (Wortman & Dunkel-Schetter, 1979, Note 6). A fourth type of social support is the provision of material aid (Kahn, 1979; Kahn & Antonucci, in press; Pinneau, 1975). Finally, support may be conveyed by providing information that the distressed person is part of a network (Cobb, 1976, 1979; Kahn & Antonucci, in press; Walker et al., 1977) or support system (Caplan, 1976) of mutual obligation or reciprocal help. To our knowledge, these particular components of social support have not been assessed separately in research. Thus, it is not clear which parameters are most important in the process of coping with life crises. (For a more detailed discussion of the construct of social support, see Caplan, 1979; Cobb, 1976; Heller, 1979; House, in press; and Walker et al., 1977.)

How does social support influence or facilitate the coping process? Both Cobb (1979) and Caplan (1979) have suggested that social support might provide a climate in which self-identity changes can more readily occur. According to Caplan (1979), people who receive adequate social support are less likely to employ counterproductive "defensive mechanisms" such as denial or distortion when they encounter information that does not confirm their perceptions or beliefs. Similarly, Cobb (1979) has argued that individuals who receive support are likely to develop greater self-confidence, and thus are able to change themselves to adapt to any modifications that occur in the environment. He has maintained that such individuals may also be more likely to develop feelings of autonomy, therefore making more attempts to control and modify their environment. Kemp and Vash (1971) have suggested that supportive others may be quite helpful in reinforcing realistic, goal-setting behavior. This may be particularly important for physically disabled or chronically ill populations who face a long and difficult course of rehabilitation and/or treatment.

The mechanisms through which perceived support influences health outcomes is not well understood at present, although some initial speculations have been offered by Cobb (1976, 1979). He has noted two possibilities: a direct effect through neuroendocrine pathways, or an indirect effect through the facilitation of compliance with prescribed medical regimens. With regard to the latter possibility, there is abundant evidence indicating that patients who receive social support are more likely to stay in treatment and follow the recommendations of their doctors. Baekeland and Lundwall (1975) reviewed studies on the predictors of dropping out of treatment and found a relationship between social isolation and dropout rate in every one of the 19 studies that had assessed both variables. In fact, Cobb (1979) has concluded that the association of cooperative patient behavior with various components of the social support complex is "one of the best documented relationships in all of medical sociology [p. 98]."

For the most part, both theorists and researchers in this area have emphasized the presumed benefits of social support. In our judgment, more attention should be paid to the possible deleterious effect of behaviors that are intended to be supportive. For example, several investigators have noted that others' attempts to encourage false hopes or maladaptive denial can make it more difficult for persons to accept the reality of the situation and thereby impede effective adjustment (Caplan, 1960; Visotsky et al., 1961). Similarly, Friedman et al. (1963) pointed out that the parents of leukemic children they studied were often distressed by optimistic statements of others (e.g., the child "could not possibly have leukemia as he looked too well [p. 618]"). Such well-intentioned remarks placed parents "in the uncomfortable position of having to 'defend' their child's diagnosis and prognosis, sometimes experiencing the feeling that others thought they were therefore 'condemning' their own child [p. 618]." In a systematic investigation of the perceived helpfulness of others' attempts to provide support, Maddison and Walker (1967) asked widows to indicate how people had responded to them during the first 3 months after their loss, and to indicate further which reactions were helpful. They report that a number of responses that are frequently made to widows (e.g. being told "about the need to get out among people again and make new friends" or being told that "I must control myself and pull myself together [p. 1066]") were actually regarded as unhelpful.

Why do attempts to provide support sometimes fail? Caplan (1979) has suggested that certain types of support may threaten the person's freedom to make his or her own decisions, and thus elicit a negative reaction. In his discussion of "mothering–smothering," Cobb (1979) has argued that some attempts to be supportive may interfere with the development of coping mechanisms. Similarly, Brickman and his associates have pointed out that help often fosters dependence and passivity among recipients (Brickman, Rabinowitz, Coates, Cohn, & Karuza, Note 8). Brickman et al. maintain that the very label of "help" or "support" often carries the implicit assumption that people are incapable of solving their own problems, and therefore "works against the perception of recipients as active, responsible agents [p. 20]." Finally, Wortman and her associates (Coates & Wortman, 1980; Coates et al., 1979; Wortman & Dunkel-Schetter, 1979, Note 6) have provided a theoretical analysis that illustrates how others well-intentioned statements (e.g., "cheer up," "it's not as bad as it seems") can hamper meaningful communication about the crisis. They suggest that others can best support the distressed person by providing an opportunity for the free expression of feelings and concerns. This latter topic is considered in greater detail in the following section.

The Opportunity for Ventilation or Free Expression of Feelings

Those who are confronted with undesirable life events may wish to talk about their experiences with others. This may reflect not only a desire to obtain support, but also a desire to express one's feelings and concerns, and to receive feedback that those feelings are understood by others and are appropriate under the circumstances (Coates & Wortman, 1980; Coates et al., 1979; Wortman & Dunkel-Schetter, 1979, Note 6). Unfortunately, people who are in the throes of serious life crises often report that they are encouraged to be "strong" and are prevented from a free expression of their feelings, and are thus denied the ventilation they frequently need and want (Andreasen & Norris, 1972; Glick et al., 1974; Helmrath & Steinitz, 1978; McCombie, 1975; Mitchell & Glicksman, 1977; Schwab et al., 1975). For example, Helmrath and Steinitz (1978) interviewed couples who lost newborn infants and reported that "each [mother] described a strong need to talk about the physical characteristics of the baby, the details of the hospital course and death, and her desires, expectations and fantasies for the baby. . . . At the same time, friends and family steadfastly avoided mentioning the infant or the death [pp. 787–788]."

Although open encounters appear to be infrequent, evidence does suggest that victims appreciate the opportunity to express their feelings. While less than one-half of Glick et al.'s (1974) sample of widows were able to express their grief freely with at least one other person, 67% reported that those who allowed or encouraged such conversations were helpful. Over 88% of those bereaved surveyed by Schoenberg, Carr, Peretz, Kutscher, and Cherico (1975) felt that "expression rather than repression of feelings, and crying, should be encouraged at least sometimes [p. 365]." Similarly, Mitchell and Glicksman (1977) report that 86% of the cancer patients they studied wished that they could discuss their situation more fully with someone. Perhaps for this reason, researchers investigating reactions to undesirable life events have reported that many respondents are quite eager to discuss their experiences and concerns and readily cooperate with an interviewer (Bulman & Wortman, 1977; Hamburg & Adams, 1967; Hinton, 1963; Marris, 1958; McCubbin, Hunter, & Metres, 1974a; Schwab et al., 1975).

There is also some evidence to suggest that the opportunities to discuss one's feelings are beneficial and that, conversely, lack of communication may intensify the strain of a victimization. Vachon, Freedman, Formo, Rogers, Lyall, and Freeman (1977) found that 81% of those cancer widows they interviewed who openly discussed death with their dying spouses reported that talking about death made it easier to face the bereavement. In fact, although a majority of those widows who had not talked about death with their terminally ill husbands said it made no difference in their bereavement experience, a sizable percentage (36%) said that not talking about death made things more difficult. Kennell, Slyter, and Klaus (1970) studied women who suffered the loss of a newborn infant, and found that a high degree of mourning was marginally associated with a lack of communication between the infant's mother and her husband. Burgess and Holmstrom (1974) report that when a rape or assault is not discussed with anyone, a "tremendous psychological burden" (p. 985) is carried with the victim for years, and these unresolved feelings may resurface at a later date. Finally, Maddison and Walker (1967) interviewed women approximately 13 months after the loss of their spouses and attempted to identify those factors associated with a decline in physical and/or mental health during the first year of bereavement. Those widows who experienced such a deterioration retrospectively reported a large number of unhelpful interactions at the time of the loss in which expression of negative feelings was directly or indirectly blocked. The authors conclude that the widow who showed a poor outcome may have "felt that she needed more encouragement, support, and understanding to permit her to indulge in a freer expression of affects, particularly grief and anger; [in addition] she may have felt a need to talk more actively and in greater detail about her husband and their past life together, but had experienced the environment as failing to provide an opportunity for this [p. 1062]."

The value of many intervention studies reviewed earlier may stem not only from their provision of information and emotional support, but also from their ability to offer an opportunity for ventilation. Such interventions typically provided an environment in which expression of feelings was encouraged in the presence of supportive others, whether they were health care professionals (Gerber et al., 1975; Gruen, 1975; Parkes, 1975a; Raphael, 1977), peers (Ferlic et al., 1979), or both (Bloom & Ross, Note 7). For example, Raphael (1977) specifically described her intervention with widows at risk for post bereavement morbidity as involving "support for the expression of grieving affects such as sadness, anger, anxiety, hopelessness, helplessness and despair [p. 1451]." This treatment was continued for a maximum of 3 months and included an average of only four sessions per widow. Nonetheless, when assessed 13 months after their spouses' deaths, women who had been randomly assigned to the intervention group reported significantly better psychological and physical health than those assigned to a no-treatment control group.

Although there is some evidence that ventilation of one's feelings may facilitate coping, a number of critical issues remain to be resolved. One important question concerns precisely how talking about one's feelings influences the nature and magnitude of these feelings, as well as subsequent coping. There are a number of intriguing possibilities. Some have suggested that expressing one's feelings is necessary for adjustment to occur (see, e.g., Lindemann, 1944). Theoretically, such expression leads to a "catharsis" or draining of the intensity of the feelings. This view was held by some of the widows studied by Glick et al. (1974), who believed that "sorrow can be treated as an entity that exists in a certain quantity, and that expressing sorrow uses it up or expels it. Therefore, it should be possible for the individual to 'get it all out,' to fully externalize or discharge it [pp. 58–59]." Expressing one's feelings might also be beneficial because it enables a person to receive information about the appropriateness of those feelings. Learning that certain emotions or reactions are common or justified may lessen the anxiety and distress associated with them. Finally, discussion of one's feelings may facilitate active problem-solving, or may enable people to view their situation from a more meaningful perspective.

In subsequent research, it is also important to identify any limiting conditions on the value of discussing one's feelings. Are the benefits of ventilation dependent on the type of feedback one receives from others? Are victims who express their feelings but elicit negative responses from others better off than those who withhold their feelings? Under what conditions are others most likely to respond empathically to a victim's displays of anguish and distress, and when will they come to regard ventilation as merely dwelling on problems? Is beneficial feedback more likely to occur when discussing one's feelings with some targets (e.g., similar others) than others? Wortman and Dunkel-Schetter (1979) have suggested, for example, that it may be particularly useful for cancer patients to discuss their feelings with other patients, since they may be more capable of providing validating feedback than others. Are certain types of people less likely to profit from open discussion of feelings? For example, some investigators have reported that males have less desire to ventilate than females (Carey, 1977; Glick, et al., 1974). Is this because they are less in need of clarifying feedback or because they fear others will be intolerant of their emotional displays?

If victims show little interest in sharing their feelings, should others encourage them to do so? By encouraging others to express their feelings, do we intensify their short-term distress and unhappiness? Data bearing on this final point were collected in an interesting intervention study conducted by Bloom and Ross (Note 7). Women facing breast biopsy were allowed to ventilate their feelings as part of a comprehensive counseling and information treatment. Within a few days of mastectomy, those women in the intervention group reported significantly more depression, anxiety, hostility, and confusion than a control group who received no such intervention. However, 2 months later, the treatment group showed higher levels of self-esteem and self-efficacy than the controls. Although the authors do not report a longer follow-up, this study suggests that both the immediate and long-term effects of open expression of feelings must be considered in any future research effort.

The Ability to Find Meaning in the Outcome

When a person is suddenly, uncontrollably victimized by criminal assault, disease, physical disability, or loss of a loved one, psychological adjustment may well be influenced by the individual's ability to find meaning or purpose in his or her misfortune. Such traumas often shatter people's views of living in an orderly, understandable, meaningful world (Cornwell et al., 1977; Glick et al., 1974; Parkes, 1971). As Glick et al. (1974) describe: "Widows and widowers sustain a loss of a major part of their lives and with it, of assumptions about themselves and their futures, about their roles and responsibilities, about the fundamental meaning of their lives [p. 300]."

A number of investigators have commented that after a crisis occurs, respondents seem compelled to make sense out of their experiences (Bulman & Wortman, 1977; Chodoff et al., 1964; Cornwell et al., 1977; Glick et al., 1974). In fact, Frankl (1963) has suggested that the search for meaning may be a powerful human motivation. Glick et al. (1974) write that their widows "return in their minds again and again to the events of their husband's death, compulsively reviewing the course of the illness or accident . . .. Again and again they asked themselves why it had happened [p. 126]." Similarly, Helmrath and Steinitz (1978) report that mothers who had lost a newborn infant asked themselves such questions as " 'What did I do during the pregnancy to cause this?' 'What didn't I do?' 'What should I have done differently?' 'What am I being punished for' [p. 787]?"

Apparently, many people come to view their aversive experience from a purposeful or meaningful perspective. For example, Cornwell et al. (1977) report that, in trying to come to terms with the death of their infant, several parents rationalized that had he or she lived, the child would have been "physically, intellectually or morally defective [p. 658]." Following the drowning of a mentally retarded youngster in a public pool, lifeguards dismissed the death with the notion that the child and his family were actually better off now that he was dead (Doka & Schwarz, 1978). Chodoff et al. (1964) report that many parents of leukemic children they studied "took comfort in the thought that the treatment administered to their child, even though bound to fail, would contribute to scientific progress . . . and thus to the saving of some other child in the future [p. 747]." A number of the severely burned patients interviewed by Andreasen and Norris (1972) saw their injury as helping to make them better people, and saw the experience as "a trial by fire or a purgatory through which they have passed, having proved themselves and improved themselves by surviving [p. 359]." Many were also "appreciative of being given a second chance to show their love for their partner [p. 359]." Finally, Helmrath and Steinitz (1978) found that five out of the seven couples they interviewed came to view the death of their baby as an opportunity for growth in their lives, and all couples felt that their relationships had been deepened and improved because of the death.

Do those individuals who are able to find some meaning in an aversive life event respond differently to the misfortune than those who are unable to do so? Although the evidence bearing on this question is extremely limited, a few studies suggest that ability to find meaning may be important. In a study of parents with fatally ill children, Natterson and Knudson (1960) report an association between calm acceptance of their child's death and a "tendency to see the medical problem in its broader aspects, with the beginning of an expressed desire to help all children [p. 463]." Similarly, Weisman and Worden (1976) suggest that those cancer patients who were able to find something favorable in their illness were the least distressed by the disease. In contrast, anger toward God following loss of a spouse, perhaps representing an inability to find meaning in the experience, was found to be a strong predictor of intense grief and depression among women who had been widowed an average of five years (Barrett & Larson, Note 9).

There are, of course, many different ways in which an individual can view an aversive life event from a meaningful perspective. In a systematic investigation of this issue, Bulman and Wortman (1977) asked 29 spinal cord injured patients whether they had ever posed the question "Why me?" and if so, how they had answered it. All respondents had asked themselves this question, and all but one had come up with an explanation. These explanations were highly varied: Some individuals felt that God had a reason for what had happened to them (e.g., "He's trying to help me learn about Him"); others reinterpreted the consequences of their accident as positive (e.g., "I see the accident as the best thing that could have happened because it brought me and my girlfriend closer together"); others maintained that the accident had been predetermined (e.g., "Things are always planned before your time by a Supreme Power"); and still others regarded their accident as deserved because of past misdeeds. Are some of these ascriptions of meaning more adaptive for successful coping than others? Unfortunately, the sample size in Bulman and Wortman's (1977) study was too small to provide an answer to this question and as yet, no other studies have specifically addressed this issue.

If subsequent research should support the notion that certain ascriptions of meaning are associated with improved long-term adjustment, should caregivers then encourage these views or beliefs among others? We think not. The limited evidence that is available suggests that others' well-intentioned attempts to impart meaning do not have a beneficial effect. Although widows are frequently told that the death of their spouse is the "will of God," for example, such comments are generally not seen as helpful (Glick et al., 1974; Maddison & Walker, 1967). In fact, Maddison and Walker (1967) observed that "subjects who had beliefs of this type tended to regard such interventions as gratuitous and unnecessary, while other subjects without any profound religious conviction found such attempts at comfort meaningless and often extremely irritating [p. 1063]." Similarly, being told that the loss of an older child would have been worse than the loss of a newborn only led to anger and resentment in mourning parents interviewed by Helmrath and Steinitz (1978). We might postulate that a more effective strategy would be to provide an opportunity for distressed people to ventilate their feelings in the presence of a supportive other, and let them generate such meaningful explanations on their own.

Of course, the ability to find meaning may be more difficult when the circumstances surrounding a crisis are particularly unjust. This may be the case when one is injured by a perpetrator (e.g., a drunk driver) who walks away from an accident unharmed (cf. Bulman & Wortman, 1977). Ascriptions of meaning may also be difficult when one's life has been repeatedly disappointing and unfulfilled in the past. As Hinton (1967) has written, "death can be very distressing if viewed as the final disillusionment, and this can well occur in those who have seen their lives as a sequence of blighted hopes [p. 88]." A similar difficulty can arise when one's life had been changing for the better, only to be unfairly interrupted by misfortune. Glick et al. (1974) report in their study of young widows: "As if to underline the injustice, a number of respondents stressed how their lives had only recently become easier, how their husband had just begun earning more money, how their marital relationship had just improved, or how the children were doing better in school, when death came along to make it all futile [p. 131]." Because the death of a child is often seen as a violation of nature, it is perhaps one of the most painful of all life crises (DeFrain & Ernst, 1978; Szybist, 1978). In fact, Vachon, Formo, Freedman, Lyall, Rogers, and Free-man (1976) report that many of the recently bereaved widows they inter-viewed "stated spontaneously that as difficult as the loss of their husband was, the loss of a child would have been worse [p. 29]." Finally, coping may be more difficult when a crisis occurs during young adulthood, since the person may feel cheated from achieving desired goals. In support of this notion, age has been found to be a significant factor in the adjustment process to some life crises, with more difficulty occuring in younger persons who develop cancer (Craig & Abeloff, 1974; Hinton, 1963; Plumb & Hol-land, 1977); lose a limb (Randall et al., 1945), or experience the death of their spouse (Carey, 1977; Maddison & Walker, 1967).

Experience with Other Stressors

How is an individual's adjustment to a particular life crisis influenced by past crises or by concomitant stressors? Will a woman who has previously lost a close friend or relative react differently to a criminal assault, for example, than a woman who has not encountered such a loss? Are people strengthened with each crisis, and made more capable of dealing with sub-sequent stressors? Or do life crises have a cumulative effect and become more difficult to cope with over time? Theorists have offered conflicting answers to these questions.

It has been suggested that experiencing prior losses may bolster a per-son's ability to cope with later losses (Huston, 1971). For example, Shontz (1975) has argued that the coping process "can ultimately produce a more healthy, mature, and satisfying personality than existed before the crisis [p. 166]." Hamburg and Adams (1967) contend that an individual will develop new coping strategies as a response to distress of "high intensity or long duration." They write that if effective, these strategies "are likely to become available for use in future crises, and indeed may broaden the individual's problem solving capacity [p. 283]." In contrast, others argue that losses may be cumulative in their effects (e.g., Engel, 1964). Some maintain that the negative effects of a previous experience are especially likely if the prior crisis has not been satisfactorily resolved (Caplan, 1964; Moos & Tsu, 1977; Visotsky et al., 1961). Haan (1977) has noted, for example, that a crisis may trigger "ominous meaning" or associations for people because of past unresolved conflicts. What specific factors might explain the influence of past stressors? Are some aversive life events more "strengthening" than others? What is the impact on coping of having previously experienced a similar trauma, as opposed to a different type of crisis? Of concomitant as opposed to prior stressors? Some intriguing conclusions are suggested by the limited research that has addressed this topic.

Prior Stressors

Among mothers who had lost a newborn infant, Kennell et al. (1970) found that a high degree of mourning assessed shortly after the loss was significantly associated with a previous loss through miscarriage or a newborn infant's death. However, Bornstein et al. (1973) found that previously experiencing the death of a relative aided in the adjustment of the bereaved men and women they studied. Those respondents who were found to be depressed 13 months after the loss of their spouse were significantly more likely than the nondepressed never to have encountered a previous loss. Few investigators have examined the effect of prior loss of a loved one on coping with one's own illness and disability, and the limited evidence is inconsistent. Carey (1974) found that having a close relationship with a dying person had a positive influence, particularly if this person had "accepted death with inner peace [p. 436]," rather than having been angry and upset until he or she died. It has also been suggested that experiencing a recent bereavement may lead to increased distress following being severely burned (Pavlovsky, 1972). Perhaps coping with one's own illness or severe disability is more difficult following loss of another because it leads to feelings of increased vulnerability, pessimism and fear regarding one's own future. However, after recognizing one's illness as being fatal, adjustment may be facilitated by a strong role model.

The above research suggests that various types of prior stressors may influence subsequent coping very differently, sometimes having a positive effect and sometimes proving deleterious. However, it is difficult to compare the impact of different life crises from one research report to another. Fortunately, one study has contrasted the effect of two different crises, bereavement and criminal victimization, on coping with a subsequent rape. In a 4- to 6-year longitudinal investigation, Burgess and Holmstrom (1978) found .that women who had experienced a criminal assault prior to the rape (sexual assault, physical assault, mugging, or verbal or physical sexual harrassment) took significantly longer to recover than individuals who had experienced no such victimization. However, women who had previously lost a parent, spouse or child through death, divorce or separation, recovered significantly more rapidly from the rape than women who had not had such an experience.

Taken together, this evidence suggests that experiencing the loss of a child twice or repeated criminal victimization may be extremely difficult, whereas losing a relative may facilitate adjustment to subsequent loss or rape. Why might this be the case? Burgess and Holmstrom (1978) have speculated that the successful resolution of "family grief" may facilitiate the development of coping skills that are useful in other situations, and may also "strengthen a person psychologically [p. 173]." It is unclear, however, why these skills and self-insights are not imparted to victims of repeated assault or loss of a child. There are a number of intriguing possibilities that may be worthwhile investigating in subsequent research. First, people often react to the loss of a child or to criminal victimization with feelings of self-blame (Burgess & Holmstrom, 1974; DeFrain & Ernst, 1978; Friedman, 1974). For example, rape victims commonly attribute the attack to some modifiable aspect of their behavior [(e.g., "I should have been more careful"; "I should not have been out so late at night" (Janoff-Bulman, 1979)]. Such an attribution implies that a change in the behavior in question will protect the individual from encountering the outcome in the future. If the event happens again, it may shatter one's previous resolution, and may make the victim feel especially vulnerable and helpless (cf. Abramson et al., 1978).

Alternatively, repeated criminal assaults might create difficulties in coping by intensifying one's feelings of personal inadequacy. A victim may feel that there must really be something wrong with his or her behavior if such an event happens more than once. Moreover, reactions of others may change for the worse when the victimization occurs a second time. The first time a woman is raped or loses a child, significant others may be willing to believe that it was not her fault and that there was nothing she could have done to prevent it. But if she is raped or victimized again, others may feel that she must be doing something wrong or must be "asking for it." Of course, direct or implied blame from others may hamper open communication and limit social support. These interpersonal difficulties would certainly be exacerbated for people who had been victimized more than once.

Another possibility is that certain kinds of undesirable life events, such as violent assault or loss of a child, are likely to result in feelings of injustice. Such losses may be more difficult to view from a meaningful perspective than other stressors—particularly if they occur more than once. One outcome that may be especially likely to engender feelings of overwhelming injustice, as well as the inability to find meaning, is the concentration camp experience. In fact, this may help to account for the widespread pathology often observed among concentration camp survivors, as well as their apparent enhanced vulnerability to subsequent stressors (Benner et al., 1980). Benner et al. suggest that survivors may react in this manner, rather than with a sense of power or mastery, because they are unable to generate a meaningful explanation for such events. According to these investigators, survivors find themselves "isolated and cut off from a meaningful cultural framework. To know that life is absurd is bad enough, but to struggle with this knowledge in a world where others are unaware of or uninterested in the catastrophe is far worse [p. 54]."

The notion that exposure to repeated stressors can change one's conception of oneself or the world, and thus result in subsequent decrements, is consistent with the models proposed by Wortman and Brehm (1975) and by Seligman and his associates (Abramson et al., 1978; Seligman, 1975). In fact, these models suggest that exposure to stressors not only influences one's reaction to subsequent crises, but behavior in non-crisis situations as well. As noted earlier, however, these models are based on laboratory research involving many trials. Can exposure to a single life crisis produce fundamental changes in one's beliefs, and thereby alter one's behavior in subsequent settings? Benner et al. (1980) have suggested that the concentration camp experience has had this kind of impact, and hypothesize that it

> permanently altered the individual's evaluation of his or her relationship with the world . . . . The person has learned that he or she is living in a potentially hostile environment with inadequate resources for mastery. Having experienced what humans can do, every new encounter carries with it the potential for the most savage attack against which one is relatively helpless [pp. 36–37].

At present, it remains to be demonstrated whether exposure to a single life crisis, or even to a small number of similar or dissimilar crises widely separated in time, can result in long-term helplessness effects that generalize to other settings. These models appear to have particular relevance, however, for individuals who repeatedly encounter an uncontrollable stressor. This may be the case for epileptics, for example, who frequently experience severe and uncontrollable seizures. In fact, DeVellis, DeVellis, Wallston, and Wallston (Note 10) found that depression and attenuated expectations of control were more prevalent among these individuals than a normative population. Interestingly, such feelings were intensified for epileptics who were unable to predict or control their seizures. Similarly, Belle (Note 11) has found a significant association between the amount of chronic stress experienced by low-income mothers [e.g., "poor housing, dependence on social agencies for the necessities of life, entrapment in low-paying, low-status, dead-end jobs, and the experience of discrimination and violent crime (p. 434)"] and depressive symptomology.

Wortman and Brehm (1975) have suggested that individuals who are repeatedly exposed to uncontrollable outcomes respond initially with anger or invigoration, but become increasingly helpless over time. It is difficult to validate this prediction, since there is virtually no longitudinal research on reactions to repeated life crises. An intriguing and carefully controlled study of primate reactions to repeated separations, however, suggests that this may be the case. Suomi, Mineka, and Delizio (in press) report two experiments in which subjects were exposed to 16 or 24 weekly peer separations, each of a duration of 4 days. Most of the subjects in each study showed severe protest–despair reactions to the first few separations. Over time, however, the protest behaviors gradually disappeared, and subjects began showing "despair" reactions as soon as each separation began.

Concomitant Stressors

What is the effect of chronic stress on coping with an aversive life event? Is an event such as rape less traumatic to a person with many other problems because it is less salient? Or is coping with a new crisis more difficult when one is under stress (cf. Coleman, 1973)? As noted earlier, Klinger's (1975, 1977) model would suggest that individuals who are experiencing many problems simultaneously may have difficulty, since the incentive-disengagement cycles for each loss combine to determine their emotional state.

At present, there is limited research that has addressed this question. Maddison and Raphael (1975) contend that the presence of additional concurrent crises among the bereaved leads to health deterioration. They maintain that such individuals are "facing such an overwhelming mass of problems demanding solution that the coping requirements are likely to be beyond the adaptive capacities of most people [p. 31]." Weisman (1979) found that cancer patients who exhibited higher levels of emotional distress had long-standing marital problems, came from lower socioeconomic strata, and had marginal resources. Similarly, Kupst and Schulman (Note 3) report that those parents who coped poorly with their child's leukemia had "pre-existing multiple problems, such as marital, relationship, financial, and occupational [p. 23]" difficulties. However, in a systematic investigation of the predictors of emotional distress over a 24-month period, Vachon (Note 4) found that little variance was accounted for by concomitant stress among the bereaved.

Burgess and Holmstrom (1978) also examined the effects of chronic stress in their investigation of recovery from rape. They found that those women who were experiencing chronic life stressors, such as economic stress, lack of social support or "preexisting biopsychosocial problems such as psychosis, alcoholism, drug use, mental retardation or homosexuality [pp. 170–171]" tended to have long-term difficulty recovering from the rape. Unfortunately, the authors' statistical analysis does not allow for a determination of the relative influence of each of these stressors on subsequent adjustment. Nonetheless, it appears that for some people, particularly those with limited social support, daily struggling with problems such as poverty or alcoholism may "use up" one's coping reserves, and leave one especially vulnerable for adjustment problems should a crisis occur.

POSSIBLE DIRECTIONS FOR SUBSEQUENT WORK

Our review of past theories and their inability to account for the diverse empirical results concerning responses to negative life events led us to suggest some variables that might mediate individual reactions. As we described, such variables might be incorporated into future theoretical formulations in this area. In this section of the chapter, we suggest further areas for subsequent work in the field of coping with life crises, on both theoretical and empirical grounds. Two general areas are explored in some detail. We first draw from our previous discussions to summarize implications of past work for future theoretical development. We discuss the need for theoretical statements that capture the complexity of the coping process, yet make precise predictions regarding the relationships among particular variables and successful coping or resolution. We then explore the problems associated with providing a clear conceptual definition of successful coping. We discuss how the difficulties with present conceptualizations of good coping have hampered theoretical and empirical work in this area, and consider possible solutions to these problems.

Theoretical Development

Our discussion of past theories, as well as the existing empirical research, has suggested some promising directions for the development of theory in this area. Earlier, we noted that the perspectives we presented contrast markedly in their breadth of focus and in their precision. Lazarus (Note 1; Lazarus & Launier, 1978) highlights the full variety of coping responses that can be made when confronted with a life crisis. Shontz's (1965, 1975) account of the adjustment process is filled with provocative insights from his experience in health-care settings. Klinger (1975, 1977) draws from work in many areas of psychology to provide a stimulating account of how life crises can dominate our thoughts and fantasies. Although each of these models provides a rich discussion of the coping process, none offers a basis for predicting the nature, sequence, or duration of particular responses elicited by victims of life crises. Wortman and Brehm (1975) and Abramson et al. (1978), on the other hand, have included mediating variables that afford more precise predictions about when people will become angry or depressed (Wortman & Brehm, 1975), and how far depressive reactions will generalize (Abramson et al., 1978). Perhaps because of their laboratory origins, however, these models fail to capture the complexity of coping with significant negative outcomes. Clearly, theoretical formulations that incorporate the best features of each of these models are desirable. Hopefully, such models will include a broad range of cognitions, emotional reactions, and coping responses, as well as incorporate mediating variables that specify when particular reactions will occur.

The importance of incorporating a broad range of emotional responses and coping strategies was also suggested in our review of the available research on reactions to life crises. One clear implication of the empirical research is that those models which have focused almost entirely on depression (Abramson et al., 1978; Seligman, 1975) or on both anger and depression (Klinger, 1975, 1977; Wortman & Brehm, 1975) are unnecessarily restrictive. The available research suggests that other reactions, particularly shock and anxiety, are widely experienced and are thus in need of increased theoretical attention. Similarly, past research suggests that people employ many different kinds of coping strategies, including denial and information seeking, as well as efforts to change the outcome in question. Unfortunately, some theories have limited their focus to predictions regarding a single strategy, such as when people will try to alter the outcome and when they will give up (Abramson et al., 1978; Wortman & Brehm, 1975). In our judgment, such theories are likely to have little predictive power in accounting for the diverse reactions to most life crises.

The empirical work reviewed also highlights the importance of incorporating mediating variables into subsequent theoretical statements. Perhaps the most striking feature of available research, considered as a whole, is the variability in the nature and sequence of people's emotional reactions and coping mechanisms as they attempt to resolve their crises. How can we account for the fact that depression is a fairly common initial reaction to some life crises (e.g., bereavement) but not to others (e.g., rape)? Within a particular life crisis, like rape, why do some women show intense emotional reactions while others appear numb or calm? Similarly, when do people decide to fight a fatal diagnosis, and when do they instead deny the diagnosis or its ramifications? Perhaps by incorporating mediating variables such as perceived social support, the opportunity for free expression of feelings, the ability to find meaning in the crisis, or experience with other stressors, future theoretical statements can offer more precise predictions about the conditions under which particular reactions will occur.

The empirical research documents considerable variability not only in the initial reaction to the negative event and in the coping strategies employed, but also in the time necessary for successful resolution of the crisis. Why do 40% of the bereaved continue to experience intense anxiety 2–4 years after their loss (Glick et al., 1974)? What factors are helpful in determining why one-quarter of rape victims do not feel recovered from a rape as long as 4–6 years later (Burgess & Holmstrom, 1978)? It is important that mediating variables be incorporated into future theories as a way of enhancing their ability to identify those individuals especially likely to experience subsequent difficulties.

Conceptual Problems in Defining Successful Adjustment

In order to develop precise theoretical statements about the relationship among particular variables and successful resolution or adjustment to a crisis, it is necessary to address a central question: What *is* successful adjustment? In our judgment, the difficulties involved in providing a clear conceptual definition of effective coping have hindered potential advancement in this field. Many characteristics thought to reflect successful recovery or adaptation have been identified, including keeping one's distress within manageable limits, maintaining a realistic appraisal of the situation, being able to function or carry out socially desired goals, maintaining a positive self-concept, and maintaining a positive outlook on the situation (see, e.g., Friedman et al., 1963; Haan, 1977; Hamburg & Adams, 1967; Myers, Friedman, & Weiner, 1970). To what extent can we assume that these qualities are synonymous with successful coping?

In order to illustrate some of the complexities involved in regarding these qualities as indicative of good coping, let us consider one of them in some detail. The view that people who are coping well are able to control their emotional distress, and keep their anxiety within manageable limits, appears to be quite common (cf. Friedman et al., 1963; Haan, 1977; Hamburg & Adams, 1967; Mechanic, 1962). This focus on emotional regulation (cf. Lazarus & Launier, 1978) is not surprising, since there is some evidence that high levels of emotional distress can disrupt coping behavior in a natural setting (cf. Anderson, 1976). Moreover, emotional stress may be associated with endocrine changes (Mason, 1975) and with poor physical prognosis among people who are seriously ill (see, e.g., Achte & Vauhkonen, 1971; Garrity & Klein, 1975). (See Cohen, 1979, for a review of the role of stress in the development of physical illness, and for a full discussion of possible mediating mechanisms underlying such a relationship.) In fact, it has even been suggested that encouraging the expression of positive emotions like joy and laughter at a time of crisis can reverse the course of a progressive disease (Cousins, 1976).

While most theorists have assumed that the inability to keep one's emotional distress within manageable limits is indicative of poor adjust-ment, recent work suggests that this might not always be the case. Wortman and Dintzer (1978) have argued that relatively intense distress can play an important role in motivating individuals to initiate coping attempts. Consis-tent with this view, Goldsmith (1955) reports that patients with spinal cord injuries who were actively upset about their disability, and who expressed angry and aggressive feelings about what happened to them, were subse-quently judged as showing more progress in rehabilitation than patients who appeared to be less distressed. In fact, there is even some recent evidence suggesting that reacting to a crisis with expressions of emotional distress may favorably influence a person's physical prognosis. Derogatis, Abeloff, and Melisaratos (1979) collected a variety of psychological mea-sures on 35 women with breast cancer and correlated the results with length of survival. Interestingly, those women who reported higher levels of hostili-ty, anxiety, and dysphoric mood at the initial assessment were likely to survive the longest. Moreover, long-term survivors were rated by their on-cologists as less well adjusted to their illness. Consistent findings were also obtained in a prospective study of patients with malignant melanoma (Ro-gentine, van Kammen, Fox, Docherty, Rosenblatt, Boyd, & Bunney, 1979). Respondents were asked to indicate how much adjustment was needed to cope with their disease. Those who reported that little adjustment was re-quired, thus suggesting that their illness had caused them little distress, were significantly more likely to experience a relapse 1 year later. Interestingly, this variable was found to be independent of known biological prognostic factors, including the number of positive lymph nodes.

At present, these results are merely suggestive, and we can only specu-late about the mediating mechanisms. What causes the pathogenic impact found in the aforementioned studies? The respondents in Rogentine et al.'s (1979) study indicated that little coping effort was required, but it is unclear whether they experienced little distress or were unable or unwilling to admit to their feelings. Does health deteriorate because the suppression of negative feelings "use up" energy that could be used in fighting the disease, as Klopfer (1957) has suggested? Or is emotional distress simply more likely to be expressed by patients who have a desire to fight the disease? Does a desire to fight an illness, or suppression of one's emotions, influence physical prognosis via the immune or endocrine systems (cf. Cohen, 1979; Lazarus, Cohen, Folkman, Kanner, & Schaefer, 1980; Pettingale, Greer, & Tee, 1977; Solomon, 1969a, b)? Or do people who are more distressed about what is happening to them show a better prognosis because they are more likely to take other actions (e.g., seeking out better doctors; getting more information about treatments) than people who are less distressed? Do individuals who express anger and frustration show the same physiological reactions as individuals who voice helplessness and despair (cf. Mason, 1975; Mason, Maher, Hartley, Mougey, Perlow, & Jones, 1976)? While a full discussion of these issues is beyond the scope of this chapter, several studies suggest that the ability to keep one's distress manageable or controllable may not always be synonymous with good adjustment, and may in fact entail certain costs.

When one examines other factors often considered to be indicative of effective coping, similar problems emerge. This is the case for the ability to maintain a positive attitude, which has been mentioned by several investigators as characteristic of good adjustment (see, e.g., Visotsky et al., 1961). Like controlling one's emotional expression, however, focusing on the positive may result in subsequent difficulties. For example, Derogatis et al. (1979) found that those breast cancer patients who survived the longest were rated by their oncologists as possessing more negative attitudes toward their illness and its treatment, and were judged by interviewers as manifesting significantly poorer attitudes toward their physicians. The ability to maintain a positive self-concept has also been mentioned by several researchers as indicative of good adjustment (e.g., Hamburg & Adams, 1967; Visotsky et al., 1961). In fact, measures of self-esteem have comprised the central operational definition of coping in several studies (see, e.g., Bloom & Ross, Note 7). Yet, individuals whose self-esteem is threatened by the crisis may be especially likely to engage in coping efforts. For example, Litman (1962) found that, at least early in hospitalization, physically disabled

> patients with negative conceptions of self . . . exhibited a great deal of motivation and were considered excellent rehabilitation candidates by the clinical staff. [This type of patient] possessed such a distasteful conception of himself that every effort was directed toward alteration of the physical state believed to be the cause of it [p. 252].

Taken as a whole, this work suggests that providing a conceptual definition of effective coping may be extremely complex. In our judgment, there are a number of points that may be worth considering when attempting to develop operational definitions of successful adjustment. Since different ways of coping are unlikely to be correlated positively with one another, it may be unwise to formulate theoretical hypotheses concerning the relationship between specific variables and "good coping" in a general sense. It is also clear from our discussion of past work that certain factors may influence some types of coping but not others. For example, an individual who denies the seriousness of his or her child's leukemia may be relatively free from emotional distress, but may fail to carry out the functions necessary for the child's care. Ideally, our theoretical statements should be more precise, indicating specifically how particular variables are related to particular components of effective adjustment. Finally, the lack of association among the various components of effective coping also suggests that empirical researchers should employ multiple measures of this construct. In studying the predictors of successful adjustment to spinal cord injury, for example, investigators may wish to assess many specific types of effective coping, including absence of somatic complaints, freedom from extreme emotional distress, cooperation with rehabilitation treatment regimens, and resumption of social and vocational activities (see Wortman et al., 1980).

Another conclusion that might be drawn from the aforementioned work is that the relationships that emerge among particular variables and indices of successful adjustment may not remain stable over time. Responses that are functional at one point in time may prove to be counterproductive as the situation changes (cf. Pearlin & Schooler, 1978). Specifically, there is evidence to suggest that denying the implications of one's predicament may be helpful in alleviating distress in the short run but dysfunctional in the long run. For example, Kimball (1969) identified a group of patients who appeared "euphoric" after open heart surgery, "greeting the staff enthusiastically as though the operation had been 'nothing at all' [p. 100]." Although this group had the fewest early complications and were transferred out of intensive care sooner than other patients, they "demonstrated a number of complications, e.g., conversion reactions, gastrointestinal hemorrhages, and pyrexias of undetectable etiology [p. 100]" days later. (See Lazarus, Note 12, for a more complete discussion of the consequences of denial.)

In past theoretical and empirical work, the various components of effective coping have been frequently conceptualized as dependent variables. The research we have reviewed, however, suggests that causal relationships among such variables as emotional reactions, coping strategies, and indices of effective coping are likely to be complex and multidirectional. For example, lack of social support may result in greater expression of emotional distress, which may in turn reduce social support still further. Moreover, the various indices of coping that we have discussed may causally influence one another. Carrying out appropriate functions at the time of crisis, for example, may lead to an increase in one's self-concept. A central question concerns how the broad classes of variables influence one another and change over time as the coping process unfolds. In our judgment, the relationships among these variables can best be explored in longitudinal designs that include frequent and repeated assessments of these variables. In light of the evidence that life crises may have impact on an individual for a considerable period of time, long-term follow-up is clearly desirable. As we noted earlier, however, investigators must devote considerable attention to the problems of reactivity, attrition, and the ethical considerations that normally accompany this type of research (see also Wortman et al., 1980).

Since individual indices of coping are unlikely to be correlated with one another and may change over time, how are we to differentiate those people who are coping poorly from those who are coping well? In our judgment, there are a number of factors that should be considered by those interested in making such distinctions. First, as other investigators have noted, the decision of what comprises good coping is intricately tied up with questions of values (cf. Lazarus & Launier, 1978). Most people would probably agree that a mother who is caring effectively for her fatally ill child, showing few somatic complaints, maintaining a realistic appraisal of the situation and keeping her emotions under control is coping more effectively than a woman who is having difficulty in all of these areas. Our discussion has suggested, however, that such clear-cut cases will rarely occur. More frequently, we will be faced with the following dilemma: Is a mother who is caring effectively for her child but subjecting herself to repeated and continual distress coping more effectively than one who spends very little time with the ill child, but is less stressed? The latter mother may be less capable of caring for her ill child, but may be more available to her spouse and other children.

Second, we believe that it may be difficult to conceptualize or define good coping with a particular life crisis in the absence of normative data regarding how people respond to that event. For example, it is difficult to regard "freedom from intense emotional distress" as an indication of good coping among the recently bereaved, since the available evidence suggests that virtually all bereaved manifest such distress. Because it is now recognized that depression is a common feature of the bereavement experience, this symptom may no longer be regarded as having diagnostic value. In fact, depression following the loss of a loved one has been dropped from the diagnostic categories of the *Diagnostic and Statistical Manual of Mental Disorders* (American Psychiatric Association, 1980).

Our previous review has shown, however, that such normative data are rarely available. It is therefore difficult to make judgments about good and bad coping in particular instances. Respondents in a study conducted by Coates et al. (1979) rated a rape victim as maladjusted and in need of professional help when she indicated, 6 months after the assault, that she was still having some difficulty in dealing with the rape. Would they have made so harsh a judgment had they known that 25% of rape victims do not regard themselves as recovered from the assault as long as 4 to 6 years later (cf. Burgess & Holmstrom, 1978)?

CONCLUSIONS AND IMPLICATIONS

What conclusions can be drawn from the diverse material that we have attempted to synthesize in this chapter? We have considered several general theoretical statements which address the issue of how people respond to undesirable life events, and the body of research that bears on the topic. Our examination of this material has suggested some intriguing discrepancies between theoretical and empirical work. Most theoretical statements indicate that people will respond to crises with a consensual pattern of response, and many theorists predict that these responses will fall into an orderly sequence of stages. In contrast, the empirical data reveal extreme variability of response and offer no clear evidence for stages. Similarly, while many theorists imply that people will recover from life crises and resume their lives, the available data suggest that the difficulties following a crisis may be experienced indefinitely.

Taken together, this past work suggests that theorists have often made inaccurate predictions about how people will react to undesirable life events. This possibility raises a series of intriguing questions. First, how widespread are such inaccurate expectations? Are they shared by care-givers, significant others, or distressed individuals themselves? Second, why might others maintain expectations concerning reactions to life crises that are so discrepant from the distressed person's experience? Finally, if such views about the course and impact of life crises are widely believed in our society, what are the implications of these beliefs for the care and treatment received by the distressed? Answers to these questions are considered in some detail below.

The Belief in a Consensual Pattern or Stage Model

As demonstrated earlier, there is a surprising lack of methodologically rigorous data indicating that individuals respond to aversive life events with a predictable pattern of emotional reactions. Despite the absence of any sound empirical evidence for the existence of sequential stage models for any negative outcomes, however, there is a pervasive belief among care-givers and helping professionals in such models of emotional response. So widespread is this belief that references to stage models can be found in books and articles written by and for nurses (Engel, 1964; Stitt, 1971; Zahourek & Jensen, 1973), therapists (Bromley, 1976), social workers (Weller & Miller, 1977a,b), clergymen (Nighswonger, 1971), health-care professionals (Bernstein, Bernstein, & Dana, 1974), and patients and their families (Kubler-Ross, 1969; Meyer, Meyer, & Garrett, 1977). For example, the following statements have been written by care-givers to provide guidance to others in their field:

Awareness of the normal stages of dying and the behavior and feelings likely to appear at each of them will assist the health professional . . . to enable the patient to achieve a state of relatively peaceful acceptance. In this manner death with dignity can be achieved [Bernstein et al., 1974, p. 188].

In order to give real assistance, care-givers should be competent in four areas. First, they must know what the usual responses to a given illness situation are, including the sequence of stages in emotional processes like mourning . . . . Staff should understand the time dimension involved, for example, in grieving for a loss. . . . It entails a progression from an initial reaction of numbness or disbelief . . . [Moos & Tsu, 1977, p. 18].

Similarly, the statement below appeared in a pamphlet for patients with spinal cord injuries and their families:

Patients react to spinal cord injury in a similar fashion as those who respond to the death of a loved one—'mourning.' The process of mourning has several stages, the first being Depression [Meyer et al., 1977, p. 36].

Of course, if it truly exists, there is much utility in a clinical stage model. Not only would it enable the care-giver to better prepare both distressed persons and their loved ones for the type and length of expected reactions, but it would also enable health-care professionals to identify those individuals who, in manifesting unusual reactions, are in need of professional assistance (Bernstein et al., 1974; Fitzgerald, 1970). As Parkes (1975a) has suggested, a stage model would also afford the professional "some kind of yardstick by which we can assess progress and evaluate the consequences of our care [p. 1274]."

In the absence of validating data, however, and data indicating the extreme variability of response to the contrary, the pervasive belief in the stage concept may have unfortunate consequences for victimized individuals. Pattison (1977) reports that, as a result of the widely held belief in Kubler-Ross' (1969) stages of dying, "dying persons who did not follow these stages were labeled 'deviant,' 'neurotic,' or 'pathological dyers.' Clinical personnel became angry at patients who did not move from one stage to the next. . . . I began to observe professional personnel demand that the dying person 'die in the right way' [p. 304]." Kastenbaum and Costa (1977) contend that acceptance of such a model "encourages an attitude in which, for example, staff or family can say 'He's just going through the anger stage' when there may, in fact, be specific realistic factors that are arousing the patient's ire [p. 242]." Thus, as Goldiamond (1976) argues, hospital staff may be "relieved of the necessity for asking how their actions might have helped cause these reactions [p. 122]."

Such widespread beliefs of family and care-givers, as well as researchers, make the stage model particularly resistant to disconfirming evidence. Nisbett and Ross (1980) have provided a detailed and cogent analysis of how a researcher's, clinician's, or layperson's interpretation of data is strongly biased by expectations based on implicit theories. They review numerous studies indicating that "people tend to seek out, recall, and interpret evidence in a manner that sustains beliefs [p. 192]." Similarly, Goldiamond (1975) has explained that "one not only superimposes a classification system, but the very classification system will dictate categories and therefore what it is that will be admitted for categorization; that is, the data [p. 107]." In summarizing the research on this problem, Nisbett and Ross (1980) have concluded that people not only recall ambiguous data as supporting their beliefs, but also dismiss any evidence that contradicts or opposes their assumptions: "If the evidence cannot be discredited outright, it may nonetheless be given little weight and treated as if it were of little consequence [p. 169]." According to these authors, such errors in information processing make people's theories "almost impervious to data [p. 169]." This work may explain why the stage model has persisted tenaciously in the absence of empirical support. Nonetheless, until methodologically sophisticated research has documented specific reactions and confirmed the existence of stages of response, re-education of the public as well as health-care professionals should be our necessary, albeit difficult, goal.

The Belief in Recovery or Acceptance

An implicit assumption of the pervasive belief in the stage model is the expectation that people will accept or recover from their crises. We reported earlier, however, that there is evidence indicating that for a sizable minority, such an assumption is unfounded. Despite this fact, the belief that people will ultimately reach a final stage of acceptance of the event, and presumably move on to the next stage in their lives, appears to be quite common.

Schoenberg, Carr, Peretz, and Kutscher (1969) surveyed physicians and found that 52% expect the bereaved to have early "experiences of pleasure" —within a few weeks after the death of a spouse. In contrast, only 19% of the bereaved widows and widowers they surveyed anticipate such pleasant feelings (Schoenberg et al.,1975). The lay public appears even less aware of the adjustment problems of the individual coping with an undesirable life event. As Vachon (Note 4) indicates: "The woman with breast cancer is expected to quickly 'get back on her feet'; resume her role within the family. The assumption is that once treatment is completed, the disease shouldn't have much effect on her life [p. 12]." Similarly, in their review of the literature on the bereavement crisis, Walker et al. (1977) conclude that "widows frequently report that even intimates do not support the need to mourn their loss beyond the first few days after the death [p. 38]."[1]

It is also apparent that because recovery is expected, progression to the next stage in one's life is encouraged rather quickly. For example, the topic of remarriage seems to be brought up by others quite early in the bereavement period. Maddison and Walker (1967), in their study of bereaved widows, found that "it was not uncommon for this topic to have been introduced within a few days or weeks of the husband's death, particularly with the younger widows [p. 1063]." Widows in the sample studied by Glick et al. (1974) report similar encounters: Others "tactfully suggested that they make themselves available for dating or plan eventually to remarry [p. 222]" by the second month after the death of their spouse. In their discussion of the expectation for rapid recovery among parents who lost a newborn infant, Helmrath and Steinitz (1978) indicate that "the external expectations were that the couple would not grieve and would 'put the death behind them and get on with life.' " Couples were also reminded that "you're young, you can always have another one [p. 788]."

Although statements by others encouraging "moving on" may be well-intentioned, there is some indication that they are not viewed favorably by the victimized individual. In fact, rather than being seen as helpful, directions toward one's future life after a crisis often lead to feelings of frustration and disappointment (see, e.g., Helmrath & Steinitz, 1978). Maddison and Walker (1967) report that "conversations which aroused interest in new activities, development of new friendships, resumption of old hobbies or occupations [p. 1063]" during the first 3 months after death of a spouse were greeted with hostility. Similarly, Glick et al. (1974) report that "widows invariably found early suggestions that they consider remarriage unpleasant and even jarring [p. 222]."

The aforementioned evidence, while limited, is consistent in suggesting a discrepancy between the way a person is expected to respond to a negative life event, and the way he or she actually reacts. Outsiders apparently unaware of the impact of a life crisis are quick to encourage the distressed

[1]It must also be noted that while most individuals expect the victim of a life crisis to recover, norms also dictate that he or she should experience some period of initial distress. A spinal cord injured person who was not depressed following his injury has noted that he "adjusted to the fact so quickly that they sent me to a psychiatrist to find out if I was okay [Goldiamond, 1976, p. 134]." A widow who remarries a few months after her spouse's death "might well be censured for displaying too little grief for her loss [Glick et al., 1974, p. 222]." Finally, Calhoun, Cann, Selby, and Magee (in press) have found that a rape victim who appears controlled immediately after the attack may be judged more negatively by others, and even viewed as less credible than a victim who is more emotional. (See also Friedman et al., 1963, and Benson et al., 1974, for a discussion of the particular problems encountered by victims whose behaviors fail to meet the expectations of those in their social environment.)

to move on with their lives. We believe that others' misconceptions about the recovery process may lead them to behave toward the distressed in ways that are unintentionally harmful, and thus intensify the strain from the life crisis itself. For example, the death of a newborn child commonly elicits such responses as "It was only a baby whom you didn't know"; "It's worse to lose a child you know" (Helmrath & Steinitz, 1978, p. 788). There is apparently no acknowledgment of the fact that, as Kennell et al. (1970) found, "clearly identifiable mourning was present in the mother of each infant who died—whether the infant lived for one hour or for 12 days, whether the infant was 3000 grams or a nonviable 580 grams . . . whether or not the mother had touched the baby [p. 348]." What factors might explain why others' expectations about responses to undesirable life events are so discrepant from the reactions that apparently occur? We know of virtually no systematic research of direct relevance to this issue. Because we believe that this problem is of paramount importance, however, we draw from the limited information available to discuss some possible mechanisms that may underlie this intriguing phenomenon.

Differences in Salience and Information

One explanation for the discrepancy between outsiders' expectations and the experiences of the victimized may simply be a difference in the amount and kinds of information to which the observers are privy (cf. Jones & Nisbett, 1972). Others may regard the inability to walk as the major problem faced by the spinal cord injured. They may not realize that permanent paralysis can be associated with a host of other difficulties, including the possible development of debilitating pressure ulcers or the worry of potential embarrassment from a broken catheter bag. Similarly, the experience of rape may frequently involve repeated sex acts or such degrading behavior as the assailant urinating on the victim (McCombie, 1975)—information to which outsiders may be unaware. Such memories are undoubtedly more salient to the victim, and may be withheld from the observer out of shame. Other pieces of information that may be available to the distressed person but not to the observer are such experiences as repeated visual or auditory hallucinations of the lost object (e.g., amputated limb) or of the deceased (see, e.g., Cornwell et al., 1977; Glick et al., 1974; Lindemann, 1944; Marris, 1958; Parkes, 1972, 1975a). In fact, the observer is unlikely to be aware that such common bereavement experiences as seeing one's dead spouse or hearing his voice or footsteps (cf. Marris, 1958) continue long after the death, and that a persistent sense of the dead person's presence does not appear to diminish for several years (Glick et al., 1974). Because such information is unavailable to outsiders, they may not be able to comprehend what the victim is going through. It is likely that such differences will interfere with the delivery of empathic responses to distressed individuals by others around them.

The Generation of Future Plans

Another factor that might explain why those involved in life crises react with more intense and prolonged distress than others expect is because the distressed individual must contend, not only with the loss itself, but with the simultaneous destruction of future plans and fantasies (Carr, 1975; Parkes, 1971). For example, the parent who experiences a miscarriage, stillbirth or loss of a child must cope with loss of hopes and dreams he or she had held for the baby (cf. Cornwell et al., 1977). The parent may have fantasized, perhaps before the baby was conceived, of buying clothes and toys for the child, of taking the child to sporting events, or even of helping the child in the choice of a career. It is unlikely, however, that others generate such thoughts, or are aware that they are salient for those involved in life crises. As Helmrath and Steinitz (1978) have noted, the loss of a fetus or newborn may appear to the observer as an "it" without an identity.

This tendency to generate future plans that are vitiated with the life crisis may also help explain why the ramifications of the loss may be very salient to the distressed person years later. A young widow who had expected her husband to assist in the raising of their children may grieve the loss if she encounters difficulties when the children become teenagers. Similarly, a mother who loses a newborn baby may become distressed each time she thinks of the child growing up. This latter point was poignantly illustrated in a poem written by a mother who had lost her baby to Sudden Infant Death Syndrome 14 years earlier:

> My mind does not mourn yesterday
> It mourns today
> The images that pass before my eyes
> Do not recall the infant son
> But see you running through my house
> A teenage child in search of food and gym shoes and maybe me.
>
> I do not mourn your for what you were,
> But for what can't be . . . [Anonymous, 1979].

This disruption of future hopes and plans is unlikely to be apparent to outsiders, who might be puzzled by displays of distress years after the life crisis.

Generalization of the Experience

As noted earlier, one of the most devastating aspects of many undesirable life events may be their tendency to alter one's view of the world. The distress associated with a rape may stem, not only from the violent act, but also from the resultant feeling that people cannot be trusted (cf. McCombie, 1975). Learning that one has heart disease or cancer is likely to highlight the unpredictability and uncontrollability of one's life in the future. Such permanent alterations following a temporary event are probably not salient to the observer, whose broader perspectives may not have been modified by the experience.

The Involuntary Nature of Cognitions and Emotional Reactions

Another reason why others may encourage victims to move on with their lives may stem from their belief that thoughts and emotions surrounding the crisis are voluntary. On the contrary, it appears that, at least in the early period of coping with an aversive event, the distressed person's illusions and reactions are often involuntary in nature. Marris (1958) writes that widows were "troubled by illusions of [their spouses'] presence or obsessive memories of the dead man and the circumstances in which he died [p. 14]." Kaltreider et al. (1979) noted the frequent appearance of "intrusive symptoms such as 'flooding with memories in response to sudden reminders' and 'unwanted thoughts about the surgery' [p. 1501]" among women who had undergone hysterectomies. In their discussion of the common "obsessional review" of a husband's death among widows who had recently lost their spouses, Glick et al. (1974) note that these women "seemed to have little control over 'dwelling' so on their experience [p. 126]." It is probable that outsiders find it difficult to believe that such thoughts and feelings are not volitional. The fact that others often implore distressed persons to control their expressions of grief, and to stop "dwelling" on their problems (cf. Glick et al. 1974; Maddison & Walker, 1967), suggests that they believe that distressed individuals could behave more appropriately if they wished.

Implications for Those Who Encounter Undesirable Life Events

Throughout this section of the chapter, we have suggested that outsiders frequently underestimate the nature and duration of the distress encountered by victims. We have also identified several factors that may make it difficult for outsiders to comprehend what the distressed person is going through. What are the implications of these erroneous expectations for the victims themselves? The transition from an outsider to the ranks of the victimized often happens within minutes. One suddenly learns that he or she has cancer, has lost a spouse, or will be permanently paralyzed. In all likelihood, views concerning how people should respond to crises have been internalized by the distressed person even before the negative outcome is experienced. For this reason, individuals are likely to hold unrealistic expectations regarding the nature and duration of their own responses. Unfortunately, this in turn may serve to intensify their distress. Kennell et al. (1970) report that the parents who lost infants in their study "were not well prepared for their own mourning responses—their reactions worried and perplexed them [p. 347]." Pattison (1977) writes of a woman who, during the course of her own dying experience, "began to doubt her own sanity when her self-observations revealed that she did not follow the stages of dying [p. 304]." The appearance of illusions and recurrent feelings of anxiety and depression over time may also be viewed by the individual experiencing them as a sign of "going crazy" (Kaltreider et al., 1979). In fact, fears of approaching insanity or of losing one's mind have frequently been reported among the bereaved (Bergman, Pomeroy, & Beckwith, 1969; Lindemann, 1944).

In addition to enhancing their difficulties, the view that one's behavior is inappropriate may prevent persons from seeking support from others in their time of distress. Kaltreider et al. (1979) found that although almost one-third of the young women who had undergone a hysterectomy were still experiencing intrusive feelings, nightmares, and other symptoms of stress a year after their operation, they "were hesitant to seek medical or psychological help because they thought they should be able to cope with this normal crisis [p. 1503]."

It behooves the health-care professional to legitimize the feelings and reactions that commonly occur among people who have encountered negative life events. The value of peer support groups (see, e.g., D'Afflitti & Weitz, 1977; Vachon, Lyall, Rogers, Formo, Freedman, Cochrane, & Freeman, 1979) may stem in part from their ability to help realign the norms of the distressed. Thus, a group of peers can assist the distressed in forming more accurate perceptions of what behaviors are, in fact, normative. Since outsiders may have a false understanding of the common experiences of victimized individuals, they may see such support groups as having a detrimental influence. As a woman who became involved in one of these groups writes:

> The majority of my relatives and friends, particularly my health professional friends, were concerned and fearful that this kind of activity could only be destructive— especially three years later. How could I go about the business of forgetting, which I should have already done, and at the same time associate with families who had lost children [Szybist, 1978, p. 286]?"

In general, outsiders must be sensitive to the fact that for most people, an aversive life event is never really forgotten and the experience is likely to be carried with them for the remainder of their lives. The transient return of unresolved feelings must not be viewed as an indication of instability or mental illness, but rather as an acceptable way of living with the crisis. It still remains to be determined whether preparing the individual for the variety of responses he or she may encounter and the length of time they may persist will be beneficial for all those who experience aversive outcomes. For example, will expectations of possible long-term difficulties result in added distress for those who are able to adjust more quickly? Nonetheless, it is our hope that a recognition of the issues discussed in this chapter will encourage further research, as well as more sensitive, empathic, and helpful treatment of those who are coping with undesirable life events.

ACKNOWLEDGMENTS

The authors would like to thank Philip Brickman and Joan Robinson for helpful comments on an earlier version of this chapter.

REFERENCE NOTES

1. Lazarus, R. S. *The stress and coping paradigm*. Paper presented at conference entitled "The critical evaluation of behavioral paradigms for psychiatric science," Gleneden Beach, Oregon, November 1978.
2. Garrity, T. F. *Behavioral adjustment after myocardial infarction: A selective review of recent descriptive, correlational and intervention research*. Paper presented at the meeting of the Academy of Behavioral Medicine Research, Snowbird, Utah, June 1979.
3. Kupst, M. J., & Schulman, J. L. *Family coping with childhood leukemia: The first six months*. Unpublished manuscript, Northwestern University Medical School, 1980.
4. Vachon, M. L. S. *The importance of social support in the longitudinal adaptation to bereavement and breast cancer*. Paper presented at the meeting of the American Psychological Association, New York, September 1979.
5. Shadish, W. R., Hickman, D., & Arrick, M. C. *Psychological adjustment to spinal cord injury: The moderating effect of time and locus of control*. Unpublished manuscript, Northwestern University, 1980.
6. Wortman, C. B., & Dunkel-Schetter, C. *Dilemmas of social support: Parallels between victimization and aging*. Paper presented at National Research Council Committee on Aging workshop entitled "The future of the elderly," Annapolis, Maryland, May 1979.
7. Bloom, J. R., & Ross, R. D. *Comprehensive psychosocial support for initial breast cancer: Preliminary report of results*. Paper presented at the meeting of the American Psychological Association, San Francisco, September 1977.
8. Brickman, P., Rabinowitz, V. C., Coates, D., Cohn, E., & Karuza, J. *Helping*. Unpublished manuscript, University of Michigan, 1979.
9. Barrett, C. J., & Larson, D. W. *Psychological functions of religion in widowhood: Attribution versus evidence*. Unpublished manuscript, Wichita State University, 1977.
10. DeVellis, R. F., DeVellis, B. M., Wallston, B. S., & Wallston, K. A. *Epilepsy and learned helplessness*. Unpublished manuscript, University of North Carolina at Chapel Hill, 1979.
11. Belle, D. (Ed.). *Lives in stress: A context for depression*. Unpublished manuscript, Harvard University, 1980.
12. Lazarus, R. S. *The power of positive thinking; or, was Norman Vincent Peale right?* Paper presented at conference entitled "Effectiveness and costs of denial," Haifa University, June 1979.

References

Abramson, L. Y., Garber, J., Edwards, N. B., & Seligman, M. E. P. Expectancy changes in depression and schizophrenia. *Journal of Abnormal Psychology,* 1978, *87,* 102–109.

Abramson, L. Y., & Sackeim, H. A. A paradox in depression: Uncontrollability and self-blame. *Psychological Bulletin,* 1977, *84,* 838–851.

Abramson, L. Y., Seligman, M. E. P., & Teasdale, J. Learned helplessness in humans: Critique and reformulation. *Journal of Abnormal Psychology,* 1978, *87,* 49–74.

Achte, K. A., & Vauhkonen, M. L. Cancer and the psyche. *Omega,* 1971, *2,* 46–56.

Adler, A. *Practice and theory of individual psychology.* New York: Harcourt, Brace, & World, 1927.

Adler, R. Experimentally inducted gastric lesions: Results and implications of studies in animals. *Advances in Psychosomatic Medicine,* 1971, *6,* 1–39.

Akiskal, H. S., & McKinney, W. T. Overview of recent research in depression: Ten conceptual models. *Archives of General Psychiatry,* 1975, *32,* 285–305.

Alloy, L. B., & Abramson, L. Y. Judgement of contingency in depressed and nondepressed students: Sadder but wiser? *Journal of Experimental Psychology: General,* 1979, *108,* 441–485.

Alloy, L. B., & Seligman, M. E. P. On the cognitive component of learned helplessness and depression. In G. H. Bower (Ed.), *The psychology of learning and motivation.* (Vol. 13) New York: Academic Press, 1979

American Psychiatric Association, *Diagnostic and statistical manual of mental disorders (DSM-III) Third edition.* Washington, D.C.: American Psychiatric Association, 1980.

Anastasi, A. *Differential psychology; individual and group differences in behavior* (3rd ed.) New York: Macmillan, 1958.

Anderson, C. R. Coping behaviors as intervening mechanisms in the inverted-U stress-performance relationship. *Journal of Applied Psychology,* 1976, *61,* 30–34.

Andreasen, N. J. C., & Norris, A. S. Long-term adjustment and adaptation mechanisms in severely burned adults. *Journal of Nervous and Mental Disease,* 1972, *154,* 352–362.

Angst, J. *Zur Atiologie und Nosologie endogener depressiver Psychosen.* Berlin: Springer, 1966.

Anonymous. The tenth of July. *Pediatrics,* 1979, *63,* 615.

Appley, M., & Trumbell, R. (Eds.) *Psychological Stress.* New York: Appleton, 1967.

Ardlie N. G., Glew, G., & Schwartz, C. J. Influence of catecholamines on nucleotide-induced platelet aggregation. *Nature,* 1966, *212,* 415–417.

Arieti, S. Manic-depressive psychosis. In S. Arieti (ed.), *American handbook of Psychiatry* (1st ed., Vol I). New York: Basic Books, 1959.

Arieti, S., & Bemporad, J. *Severe and mild depressions: The psychotherapeutic approach.* New York: Basic Books, 1978.

Asch, S. Forming impressions of personality. *Journal of Abnormal and Social Psychology,* 1946, *41,* 258–290.

Asher, S. R., & Markel, R. A. Sex differences in reading comprehension of high-and low- interest material. *Journal of Educational Psychology,* 1974, *66,* 680–687.

Atkinson, J. W. *An introduction to motivation.* Princeton, N.J.: Van Nostrand, 1964.

Averill, J. R. Personal control over aversive stimuli and its relationship to stress. *Psychological Bulletin,* 1973, *80,* 286–303.

Averill, J. R., O'Brien, L., & DeWitt, G. W. The influence of response effectiveness on the preference for warning and on psychophysiological stress reactions. *Journal of Personality,* 1977, *45,* 395–418.

Averill, J. R., Opton, E. M., & Lazarus, R. S. Cross-cultural studies of psychophysiological responses during stress and emotion. *International Journal of Psychology,* 1969, *4,* 83–102.

Averill, J. R., & Rosenn, M. Vigilant and nonvigilant coping strategies and psychophysiological stress reactions during the anticipation of an electric shock. *Journal of Personality and Social Psychology,* 1972, *23,* 128–141.

Ayeroff, F., & Abelson, R. ESP and ESB: Belief in personal success at mental telepathy. *Journal of Personality and Social Psychology,* 1976, *34,* 240–247.

Baekeland, F., & Lundwall, L. Dropping out of treatment: A critical review. *Psychological Bulletin,* 1975, *82,* 738–783.

Balke B. Optimale Koerperliche Leistungsfaehigkeisihre Messung und Veraenderung infrolage Arbeitsermuedung. *Arbeitsphysiologie,* 1954, *15,* 311–323.

Balke, B., Grillo, G. P., Konecci, E. B., & Luft, U. C. Work capacity after blood donation. *Journal of Applied Physiology,* 1954, *7,* 231–238.

Ball, T. S., Vogler, R. E. Uncertain pain and the pain of uncertainty. *Perceptual and Motor Skills,* 1971, *33,* 1195–1203.

Bandura, A. *Social learning theory.* Englewood Cliffs, N.J.: Prentice-Hall, 1977.

Bandura, A. Self-efficacy: Toward a unifying theory of behavioral change. *Psychological Review,* 1977, *84,* 191–215.

Bandura, A., Adams, N. E., & Beyer, J. Cognitive processes mediating behavioral changes. *Journal of Personality and Social Psychology,* 1977, *35,* 125–139.

Bard M., & Waxenberg, S. Relationship of Cornell Medical Index to post-surgical invalidism. *Journal of Clinical Psychology,* 1957, *13,* 151–153.

Baum, A., Aiello, J. R., & Calesnick, L. E. Crowding and personal control: Social density and the development of learned helplessness. *Journal of Personality and Social Psychology,* 1978, *36,* 1000–1011.

Beard, B. H. Fear of death and fear of life: The dilemma in chronic renal failure, hemodialysis, and kidney transplantation. *Archives of General Psychiatry,* 1969, *21,* 373–380.

Beck, A. T. A systematic investigation of depression. *Comprehensive Psychiatry,* 1961, *2,* 163–170.

Beck, A. T. Thinking and depression: 1. Idiosyncratic content and cognitive distortions. *Archives of General Psychiatry,* 1963, *9,* 324–333.

Beck, A. T. Thinking and depression: 2. Theory and Therapy. *Archives of General Psychiatry,* 1964, *10,* 561–571.

Beck, A. T. *Depression: Clinical, experimental, and theoretical aspects.* New York: Harper & Row, 1967.

Beck, A. T. Cognitive therapy: Nature and relation to behavior therapy. *Behavior Therapy,* 1970, *1,* 184–200.

Beck, A. T. Cognition, affect, and psychopathology. In H. London and R. E. Nisbett (Eds.) *Thought and feeling.* Chicago, Ill.: Aldine, 1974.

Beck. A. T. *Cognitive therapy and emotional disorders.* New York: International Universities Press, 1976.

Beck, A. T., & Hurvich, M. S. Psychological correlates of depression: I. Frequency of "masochistic" dream content in a private practice sample. *Psychosomatic Medicine,* 1959, *21,* 50–55.

Beck, A. T., Rush. A. J., Shaw, B. F., & Emery, G. *Cognitive therapy of depression: A treatment manual.* New York: Guilford, 1979.

Beck, A. T., & Ward, C. H. Dreams of depressed patients: Characteristic themes in manifest content. *Archives of General Psychiatry,* 1961, *5,* 462–467.

Beck, A. T., Ward, C. H., Mendelson, M., Mock, J. E., & Erbaugh, J. K. An inventory for measuring depression. *Archives of General Psychiatry,* 1961, *4,* 561–571.

Becker, W. C., & Matteson, H. H. GSR conditioning, anxiety, and extraversion. *Journal of Abnormal and Social Psychology,* 1961, *62,* 427–430.

Bem, D. J. Self-perception: An alternative interpretation of cognitive dissonance phenomena. *Psychological Review,* 1967, *74,* 183–200.

Benner, P., Roskies, E., & Lazarus, R. S. Stress and coping under extreme conditions. In J. E. Dimsdale (Ed.), *Survivors, victims, and perpetrators: Essays on the Nazi holocaust.* Washington, D. C.: Hemisphere, 1980.

Benson, D., McCubbin, H. I., Dahl, B. B., & Hunter, E. J. Waiting: The dilemma of the MIA wife. In H. I. McCubbin, B. B. Dahl, P. J. Metres, E. J. Hunter, & J. A. Plag (Eds.), *Family separation and reunion: Families of prisoners of war and servicemen missing in action.* Washington, D.C.: U.S. Government Printing Office, 1974.

Benson, J. S., & Kennelly, K. J. Learned helplessness: The result of uncontrollable reinforcements or uncontrollable aversive stimuli? *Journal of Personality and Social Psychology,* 1976, *34,* 138–145.

Bergman, A. B., Pomeroy, M. A., & Beckwith, J. B. The psychiatric toll of the Sudden Infant Death Syndrome. *General Practitioner,* 1969, *40,* 99–103.

Berlyne, D. E. *Conflict, arousal and curiosity.* New York: McGraw-Hill, 1960.

Bernstein, L., Bernstein, R. S., & Dana, R. H. *Interviewing: A guide for health professionals.* New York: Appleton-Century-Crofts, 1974.

Bertelson, A., Harvald, B., & Hauge, M. A Danish twin study of manic-depressive disorders. *British Journal of Psychiatry,* 1977, *130,* 330–351.

Bibring, E. The mechanism of depression. In P. Greenacre (Ed.), *Affective disorders: Psychoanalytic contributions to their study.* New York: International Universities Press, 1953.

Bitterman, M., & Holtzman, W. Conditioning and extinction as a function of anxiety. *Journal of Abnormal and Social Psychology,* 1952, *47,* 615–623.

Björkstrand, P. Electrodermal responses as affected by subject- versus experimenter-controlled noxious stimulation. *Journal of Experimental Psychology,* 1973, *97,* 365–369.

Blaney, P. H. Contemporary theories of depression: Critique and comparison. *Journal of Abnormal Psychology*, 1977, *86*, 203–223.

Blatt, S. J., D'Afflitti, J. P., & Quinlan, D. M. Experiences of depression in normal young adults. *Journal of Abnormal Psychology*, 1976, *85*, 383–389.

Block, J. Recognizing the coherence of personality. In D. Magnusson & N. S. Endler (Eds.), *Personality at the Crossroads*, Hillsdale N.J. : Lawrence Erlbaum Associates, 1977.

Bolles R. C. Reinforcement, expectancy, and learning. *Psychological Review*, 1972, *79*, 394–409.

Bornstein, P. E., & Clayton, P. J. The anniversary reaction. *Diseases of the Nervous System*, 1972, *33*, 470–472.

Bornstein, P. E., Clayton, P. J., Halikas, J. A., Maurice, W. L., & Robins, E. The depression of widowhood after thirteen months. *British Journal of Psychiatry*, 1973, *122*, 561–566.

Bowden, D. M., & McKinney, W. T. Behavioral effects of peer separation, isolation, and reunion on adolescent male rhesus monkeys. *Developmental Psychobiology*, 1972, *5*, 353–362.

Bower, G. H. Contacts of cognitive psychology with social learning theory. *Cognitive Therapy and Research*, 1978, *2*, 123–146.

Bowers, K. S. Pain, anxiety, and perceived control. *Journal of Consulting and Clinical Psychology*, 1968, *32*, 596–602.

Bowlby, J. Grief and mourning in infancy and early childhood. *Psychoanalytic Study of the Child*, 1960, *15*, 9–52.

Bowlby, J. Processes of mourning. *The International Journal of Psychoanalysis*, 1961, *42*, 317–340.

Bowlby, J. *Attachment and loss (Vol. 2): Separation: Anxiety and anger*. New York: Basic Books, 1973

Brand, R. J., Rosenman, R. H., Sholtz, R. I., & Friedman, M. Multivariate prediction of coronary heart disease in the Western Collaborative Group Study compared to the findings of the Framingham Study. *Circulation*, 1976, *53*, 348–355.

Braud, W., Wepman, B., & Russo, D. Task and species generality of the "helplessness" phenomenon. *Psychonomic Science*, 1969, *16*, 154–155.

Bray, G. P. Rehabilitation of spinal cord injured: A family approach. *Journal of Applied Rehabilitation Counseling*, 1978, *9*, 70–78.

Brehm, J. W. *Response to loss of freedom: A theory of psychological reactance*. New York: Academic Press, 1966.

Brewer, W. F. There is no convincing evidence for operant and classical conditioning in humans. In W. B. Weimer & D. S. Palermo (Eds.), *Cognitions and symbolic processes*. Hillsdale N.J.: Lawrence Erlbaum Associates, 1974.

Broadhurst, P. L. The interaction of task difficulty and motivation: The Yerkes-Dodson law revived. *Acta Psychologica*, 1959, *16*, 321–338.

Bromley, I. *Tetraplegia and paraplegia: A guide for physiotherapists*. Edinburgh: Churchill Livingstone, 1976.

Brophy, J. E., & Good, T. L. *Teacher-student relationships: Causes and consequences*. New York: Holt, Rinehart, Winston, 1974.

Brown, F. S. Heredity in the psychoneurosis. *Proceedings of the Royal Society of Medicine*, 1942, *35*, 785–790.

Brown, I., & Inouye, D. K., Learned helplessness through modeling: The role of perceived similarity in competence. *Journal of Personality and Social Psychology*, 1978, *36*, 900–908.

Brown, J. S. *The motivation of behavior* New York: McGraw-Hill, 1961.

Bruhn, J. G., Thurman, A. E., Chandler, B. C., & Bruce, T. A. Patients' reactions to death in a coronary care unit. *Journal of Psychosomatic Research*, 1970, *14*, 65–70.

Bryant, B. K., & Trockel, J. F. Personal history of psychological stress related to locus of control orientation among college women. *Journal of Consulting and Clinical Psychology, 1976, 44*, 266–271.

Buchwald, A. M., Coyne, J. C., & Cole, C. S. A critical evaluation of the learned helplessness model of depression. *Journal of Abnormal Psychology, 1978, 87*, 180–193.

Bulman, R. J., & Wortman, C. B. Attributions of blame and coping in the "real world": Severe accident victims react to their lot. *Journal of Personality and Social Psychology, 1977, 35*, 351–363.

Burgess, A. W., & Holmstrom, L. L. Rape trauma syndrome. *American Journal of Psychiatry, 1974, 131*, 981–986.

Burgess, A. W., & Holmstrom, L. L. Coping behavior of the rape victim. *American Journal of Psychiatry, 1976, 133*, 413–418.

Burgess, A. W., & Holmstrom, L. L. Recovery from rape and prior life stress. *Research in Nursing and Health, 1978, 1*, 165–174.

Burgess, A. W., & Holmstrom, L. L. Adaptive strategies and recovery from rape. *American Journal of Psychiatry, 1979, 136*, 1278–1282.

Burnam, M. A., Pennebaker, J. W. , & Glass, D. C. Time consciousness, achievement striving and the Type A coronary-prone behavior pattern. *Journal of Abnormal Psychology, 1975, 84*, 76–79.

Buss, A. H. *The psychology of aggression.* New York: Wiley, 1961.

Butensky, A., Faralli, V., Heebner, D., & Waldron, I. Elements of the coronary prone behavior pattern in children and teenagers. *Journal of Psychosomatic Research, 1976, 20*, 439–444.

Butterfield, E. C. The role of competence motivation in interrupted task recall and repetition choice. *Journal of Experimental Child Psychology, 1965, 2*, 354–370.

Cairns, R. B. Meaning and attention as determinants of social reinforcer effectiveness. *Child Development, 1970, 41*, 1067–1082.

Calhoun, L. G., Cann, A., Selby, J. W., & Magee, D. L. Victim emotional response: Effects on social reaction to victims of rape. *British Journal of Social and Clinical Psychology,* in press.

Caplan, G. Patterns of parental response to the crisis of premature birth: A preliminary approach to modifying the mental-health outcome. *Psychiatry, 1960, 23*, 365–374.

Caplan, G. *Principles of preventive psychiatry.* New York: Basic Books, 1964.

Caplan, G. The family as a support system. In G. Caplan & M. Killilea (Eds.), *Support systems & mutual help: Multidisciplinary explorations.* New York: Grune & Stratton, 1976.

Carey, R. Emotional adjustment in terminal patients: A quantitative approach. *Journal of Counseling Psychology, 1974, 21*, 433–439.

Carey, R. G. The widowed: A year later. *Journal of Counseling Psychology, 1977, 24*, 125–131.

Carr, A. C. Bereavement as a relative experience. In B. Schoenberg, I. Gerber, A. Wiener, A. H. Kutscher, D. Peretz, & A. C. Carr (Eds.), *Bereavement: Its psychosocial aspects.* New York: Columbia University Press, 1975.

Carroll, J. S., & Payne, J. W. The psychology of the parole decision process: A joint application of attribution theory and information processing psychology. In J. S. Carroll and J. W. Payne (Eds.), *Cognition and social behavior.* Hillsdale, N.J.: Erlbaum Press, 1976.

Carroll, J. S., & Payne, J. W. Judgments about crime and the criminal: A model and a method for investigating parole decision. In B. D. Sales (Ed.), *Prospectives in law and psychology. Vol. 1: The criminal justice system.* New York: Plenum, 1977.

Carver, C. S., Coleman, A. E., & Glass, D. C. The coronary-prone behavior pattern and the suppression of fatique on a treadmill test. *Journal of Personality and Social Psychology, 1976, 33*, 460–466.

Carver, C. S., & Glass, D. C. The coronary prone behavior pattern and interpersonal aggression. *Journal of Personality and Social Psychology*, 1978, *36*, 361–366.

Cassem, N. H., & Hackett T. P. Psychiatric consultation in a coronary care unit. *Annals of Internal Medicine*, 1971, *75*, 9.

Chapman, L. Illusory correlation in observational report. *Journal of Verbal Learning and Verbal Behavior*, 1967, *6*, 151–155.

Chapman, L., & Chapman, J. Illusory correlation as an obstacle to the use of valid psychodiagnostic signs. *Journal of Abnormal Psychology*, 1969, *74*, 271–280.

Chesser, E. S., & Anderson, J. L. Psychological considerations in cancer of the breast. *Proceedings of the Royal Society of Medicine*, 1975, *68*, 793–795.

Chodoff, P., Friedman, S. B., & Hamburg, D. A. Stress, defenses, and coping behavior: Observations in parents of children with malignant disease. *American Journal of Psychiatry*, 1964, *120*, 743–749.

Church, R. M. Systematic effect of random error in the yoked control design. *Psychological Bulletin*, 1964, *62*, 122–131.

Clark, K. B., & Clark, M. P. The development of consciousness of self and the emergence of racial identification in Negro preschool children. *Journal of Social Psychology*, 1939, *10*, 591–599.

Clayton, P. J., Desmarais, L., & Winokur, G. A study of normal bereavement. *American Journal of Psychiatry*, 1968, *125*, 168–178.

Clayton, P. J., Halikas, J. A., & Maurice, W. L. The depression of widowhood. *British Journal of Psychiatry*, 1972, *120*, 71–78.

Coates, D., & Wortman, C. B. Depression maintenance and interpersonal control. In A. Baum & J. Singer (Eds.), *Advances in environmental psychology* (Vol. 2). Hillsdale N.J.: Lawrence Erlbaum Associates, 1980.

Coates, D., Wortman, C. B., & Abbey, A. Reactions to victims. In I. H. Frieze, D. Bar-tal, & J. S. Carroll, (Eds.), *New approaches to social problems*. San Francisco: Jossey-Bass, 1979.

Cobb, S. Social support as a moderator of life stress. *Psychosomatic Medicine*, 1976, *38*, 300–314.

Cobb, S. Social support and health through the life course. In M. White Riley (Ed.). *Aging from birth to death: Interdisciplinary perspectives*. Boulder, Col.: Westview Press, 1979.

Cobb S., & Kasl, S. *Termination: The consequences of job loss*. (Publication #LR77-224). Washington, D.C.: DHEW (NIOSH), 1977.

Cohen, F. Personality, stress, and the development of physical illness. In G. C. Stone, F. Cohen, & N. E. Adler (Eds.), *Health psychology: A handbook*. San Francisco: Jossey-Bass, 1979.

Cohen, M. E. The high familial prevalence of neurocirculatory aesthenia (anxiety neurosis, effort syndrome). *American Journal of Human Genetics*, 1951, *3*, 126–158.

Cohen, S., Rothbart, M., & Phillips, S. Locus of control and the generality of learned helplessness in humans. *Journal of Personality and Social Psychology*, 1976, *34*, 1049–1056.

Cohn, N. K. Understanding the process of adjustment to disability. *Journal of Rehabilitation*, 1961, *27*, 16–18.

Cole, C. S., & Coyne, J. C. Situational specifity of laboratory-induced learned helplessness. *Journal of Abnormal Psychology*, 1977, *86*, 615–623.

Coleman, J. C. Life stress and maladaptive behavior. *American Journal of Occupational Therapy*, 1973, *27*, 169–180.

Coopersmith, S. *The antecedents of self-esteem*. San Francisco: Freeman, 1967.

Coppen, A. J. Depressed states and indolealkylamines. *Advances in Pharmacology*, 1968, *6B*, 283–291.

Corah, N. L., & Boffa, J. Perceived control, self-observation, and response to aversive stimulation. *Journal of Personality and Social Psychology*, 1970, *16*, 1–4.

Cornwell, J., Nurcombe, B., & Stevens, L. Family response to loss of a child by Sudden Infant Death Syndrome. *The Medical Journal of Australia*, 1977, *1*, 656–658.

Costello, C. G., & Comrey, A. L. Scales for measuring depression and anxiety. *Journal of Psychology*, 1967, *66*, 303–313.

Cousins, N. Anatomy of an illness (as perceived by the patient). *The New England Journal of Medicine*, 1976, *295*, 1458–1463.

Covi, L., Lipman, R. S., Derogatis, L. R., Smith, J. E., & Pattison, J. H. Drugs and group psychotherapy in neurotic depression. *American Journal of Psychiatry*, 1974, *131*, 191–197.

Covington, M. V., & Berry, R. G. *Self-worth and school learning*. New York: Holt, Rinehart & Winston, 1976.

Coyne, J. C., & Lazarus, R. S. Cognition, stress, and coping: A transactional perspective. In I. L. Kutash & L. B. Schlesinger (Eds.), *Pressure point: Perspectives on stress and anxiety*. San Francisco: Jossey-Bass, in press.

Craig, T. J., & Abeloff, M. D. Psychiatric symptomatology among hospitalized cancer patients. *The American Journal of Psychiatry*, 1974, *131*, 1323–1327.

Craighead, W. E. Behavior therapy for depression: Issues resulting from treatment studies. In L. P. Rehm (Ed.), *Behavior therapy for depression: Present status and future directions*. New York: Academic Press, in press.

Crandall, V. C., Katkovsky, W. E., Crandall, V. J. Children's beliefs in their control of reinforcements in intellectual achievement behavior. *Child Development*, 1965, *36*, 91–109.

Crandall, V. J., & Rabson, A. Children's repetition choices in an intellectual achievement situation following success and failure. *Journal of Genetic Psychology*, 1960, *97*, 161–168.

Croog, S. H., Levine, S., & Lurie, Z. The heart patient and the recovery process: A review of the directions of research on social psychological factors. *Social Science and Medicine*, 1968, *2*, 111–164.

D'Afflitti, J. G., & Weitz, G. W. Rehabilitating the stroke patient through patient-family groups. In R. H. Moos (Ed.), *Coping with physical illness*. New York: Plenum, 1977.

Davitz, J. R. *The language of emotion*. New York: Academic Press, 1969.

Dawber, T. R., & Kannel, W. B. Susceptibility to coronary heart disease. *Modern Concepts in Cardiovascular Disease*, 1961, *30*, 671–676.

Dawson, M. E., & Furedy, J. J. The role of awareness in human differential autonomic classical conditioning: The necessary-gate hypothesis. *Psychophysiology*, 1976, *13*, 50–53.

Dawson, M. E., Schell, A. M., & Catania, J. A. Autonomic correlates of depression and clinical improvement following electroconvulsive shock therapy. *Psychophysiology*, 1977, *14*, 569–578.

de Araujo, G., van Arsdel, P. P., Holmes, T. H., & Dudley, D. L. Life change, coping ability, and chronic intrinsic asthma. *Journal of Psychosomatic Research*, 1973, *17*, 359–363.

de Charms, R. *Personal causation*. New York: Academic Press 1968.

Deci, E. L. *Intrinsic motivation*. New York: Plenum, 1975.

DeFrain, J. D., & Ernst, L. The psychological effects of Sudden Infant Death Syndrome on surviving family members. *The Journal of Family Practice*, 1978, *6*, 985–989.

Dembo, T., Leviton, G. L., & Wright, B. A. Adjustment to misfortune: A problem of social-psychological rehabilitation. *Artificial Limbs*, 1956, *3*, 4–62.

Dembroski, T. M., MacDougall, J. M., & Shields, J. L. Physiological reactions to social challenge in persons evidencing the Type A coronary-prone behavior pattern, *Journal of Human Stress*, 1977, *3*, 2–10.

DeMonbreum, B. G., & Craighead, W. E. Distortion of perception and recall of positive and neutral feedback in depression. *Cognitive Therapy and Research*, 1977, *1*, 311–330.

Depue, R. A., & Monroe, S. M. Learned helplessness in the perspective of depressive disorders: Conceptual and definitional issues. *Journal of Abnormal Psychology*, 1978, *87*, 3–20.

Derogatis, L. R., Abeloff, M. D. , & Melisaratos, N. Psychological coping mechanisms and survival time in metastatic breast cancer. *Journal of the American Medical Association,* 1979, *242,* 1504–1508.

Derogatis, L. R., Lipman, R. S., Covi, L., & Rickels, K. Factorial invariance of symptom dimensions in anxious and depressive neuroses. *Archives of General Psychiatry,* 1972, *27,* 659–665.

DesPres, T. *The Survivor.* New York: Oxford University Press, 1976.

DeVellis, R. F., DeVellis, B. M., & McCauley, C. Vicarious acquisition of learned helplessness. *Journal of Personality and Social Psychology,* 1978, *36,* 886–893.

Diener, C. I., & Dweck, C. S. An analysis of learned helplessness: Continuous changes in performance strategy, and achievment cognitions following failure. *Journal of Personality and Social Psychology,* 1978, *36,* 451–462.

Diener, C. I., & Dweck, C. S. An analysis of learned helplessness: II. The processing of success. *Journal of Personality and Social Psychology,* in press.

Diggory, J. C., Riley, E. J., & Blumenfeld, R. Estimated probability of success for a fixed goal. *American Journal of Psychology,* 1960, *73,* 41–55.

Digman, J. M. Principal dimensions of child personality as inferred from teachers' judgments. *Child Development,* 1963, *34,* 43–60.

Dinardo, Q. *Psychological adjustment to spinal cord injury.* Unpublished doctoral dissertation, University of Houston, 1971.

Dlin, B. M., Fischer, H. K., & Huddell, B. Psychologic adaptation to pacemaker and open-heart surgery. *Archives of General Psychiatry,* 1968, *19,* 599–610.

Doehrman, S. R. Psycho-social aspects of recovery from coronary heart disease: A review. *Social Science and Medicine,* 1977, *11,* 199–218.

Dohrenwend, B. S., & Dohrenwend, B. P. *Stressful life events: Their nature and effects.* New York: Wiley, 1974.

Doka, K. J. & Schwarz, E. Assigning blame: The restoration of the "sentimental order" following an accidental death. *Omega,* 1978-79, *9,* 279–285.

Dollard, J. & Miller, N. *Personality and psychotherapy.* New York: McGraw-Hill, 1950.

Douglas D., & Anisman, H. Helplessness or expectation incongruency: Effects of aversive stimulation on subsequent performance. *Journal of Experimental Psychology: Human Perception and Performance,* 1975, *1,* 411–417.

Downing, R. W., & Rickels, K. Mixed anxiety-depression—fact or myth? *Archives of General Psychiatry,* 1974, *30,* 312–317.

Ducette, J., Wolk, S., & Soucar, E. Atypical pattern in locus of control and nonadaptive behavior. *Journal of Personality.* 1972, *40,* 287–297.

Duffy, E. The conceptual categories of psychology: A suggestion for revision. *Psychological Review,* 1941, *48,* 177–203.

Duffy, E. *Activation and behavior.* New York: Wiley, 1962.

Duguid, J. B. Thrombosis as a factor in the pathogenesis of coronary artherosclerosis. *Journal of Pathology and Bacteriology,* 1946, *58,* 207–212.

Dulaney, D. E. Awareness rules and propositional control: A confrontation with S-R behavior theory. In T. R. Dixon & D. L. Horton (Eds.), *Verbal behavior and general behavior.* Englewood Cliffs, N.J.: Prentice-Hall, 1968.

Dweck, C. S. The role of expectations and attributions in the alleviation of learned helplessness. *Journal of Personality and Social Psychology,* 1975, *31,* 674–685.

Dweck, C. S. Children's interpretation of evaluative feedback: The effect of social cues on learned helplessness. In C. S. Dweck, K. T. Hill, W. H. Reed, W. M. Steihman, & R. D. Parke. The impact of social cues on children's behavior. *Merrill-Palmer Quarterly,* 1976, *22,* 83–123.

Dweck C. S., & Bush, E. S. Sex differences in learned helplessness: I. Differential debilitation with peer and adult evaluators. *Developmental Psychology,* 1976, *12,* 147–156.

Dweck, C. S., Davidson, W., Nelson, S., & Enna, B. Sex differences in learned helplessness: II. The contingencies of evaluative feedback in the classroom and III. An experimental analysis. *Developmental Psychology,* 1978, *14,* 268–276.

Dweck, C. S., & Gilliard, D. Expectancy statements as determinants of reactions to failure: Sex differences in persistence and expectancy change. *Journal of Personality and Social Psychology,* 1975, *32,* 1077–1084.

Dweck, C. S., Goetz, T. E., & Strauss, N. Sex differences in learned helplessness: IV. An experimental and naturalistic study of failure generalization and its mediators. *Journal of Personality and Social Psychology,* in press.

Dweck C. S., & Repucci, N. D. Learned helplessness and reinforcement responsibility in children. *Journal of Personality and Social Psychology,* 1973, *25,* 109–116.

Dweck, C., & Wortman, C. B. Achievement, text anxiety and learned helplessness: Adaptive and maladaptive cognitions. In H. W. Krohne & L. Laux (Eds.), *Achievement, stress and anxiety.* Washington, D.C.: Hemisphere, 1980.

Eckberg, D. L., Drabinsky, M., & Braunwald, E. Defective cardiac para-sympathetic control in patients with heart disease. *New England Journal of Medicine,* 1971, *285,* 877–883.

Eisenberger, R., Kaplan, R. M., & Singer, R. D. Decremental and nondecremental effects of noncontingent social approval. *Journal of Personality and Social Psychology,* 1974, *30,* 716–722.

Eisendrath, R. M. The role of grief and fear in the death of kidney transplant patients. *American Journal of Psychiatry,* 1969, *126,* 381–387.

Elig, T. W., & Frieze, I. H. A multi-dimensional scheme for coding and interpreting perceived causality for success and failure events: The Coding Scheme of Perceived Causality (CSPC). *SAS Catalog of Selected Documents in Psychology,* 1975, *5,* 313.

Eliot, R. S. (Ed.) *Stress and the heart.* Mount Kisco, N.Y.: Futura, 1974.

Ellis, A. *Reason and emotion in psychotherapy.* New York: Stuart, 1962.

Ellis, A., & Grieger, R. (Eds.) *Handbook of rational–emotive therapy.* New York: Springer, 1977.

Ellis, A., & Harper, R. A. *A new guide to rational living.* Englewood Ciffs N.J.: Prentice-Hall, 1975.

Engel, G. L. *Psychological development in health and disease.* Philadelphia: Saunders, 1962.

Engel, G. L. Grief and grieving. *American Journal of Nursing,* 1964, *64,* 93–98.

Engel, G. L. A life setting conductive to illness: The giving-up–given-up complex. *Annals of Internal Medicine,* 1968, *69,* 293–300.

Engel, G. L. Sudden death and the "medical model" in psychiatry. *Canadian Psychiatric Association Journal,* 1970, *15,* 527–538.

English, H. B., & English, A. C. *A comprehensive dictionary of psychological and psychoanalytic terms: A guide to usage.* New York: McKay, 1958.

Enzle M. E., Hansen, R. D., & Lowe C. A. Causal attribution in the mixed-motive game: Effects of facilitory and inhibitory environmental forces. *Journal of Personality and Social Psychology,* 1975, *31,* 50–54.

Epstein, S. The nature of anxiety with emphasis upon its relationship to expectancy. In C. D. Spielberger (Ed.), *Anxiety: Current trends in theory and research.* New York: Academic Press, 1972.

Epstein, S. Traits are alive and well. In D. Magnusson & N. S. Endler (Eds.) *Personality at the crossroads.* Hillsdale, N.J.: Lawrence Erlbaum Associates, 1977.

Erwin, J., Mobaldi, J., & Mitchell, G. Separation of rhesus monkey juveniles of the same sex. *Journal of Abnormal Psychology,* 1971, *78,* 134–139.

Estes W. K. (Ed.) . *Handbook of learning and cognitive processes* (Vols. 1–5), Hillsdale N.J.: Erlbaum Press, 1975.

Estes, W. K., & Skinner, B. F. Some quantitative properties of anxiety. *Journal of experimental Psychology,* 1941, *29,* 390–400.

Eysenck, H. J. *Behavior therapy and the neuroses.* London: Pergamon, 1960.

Feather, N. T. Valence of outcome and expectation of success in relation to task difficulty and perceived locus of control. *Journal of Personality and Social Psychology,* 1967, *7,* 552–561.

Feather, N. T. Attribution of responsibility and valence of success and failure in relation to initial confidence and task performance. *Journal of Personality and Social Psychology,* 1969, *13,* 129–144.

Feather, N. T., & Simon, J. G. Casual attributions for success and failure in relation to expectations of success based upon selective or manipulative control. *Journal of Personality,* 1971, *39,* 527–554.

Fenichel, O. *The psychoanalytic theory of neurosis.* New York: Norton, 1945.

Fennema, E., & Sherman, J. Sex-related differences in mathematics achievement, spatial visualization, and affective factors. *American Educational Research Journal,* 1977, *14,* 51–71.

Fenz, W. D., & Dronsejko, K. Effects of real and imagined threat of shock on GSR and heart rate as a function of trait anxiety. *Journal of Experimental Research in Personality,* 1969, *3,* 187–196.

Ferlic, M., Goldman, A., & Kennedy, B. J. Group counseling in adult patients with advanced cancer. *Cancer,* 1979, *43,* 760–766.

Ferster, C. B. Classification of behavioral pathology. In L. Krasner & L. P. Ullman (Eds.), *Research in behavior and modification.* New York: Holt, Rinehart & Winston, 1965.

Festinger, L. A theory of social comparison processes. *Human Relations,* 1954, *7,* 117–140.

Fischer, W. F. *Theories of anxiety.* New York: Harper & Row, 1970.

Fishbein, M., & Ajzen, I. Attitudes and opinions. *Annual Review of Psychology,* 1972, *23,* 487–544.

Fitch, G. Effects of self-esteem, perceived performance, and choice on causal attributions. *Journal of Personality and Social Psychology,* 1970, *16,* 311–315.

Fitzgerald, R. C. Reactions to blindness: An exploratory study of adults with recent loss of sight. *Archives of General Psychiatry,* 1970, *22,* 370–379.

Flanagan, J. C., Davis, F. B., Dailey, J. T., Shaycoft, M. F., Orr, D. B., Goldberg, I., & Neyman, C. A. Jr. *The American high-school student.* Pittsburgh: University of Pittsburgh, 1964.

Folkes, V. S. *Causal communications in the early stages of affiliative relationships.* Unpublished doctoral dissertation, University of California, Los Angeles, 1978.

Fontaine, G. Social comparison and some determinants of expected personal control and expected performance in a novel task situation. *Journal of Personality and Social Psychology,* 1974, *29,* 487–496.

Fosco, F., & Geer, J. H. Effects of gaining control over aversive stimuli after differing amounts of no control. *Psychological Reports,* 1971, *29,* 1153–1154.

Fox, L. H. Sex differences in mathematical precocity: Bridging the gap. In D. P. Keating (Ed.), *Intellectual talent: Research and development.* Baltimore, Md.: The Johns Hopkins University Press, 1976.

Frankel, A., & Snyder, M. L. Poor performance following unsolvable problems: Learned helplessness or egotism? *Journal of Personality and Social Psychology,* 1978, *36,* 1415–1424.

Frankl, V. *Man's search for meaning.* New York: Washington Square Press, 1963.

Frankenhaeuser, M. Behavior and circulating catecholamines. *Brain Research,* 1971, *31,* 241–262.

Frankenhaeuser, M. The role of peripheral catecholamines in adaptation to understimulation and overstimulation. In G. Serban (Ed.), *Psychopathology of human adaptation.* New York: Plenum, 1976.

French, J. R. P., Rodgers, W., & Cobb, S. Adjustment as person-environment fit. In G. V. Coelho, D. A. Hamburg, & J. E. Adams (Eds.), *Coping and adaptation.* New York: Basic Books, 1974.

Freud, S. (1926) Inhibitions, symptoms, and anxiety. *Standard Edition,* Vol. 20. London: Hogarth Press, 1959.

Freud, S. Mourning and melancholia. In J. Strachey (Ed. and trans.), *Standard edition of the complete psychological works of Sigmund Freud,* Vol. 14. London: Hogarth Press, 1957 (Originally published, 1917).

Friedberg, C. K. *Diseases of the heart* .(3rd ed.). Philadelphia: Saunders, 1966.

Friedman, A. S. Minimal effect of severe depression on cognitive functioning. *Journal of Abnormal and Social Psychology,* 1964, *69,* 237–243.

Friedman, A. S. Interaction of drug therapy with marital therapy in depressed patients. *Archives of General Psychiatry,* 1975, *32,* 619–637.

Friedman, M. *Pathogenesis of coronary artery disease.* New York: McGraw-Hill, 1969.

Friedman, M., Byers, S. O., Diamant, J., & Rosenman, R. H. Plasma catecholamine response of coronary-prone subjects (Type A) to a specific challenge. *Metabolism,* 1975, *24,* 205–210.

Friedman, M., & Rosenman, R. H. Association of specific overt behavior pattern with blood and cardiovascular findings. *Journal of the American Medical Association,* 1959, *169,* 1286–1296.

Friedman, M., Rosenman, R. H., & Carroll, V. Changes in the serum cholesterol and blood-clotting time in men subjected to cyclic variation of occupational stress. *Circulation,* 1958, *17,* 853–861.

Friedman, M., St. George, S., Byers, S. O., & Rosenman, R. H. Excretion of catecholamines, 17-ketosteroids, 17-hydroxycorticoids, and 5-hydroxyindole in men exhibiting a particular behavior pattern associated with high incidence of clinical coronary disease. *Journal of Clinical Investigation,* 1960, *39,* 758.

Friedman, R. J., & Katz, M. N. (Eds.), *The psychology of depression: Contemporary theory and research.* Washington, D. C: V. H. Winston, 1974.

Friedman, S. B. Psychological aspects of sudden unexpected death in infants and children. *Pediatric Clinics of North America,* 1974, *21,* 103–111.

Friedman, S. B., Chodoff, P., Mason, J. W., & Hamburg, D. A. Behavioral observations on parents anticipating the death of a child. *Pediatrics,* 1963, *32,* 610–625.

Frieze, I. H. Causal attributions and information seeking to explain success and failure. *Journal of Research in Personality,* 1976, *10,* 293–305.

Frieze, I. H., & Weiner, B. Cue utilization and attributional judgements for success and failure. *Journal of Personality,* 1971, *39,* 591–606.

Fromm, E. *Escape from freedom.* New York: Rinehart, 1941.

Frumkin, K., & Brookshire, K. H. Conditioned fear training and later avoidance learning in goldfish. *Psychonomic Science,* 1969, *16,* 159–160.

Fuchs, C. Z., & Rehm, L. P. A self-control behavior therapy program for depression. *Journal of Consulting and Clinical Psychology,* 1977, *45,* 206–215.

Funkenstein, D. H., King, S. H., & Drolette, M. E. *Mastery of stress.* Cambridge, Mass.: Harvard University Press, 1957.

Ganzer, V. J. Effects of audience presence and test anxiety on learning and retention in a social learning situation. *Journal of Personality and Social Psychology,* 1968, *8,* 194–199.

Garber, J., & Hollon, S. D. Universal versus personal helplessness: Belief in uncontrollability or incompetence? *Journal of Abnormal Psychology,* 1980, *89,* 56–66.

Garber, J., Miller, W. R., & Seaman, S. F. Learned helplessness, stress, and the depressive disorders. In R. A. Depue (Ed.), *The psychobiology of the depressive disorders: Implication for the effects of stress.* New York: Academic Press, 1979.

Garrity, T. F., & Klein, R. F. Emotional response in clinical severity as early determinants of severity as early determinants of six-month mortality after myocardial infarction. *Heart and Lung,* 1975, *4,* 730–737.

Gatchel, R. J., McKinney, M. E., & Koebernick, L. F. Learned helplessness, depression, and physiological responding. *Psychophysiology,* 1977, *14,* 25–31.

Gatchel, R. J., Paulus, P. B., & Maples, C. W. Learned helplessness and self-reported affect. *Journal of Abnormal Psychology,* 1975, *84,* 732–734.

Gatchel, R. J., & Proctor, J. D. Physiological correlates of learned helplessness in man. *Journal of Abnormal Psychology,* 1976, *85,* 27–34.

Geer, J., Davison, G. C., & Gatchel, R. J. Reduction of stress in humans through nonveridical perceived control of aversive stimulation. *Journal of Personality and Social Psychology,* 1970, *16,* 731–738.

Geer, J. H., & Maisel, E. Evaluating the effects of the prediction-control confound. *Journal of Personality and Social Psychology,* 1972, *23,* 314–319.

Gerber, I., Wiener, A., Battin, D., & Arkin, A. Brief therapy to the aged bereaved. In B. Schoenberg, I. Gerber, A. Wiener, A. H. Kutscher, D. Peretz, & A. C. Carr (Eds.), *Bereavement: Its psychosocial aspects.* New York: Columbia University Press, 1975.

Gershon, E. S., Mark, A., Cohen, N., Belison, N., Baron, M., & Knobe, K. Transmitted factors in the morbid risk of affective disorder: A controlled study. *Journal of Psychiatric Research,* 1975, *12,* 283.

Gilmore, T. M., & Minton, H. L. Internal versus external attribution of task performance as a function of locus of control, initial confidence and success–failure outcome. *Journal of Personality,* 1974, *42,* 159–174.

Glass, D. C. *Behavior patterns, stress, and coronary disease.* Hillsdale, N. J.: Lawrence Erlbaum Associates, 1977.

Glass, D. C., Reim, B., & Singer, J. R. Behavioral consequences of adaptation to controllable and uncontrollable noise. *Journal of Experimental Social Psychology,* 1971, *7,* 244–257.

Glass, D. C., & Singer, J. E. *Urban stress: Experiments on noise and social stressors.* New York: Academic Press, 1972.

Glass, D. C., Singer, J. E., Friedman, L. N. Psychic cost of adaptation to an environmental stressor. *Journal of Personality and Social Psychology,* 1969, *12,* 200–210.

Glass, D. C., Singer, J. E., Leonard, H. S., Krantz, D., Cohen, S., & Cummings, H. Perceived control of aversive stimulation and the reduction of stress responses. *Journal of Personality,* 1973, *41,* 577–595.

Glass, D. C., Snyder, M. L., & Hollis, J. F. Time urgency and the Type A coronary-prone behavior pattern. *Journal of Applied Social Psychology,* 1974, *4,* 125–140.

Glick, I. O., Weiss, R. S., & Parkes, C. M. *The first year of bereavement.* New York: Wiley, 1974.

Goldiamond, I. Insider-outsider problems: A constructional approach. *Rehabilitation Psychology,* 1975; *22,* 103–116.

Goldiamond, I. Coping and adaptive behaviors of the disabled. In G. L. Albrecht (Ed.), *The sociology of physical disability and rehabilitation.* Pittsburgh: University of Pittsburgh Press, 1976.

Goldsmith, H. *A contribution of certain personality characteristics of male paraplegics to the degree of improvement in rehabilitation.* Unpublished doctoral dissertation, New York University, 1955.

Goldstein, I. B. The relationship of muscle tension and autonomic activity to psychiatric disorders. *Psychosomatic Medicine,* 1965, *27,* 39–52.

Golin, S., & Terrell, F. Motivational and associative aspects of mild depression in skill and chance. *Journal of Abnormal Psychology,* 1977, *86,* 389–401.

Goodkin, F. Rats learn the relationship between responding and environmental events: An expansion of the learned helplessness hypothesis. *Learning and Motivation,* 1976, *7,* 382–393.

Gordon, S. *Lonely in America.* New York: Simon & Schuster, 1976.

Greene, W. A., Goldstein, S., & Moss, A. J. Psychosocial aspects of sudden death: A preliminary report. *Archives of Internal Medicine,* 1972, *129,* 725–731.

Gregory, W. L. Locus of control for positive and negative outcomes. *Journal of Personality and Social Psychology,* 1978, *36,* 840–849.

Griffiths, M. Effects of noncontingent success and failure on mood and performance. *Journal of Personality,* 1977, *45,* 442–457.

Grings, W. W. Cognitive factors in electrodermal conditioning. *Psychological Bulletin,* 1973, *79,* 200–210.

Grinker, R. R., & Nunnally, J. C. The phenomena of depressions. In M. M. Katz, J. O. Cole, & W. F. Barton (Eds.), *The role and methodology of classification in psychiatry and psychopathology.* Chevy Chase, Maryland: U.S. Public Health Service, 1968.

Gruen, W. Effects of brief psychotherapy during the hospitalization period on the recovery process in heart attacks. *Journal of Consulting and Clinical Psychology,* 1975, *43,* 223–232.

Gullo, S. V., Cherico, D. J., & Shadick, R. Suggested stages and response styles in life-threatening illness: A focus on the cancer patient. In B. Schoenberg, A. C. Carr, A. H. Kutscher, D. Peretz, & I. K. Goldberg (Eds.), *Anticipatory grief.* New York: Columbia University Press, 1974.

Gunther, M. S. Emotional aspects. In D. Ruge (Ed.), *Spinal cord injuries.* Springfield, Mass.: Charles C. Thomas, 1969.

Gurin, P., Gurin, G., Lao, R. C., & Beattie, M. Internal-external control in the motivational dynamics of Negro youth. *Journal of Social Issues,* 1969, *25,* 29–53.

Guttmann, L. *Spinal cord injuries: Comprehensive management and research* (2nd ed.), Oxford: Blackwell Scientific Publications, 1976.

Haan, N. Proposed model of ego functioning: Coping and defense mechanisms in relationship to IQ change. *Psychological Monographs,* 1963, *77,* (8, Whole No. 571).

Haan, N. A tripartite model of ego functioning: Values and clinical research applications. *Journal of Nervous and Mental Disease,* 1969, *148,* 14–30.

Haan, N. *Coping and defending: Processes of self-environment organization.* New York: Academic Press, 1977.

Haggard, E. A. Experimental studies in affective processes: I. Some effects of cognitive structure and active participation on certain autonomic reactions during and following experimentally induced stress. *Journal of Experimental Psychology,* 1943, *33,* 257–284.

Hamburg, D. A., & Adams, J. E. A perspective on coping behavior: Seeking and utilizing information in major transitions. *Archives of General Psychiatry,* 1967, *17,* 277–284.

Hamburg, D. A., Hamburg, B., & DeGoza, S. Adaptive problems and mechanisms in severely burned patients. *Psychiatry,* 1953, *16,* 1–20.

Hamilton, D., & Gifford, R. Illusory correlations in interpersonal perception: A cognitive basis of stereotype judgments. *Journal of Experimental Social Psychology,* 1976, *12,* 392–404.

Hammen, C. L., & Krantz, S. Effect of success and failure on depressive cognitions. *Journal of Abnormal Psychology,* 1976, *85,* 577–586.

Hanusa, B. H., & Schulz, R. Attributional mediators of learned helplessness. *Journal of Personality and Social Psychology,* 1977, *35,* 602–611.

Harrison, R. V. Person-environment fit and job stress. In C. L. Cooper & R. Payne (Eds.), *Stress at work.* New York: Wiley, 1978.

Harvey, J. H., Ickes, W. J., & Kidd, R. F. *New directions in attribution research;* (Vol. 1), Hillsdale, N. J.: Lawrence Erlbaum Associates, 1976.

Hauri, P. Dreams in patients remitted from reactive depression. *Journal of Abnormal Psychology,* 1976, *85,* 1–10.

Heckhausen, H. *The anatomy of achievement motivation.* New York: Academic Press, 1967.

Heider, F. *The psychology of interpersonal relations.* New York: Wiley, 1958.

Heinicke, C. Some effects of separating two-year-old children from their parents: A comparative study. *Human Relations,* 1956, *9,* 105–176.

Heinicke, C., & Westheimer, I. *Brief separations.* New York: International Universities Press, 1966.

Heller, K. The effects of social support: Prevention and treatment implications. In A. P. Goldstein & F. H. Kanfer (Eds.), *Maximizing treatment gains: Transfer enhancement in psychotherapy.* New York: Academic Press, 1979.

Helmrath, T. A., & Steinitz, E. M. Death of an infant: Parental grieving and the failure of social support. *The Journal of Family Practice,* 1978, *6,* 785–790.

Heneman, H. G., & Schwab, D. P. Evaluation of research on expectancy theory predictions of employee performance. *Psychological Bulletin,* 1972, *78,* 1–9.

Hetherington, E. M. Effects of father absence on personality development in adolescent daughters. *Developmental Psychology,* 1972, *7,* 313–326.

Hilton, T. L., & Berglund, G. W. Sex differences in mathematics achievement—a longitudinal study. *Journal of Education Research,* 1974, *67,* 231–237.

Hinde, R. A., Spencer-Booth, Y., & Bruce, M. Effects of 6-day maternal deprivation on rhesus monkey infants. *Nature,* 1966, *210,* 1021–1033.

Hinton, J. M. *Dying.* Baltimore, Maryland: Penguin Books, 1967.

Hinton, J. M. The physical and mental distress of the dying. *Quarterly Journal of Medicine,* 1963, *32,* 1–21.

Hiroto, D. S. Locus of control and learned helplessness. *Journal of Experimental Psychology,* 1974, *102,* 187–193.

Hiroto, D. S., & Seligman, M. E. P. Generality of learned helplessness in man. *Journal of Personality and Social Psychology,* 1975, *31,* 311–327.

Hodges, W. F. Effects of ego threat and threat of pain on state anxiety. *Journal of Personality and Social Psychology,* 1968, *8,* 364–372.

Hodges, W. F., & Spielberger, C. D. The effects of threat of shock on heart rate for subjects who differ in manifest anxiety and fear of shock. *Psychophysiology,* 1966, *2,* 287–294.

Hohmann, G. W. Psychological aspects of treatment and rehabilitation of the spinal cord injured person. *Clinical Orthopaedics and Related Research,* 1975, *112,* 81–88.

Hollon, S. D. Behavioral and cognitive-behavioral therapies in depression: Comparisons and combinations with alternative approaches. In L. P. Rehm (Ed.), *Behavior therapy for depression: Present status and future directions.* New York: Academic Press, in press.

Hollon, S. D., & Beck, A. T. Psychotherapy and drug therapy: Comparisons and combinations, In S. L. Garfield & A. E. Bergin (Eds.), *The handbook of psychotherapy and behavior change: An empirical analysis.* New York: Wiley, 1978.

Hollon, S. D., & Beck, A. T. Cognitive–behavioral intervention for depression. In P. C. Kendall & S. D. Hollon (Eds.), *Cognitive–behavioral interventions: Theory, research and procedures.* New York: Academic Press, 1979.

Hollon, S. D., & Kendall, P. C. Cognitive–behavioral interventions: Theory and procedure. In P. C. Kendall & S. D. Hollon (Eds.), *Cognitive–behavioral interventions: Theory, research, and procedure.* New York: Academic Press, 1979.

Holmes, T. H., & Masuda, M. Life change and illness susceptibility. In B. S. Dohrenwald & B. P. Dohrenwald (Eds.), *Stressful life events: Their nature and effects.* New York: Wiley, 1974.

Holmes, T. H., & Rahe, R. H. The social readjustment rating scale. *Journal of Psychosomatic Research,* 1967, *11,* 213–218.

Horney, K. *Neurotic personality of our times.* New York: Norton, 1937.

House, J. S. Occupational stress as a precursor to coronary disease. In W. D. Gentry & R. B. Williams, Jr. (Eds.), *Psychological aspects of myocardial infarction and coronary care.* St. Louis: Mosby, 1975.

House, J. S. *Work, stress, and social support.* Reading, Mass.: Addison-Wesley, in press.

Howe, E. S. GSR conditioning in anxiety states, normals, and chronic functional schizophrenic subjects. *Journal of Abnormal and Social Psychology,* 1958, *56,* 183–189.

Huston, P. E. Neglected approach to cause and treatment of psychotic depression. *Archives of General Psychiatry,* 1971, *24,* 505–508.

Ickes, W. J., & Kidd, R. F. An attributional analysis of helping behavior. In J. H. Harvey, W. J. Ickes, and R. F. Kidd (Eds.), *New directions in attribution research* (Vol. 1). Hillsdale, N. J.: Erlbaum Press, 1976.

Ickes, W. J., & Layden, M. A. Attributional styles. In J. Harvey, W. Ickes, R. Kidd (Eds.), *New directions in attributional research* (Vol. 2). Hillside, N. J.: Lawrence Erlbaum Associates, 1978.

Imbus, S. H., & Zawacki, B. E. Autonomy for burned patients when survival is unprecedented. *The New England Journal of Medicine,* 1977, *297,* 308–311.

Irwin, R. W. *Intentional behavior and motivation: A cognitive view.* Philadelphia: Lippincott, 1971.

Isen, A. M., Shalker, T. E., Clark, M., & Karp, L. Affect, accessibility of material in memory, and behavior: A cognitive loop? *Journal of Personality and Social Psychology,* 1978, *36,* 1–12.

Jacobson, E. *Depression: Comparative studies of normal, neurotic, and psychotic conditions,* New York: International University Press, 1971.

James, W. H. *Internal versus external control of reinforcement as a basic variable in learning theory.* Unpublished doctoral dissertation, Ohio State University, 1957.

James, W. H., & Rotter, J. B. Partial and one hundred percent reinforcement under chance and skill conditions. *Journal of Experimental Psychology,* 1958, *55,* 397–403.

Jamison, K. R., Wellisch, D. K., & Pasnau, R. O. Psychosocial aspects of mastectomy I: The woman's perspective. *American Journal of Psychiatry,* 1978, *135,* 432–436.

Janis, I. *Psychological stress.* New York: Wiley, 1958.

Janoff-Bulman, R. Characterological versus behavioral self-blame: Inquiries into depression and rape. *Journal of Personality and Social Psychology,* 1979, *37,* 1798–1809.

Jarvik, M. E. Negative recency effect in probability learning. *Journal of Experimental Psychology,* 1951, *41,* 291–297.

Jenkins, C. D. Psychologic and social precursors of coronary disease. *New England Journal of Medicine,* 1971, *284,* 244–255, 307–317.

Jenkins, C. D. Recent evidence supporting psychologic and social risk factors for coronary disease. *New England Journal of Medicine,* 1976, *294,* 987–994, 1033–1038.

Jenkins, C. D., Rosenman, R. H., & Friedman, M. Replicability of rating the coronary-prone behavior pattern. *British Journal of Preventive and Social Medicine,* 1968, *22,* 16–22.

Jenkins, C. D., Rosenman, R. H., & Zyzanski, S. J. *The Jenkins Activity Survey for Health Prediction,* (Form B). Boston: Authors, 1972.

Jenkins, C. D., Zyzanski, S. J., & Rosenman, R. H. Risk of new myocardial infarction in middle-aged men with manifest coronary heart disease. *Circulation,* 1976, *53,* 342–347.

Jenkins, H. M., & Ward, W. C. Judgment of contingency between responses and outcomes. *Psychological Monographs,* 1965, *79,* (1, Whole No. 594).

Jennings, D., Amabile, T., & Ross, L. The intuitive scientist's assessment of covariation: data-based vs. theory-based judgments. In Tversky, A., Kahneman, D., & Slovic, P. (Eds.), *Judgment under uncertainty: Heuristics and biases.* New York: Cambridge University Press, 1980.

Jessor, R., Graves, T. C., Hanson, R. C., & Jessor, S. L. *Society, personality and deviant behavior.* New York: Holt, Rinehart, & Winston, 1968.

Johnson, J. E., & Leventhal, H. Effects of accurate expectations and behavioral instructions on reactions during a noxious medical examination. *Journal of Personality and Social Psychology,* 1974, *29,* 710–718.

Jones, B. C., & Clark, D. L. Mother-infant separation in squirrel monkeys living in a group. *Developmental Psychobiology,* 1973, *6,* 259–269.

Jones, E. E., & Davis, K. E. From acts to dispositions: The attributional process in person perception. In L. Berkowitz (Ed.), *Advances in experimental social psychology* (Vol. 2). New York: Academic Press, 1965.

Jones, E. E., & Nisbett, R. E. The actor and the observer: Divergent perceptions of the causes of behavior. In E. E. Jones, D. E. Kanouse, H. H. Kelley, R. E. Nisbett, S. Valins, & B. Weiner (Eds.), *Attribution: Perceiving the causes of behavior.* Morristown, N.J.: General Learning Press, 1972.

Jones, G. E., Kanouse, D. E., Kelley, H. H., Nisbett, R. E., Valins, S., & Weiner, B. *Attribution: Perceiving the causes of behavior.* Morristown, N. J.: General Learning Press, 1972.

Jones, R. G. *A factored measure of Ellis' irrational belief system.* Wichita, Kansas: Test Systems, Inc., 1968.

Jones, S. L., Nation, J. R., & Massad, P. Immunization against learned helplessness in man. *Journal of Abnormal Psychology,* 1977, *86,* 75–83.

Jurko, M., Jost, H., & Hill, T. S. Pathology of the energy system. *Journal of Psychology,* 1952, *33,* 183–198.

Kahn, R. L. *Conflict and ambiguity: Studies in organizational roles and personal stress.* New York: Wiley, 1964.

Kahn, R. L. Aging and social support. In M. White Riley (Ed.), *Aging from birth to death: Interdisciplinary perspectives.* Boulder, Col.: Westview Press, 1979.

Kahn, R. L., & Antonucci, T. Convoys over the life course: Attachment roles and social support. In P. B. Baltes & O. Brim (Eds.), *Life-span development and behavior,* Vol. 3, Boston: Lexington Press, in press.

Kahneman, D., & Tversky, A. On the psychology of prediction. *Psychological Review,* 1973, *80,* 237–251.

Kallman, F. Genetic principles in manic-depressive psychosis. In P. H. Hoch & J. Zubin (Eds.), *Depression.* New York: Grune & Stratton, 1954.

Kaltreider, N. B., Wallace, A., & Horowitz, M. J. A field study of the stress response syndrome: Young women after hysterectomy. *Journal of the American Medical Association,* 1979, *242,* 1499–1503.

Kaplan, J. The effects of separation and reunion on the behavior of mother and infant squirrel monkeys. *Developmental Psychobiology,* 1970, *3,* 43–52.

Kaplan, R. Social support, person-environment fit and coping. In L. A. Ferman & J. P. Gordus (Eds.), *Mental health and the economy,* Kalamazoo, Michigan: The Upjohn Institute, 1979.

Kastenbaum, R., & Aisenberg, R. *The psychology of death.* New York: Springer, 1972.

Kastenbaum, R., & Costa, P. T. Psychological perspectives on death. *Annual Review of Psychology,* 1977, *28,* 225–249.

Kastenbaum, R., & Weisman, A. D. The psychological autopsy as a research procedure in gerontology. In D. P. Kent, R. Kastenbaum, & S. Sherwood (Eds.), *Research planning and action for the elderly: The power and potential of social science.* New York: Behavioral Publications, 1972.

Katkin, E. S. *The relationship between self-report and physiological indices of anxiety during differentially stressed situations.* Doctoral dissertation, Duke University. Ann Arbor, Michigan: University Microfilms, 1964, No. 64–5596.

Katkin, E. S. Relationship between manifest anxiety and two indices of autonomic response to stress. *Journal of Personality and Social Psychology,* 1965, *2,* 324–333.

Katkin, E. S., & McCubbin, R. J. Habituation of the orienting response as a function of individual differences in anxiety and autonomic lability. *Journal of Abnormal Psychology,* 1965, *74,* 54–60.

Katz, J. L., Weiner, H., Gallagher, T. F., & Hellman, L. Stress, distress, and ego defenses: Psychoendocrine response to impending breast tumor biopsy. *Archives of General Psychiatry*, 1970, *23*, 131–142.

Kaufman, I. C., & Rosenblum, L. A. The reaction to separation in infant monkeys: Anaclitic and conservation withdrawal. *Psychosomatic Medicine*, 1967, *29*, 648–675.

Kellner, R., Simpson, G., & Winslow, W. W. The relationship of depressive neurosis to anxiety and somatic symptoms. *Psychosomatics*, 1972, *13*, 358–362.

Kelly, D. H., Brown, C., & Shaffer, J. A. A comparison of physiological and psychological measurements on anxious patients and normal controls. *Psychophysiology*, 1970, *6*, 429–441.

Kelly, D. H., & Walter, C. J. S. The relationship between clinical depression and anxiety assessed by forearm blood flow and other measurements *British Journal of Psychiatry*, 1968, *114*, 611–627.

Kelly, D. H., & Walter, C. J. S. A clinical and physiological relationship between anxiety and depression. *British Journal of Psychiatry*. 1969, *115*, 401–406.

Kelley, H. H. The warm-cold variable in first impressions of persons. *Journal of Personality*, 1950, *18*, 431–439.

Kelley, H. H. Attribution theory in social psychology. In D. Levine (Eds.), *Nebraska Symposium on Motivation* (Vol. 15). Lincoln: University of Nebraska Press, 1967.

Kelley, H. H. *Attribution in social interaction*. New York: General Learning Press, 1971.

Kelman, H. R., Lowenthal, M., & Muller, J. N. Community status of discharged rehabilitation patients: Results of a longitudinal study. *Archives of Physical Medicine and Rehabilitation*, 1966, *47*, 670–675.

Kemp, B. J., & Vash, C. L. Productivity after injury in a sample of spinal cord injured persons: A pilot study. *Journal of Chronic Disease*, 1971, *24*, 259–275.

Kennell, J. H., Slyter, H., & Klaus, M. H. The mourning response of parents to the death of a newborn infant. *The New England Journal of Medicine*, 1970, *283*, 344–349.

Kerr, T. A., Schapira, K., Roth, M., & Garside, R. F. The relationship between the Maudsley Personality Inventory and the course of affective disorders. *British Journal of Psychiatry*, 1970, *116*, 11–19.

Kessen, W., & Mandler, G. Anxiety, pain and the inhibition of distress. *Psychological Review*, 1961, *68*, 396–404.

Kihlstrom, J., & Nasby, W. Cognitive tasks in clinical assessment: An exercise in applied psychology. In P. C. Kendall & S. D. Hollon (Eds.) *Cognitive-behavioral interventions: Assessment methods*. New York: Academic Press, in press.

Kilpatrick-Tabak, B., & Roth, S. An attempt to reverse performance deficits associated with depression and experimentally induced helplessness. *Journal of Abnormal Psychology*, 1978, *87*, 141–154.

Kimball, C. P. Psychological responses to the experience of open-heart surgery. *American Journal of Psychiatry*, 1969, *126*, 96–107.

Kirscht, J. P. Perception of control and health beliefs. *Canadian Journal of Behavioral Science*, 1972, *4*, 225–237.

Klee, S., & Meyer, R. G. Prevention of learned helplessness in humans. *Journal of Consulting and Clinical Psychology*, 1979, *47*, 411–412.

Klein, D. C., Fencil-Morse, E., & Seligman, M. E. P. Learned helplessness, depression, and the attribution of failure. *Journal of Personality and Social Psychology*, 1976, *33*, 508–516.

Klein, D. C., & Seligman, M. E. P. Reversal of performance deficits in learned helplessness and depression. *Journal of Abnormal Psychology*, 1976, *85*, 11–26.

Klerman, G. L., DiMascio, A., Weissman, M., Prusoff, B., & Paykel, E. Treatment of depression by drugs and psychotherapy. *American Journal of Psychiatry*, 1974, *131*, 186–191.

Klinger, E. Consequences of commitment to and disengagement from incentives. *Psychological Review,* 1975, *82,* 1–25.

Klinger, E. *Meaning and void: Inner experience and the incentives in people's lives.* Minneapolis: University of Minnesota Press, 1977.

Klopfer, B. Psychological variables in human cancer. *Journal of Projective Techniques,* 1957, *21,* 331–340.

Koepke, J. E., & Pibram, K. H. Habituation of GSR as a function of stimulus duration and spontaneous activity. *Journal of Comparative and Physiological Psychology,* 1966, *61,* 442–448.

Kolb, L. C. *Modern clinical psychiatry.* Philadelphia: W. B. Saunders, 1973.

Koller, P. S., & Kaplan, R. M. A two-process theory of learned helplessness. *Journal of Personality and Social Psychology,* 1978, *36,* 1177–1183.

Krantz, D. S., Glass, D. C., & Snyder, M. L. Helplessness, stress level, and the coronary prone behavior pattern. *Journal of Experimental Social Psychology,* 1974, *10,* 284–300.

Krantz, D. S., & Schulz, R. Personal control and health: Some applications to crisis of middle and old age. In J. Singer and A. Baum (Eds.), *Advances in environmental psychology,* Hillsdale, N.J.: Lawrence Erlbaum Associates, 1980.

Kubler-Ross, E. *On death and dying.* New York: Macmillan, 1969.

Kuiper, N. A. Depression and causal attributions for success and failure. *Journal of Personality and Social Psychology,* 1978, *36,* 236–246.

Kun, A., & Weiner, B. Necessary versus sufficient causal schemata for success and failure. *Journal of Research in Personality,* 1973, *7,* 197–207.

Kuypers, J. A., & Bengston, V. L. Social breakdown and competence. *Human Development,* 1973, *16,* 181–201.

Lader, M. H. Palmer skin conductance measures in anxiety and phobic states. *Journal of Psychosomatic Research,* 1967, *11,* 271–281.

Lader, M. H. The psychophysiology of anxious and depressed patients. In D. C. Fowles (Ed.), *Clinical applications of psychophysiology.* New York: Columbia University Press, 1975.

Lader, M. H., & Noble, P. J. The affective disorders. In P. H. Venables & M. J. Christie (Eds.), *Research in psychophysiology.* New York: Wiley, 1975.

Lader, M. H., & Wing, L. *Physiological measures, sedative drugs and morbid anxiety.* Maudsley Monographs No. 14. London: Oxford University Press, 1966.

Lader, M. H., & Wing, L. Physiological measures in agitated and retarded depressed patients. *Journal of Psychiatric Research,* 1969, *7,* 89–100.

Langer, E. The illusion of control. *Journal of Personality and Social Psychology,* 1975, *32,* 311–328.

Langer, E. Rethinking the role of thought in social interaction. In J. Harvey, W. J. Ickes, R. F. Kidd (Eds.), *New directions in attribution research* (Vol. 2). Potomac, Md.: Lawrence Erlbaum Associates, 1978. a

Langer, E. The psychology of chance. *Journal for the Theory of Social Behavior,* 1978, *7,* 185–207. b

Langer, E. The illusion of incompetence. In L. Perlmutter & R. Monty (Eds.) *Choice and perceived control,* Potomac, Md.: Lawrence Erlbaum Associates, 1979.

Langer, E. Old age: An artifact? *Biology, Behavior & Aging.* National Council publication, in press. a

Langer, E. Playing the middle against both ends: The usefulness of adult cognitive activity as a model for cognitive activity in childhood and old age. In S. R. Yussen (Ed.), *The Growth of Insight in Children,* New York: Academic Press, in press. b

Langer, E., Blank, A., & Chanowitz, R. The mindlessness of ostensibly thoughtful action: The role of placebic information in interpersonal interaction. *Journal of Personality and Social Psychology,* 1978, *36,* 635–642.

Langer, E., & Imber, L. Mindlessness and susceptibility to the illusion of incompetence. *Journal of Personality and Social Psychology,* 1979, *37,* 2014–2025.

Langer, E., Janis, I. L., & Wolfer, J. A. Reduction of psychological stress in surgical patients. *Journal of Experimental Social Psychology,* 1975, *11,* 155–165.

Langer, E., & Newman, H. The role of mindlessness in a typical social psychological experiment. *Personality and Social Psychology Bulletin.* 1979, *5,* 295–298.

Langer, E. J., & Rodin, J. The effects of choice and enhanced personal responsibility for the aged: A field experiment in an institutional setting. *Journal of Personality and Social Psychology,* 1976, *34,* 191–198.

Langer, E., & Roth, J. Heads I win, tails it's chance: The illusion of control as a function of the sequence of outcomes in a purely chance task. *Journal of Personality and Social Psychology,* 1976, *32,* 951–953.

Lanzetta, J. T., & Driscoll, J. M. Preference for information about an uncertain but unavoidable outcome. *Journal of Personality and Social Psychology,* 1966, *3,* 96–102.

Lanzetta, J. T., & Hannah, T. E. Reinforcing behavior of "naive" trainers. *Journal of Personality and Social Psychology,* 1969, *11,* 245–252.

Lawson, N. C. *Depression after spinal cord injury: A multi-measure longitudinal study.* Unpublished doctoral dissertation, University of Houston, 1976.

Lawson, N. C. Significant events in the rehabilitation process: The spinal cord patient's point of view. *Archives of Physical Medicine and Rehabilitation,* 1978, *59,* 573–579.

Lazarus, A. A. Learning theory and the treatment of depression. *Behavior Research and Theory,* 1968, *6,* 83–89.

Lazarus, R. S. *Psychological stress and the coping process.* New York: McGraw-Hill, 1966.

Lazarus, R. S., & Alfert, E. The short-circuiting of threat. *Journal of Abnormal and Social Psychology,* 1964, *69,* 195–205.

Lazarus, R. S., & Averill, J. R. Emotion and cognition: With special reference to anxiety. In C. D. Spielberger (Ed.), *Anxiety: Current trends in theory and research.* New York: Academic Press, 1972.

Lazarus, R. S., Averill, J. R., & Opton, E. M. Towards a cognitive theory of emotion. In M. Arnold (Ed.), *Third international symposium on feelings and emotions.* New York: Academic Press, 1970.

Lazarus, R. S., Averill, J. R., & Opton, E. M. The psychology of coping: Issues of research and assessment. In G. V. Coelho, D. A. Hamburg, & J. E. Adams (Eds.), *Coping and adaptation.* New York: Basic Books, 1974.

Lazarus, R. S., Cohen, J. B., Folkman, S., Kanner, A., & Schaefer, C. Psychological stress and adaptation: Some unresolved issues. In H. Selye (Ed.), *Selye's guide to stress research, Vol. 1.* New York: Van Nostrand Reinhold Co. 1980.

Lazarus, R. S., & Launier, R. Stress-related transactions between person and environment. In L. A. Pervin & M. Lewis (Eds.), *Perspectives in interactional psychology.* New York: Plenum, 1978.

Lazarus, R. S., & Opton, E. M. The study of psychological stress: A summary of theoretical formulations and experimental findings. In C. D. Spielberger (Ed.), *Anxiety and behavior.* New York: Academic Press, 1966.

Lefcourt, H. M. *Locus of Control,* Hillsdale, N.J.: Lawrence Erlbaum Associates, 1976.

Lefcourt, H. M. Locus of control and coping with life's events. In F. Staub (Ed.), *Personality.* Englewood Cliffs, N.J.: Prentice-Hall, 1979.

Lefcourt, H. M., Hogg, E., Struthers, S., & Holmes, C. Causal attributions as a function of locus of control, initial confidence, and performance outcomes. *Journal of Personality and Social Psychology,* 1975, *32,* 391–397.

Lefcourt, H. M., Von Baeyer, C., Ware, E. E., & Cox, D. The multidimensional-multiattributional causality scale. *Canadian Journal of Behavioral Science.* 1979, *11,* 286–304.

Leon, G. R., Kendall, P. C., & Garber, J. Depression in children: Parent, teacher, and child perspectives. *Journal of Abnormal Child Psychology,* in press.

Leonhard, K. *Aufteilung der endogenen psychosen* (2nd ed.). Berlin: Akademie Verlag, 1959.

Leopold, R. L., & Dillon, H. Psychiatric considerations in whiplash injuries of the neck. *The Pennsylvania Medical Journal,* 1960, *63,* 385–389.

Lepley, W. M. The maturity of the chances: A gambler's fallacy. *Journal of Psychology,* 1963, *56,* 69–72.

LeShan, L. A basic psychological orientation apparently associated with malignant disease. *Psychiatric Quarterly,* 1961, *35,* 314–330.

Levenson, H. Multidimensional locus of control in psychiatric patients. *Journal of Consulting and Clinical Psychology,* 1973, *41,* 397–404.

Leventhal, G. S., & Michaels, J. W. Locus of cause and equity motivation as determinants of reward allocation. *Journal of Personality and Social Psychology,* 1971, *17,* 229–235.

Levis, D. J. Learned helplessness: A reply and an alternative S-R interpretation. *Journal of Experimental Psychology: General,* 1976, *105,* 47–65.

Lewin, K. *A dynamic theory of personality.* New York: McGraw-Hill, 1935.

Lewinsohn, P. M. A behavioral approach to depression. In R. J. Friedman & M. M. Katz (Eds.), *The psychology of depression: Contemporary theory and research.* Washington, D.C.: V. H. Winston, 1974.

Lewinsohn, P. M., & Graf, M. Pleasant activities and depression. *Journal of Consulting and Clinical Psychology,* 1973, *41,* 261–268.

Lewinsohn, P. M., & Libet, J. Pleasant events, activity schedules, and depression. *Journal of Abnormal Psychology,* 1972, *79,* 291–295.

Lewinsohn, P. M., Lobitz, W. C., & Wilson, S. "Sensitivity" of depressed individuals to aversive stimuli. *Journal of Abnormal Psychology,* 1973, *81,* 259–263.

Lewinsohn, P. M., & MacPhillamy, D. J. The relationship between age and engagement in pleasant activities. *Journal of Gerontology,* 1974, *29,* 290–294.

Lewis, A. J. Depression. In R. B. Scott (Ed.), *Price's textbook of the practice of medicine.* London: Oxford University Press, 1966.

Lewis, J. K., McKinney, W. T., Young, L. D., & Kraemer, G. W. Mother-infant separation in rhesus monkeys as a model of human depression. *Archives of General Psychiatry,* 1976, *33,* 699–705.

Lichtenberg, P. A. A definition and analysis of depression. *Archives of Neurology and Psychiatry,* 1957, *77,* 516–527.

Lieberman, M. A. Psychological correlates of impending death: Some preliminary observations. *Journal of Gerontology,* 1965, *20,* 181–190.

Lief, H. I., & Fox , R. C. Training for detached concern in medical students. In H. I. Lief and N. R. Lief (Eds.), *The psychological basis of medical practice.* New York: Harper & Row, 1963.

Lindemann, E. Symptomatology and management of acute grief. *American Journal of Psychiatry,* 1944, *101,* 141–148.

Lipowski, Z. J. Physical illness, the individual and the coping processes. *Psychiatry in Medicine,* 1970, *1,* 91–102.

Lishman, W. A. Selective factors in memory: II. Affective disorders. *Psychological Medicine,* 1972, *2,* 248–253.

Litman, T. J. The influence of self-conception and life orientation factors in the rehabilitation of the orthopedically disabled. *Journal of Health and Human Behavior,* 1962, *3,* 249–256.

Litman-Adizes, T. *An attributional model of depression: Laboratory and clinical investigations.* Unpublished doctoral dissertation, University of California, Los Angeles, 1978.

Livingston, P. B., & Zimet, C. N. Death anxiety, authoritarianism and choice of specialty in medical students. *Journal of Nervous and Mental Disease,* 1965, *140,* 222–230.

Lloyd, G. G., & Lishman, W. A. Effect of depression on the speed of recall of pleasant and unpleasant experiences. *Psychological Medicine*, 1975, *5*, 173–180.

Loeb, A., Beck, A. T., & Diggory, J. Differential effects of success and failure on depressed and nondepressed patients. *Journal of Nervous and Mental Disease*, 1971, *152*, 106–114.

Maccoby, E. E. *The development of sex differences.* Stanford, Calif.: Stanford University Press, 1966.

Maccoby, E. E., & Feldman, S. S. Mother-attachment and stranger-reactions in the third year of life. *Monograph of Social Research and Child Development*, 1972, *37*, 1–9.

Maccoby, E. E., & Jacklin, C. N. *The psychology of sex differences.* Stanford, Calif.: Stanford University Press, 1974.

Maddison, D., & Raphael, B. Conjugal bereavement and the social network. In B. Schoenberg, I. Gerber, A. Wiener, A. H. Kutscher, D. Peretz, & A. C. Carr (Eds.), *Bereavement: Its psychosocial aspects.* New York: Columbia University Press, 1975.

Maddison, D., & Walker, W. L. Factors affecting the outcome of conjugal bereavement. *British Journal of Psychiatry*, 1967, *113*, 1057–1067.

Magnussen, D., & Endler, N. S. (Eds.). *Personality at the crossroads.* Hillsdale, N.J.: Lawrence Erlbaum Associates, 1977.

Maguire, G. P. Psychiatric problems after mastectomy. In P. C. Brand & P. A. van Keep (Eds.), *Breast cancer: Psycho-social aspects of early detection and treatment.* Baltimore: University Park Press, 1978.

Maguire, G. P., Lee, E. G., Bevington, D. J., Kuchemann, C. S., Crabtree, R. J., Cornell, C. E. Psychiatric problems in the first year after mastectomy. *British Medical Journal*, 1978, *1*, 963–965.

Mahoney, J. J. Reflections in the cognitive-learning trend in psychotherapy. *American Psychologist*, 1977, *32*, 5–13.

Maier, S. F., Albin, R. W., & Testa, T. J. Failure to learn to escape in rats previously exposed to inescapable shock depends on nature of escape response. *Journal of Comparative and Physiological Psychology*, 1973, *85*, 581–592.

Maier, S. F., & Seligman, M. E. P. Learned helplessness: Theory and evidence. *Journal of Experimental Psychology: General*, 1976, *105*, 3–46.

Maier, S. F., Seligman, M. E. P., & Solomon, R. L. Pavlovian fear conditioning and learned helplessness. In B. A. Campbell & R. M. Church (Eds.), *Punishment.* New York: Appleton-Century-Crofts, 1969.

Maier, S. F., & Testa, R. J. Failure to learn to escape by rats previously exposed to inescapable shock is partly produced by associative interference. *Journal of Comparative and Physiological Psychology*, 1975, *88*, 554–564.

Malmo, R. B. Studies of anxiety: Some clinical origins of the activation concept. In C. D. Spielberger (Ed.), *Anxiety and behavior.* New York: Academic Press, 1966.

Malmo, R. B., & Shagass, C. Physiologic studies of reaction to stress in anxiety and early schizophrenia. *Psychosomatic Medicine*, 1949, *11*, 9–24.

Malmo, R. B., Shagass, C., & Davis, J. F. Electromyographic studies of muscular tension in psychiatric patients under stress. *Journal of Clinical Experimental Psycho-pathology*, 1951, *12*, 45–66.

Mandler, G. The interruption of behavior. In D. Levine (Ed.), *Nebraska symposium on motivation.* Lincoln, Nebraska: University of Nebraska Press, 1964.

Mandler, G. Helplessness: Theory and research in anxiety. In C. D. Spielberger (Ed.), *Anxiety: Current trends in theory and research.* New York: Academic Press, 1972.

Mandler, G., & Watson, D. L. Anxiety and the interruption of behavior. In C. D. Spielberger (Ed.), *Anxiety and behavior.* New York: Academic Press, 1966.

Mann, L. On being a sore loser: How fans react to their team's failure. *Australian Journal of Psychology*, 1974, *26*, 37–47.

Mapother, E. Discussion on manic-depressive psychosis. *British Medical Journal,* 1926, *2,* 872–879.

Marlett, N. J., & Watson, D. Test anxiety and immediate or delayed feedback in a test-like avoidance task. *Journal of Personality and Social Psychology,* 1968, *8,* 200–203.

Marris, P. *Widows and their families.* London: Routledge & Kegan Paul, 1958.

Martin, I. Levels of muscle activity in psychiatric patients. *Acta Psychologica,* 1956, *12,* 326–341.

Maselli, M. D., & Altrocchi, J. Attribution of intent. *Psychological Bulletin,* 1969, *71,* 445–454.

Mason, J. W. Organization of psychoendocrine mechanisms: A review and reconsideration of research. In N. S. Greenfield and R. A. Sternbach (Eds.), *Handbook of psychophysiology,* New York: Holt, Rinehart & Winston, 1972.

Mason, J. W. Emotion as reflected in patterns of endocrine regulation. In L. Levi (Ed.), *Emotions: Their parameters and measurement.* New York: Raven Press, 1975.

Mason, J. W., Maher, J. T., Hartley, L. H., Mougey, E., Perlow, M. J., & Jones L. G. Selectivity of corticosteroid and catecholamine response to various natural stimuli. In G. Serban (Ed.), *Psychopathology of human adaptation.* New York: Plenum, 1976.

Masserman, J. H. The principle of uncertainty in neurotigenesis. In H. D. Kimmel (Ed.), *Experimental psychopathology.* New York: Academic Press, 1971.

Matthews, K. A., & Brunson, B. I. Allocations of attention and the Type A coronary-prone behavior pattern. *Journal of Personality and Social Psychology,* 1979, *37,* 2081–2090.

Matthews, K. A., & Krantz, D. S. Resemblance of twins and their parents in Pattern A behavior. *Psychosomatic Medicine,* 1976, *38,* 140–144.

May, J. R., & Johnson, H. J. Physiological activity to internally elicited arousal and inhibitory thoughts. *Journal of Abnormal Psychology,* 1973, *82,* 239–245.

McCandless, B. R., Roberts, A., & Starnes, T. Teachers' marks, achievement test scores, and aptitude relations with respect to social class, race, and sex. *Journal of Educational Psychology,* 1972, *63,* 153–159.

McCarron, L. T. Psychophysiological discriminants of reactive depression. *Psychophysiology,* 1973, *10,* 223–230.

McClelland, D. C., Atkinson, J. W., Clark, R. A., & Lowell, E. L. *The achievement motive.* New York: Appleton, Century-Crofts, 1953.

McCombie, S. L. Characteristics of rape victims seen in crisis interviewing. *Smith College Studies in Social Work,* 1975, *46,* 137–158.

McCubbin, H. I., Dahl, B. B., Lester, G. R., Benson, D., & Robertson, M. L. Coping repertoires of families adapting to prolonged war-induced separations. *Journal of Marriage and the Family,* 1976, *38,* 461–471.

McCubbin, H. I., Hunter, E. J., & Metres, P. J. Adaptation of the family to the prisoner of war and missing in action experience: An overview. In H. I. McCubbin, B. B. Dahl, P. J. Metres, E. J. Hunter, & J. A. Plag (Eds.), *Family separation and reunion: Families of prisoners of war and servicemen missing in action.* Washington, D.C.: U.S. Government Printing Office, 1974. a

McCubbin, H. I., Hunter, E. J., Metres, P. J. Children in limbo. In H. I. McCubbin, B. B. Dahl, P. J. Metres, E. J. Hunter, & J. A. Plag (Eds.), *Family Separation and reunion: Families of prisoners of war and servicemen missing in action.* Washington, D.C.: U.S. Government Printing Office, 1974. b

McDaniel, J. W. *Physical disability and human behavior,* (2nd ed.), New York: Pergamon Press, 1976.

McDaniel, J. W., & Sexton, A. W. Psychendocrine studies of patients with spinal cord lesions. *Journal of Abnormal Psychology,* 1970, *76,* 117–122.

McGinn, N. F., Harburg, E., Julius, S., & McLeod, J. M. Psychological correlates of blood pressure. *Psychological Bulletin,* 1964, *61,* 209–219.

McInnes, R. G. Observations on heredity in neurosis. *Proceedings of the Royal Society of Medicine,* 1937, *30,* 895–904.

McKegney, F., & Lange, P. The decision to no longer live on chronic dialysis. *American Journal of Psychiatry*, 1971, *128*, 267.

McKinney, W. T., Suomi, S. J., & Harlow, H. P. Repetitive peer separation of juvenile-age rhesus monkeys. *Archives of General Psychiatry*, 1972, *27*, 200–203.

McLean, P. D., & Hakstian, A. R. Clinical depression: Comparative efficacy of outpatient treatments. *Journal of Consulting and Clinical Psychology*, 1979, *47*, 818–836.

McMahan, I. Relationships between causal attributions and expectancy of success. *Journal of Personality and Social Psychology*, 1973, *28*, 108–114.

McNitt, P. C., & Thornton, D. W. Depression and perceived reinforcement: A reconsideration. *Journal of Abnormal Psychology*, 1978, *87*, 137–140.

Mechanic, D. *Students under stress*. New York: Free Press, 1962.

Melges, F. T., & Bowlby, J. Types of hopelessness in psychopathological process. *Archives of General Psychiatry*, 1969, *20*, 690–699.

Melges, F. T., & Weisz, A. E. The personal future and suicidal ideation. *Journal of Nervous and Mental Diseases*, 1971, *153*, 244–250.

Mendels, J., Stern, S., & Frazer, A. Biological concepts of depression. In D. M. Gallant & G. M. Simpson (Eds.), *Depression: Behavioral, biochemical, diagnostic and treatment concepts*. New York: Spectrum, 1976.

Mendels, J., Weinstein, N., & Cochrane, C. The relationship between depression and anxiety. *Archives of General Psychiatry*, 1972, *27*, 649–653.

Mendlewicz, J., & Rainer, J. D. Adoption study supporting genetic transmission in manic-depressive illness. *Nature*, 1977, *268*, 327–328.

Meyer, P. R., Meyer, E., & Garrett, A. *Spinal cord injury: A guide for patients and their families*. Chicago: Midwest Regional Spinal Cord Injury Care System, 1977.

Meyerowitz, B. E. Psychosocial correlates of breast cancer and its treatments. *Psychological Bulletin*, 1980, *87*, 108–131.

Meyers, B. A., Friedman, S. B., & Weiner, I. B. Coping with a chronic disability: Psycho-social observations of girls with scoliosis. *American Journal of Diseases of Children*, 1970, *120*, 175–181.

Miller, I. W., & Norman, W. H. Learned helplessness in humans: A review and attribution theory model. *Psychological Bulletin*, 1979, *86*, 93–118.

Miller, N. E. Learnable drives and rewards. In S. S. Stevens (Ed.), *Handbook of experimental psychology*. New York: Wiley, 1951.

Miller, S. M. Coping with impending stress: Psychophysiological and cognitive correlates of choice. *Psychophysiology*, 1979, *16*, 572–581. a

Miller, S. M. Controllability and human stress: Method, evidence, and theory. *Behavior Research and Therapy*, 1979, *17*, 287–306. b

Miller, S. M. When a little information is a dangerous thing: Coping with stressful life events by monitoring versus blunting. In S. Levine & H. Ursin (Eds.), *Coping and health: Proceedings of NATO Conference*, Plennum Press, in press.

Miller, S. M., & Grant, R. P. The blunting hypothesis: A theory of predictablity and human stress. In P. O. Sjöder, S. Bates, & W. S. Dockens (Eds.), *Trends in behavior therapy*. New York: Academic Press, 1979.

Miller, W. R. Psychological deficit in depression. *Psychological Bulletin*, 1975, *82*, 238–260.

Miller, W. R., & Seligman, M. E. P. Depression and the perception of reinforcement. *Journal of Abnormal Psychology*, 1973, *82*, 62–73.

Miller, W. R., & Seligman, M. E. P. Depression and learned helplessness in man. *Journal of Abnormal Psychology*, 1975, *84*, 228–238.

Miller, W. R., & Seligman, M. E. P. Learned helplessness, depression, and the perception of reinforcement. *Behavior Research and Therapy*, 1976, *14*, 7–17.

Miller, W. R., Seligman, M. E. P., & Kurlander, H. M. Learned helplessness, depression, and anxiety. *Journal of Nervous and Mental Disease,* 1975, *161,* 347–357.

Mischel, W. *Personality and assessment.* N.Y.: Wiley, 1968.

Mitchell, G. W., & Glickman, A. S. Cancer patients: Knowledge and attitudes. *Cancer,* 1977, *40,* 61–66.

Moos, R. H., & Tsu, V. D. The crisis of physical illness: An overview. In R. H. Moos (Ed.), *Coping with physical illness.* New York: Plenum, 1977.

Morris, T., Greer, H. S., & White, P. Psychological and social adjustment to mastectomy: A two-year follow-up study. *Cancer,* 1977, *40,* 2381–2387.

Morse, S., & Gergen, K. J. Social comparison, self-consistency, and the concept of self. *Journal of Personality and Social Psychology,* 1970, *16,* 148–156.

Mowrer, O. H. A stimulus-response analysis of anxiety and its role as a reinforcing agent. *Psychological Review,* 1939, *46,* 553–565.

Murphy, L. B. & Moriarty, A. E. *Vulnerability, coping and growth: From infancy to adolescence.* New Haven: Yale University Press, 1976.

Naditch, M. P. Locus of control, discontent, and hypertension. *Social Psychiatry,* 1974, *9,* 111–117.

Naditch, M. P., Gargan, M. A., & Michael, L. B. Denial, anxiety, locus of control and the discrepancy between aspirations and achievements as components of depression. *Journal of Abnormal Psychology,* 1975, *84,* 1–9.

Nation, J. R., Cooney, J. B., & Gartrell, K. E. Durability and generizability of persistence training. *Journal of Abnormal Psychology,* 1979, *88,* 121–136.

Natterson, J. M. & Knudson, A. G. Observations concerning fear of death in fatally ill children and their mothers. *Psychosomatic Medicine,* 1960, *22,* 456–465.

Neal, J. M., & Katahn, M. Anxiety choice and stimulus uncertainty. *Journal of Personality,* 1968, *36,* 235–245.

Nelson, R. G., & Craighead, W. G. Selective recall of positive and negative feedback, self-control behaviors and depression. *Journal of Abnormal Psychology,* 1977, *86,* 379–388.

Nicholls, J. G. Causal attributions and other achievement-related cognitions: Effects of task outcome, attainment value and sex. *Journal of Personality and Social Psychology,* 1975, *31,* 379–389.

Nicholls, J. G. Effort is virtuous but it's better to have ability: Evaluative responses to perceptions of effort and ability. *Journal of Research in Personality,* 1976, *10,* 306–315.

Nighswonger, C. A. Ministry to the dying as a learning encounter. *Journal of Thanatology,* 1971, *1,* 101–108.

Nisbett, R. E., Borgida, E., Crandall, R., & Reed, H. Popular induction: Information is not necessarily informative. In J. S. Carroll & J. W. Payne (Eds.), *Cognition and social behavior.* New York: Lawrence Erlbaum Associates, 1976.

Nisbett, R. E., & Ross, L. *Human inference: Strategies and shortcomings of social judgment.* Englewood Cliffs, N.J.: Prentice-Hall, 1980.

Notman, M. T., & Nadelson, C. C. The rape victim: Psychodynamic considerations. *American Journal of Psychiatry,* 1976, *133,* 408–412.

Oskamp, S. *Attitudes and opinions,* Englewood Cliffs, N.J.: Prentice-Hall, 1977.

Overall, J. E., Hollister, L. E., Johnson, M., & Pennington, V. Nosology of depression and differential response to drugs. *The Journal of the American Medical Association,* 1966, *195,* 946–948.

Overmier, J. B., & Seligman, M. E. P. Effects of inescapable shock upon subsequent escape and avoidance learning. *Journal of Comparative and Physiological Psychology,* 1967, *63,* 28–33.

Padilla, A. M. Effects of prior and interpolated shock exposures on subsequent avoidance learning by goldfish. *Psychological Reports,* 1973, *32,* 451–456.

Padilla A. M., Padilla, C., Ketterer, T., & Giacolone, D. Inescapable shocks and subsequent avoidance conditioning in goldfish (Carrasius auratus). *Psychonomic Science,* 1970, *20,* 295–296.

Parkes, C. M., Benjamin, B., & Fitzgerald, R. G. Broken heart: A statistical study of increased mortality among widowers. *British Medical Journal,* 1969, *1,* 740–743.

Parkes, C. M. The first year of bereavement: A longitudinal study of the reactions of London widows to the death of their husbands. *Psychiatry,* 1970, *33,* 444–467.

Parkes, C. M. Psycho-social transitions: A field for study. *Social Science and Medicine,* 1971, *5,* 101–115.

Parkes, C. M. Components of the reaction to loss of a limb, spouse or home. *Journal of Psychosomatic Research,* 1972, *16,* 343–349.

Parkes, C. M. The emotional impact of cancer on patients and their families. *Journal of Laryngology and Utology,* 1975, *89,* 1271–1279. a

Parkes C. M. Unexpected and untimely bereavement: A statistical study of young Boston widows and widowers. In B. Schoenberg, I. Gerber, A. Wiener, A. H. Kutscher, D. Peretz & A. C. Carr (Eds.), *Bereavement: Its psychosocial aspects.* New York: Columbia University Press, 1975. b

Pattison, E. M. *The experience of dying.* Englewood Cliffs, N.J.: Prentice-Hall, 1977.

Pavlovsky, P. Occurence and development of psychopathologic phenomena in burned persons and their relation to severity of burns, age and premorbid personality. *Acta Chirurgiae Plasticae,* 1972, *14,* 112–119.

Paykel, E. S. Classification of depressed patients: A cluster analysis derived grouping. *British Journal of Psychiatry,* 1971, *30,* 302–309.

Paykel, E. S. Depressive typologies and response to amitriptyline. *British Journal of Psychiatry,* 1972, *120,* 147–156.

Paykel, E. S. Life stress and psychiatric disorder: Applications of the clinical approach. In B. S. Dohrenwend and B. P. Dohrenwend (Eds.), *Stressful life events: Their nature and effects.* New York: Wiley, 1974.

Pearlin, L. I., & Schooler, C. The structure of coping. *Journal of Health and Social Behavior,* 1978, *19,* 2–21.

Pearlman, J., Stotsky, B. A., & Dominick, J. R. Attitudes toward death among nursing home personnel. *Journal of Genetic Psychology,* 1969, *114,* 63–75.

Peck, A. Emotional reactions to having cancer. *American Journal of Roentgenology, Radium Therapy, and Nuclear Medicine,* 1972, *114,* 591–599.

Penman, D. T. *Coping strategies in adaptation to mastectomy.* Unpublished doctoral dissertation, Yeshiva University, 1979.

Perris, C. A study of bipolar (manic-depressive) and unipolar recurrent depressive psychoses. *Acta Psychiatrica Scandinavia,* 1966, *42,* suppl. 194.

Pervin, L. A. The need to predict and control under conditions of threat. *Journal of Personality,* 1963, *31,* 570–587.

Pettingale K. W., Greer, S., & Tee, D. E. H. Serum IgA and emotional expression in breast cancer patients. *Journal of Psychosomatic Research,* 1977, *21,* 395–399.

Phares, E. J. Expectancy change in chance and skill situations. *Journal of Abnormal and Social Psychology,* 1957, *54,* 339–342.

Phares, E. J. *Locus of control in personality.* Morristown, N.J.: General Learning Press, 1976.

Pinneau, S. R. *Effects of social support on psychological and physiological strain.* Unpublished doctoral dissertation, University of Michigan, 1975.

Plumb, M. M., & Holland, J. Cancer in adolescents: The symptom is the thing. In B. Schoenberg, A. C. Carr, A. H. Kutscher, D. Peretz, & I. K. Goldberg (Eds.), *Anticipatory grief.* New York: Columbia University Press, 1974.

Plumb, M. M., & Holland, J. Comparative studies of psychological function in patients with advanced cancer. I: Self reported depressive symptoms. *Psychosomatic Medicine, 1977, 4,* 264–275.

Preston, D. G., Baker, R. P., & Seay, B. M. Mother-infant separation in patas monkeys. *Developmental Psychology, 1970, 3,* 298–306.

Price, J. The genetics of depressive behavior. In A. Coppen & A. Walk (Eds.),Recent developments in affective disorders - A symposium. *British Journal of Psychiatry Special Publications,* No. 2. Royal Medico-Psychological Association, 1968.

Price, K. P., Tryon, W. W., & Raps, C. S. Learned helplessness and depression in a clinical population: A test of two behavioral hypotheses. *Journal of Abnormal Psychology, 1978, 87,* 113–121.

Prusoff, B., & Klerman, G. L. Differentiating depressed from anxious neurotic outpatients: Use of discriminant function analysis for separation of neurotic affective states. *Archives of General Psychiatry, 1974, 30,* 302–304.

Raab, W., Chaplin, J. P., & Bajusz, E. Myocardial necroses produced in domesticated rats and in wild rats by sensory and emotional stresses. *Proceedings of the Society of Experimental Biology and Medicine, 1964, 116,* 665–669.

Raab, W., Stark, E., MacMillan, W. H., & Gigee W. R. Sympathetic origin and antiadrenergic prevention of stress-induced myocardial lesions. *American Journal of Cardiology, 1961, 8,* 203–211.

Racinskas, J. R. *Maladaptive consequences of loss or lack of control over aversive events.* Unpublished doctoral dissertation, Waterloo University, Ontario, Canada, 1971.

Randall, G. C., Ewalt, J. R., & Blair, H. Psychiatric reaction to amputation. *Journal of the American Medical Association, 1945, 128,* 645–652.

Raphael, B. Preventive intervention with the recently bereaved. *Archives of General Psychiatry, 1977, 34,* 1450–1454.

Raskin, A. A guide for drug use in depressive disorders. *American Journal of Psychiatry, 1974, 131,* 181–185.

Ray, C. Adjustment to mastectomy: The psychological impact of disfigurement. In P. C. Brand & P. A. van Keep (Eds.), *Breast cancer: Psycho-social aspects of early detection and treatment.* Baltimore: University Park Press, 1978.

Reichsman, F., & Levy, N. B. Problems in adaptation to maintenance hemodialysis. *Archives of Internal Medicine, 1972, 130,* 859–865.

Reid, D. W., & Ziegler M. A survey of the reinforcements and activities elderly citizens feel are important for their general happiness. *Essence, 1977, 2,* 5–24.

Reim, B., Glass, D. C., & Singer, J. E. Behavioral consequences of exposure to uncontrollable and unpredictable noise. *Journal of Applied Social Psychology, 1971, 1,* 44–56.

Rescorla, R. A., & Solomon, R. L. Two-process learning theory: Relationships between Pavlovian conditioning and instrumental learning. *Psychological Review, 1967, 74,* 151–182.

Richter, C. P. On the phenomenon of sudden death in animals and man. *Psychosomatic Medicine, 1957, 19,* 191–198.

Rimm, D. C., & Litvak, S. B. Self-verbalization and emotional arousal. *Journal of Abnormal Psychology, 1969, 74,* 181–187.

Riss, W., & Scalia, F. *Functional pathways of the central nervous system.* Amsterdam: Elsevier, 1967.

Rizley, R. Depression and distortion in the attribution of causality. *Journal of Abnormal Psychology, 1978, 87,* 32–48.

Robertson, J., & Robertson, J. Young children in brief separation: A fresh look. *Psychoanalytic Study of the Child, 1971, 26,* 264–315.

Rodin, J. Density, perceived choice and response to controllable and uncontrollable outcomes. *Journal of Experimental Social Psychology, 1976, 12,* 564–578.

Rodin, J., & Langer, E. J. Long-term effects of a control-relevant intervention with the institution-alized aged. *Journal of Personality and Social Psychology, 1977, 35,* 897–902.

Rogentine, G. N., van Kammen, D. P., Fox, B. H., Docherty, J. P., Rosenblatt, J. E., Boyd, S. C., & Bunney, W. E. Psychological factors in the prognosis of malignant melanoma: A prospective study. *Psychosomatic Medicine, 1979, 41,* 647–655.

Rogers, C. R. *On becoming a person.* Boston: Houghton Mifflin, 1961.

Rogers, T., & Craighead, W. E. Physiological responses to self-statements: The effects of statement valence and discrepancy. *Cognitive Therapy and Research, 1977, 1,* 99–120.

Rokeach, M. Beliefs, attitudes, and values: A theory of organization and change. San Francisco: Jossey- Bass, 1968.

Rosanoff, A. J., Handy, I., & Pesset, I. R. The etiology of manic-depressive syndromes with special reference to their occurrence in twins. *American Journal of Psychiatry, 1935, 91,* 725–762.

Rosenbaum, R. M. *A dimensional analysis of the perceived causes of success and failure.* Unpublished doctoral dissertation, University of California, Los Angeles, 1972.

Rosenberg, M. *Society and the adolescent self-image.* Princeton, N.J.: Princeton University Press, 1965.

Rosenblum, L. A., & Kaufman, I. C. Variations in infant development and response to maternal loss in monkeys. *American Journal of Orthopsychiatry, 1968, 38,* 418–426.

Rosenman, R. H., Brand, R. J., Jenkins, C. D., Friedman, M., Straus, R., & Wurm, M. Coronary heart disease in the Western Collaborative Group Study: Final follow-up experience of 8½ years. *Journal of the American Medical Association, 1975, 233,* 872–877.

Rosenman, R. H., & Friedman, M. Neurogenic factors in pathogenesis of coronary heart disease. *Medical Clinics of North America, 1974, 58,* 269–279.

Rosenman, R. H., Friedman, M., Straus, R., Wurm, M., Jenkins, C. D., & Messinger, H. Coronary heart disease in the Western Collaborative Group Study: A follow-up experience of two years. *Journal of the American Medical Association, 1966, 195,* 130–136.

Rosenman, R. H., Rahe, R. H., Borhani, N. O., & Feinlieb, M. Heritability of personality and behavior pattern. In *Proceedings of First International Congress on Twins,* Rome, 1975.

Roth, M., Gurney, C., Garside, R. F., & Kerr, T. A. Studies in the classifications of affective disorders. *British Journal of Psychiatry, 1972, 121,* 147–161.

Roth, S. *The effects of experimentally induced expectancies of control: Facilitation of controlling behavior or learned helplessness?* Unpublished doctoral dissertation, Northwestern University, 1973.

Roth, S. A revised model of learned helplessness in humans. *Journal of Personality, 1980, 48,* 103–133.

Roth, S., & Bootzin, R. R. Effects of experimentally induced expectancies of external control: An investigation of learned helplessness. *Journal of Personality and Social Psychology, 1974, 29,* 253–264.

Roth, S., & Kubal, L. Effects of noncontingent reinforcement on tasks of differing importance: Facilitation and learned helplessness. *Journal of Personality and Social Psychology, 1975, 32,* 680–691.

Rothbart M., & Mellinger, M. Attention and responsivity to remote dangers: A laboratory simulation for assessing reactions to threatening events. *Journal of Personality and Social Psychology, 1972, 24,* 132–142.

Rotter, J. B. Generalized expectencies for internal versus external control of reinforcement. *Psychological Monographs, 1966, 80,* (1, Whole No. 609).

Rotter, J. B. Some problems and misconceptions related to the construct of internal vs. external control of reinforcement. *Journal of Consulting and Clinical Psychology, 1975, 48,* 56–67.

Rotter, J. B., Chance, J. E., & Phares, E. J. *Applications of a social learning theory of personality.* New York: Holt, Rinehart & Winston, 1972.

Rotter, J. B., Liverant, S., & Crowne, D. P. The growth and extinction of expectancies in chance controlled and skilled tasks. *Journal of Psychology*, 1961, *52*, 161–177.

Rotter, J. B., Seeman, M., & Liverant, S. Internal versus external control of reinforcement: A major variable in behavior theory. In N. F. Washburne (ed.), *Decisions, values and groups*. (Vol. 2). Oxford: Pergamon Press, 1962.

Rush, A. J., Beck, A. T., Kovacs, M., & Hollon, S. Comparative efficacy of cognitive therapy and pharmacotherapy in the treatment of depressed outpatients. *Cognitive Therapy and Research*, 1977, *1*, 17–37.

Russell, P. L., & Brandsma, J. M. A theoretical and empirical investigation of the rational-emotive and classical conditioning theories. *Journal of Consulting and Clinical Psychology*, 1974, *42*, 389–397.

Sacco, W. P., & Hokanson, J. E. Expectations of success and anagram performance of depressive in a public and private setting. *Journal of Abnormal Psychology*, 1978, *87*, 122–130.

Sainsbury, P., & Gibson, J. G. Symptoms of anxiety and tension and the accompanying physiological changes in the muscular system. *Journal of Neurology, Neurosurgery, and Psychiatry*, 1954, *17*, 214–216.

Sanders, J. B., & Kardinal, C. G. Adaptive coping mechanisms in adult acute leukemia patients in remission. *Journal of the American Medical Association*, 1977, *9*, 952–954.

Sarason, I. G. The effects of anxiety, reassurance, and meaningfulness of material to be learned in verbal learning. *Journal of Experimental Psychology*, 1958, *56*, 472–477.

Sarason, I. G. Empirical findings and theoretical problems in the use of anxiety scales. *Psychological Bulletin*, 1960, *57*, 403–415.

Schachter, S. The interaction of cognitive and physiological determinants of emotional state. In C. D. Spielberger (Ed.), *Anxiety and behavior*. New York: Academic Press, 1966.

Schachter, S., & Rodin, J. *Obese humans and rats*. Hillside, N.J.: Lawrence Erlbaum Associates, 1974.

Schaie, K. W., & Schaie, J. P. Clinical assessment and aging. In J. E. Birren and K. W. Schaie (eds.), *Handbook of the psychology of aging*. New York: Van Nostrand Reinhold, 1977.

Schildkraut, J. J., & Kety, S. S. Biogenic amines and emotion. *Science*, 1967, *156*, 21–30.

Schildkraut, V. G. The catecholamine hypothesis of affective disorders. *American Journal of Psychiatry*, 1965, *122*, 509–522.

Schlottman, R. S., & Seay, B. M. Mother-infant separation in the Jara monkey (*Macaca irus*). *Journal of Comparative Physiological Psychology*, 1972, *29*, 334–340.

Schmale A. H. Psychic trauma during bereavement. *International Psychiatric Clinics*, 1971, *8*, 147–168.

Schmale, A. H. Giving up as a final common pathway to changes in health. *Advances in Psychosomatic Medicine*, 1972, *8*, 18–38.

Schneirla, T. C. An evolutionary and developmental theory of biphasic processes underlying approach and withdrawal. In *Nebraska Symposium on Motivation*. Lincoln, Nebraska: University of Nebraska Press, 1959, 1–42.

Schoenberg, B. B., Carr, A. C., Peretz, D., & Kutscher, A. H. Physicians and the bereaved. *General Practitioner*, 1969, *40*, 105–108.

Schoenberg, B. B., Carr, A. C., Peretz, D., Kutscher, A. H., & Cherico, D. J. Advice of the bereaved for the bereaved. In B. Schoenberg, I. Gerber, A. Wiener, A. H. Kutscher, D. Peretz, & A. C. Carr (Eds.), *Bereavement: Its psychosocial aspects*. New York: Columbia University Press, 1975.

Schoenfield, D. Future committments and successful aging, I: The random sample. *Journal of Gerontology*, 1972, *32*, 323–333.

Schucker, B., & Jacobs, D. R., Jr. Assessment of behavioral risk for coronary disease by voice characteristics. *Psychosomatic Medicen*, 1977, *39*, 219–228.

Schulz R. Effects of control and predictability on the physical and psychological well-being of the institutionalized aged. *Journal of Personality and Social Psychology*, 1976, *33*, 563–573.

Schulz, R. *The psychology of death, dying and bereavement.* Reading, Mass: Addison-Wesley, 1978.

Schulz, R., & Aderman, D. Clinical research and the stages of dying. *Omega,* 1974, *5,* 137–143.

Schulz, R., & Brenner, G. Relocation of the aged: A review and theoretical analysis. *Journal of Gerontology,* 1977, *32,* 323–333.

Schütz, A. Collected papers. I. *The problem of social reality.* The Hague: Martinus Nijhoff, 1967.

Schwab, J., Chalmers, J., Conroy, S., Farris, P., & Markush, R. Studies in grief: A preliminary report. In B. Schoenberg, I. Gerber, A. Wiener, A. H. Kutscher, D. Peretz, & A. C. Carr (Eds.), *Bereavement: Its Psychosocial aspects.* New York: Columbia University Press, 1975.

Schwartz, D. A. The paranoid-depressive existential continuum. *Psychiatric Quarterly,* 1964, *38,* 690–706.

Seay, B. M. , Hansen, E. W., & Harlow, H. F. Mother-infant separation in monkeys. *Journal of Child Psychology and Psychiatry,* 1962, *3,* 123–132.

Seeman, N. Alienation and social learning in a reformatory. *American Journal of Sociology,* 1963, *69,* 270–284.

Seligman, M. E. P. Chronic fear produced by unpredictable electric shock. *Journal of Comparative and Physiological Psychology,* 1968, *66,* 402–411.

Seligman, M. E. P. Learned helplessness. *Annual Review of Medicine,* 1972, *23,* 407–412.

Seligman, M. E. P. Fall into helplessness. *Psychology Today.* June 1973, 43–48; 51–54; 88.

Seligman, M. E. P. Depression and learned helplessness. In R. J. Friedman & M. M. Katz (Eds.), *The psychology of depression: Contemporary theory and research,* Washington: V. H. Winston, 1974.

Seligman, M. E. P. *Helplessness: On depression, developmemt and death.* San Francisco: W. H. Freeman, 1975.

Seligman, M. E. P. Behavioral and cognitive therapy for depression form a learned helplessness point of view. L. P. Rehm (Ed.), *Behavior therapy for depression: Present status and future directions.* New York: Academic Press, in press.

Seligman, M. E. P., Abramson, L. Y., Semmel, A., & von Baeyer, C. Depressive attributional style. *Journal of Abnormal Psychology,* 1979, *88,* 242–247.

Seligman, M. E. P., & Beagley, G. Learned helplessness in the rat. *Journal of Comparative and Physiological Psychology,* 1975, *88,* 534–541.

Seligman, M. E. P., Klein, D. C., & Miller, W. R. Depression. In H. Leitenberg (Ed.), *Handbook of behavior modification and behavior therapy.* Englewood Cliffs, N.J.: Prentice-Hall, 1976.

Seligman, M. E. P., & Maier, S. F. Failure to escape traumatic shock. *Journal of Experimental Psychology,* 1967, *74,* 1–9.

Seligman, M. E. P., Maier, S. F., & Geer, J. The alleviation of learned helplessness in the dog. *Journal of Abnormal Psychology,* 1968, *73,* 256–262.

Seligman, M. E. P., Maier, S. F., & Solomon, R. L. Unpredictable and uncontrollable aversive events. In F. R. Brush (Ed.), *Aversive conditioning and learning.* New York: Academic Press, 1971.

Seligman, M. E. P., Rosellini, R. A., & Kozak, M. Learned helplessness in the rat: Reversibility, time course, and immunization. *Journal of Comparative and Physiological Psychology,* 1975, *88,* 542–547.

Selye, H. The general adaptation syndrome and diseases of adaptation. *Journal of Clinical Endocrinology,* 1946, *6,* 117–230.

Selye, H. *The stress of life* (Rev. ed.). New York: McGraw-Hill, 1976.

Seward, J. P., & Humphrey, G. L. Avoidance learning as a function of pretraining in the cat. *Journal of Comparative and Physiological Psychology,* 1967, *63,* 338–341.

Shaw, B. F. Comparison of cognitive therapy and behavior therapy in the treatment of depression. *Journal of Consulting and Clinical Psychology,* 1977, *45,* 543–551.

Shekelle, R. B., Schoenberger, J. A., & Stamler, J. Correlates of the JAS Type A behavior pattern score. *Journal of Chronic Diseases,* 1976, *29,* 381–394.

Sherman, J., & Fennema, E. The study of mathematics by high school girls and boys: Related variables. *American Educational Research Journal,* 1977, *14,* 159–168.

Sherrod, D. R., & Downs, R. Environmental determinants of altruism. *Journal of Experimental Social Psychology,* 1974, *10,* 468–479.

Shipley, C. R., & Fazio, A. F. Pilot study of a treatment in psychological depression. *Journal of Abnormal Psychology,* 1973, *82,* 372–376.

Shontz, F. C. Reactions to crisis. *The Volta Review,* 1965, *67,* 364–370.

Shontz, F. C. *The psychological aspects of physical illness and disability.* New York: Macmillan, 1975.

Sidle, A., Moos, R., Adams, J., & Kady, P. Development of a coping scale. *Archives of General Psychiatry,* 1969, *20,* 226–232.

Siller, J. Psychological situation of the disabled with spinal cord injuries. *Rehabilitation Literature,* 1969, *30,* 290–296.

Simpson, M. T., Olewine, D. A., Jenkins, C. D., Ramsey, F. H. Zyzanski, S. J., Thomas, G., & Hames, C. G. Exercise-induced catecholamines and platelet aggregration in the coronary-prone behavior pattern. *Psychosomatic Medicine,* 1974, *36,* 476–487.

Skinner, B. F. The process involved in the repeated guessing of alternatives. *Journal of Experimental Psychology,* 1942, *30,* 495–503.

Skinner, B. F. *Science and human behavior.* New York: MacMillan, 1953.

Slater, E., & Shields, J. Genetic aspects of anxiety. In M. H. Lader (Ed.), *Studies in anxiety. British Journal of Psychiatry Special Publication,* No. 3, 1969.

Smedslund, J. The concept of correlation in adults. *Scandanavian Journal of Psychology,* 1963, *4,* 165–173.

Smits, S. J. Variables related to success in a medical rehabilitation setting. *Archives of Physical Medicine and Rehabilitation,* 1974, *55,* 449–454.

Smolen, R. C. Expectancies, mood, and performance of depressed and nondepressed psychiatric inpatients on chance and skill tasks. *Journal of Abnormal Psychology,* 1978, *87,* 91–101.

Snyder, M., Tanke, E. O., & Berscheid, E. Social perception and interpersonal behavior: On the self-fulfilling nature of social stereotypes. *Journal of Personality and Social Psychology,* 1977, *35,* 656–666.

Sobel, H. J., & Worden, J. W. The MMPI as a predictor of psychosocial adaptation to cancer. *Journal of Consulting and Clinical Psychology,* 1979, *47,* 716–724.

Sohn, D. The affect-generating powers of effort and ability self-attributions of academic success and failure. *Journal of Educational Psychology,* 1977, *69,* 500–505.

Sokolov E. N. *Perception and the conditioned reflex.* New York: MacMillan, 1963.

Solomon, G. F. Discussions, emotions and immunity. *Annals of the New York Academy of Sciences,* 1969, *164,* 461–462. (a)

Solomon, G. F. Emotions, stress, the central nervous system, and immunity. *Annals of the New York Academy of Sciences,* 1969, *164,* 335–343. (b)

Solomon, R. L., & Corbit, J. D. An opponent-process theory of motivation: II. Cigarette addiction. *Journal of Abnormal Psychology,* 1973, *81,* 158–171.

Solomon, R. L. , & Corbit, J. D. An opponent-process theory of motivation, I: Temporal dynamics of affect. *Psychological Review,* 1974, *81,* 119–145.

Speisman, J. C., Lazarus, R. S., Mordkoff, A. M. & Davison, L. A. The experimental reduction of stress based on ego-defense theory. *Journal of Abnormal Psychology,* 1964, *68,* 367–380.

Spielberger, C. D., Goldstein, L. D., & Dahlstrom, W. G. Complex incidental learning as a function of anxiety and task difficulty. *Journal of Experimental Psychology,* 1958, *56,* 58–61.

Spitz, R. A. Anaclitic depression. *The Psychoanalytic Study of the Child,* 1946, *2,* 313–347.

Staub, E., & Kellet, D. Increasing pain tolerance by information about aversive stimuli. *Journal of Personality and Social Psychology,* 1976, *34,* 716–724.

Staub, E., Tursky, B., & Schwartz, G. E. Self-control and predictability: Their effects on reaction to aversive stimulation. *Journal of Personality and Social Psychology,* 1971, *18,* 157–162.

Stein, A. H. , & Bailey, M. M. The socialization of achievement motivation in females. *Psychological Bulletin,* 1973, *80,* 345–366.

Steiner, D. Perceived freedom. In L. Berkowitz (Ed.), *Advances in experimental social psychology,* (Vol. 5), New York: Academic Press, 1970.

Stenstedt, A. The genetics of neurotic depression. *Psychiatrica Scandinavia,* 1966, *42,* 392–409.

Stevenson, H. W., Hale, G. A., Klein, R. E., & Miller, L. K. Interrelations and correlates in children's learning and problem solving. *Monographs of the Society for Research in Child Development,* 1968, *33*(7, Serial No. 123).

Stewart M., Winokur, G., Stern, J., Guze, S., Pfeiffer, E., & Horning, F. Adaptation and conditioning GSR in psychiatric patients. *Journal of Mental Science, 1959, 105,* 1102–1111.

Stitt, A. Emergency after death. *Emergency Medicine,* 1971, *3,* 270–279.

Storms, M. D., & McCaul, D. D. Attribution processes and emotional exacerbation of dysfunctional behavior. In J. H. Harvey, W. J. Ickes, and R. F. Kidd (Eds.), *New directions in attribution research,* (Vol. 1). Hillsdale N.J.: Erlbaum Press, 1976.

Stotland, E. *The psychology of hope.* San Francisco: Jossey-Bass, Inc., 1969.

Strickland, B. R. Internal-external expectancies and health related behaviors. *Journal of Consulting and Clinical Psychology,* 1978, *46,* 1192–1211.

Strickland, B. R. Internal-external expectancies and cardiovascular functioning. In L. C. Perlmutter & R. A. Monty (Eds.), *Choice and perceived control.* Hillsdale, N.J.: Lawrence Erlbaum Assoc., 1979.

Sullivan, H. S. *The interpersonal theory of psychiatry.* New York: Norton, 1953.

Suomi, S. J., & Harlow, H. F. Effects of differential removal from group on social development of rhesus monkeys. *Journal of Child Psychology and Psychiatry,* 1975, *16,* 149–164.

Suomi, S. J., Mineka, S., & Delizio, R. Multiple peer separations in adolescent monkeys: An opponent process interpretation. *Journal of Experimental Psychology: General,* in press.

Sutherland, S., & Scherl, D. Patterns of response among victims of rape. *American Journal of Orthopsychiatry,* 1970, *40,* 503–511.

Symonds, M. Victims of violence: Psychological effects and after effects. *The American Journal of Psychoanalysis,* 1975, *35,* 19–26.

Szpiler, J. A., & Epstein, S. Availability of an avoidance response as related to autonomic arousal. *Journal of Abnormal Psychology,* 1976, *85,* 73–82.

Szybist, C. Thoughts of a mother. In O. J. Z. Sahler (Ed.) *The child and death.* St. Louis: C. V. Mosby, 1978.

Taylor, F. C., & Marshall, W. L. Experimental analysis of a cognitive-behavioral therapy for depression. *Cognitive Therapy and Research,* 1977, *1,* 59–72.

Teasdale J. D. Effects of real and recalled success on learned helplessness and depression. *Journal of Abnormal Psychology,* 1978, *87,* 155–164.

Teasdale J. D., & Bancroft, J. Manipulation of thought content as a determinant of mood and corrugator electromyographic activity in depressed patients. *Journal of Abnormal Psychology,* 1977, *86,* 235–241.

Tennen, H., & Eller, S. J. Attributional components of learned helplessness and facilitation. *Journal of Personality and Social Psychology,* 1977, *35,* 265–271.

Theorell, T. Life events before and after the onset of a premature myocardial infarction. In B. S. Dohrenwend and B. P. Dohrenwend (Eds.), *Stressful life events: Their nature and effects.* New York: Wiley, 1974.

Theorell, T., & Rahe, R. H. Life change events, ballistocardiography, and coronary death. *Journal of Human Stress*, 1975, *1*, 18–24.

Thomas, E., & Dewald, L. Experimental neurosis: Neuropsychological analysis. In J. D. Maser & M. E. P. Seligman (Eds.), *Psychopathology: Experimental models*. San Francisco: Freeman, 1977.

Thornton, J. W., & Jacobs, P. D. Learned helplessness in human subjects. *Journal of Experimental Psychology*, 1971, *87*, 369–372.

Thornton, J. W., & Powell, G. D. Immunization and alleviation of learned helplessness in man. *American Journal of Psychology*, 1974, *87*, 351–367.

Triandis, H. *The analysis of subjective culture*. New York; Wiley-Interscience, 1972.

Trieschmann, R. B. *The psychological, social, and vocational adjustment in spinal cord injury: A strategy for future research* (Final Report #13-P-59011-9-01). Washington, D.C.: Rehabilitation Services Adminstration, 1978.

Tversky, A., & Kahneman, D. Belief in the law of small numbers. *Psychological Bulletin*, 1971, *76*, 105–110.

Tyhurst, J. S. Individual reactions to community disaster: The natural history of psychiatric phenomena. *American Journal of Psychiatry*, 1951, *107*, 764–769.

Vachon, M. L. S. Grief and bereavement following the death of a spouse. *Canadian Psychiatric Association Journal*, 1976, *21*, 35–43.

Vachon, M. L. S., Formo, A., Freedman, K., Lyall, W. A. L., Rogers, J., & Freeman, S. J. J. Stress reactions to bereavement. *Essence*, 1976, *1*, 23–33.

Vachon, M. L. S., Freedman, K., Formo, A., Rogers, J., Lyall, W. A. L., & Freeman, S. J. J. The final illness in cancer: The widow's perspective. *Canadian Medical Association Journal*, 1977, *117*, 1151–1154.

Vachon, M. L. S., Lyall, W. A., Rogers, J., Formo, A., Freedman, K., Cochrane, J., & Freeman, S. J. J. The use of group meetings with cancer patients and their families. In J. Taché, H. Selye, & S. B. Day (Eds.), *Cancer, stress, and death*. New York: Plenum, 1979.

Valle, V. A., & Frieze I. H. Stability of causal attributions as a mediator in changing expectations for success. *Journal of Personality and Social Psychology*, 1976, *33*, 579–587.

Veroff, J. Development and validation of a projective measure of power motivation. *Journal of Abnormal and Social Psychology*, 1957, *54*, 1–8.

Veroff, J. Social comparison and the development of achievement motivation. In C. P. Smith (Ed.), *Achievement-related motives in children*. New York: Russell Sage, 1969.

Veroff, J., Douvan, E., & Kulka, R. *The American experience: A self-portrait over two decades*. New York: Basic Books, in press.

Verwoerdt, A., & Elmore, J. L. Psychological reactions in fatal illness, I: The prospect of impending death. *Journal of the American Geriatrics Society*, 1967, *15*, 9–19.

Visotsky, H. M., Hamburg, D. A., Goss, M. E. & Lebovits, B. Z. Coping behavior under extreme stress. *Archives of General Psychiatry*, 1961, *5*, 423–448.

Walker, K. N., MacBride, A., & Vachon, M. L. S. Social support networks and the crisis of bereavement. *Social Science and Medicine*, 1977, *11*, 35–41.

Wallston, B. S., Wallston, K. A., Kaplan, G. D., & Miades, S. A. Development and validation of the health locus of control scale. *Journal of Consulting and Clinical Psychology*, 1976, *44*, 1580–585.

Ward, W., & Jenkins, H. The display of information and the judgment of contingency. *Canadian Journal of Psychology*, 1965, *19*, 231–241.

Warren, V. L., & Cairns, R. B. Social reinforcement satiation: An outcome of frequency or ambiguity? *Journal of Experimental Child Psychology*, 1972, *13*, 249–260.

Weiner, B. *Theories of motivation: From mechanism to cognition*. Chicago: Rand McNally, 1972.

Weiner, B. (Ed.), *Achievement motivation and attribution theory.* Morristown, N.J.: General Learning Press, 1974.

Weiner, B. An attributional model for educational psychology. In L. Shulman (Ed.), *Review of research in education,* (Vol. 4), Itasca, Ill.: Peacock, 1976.

Weiner, B., Frieze, I., Kukla, A., Reed, L., Rest, S., & Rosenbaum, R. M. *Perceiving the causes of success and failure.* Morristown, N.J.: General Learning Press, 1971.

Weiner, B., Heckhausen, H., Meyer, W., & Cook, R. E. Causal ascriptions and achievement behavior: A conceptual analysis of locus of control. *Journal of Personality and Social Psychology,* 1972, *21,* 239–248.

Weiner, B., & Kukla, A. An attributional analysis of achievement motivation. *Journal of Personality and Social Psychology,* 1970, *15,* 1–20.

Weiner, B., Nierenberg, R., & Goldstein, M. Social learning (locus of control) versus attributional (causal stability) interpretations of expectancy of success. *Journal of Personality,* 1976, *44,* 52–68.

Weiner, B., Russell, D., & Lerman, D. Affective consequences of causal ascriptions. In J. H. Harvey, W. J. Ickes, and R. F. Kidd (Eds.), *New directions in attribution research,* (Vol. 2) Hillsdale N.J.: Erlbaum Press, 1978.

Weiner, B., Russell, D., & Lerman, D. The cognition-emotion process in achievement-related contexts. *Journal of Personality and Social Psychology,* 1979, *37,* 1211–1220.

Weintraub, M., Segal, R. M., & Beck, A. T. An investigation of cognition and affect in the depressive experience of normal men. *Journal of Consulting and Clinical Psychology,* 1974, *42,* 911.

Weisman, A. D. *The realization of death: A guide for the psychological autopsy.* New York: Jason Aronson, 1974.

Weisman, A. D. *Coping with cancer.* New York: McGraw-Hill, 1979.

Weisman, A. D. Early diagnosis of vulnerability in cancer patients. *American Journal of the Medical Sciences,* 1976, *271,* 187–196.

Weisman, A. D., & Worden, J. W. Psychosocial analysis of cancer deaths. *Omega,* 1975, `6, 61–75.

Weisman, A. D., & Worden, J. W. The existential plight in cancer: Significance of the first 100 days. *International Journal of Psychiatry in Medicine,* 1976, *7,* 1–15.

Weiss, J. M. Somatic effects of predictable and unpredictable shock. *Psychosomatic Medicine,* 1970, *32,* 397–408.

Weiss, J. M. Effects of coping behavior in different warning signal conditions on stress pathology in rats. *Journal of Comparative and Physiological Psychology,* 1971, *77,* 1–30.

Weiss, J. M. Psychological factors in stress and disease. *Scientific American,* 1972, *226,* 104–113.

Weiss, J. M., Glazer, H. I., & Pohorecky, L. A. Coping behavior and neurochemical changes in rats: An alternative explanation for the original "learned helplessness" experiments. In G. Serban and A. King (Eds.), *Animal models in human psychobiology.* New York: Plenum, 1976.

Weiss, J. M., Stone, E. A., & Harrell, N. Coping behavior and brain norepinephrine level in rats. *Journal of Comparative and Physiological Psychology,* 1970, *72,* 153–160.

Welker, R. L. Acquisition of a free operant appetitive response in pigeons as a function of prior experience with response-independent food. *Learning and Motivation,* 1976, *7,* 394–405.

Weller, D. J., & Miller, P. M. Emotional reactions of patient, family, and staff in acute-care period of spinal cord injury: Part 1. *Social Work in Health Care,* 1977, *2,* 369–377. (a)

Weller, D. J., & Miller, P. M. Emotional reactions of patient, family, and staff in a acute-care period of spinal cord injury: Part 2. Emotional reactions of family and staff. *Social Work in Health Care,* 1977, *3,* 7–17. (b)

Wener, A. E., & Rehm, L. P. Depressive affect: A test of behavioral hypotheses. *Journal of Abnormal Psychology,* 1975, *84,* 221–227.

Whalen, C. K., & Henker, B. Psychostimulants and children: A review and analysis. *Psychological Bulletin,* 1976, *83,* 1113–1130.

Whatmore, G. B., & Ellis, R. M. Some neurophysiological aspects of depressed states: An electromyographic study. *Archives of General Psychiatry,* 1959, *1,* 70–80.

White, B. V., & Gilden, E. F. "Cold pressor test" in tension and anxiety. A cardiochronographic study. *Archives of Neurology and Psychiatry,* 1937, *38,* 964–984.

White, R. W. Strategies of adaptation: An attempt at systematic description. In G V. Coelho, D. A. Hamburg, & J. E. Adams (eds.); *Coping and adaptation.* New York: Basic Books, 1974.

Wicklund, R. *Freedom and Reactance.* Hillsdale, N.J.: Erlbaum, 1974.

Wiener, A., Gerber, I., Battin, D., & Arkin, A. M. The process and phenomenology of bereavement. In B. Schoenberg, I. Gerber, A. Wiener, A. H. Kutscher, D. Peretz, & A. C. Carr (Eds.), *Bereavement: Its psychosocial aspects.* New York: Columbia University Press, 1975.

Willis, M. H., & Blaney, P. H. Three tests of the learned helplessness model of depression. *Journal of Abnormal Psychology,* 1978, *87,* 131–136.

Wine, J. Test anxiety and direction of attention. *Psychological Bulletin,* 1971, *76,* 92–104.

Winoker, G., Clayton, P. J., & Reich, T. *Manic depressive illness.* St. Louis: C. V. Mosby Co., Publishers, 1964.

Wishner, J. Neurosis and tension: An exploratory study of the relationship of physiological and Rorschach measures. *Journal of Abnormal and Social Psychology,* 1953, *48,* 253–260.

Woodruff, R. A., Guze S. B., & Clayton, P. J. Anxiety neurosis among psychiatric outpatients. *Comprehensive Psychiatry,* 1972, *13,* 165–170.

Wortman, C. B. Some determinants of perceived control. *Journal of Personality and Social Psychology,* 1975, *31,* 282–294.

Wortman, C. B. Causal attributions and personal control. In J. Harvey, W. Ickes, &R. F. Kidd(Eds.), *New directions in attribution research.* Hillsdale, N.J.: Lawrence Erlbaum Associates, 1976.

Wortman, C. B., Abbey, A., Holland, A. E., Silver, R. L., & Janoff-Bulman, R. Transitions from the laboratory to the field: Problems and progress. In L. Bickman (Ed.), *Applied Social Psychology Annual.* Beverly Hills, Calif.: Sage Publications, 1980.

Wortman, C. B., & Brehm, J. W. Responses to uncontrollable outcomes: An integration of reactance theory and the learned helplessness model. In L. Berkowitz (Ed.), *Advances in experimental social psychology* ,(Vol. 8) New York: Academic Press, 1975.

Wortman, C. B., & Dintzer, L. Is an attributional analysis of the learned helplessness phenomenon viable? A critique of the Abramson-Seligman-Teasdale reformulation. *Journal of Abnormal Psychology,* 1978, *87,*75–90.

Wortman, C. B., & Dunkel-Schetter, C. Interpersonal relationships and cancer: A theoretical analysis. *Journal of Social Issues,* 1979, *35,*120–155.

Wortman, C. B., Panciera, L., Shusterman, L., & Hibscher, J. Attributions of causality and reactions to uncontrollable outcomes. *Journal of Experimental Social Psychology,* 1976, *12,* 301–316.

Wyss, D. *Depth psychology: A critical history.* New York: Norton, 1966.

Yerkes R. M., & Dodson, J. D. The relation of strength of stimulus to rapidity of habit formation. *Journal of Comparative Neurological Psychology,* 1908. *18,* 459–482.

Zahourek, R., & Jensen, J. S. Grieving and the loss of the newborn. *American Journal of Nursing,* 1973, *73,*836–839.

Zajonc, R. B., & Brickman, P. Expectancy and feedback as independent factors in task performance. *Journal of Personality and Social Psychology,* 1969, *11,* 148–156.

Zeiss A. M., Lewinsohn, P. M., & Munoz, R. F. Nonspecific improvement effects in depression using interpersonal skills training, pleasant activity schedules or cognitive training. *Journal of Consulting and Clinical Psychology,* 1979, *47,* 427–439.

Zerbin-Rudin, E. Endogen psychosen. In P. E. Becker (Ed.), *Humangenetik.* Stuttgart: Georg Thieme Verlag, 1967.

Ziegler M., & Reid, D. W. Correlates of locus of desired control in two samples of elderly persons: community residents and hospitalized patients. *Journal of Consulting and Clinical Psychology,* in press.

Zuckerman, M., & Lubin, B. *Manual for the Multiple Affect Adjective Checklist.* San Diego: Educational and Industrial Testing Service, 1965.

Zuckerman, M., Lubin, B., & Robins, S. Validation of the multiple affect adjective check list in clinical situations. *Journal of Consulting and Clinical Psychology,* 1965, *29,* 594.

Zyzanski, S. J., Jenkins, C. D., Ryan, T. J., Flessas, A., & Everist, M. Psychological correlates of coronary angiographic findings. *Archives of Internal Medicine,* 1976, *136,* 1234–1237.

Author Index

Subject Index

A

Academic area, 210–212
  mathematical, 203, 210–221
  reading, 204
  verbal, 203, 210–221
Academic performance
  intellectually irrelevant, 205–207, 211, 216–218, 220
  intellectually relevant, 216, 218
Academic setting, 204
Accident victim, 255, 279, 282, 291, 294, 319
Achievement, 14, 35–39, 42, 44, 46–49, 248–251, 253, 254, 256, 258
  cognition, 198, 199, 201, 218–221
  motivation, 18, 35–37, 43, 48
  orientation, 212, 213, 218–221, 228, 230, see also Helplessness orientation; Mastery orientation
  setting, 197, 198, 203–205, 209
  striving, 225, 228
Activity level, 133–135, 153, 229, 265, 268
Activity scheduling, 190

Actual control, 72–75, 97, 114, 115, 119, 120, 122, 123
  equated for predictability, 74–75, 77, 81–83, 95
Adjustment, 262, 279, 282, 287–288, 290, 292–294, 303, 305, 310–313, 316–317, 319–322, 325–330, 334, 340
  defined, 327–332
Adoption studies, 144
Adrenalin, 225, 241, 242, 274
Adult–child interaction, 204
Affect, 8, 47–49, 52, 53, 55, 56, 177–179, 246, 256, 300, 305, 317
  negative, 48, 55, 186, 190, 194, 199, 200, 291, 328
  positive, 200, 201, 248, 249, 256, 312, 328
Affective disorder, see Depression
Affective reaction, 39, 42–44, 48–50, 52, 53, 175, 176, 180, 181, 184, 185, 245, 249, 255, 302
  in achievement, 48–50
Affiliation, 46–47, 248, 253, 254, 258

391